SACRED SUICIDE

The label 'Suicide Cults' has been applied to a wide variety of different alternative religions, from Jonestown to the Solar Temple to Heaven's Gate. Additionally, observers have asked if such group suicides are in any way comparable to Islamist suicide terrorism, or to historical incidents of mass suicide, such as the mass suicide of the ancient community of Masada. Organizationally and ideologically diverse, it turns out that the primary shared trait of these various groups is a common stereotype of religion as an irrational force that pushes fanatics to undertake acts of suicidal violence.

Offering a valuable perspective on New Religious Movements and on religion and violence, *Sacred Suicide* brings together contributions from a diverse range of international scholars of sociology, religious studies and criminology.

ASHGATE NEW RELIGIONS

Series Editors:

James R. Lewis, University of Tromsø, Norway

George D. Chryssides, University of Birmingham, UK

The popularity and significance of New Religious Movements is reflected in the explosion of related articles and books now being published. This Ashgate series offers an invaluable resource and lasting contribution to the field.

Sacred Suicide

Edited by

JAMES R. LEWIS
University of Tromsø, Norway

CAROLE M. CUSACK
University of Sydney, Australia

Routledge
Taylor & Francis Group
LONDON AND NEW YORK

First published 2014 by Ashgate Publishing

2 Park Square, Milton Park, Abingdon, Oxfordshire OX14 4RN
711 Third Avenue, New York, NY 10017

Routledge is an imprint of the Taylor & Francis Group, an informa business

First issued in paperback 2018

British Library Cataloguing in Publication Data
A catalogue record for this book is available from the British Library

The Library of Congress has cataloged the printed edition as follows:
Sacred suicide / edited by James R. Lewis and Carole M. Cusack.
pages cm. -- (Ashgate new religions)
Includes bibliographical references and index.
ISBN 978-1-4094-5086-3 (hardcover : alk. paper)
1. Death—Religious aspects. 2. Suicide—Religious aspects. 3. Suicide—Religious aspects—Islam. 4. Cults. I. Lewis, James R., editor.
BL504.S225 2014
202'.3—dc23

2014009723

ISBN 978-1-4094-5086-3 (hbk)
ISBN 978-1-138-54625-7 (pbk)

Contents

Notes on Contributors

Jan A. Ali is a sociologist of religion, with special reference to Islam. He is a Senior Lecturer in Islam and Modernity in the School of Humanities and Communication Arts and concurrently holds a post as the Community and Research Analyst in the Religion and Society Research Centre at the University of Western Sydney. Jan Ali is author of *Islamic Revivalism Encounters the Modern World: A Study of the Tablīgh Jamā'at* (New Delhi: Sterling Publishers, 2012).

Nachman Ben-Yehuda is a Professor and former Dean of the Faculty of Social Sciences at the Hebrew University in Jerusalem, Israel. He is the author of *The Masada Myth: Collective Memory and Mythmaking in Israel* (1996), *Theocratic Democracy: The Social Construction of Religious and Secular Extremism* (2010), *Sacrificing Truth* (2002), *Betrayals and Treason: Violations of Trust and Loyalty* (2001), and *Atrocity, Deviance and Submarine Warfare: Norms and Practices During the World Wars* (2013).

Henrik Bogdan is Professor in History of Religions at the University of Gothenburg. His main areas of research are Western Esotericism, New Religious Movements, and Freemasonry. He is the author of *Western Esotericism and Rituals of Initiation* (2007), editor of *Brother Curwen, Brother Crowley: A Correspondence, by Aleister Crowley and David Curwen* (2010), co-editor of *Occultism in a Global Perspective* (2013), *Sexuality and New Religious Movements* (2014), and *The Brill Handbook on Freemasonry* (2014).

Carole M. Cusack is Professor of Religious Studies at the University of Sydney. She is the author of *Conversion Among the Germanic People* (1998), *Invented Religions: Imagination, Fiction and Faith* (2010), and *The Sacred Tree: Ancient and Medieval Manifestations* (2011). She is the editor (with Christopher Hartney) of *Religion and Retributive Logic: Essays in Honour of Garry W. Trompf* (Brill, 2010) and (with Alex Norman) *Handbook of New Religions and Cultural Production* (Brill, 2012).

Helen Farley is a Senior Research Fellow in Studies in Religion at the University of Queensland. Her research interests include the cultural history of various currents of esoteric thought, particularly tarot. She is actively involved in researching religion and technology and was the project leader of the Religion Bazaar project in *Second Life*. She also is Senior Lecturer at the Australian Digital Futures Institute at the University of Southern Queensland where she researches educational technology for teaching and learning.

Mattias Gardell is Chair of the Department of the History of Religions at Uppsala University, Sweden. His publications include *In the Name of Elijah Muhammad: Louis Farrakhan and the Nation of Islam* (1996), *Rasrisk* (1998; 2003), *Gods of the Blood. White Separatism and the Pagan Revival* (2003), *Bin Laden i våra hjärtan. Globaliseringen och framväxten av politisk islam* [Bin Laden in Our Hearts. Globalization and the Rise of Political Islam] (2005), *Tortyrens återkomst* [The Return of Torture] (2008), *Islamofobi* [Islamophobia] (2010).

Lorenz Graitl is a Post-doctoral Fellow at the Berlin Graduate School of Muslim Cultures and Societies. He received his PhD in sociology from Freie Universität Berlin. His first book, *Sterben als Spektakel: Zur kommunikativen Dimension des politisch motivierten Suizids* (VS Springer, 2012), discusses the historical genesis and communicative aspects of different forms of political suicide, as well as corresponding discourses of legitimization. Currently he is working on the mediatized dispute over Telangana.

Christopher Hartney is a Lecturer in Studies in Religion at the University of Sydney where he teaches on religion and violence and religion and film. He specializes in the study of new religions in East Asia and Vietnam, and has published on Caodaism, Vietnam's largest indigenous religion. He also works on aesthetics and is the Australian delegate to the International Congress of Aesthetics. He is co-editor (with Alex Norman) of the journal *Literature and Aesthetics*.

James R. Lewis is Professor of Religious Studies at the University of Tromsø in Norway. His books have been published by Cambridge University Press, Oxford University Press, and Brill. His *Cults in America* (1998) and *The Oxford Handbook of New Religious Movements* (2004) both won CHOICE book awards. In the area of New Religions and violence, he has edited anthologies on the Branch Davidians, the Solar Temple, and a general collection on *Violence and New Religious Movements* (2011).

Rebecca Moore is Professor of Religious Studies at San Diego State University, where she teaches classes in new religions and religion in America. Former co-editor of *Nova Religio* for ten years, she maintains the widely respected website *Alternative Considerations of Jonestown and Peoples Temple*. She has written and published extensively on Peoples Temple and Jonestown, and co-edited the book *Peoples Temple and Black Religion in America* (2004). Her latest book on the subject is *Understanding Jonestown and Peoples Temple* (2009).

Lynn S. Neal is Associate Professor of Religion at Wake Forest University. Her research focuses on American religious history, particularly the relationship between religion and popular culture, as well as the history of religious intolerance. Her publications include "They're Freaks!: The Cult Stereotype in Fictional Television Shows, 1958–2008" (in *Nova Religio*, 2011), *Religious Intolerance in America: A Documentary History*, with John Corrigan (2010), and *Romancing God: Evangelical Women and Inspirational Fiction* (2006).

Katarina Plank is a historian of religion. She was awarded her doctorate by Lund University in 2011 for a thesis on Buddhism and meditation in Sweden. She is currently working as a post-doctoral researcher at Gothenburg University on a project on Thai Buddhism in Sweden, focused on migration, gender and religion. She has published several articles in Nordic journals and books on topics of materiality, sexuality, mindfulness and meditation in relation to Buddhist traditions.

Thomas Robbins is a semi-retired sociologist of religion. He received his PhD from the University of North Carolina (1974). He is the author of *Cults, Converts and Charisma* (1988) and the co-author of six collections of original papers including *Millennium, Messiahs and Mayhem* (1997) and *Misunderstanding Cults* (2001). He has published numerous articles, essays, and reviews in social science and religious studies journals.

John Walliss is Senior Lecturer in Criminology in the Department of Social Science at Liverpool Hope University, UK. He is the author of several books on aspects of contemporary millenarianism, including *Responding to Late Modernity: The Brahma Kumaris as a 'Reflexive Tradition'* (2002) and *Apocalyptic Trajectories: Millenarianism and Violence in the Contemporary World* (2004).

Introduction

James R. Lewis and Carole M. Cusack

With the possible exception of suicides committed in response to prolonged, painful illnesses, the general social consensus in advanced industrialized nations seems to be that suicide is an irrational act, explainable chiefly in terms of some form of mental derangement. As a consequence of this widespread cultural judgment, religious groups that commit mass suicide as well as individuals identified as religious-motivated suicide bombers or self-immolators are quickly categorized as people motivated by "fanaticism." In contrast, however, people who willingly sacrifice their lives for a national cause such as war are valorized as heroic. Louise Richardson, a leading expert on terrorism, notes that self-sacrifice in time of war is really not so distant from suicide terrorism:

> I will argue that in killing themselves in order to kill others they are behaving in a way that is entirely consistent with the behaviour of soldiers throughout the ages. Military historians have long ago convinced us that what drove young men over the trenches and out of the foxholes was fierce loyalty to their small band of brothers. This may appear surprising, as we tend to think of suicide attacks as individual actions, but in fact there has been no recorded case of terrorist simply deciding to become a martyr, finding the explosives and making a plan. Instead, in every known martyrdom operation, the group plays an essential role in planning the terrorist attack and in training, sustaining and supervising the volunteer. The average martyrdom operation requires a supporting cast of about ten others. In societies the world over we reserve our highest honours for those who have given their lives for their country. Public squares everywhere are filled with monuments to those who have been victorious in battle. Suicide terrorists seek honours like these and their handlers make sure they get them. (Richardson 2006: 136)

The conclusion that a suicide bomber or a strange religious group committing mass suicide is crazy is also reinforced by a broader cultural judgment that associates religion with irrationality, so that any sort of violence perpetrated by a person identified as a religious actor is immediately viewed as an example of *religious* violence that, seemingly by definition, is not open to rational examination (as discussed in, for example, Cavanaugh 2009). Additionally, in the specific case of suicide bombers who are also Muslims, Mattias Gardell, in his contribution to this volume, asks whether the actors' foreignness is a factor: Is it because this act is carried out by the Other? Is it because we see the behavior through an Orientalist lens, a dramatic outbreak of irrational barbarian violence against civilization?

Though this sort of xenophobia likely plays a role in our judgment of Middle Eastern suicide bombers and Buddhist self-immolators, we tend to make parallel evaluations when members of alternative religions carry out group suicides. Of the major violent incidents involving new religious movements (NRMs)—the Jonestown murder-suicides (1978), the ATF/FBI raid on the Mount Carmel community (1993), the Solar Temple murder-suicides (1994, 1995, and 1997), the Tokyo subway poison gas attack (1995), the Heaven's Gate suicides (1997), and the murder-suicides of the Movement for the Restoration of the Ten Commandments of God in Uganda (2000)—the focal violence of four out of six of these events were acts of mass suicide. It has also been argued (most recently by Kenneth Newport in his 2006 book *The Branch Davidians of Waco*) that the members of the Mount Carmel community intentionally committed suicide. If Newport is correct, then that would mean that every NRM involved in a major act of violence except Aum Shinrikyo was a "suicide cult." Additionally, other NRMs, from Falun Gong to Chen Dao, have been portrayed as suicidal.

When discussing "suicide cults," contemporary analysts also often refer to what they think of as being historical precedents, such as the ancient community of Masada that famously committed mass suicide rather than surrender to the Romans. Another frequently mentioned historical example of religiously motivated mass suicide is the Russian Old Believers, who burned themselves (sometimes along with others trapped inside churches they had torched) rather than adopt liturgical changes they believed would cause them to lose their salvation. Is there some common thread that unites these various phenomena?

Despite surface similarities, the situations of the communities involved in suicide violence turn out to be too diverse to bring together under one explanatory scheme. In a handful of cases, one can point to religion as being a key motivator. But in most cases, specific local sociological and political factors offer more compelling explanations. For example, Jonestown, the Solar Temple, and Heaven's Gate share certain characteristics, but, for the most part, these cannot be extended to suicide bombers and to other categories of suicide involving religious actors.

What is common across these diverse case studies is a common *stereotype* of religion as an irrational force that pushes fanatics to undertake acts of violence.

This stereotype has been thoughtlessly applied by the media to religious groups that have no suicidal inclinations, such as the Chen Dao UFO religion, which was incessantly portrayed as another Heaven's Gate during its short sojourn in the media spotlight. The stereotype of fanatical religious groups that are, by their very nature, inclined to commit suicide can also be applied by government agencies to cover other kinds of machinations, as in the case of the People's Republic of China's staging of apparent suicides by Falun Gong members. Thus, in addition to analyzing mass suicides of religious groups, many of the chapters in the present collection will provide critical examinations of the essentialist stereotype of "religious suicide."

Survey of Contents

The first two chapters examine historical group suicides. In 73 AD, a group of 967 Jewish assassins and rebels—Sicarii—were trapped on top of the fortress of Masada, near the shore of the Dead Sea, as the Imperial Roman Army erected a siege system around the fortress. When the besieged realized that there was no hope for winning or escaping, they all committed suicide on the fifteenth day of Xanthicus. Only seven of the besieged managed to hide themselves and survive the mass suicide. This historical narrative, given to us by Josephus Flavius, was transformed by secular Zionists in the twentieth century from a narrative of defeat and mass suicide of the Sicarii, into a heroic mythical tale that served as one of the founding myths of the state of Israel. In "The Sicarii Suicide on Masada and the Foundation of a National Myth," Nachman Ben-Yehuda examines this tale, contrasting the historical vs. the mythical narrative and explaining how and why the Masada mythical narrative was created, and how it served as a foundation myth.

In "Religious Mass Suicide Before Jonestown: The Russian Old Believers," Thomas Robbins examines another series of prominent historical group suicides. Over a period of several decades in late seventeenth- and early eighteenth-century Russia, tens of thousands of "Old Believers" committed suicide, generally by self-immolation. Most of the suicides were not individual acts but transpired in the context of catastrophic collective events at hermitages or monasteries. In several instances, the number of persons who perished at a burned-out settlement far exceeded the number of deaths at Jonestown. Convergences with the Peoples Temple holocaust include: a general climate of apocalyptic excitation; a sectarian Manichean outlook which perceived absolute evil triumphant in the world, and in which "political" themes became more prominent over time, and a conviction of imminent armed assault by hostile forces. Both the Old Believers and Peoples Temple experienced difficulties in resolving the tension between the impulse to violently confront a demonic state and the desire to develop a communal refuge where they could live according to their faith. Marked divergences include the degree of actual persecution, and the post-holocaust survival and growth of the Old Believers.

The second section examines four alternative religious groups that made headlines in the 1990s with spectacular mass suicides. In Chapter 3, "Purification, Illumination, and Death: The Murder-Suicides of the Order of the Solar Temple," Henrik Bogdan examines the Solar Temple. In October 1994, 53 members of the order in Switzerland and Québec were murdered or committed suicide. These tragic events were followed by two smaller group suicides in subsequent years, and the Solar Temple quickly became one of the most notorious and discussed "cults." However, it soon turned out that the Solar Temple defied the stereotypical understanding of a cult or new religious movement in that it was not a marginalized organization. On the contrary, members were affluent and were well-connected with the surrounding society. Previous attempts to understand the murder-suicides of the Solar Temple have either focused on the roles of the leaders of the group, or on the increasingly apocalyptic teachings of the movement and how these were projected on the surrounding society. Bogdan's chapter focuses more on the ritual practices of the movement and on its rank-and-file members, and asks what sort of world-view, and what ritual practices, did the members share, and how is this related to the murder-suicides of the Solar Temple?

Chapter 4, Rebecca Moore's "Suicide, Murder, and Martyrdom: The Deaths in Jonestown, Guyana," examines the first contemporary religious group involved in mass suicide. Initial reports of the deaths that occurred in Jonestown, Guyana in November 1978 characterized them as mass suicides. As accounts of the deaths of children and old people emerged, however, the events began to be described as murder, especially by conspiracy theorists. A narrative of martyrdom pervaded life in Jonestown, as well as life within Peoples Temple, the group sponsoring the agricultural commune. Jim Jones, the group's leader, appropriated and re-interpreted the Black Panther Party rhetoric of revolutionary suicide. This act of protest was rehearsed many times in Jonestown. Some survivors who lived in Jonestown challenge the assertion that residents took these rehearsals seriously, although a number of audiotapes have parents providing the justification for killing their children to save them from torture; others on tape state that they are taking their own lives as a rejection of capitalism. In any event, by killing the children first, the mass suicides of the parents seemed virtually assured.

Heaven's Gate is an almost prototypical suicide group, at least as most people understand the term. The group's 1997 "exit" in Rancho Santa Fe, California, resulted in the death of all of the group's full-time members, and today the movement is defunct. Yet Heaven's Gate did not begin as a group oriented around the idea of suicide. In "Individual Suicide and the End of the World: Destruction and Transformation in UFO and Alien-Based Religions," Carole M. Cusack situates Heaven's Gate in terms of its continuities with certain popular cultural eschatologies, such as the influential "alien messiah" film *The Day the Earth Stood Still* (1951), and in terms of its continuities with the apocalyptic eschatologies of prior UFO/alien-based new religions. Cusack also considers the roots of the group suicide in the movement's worldview, as well as the influence of Marshall Applewhite's response to the death of Bonnie Lu Nettles, his platonic partner.

In the spring of 2000, nearly a thousand members of the Movement for the Restoration of the Ten Commandments of God died in a series of murder-suicides in and around Kanungu, Uganda. While a volume of material has been produced by scholars detailing other similar cases in Europe and the US, the MRTCG has received very little interest, particularly by these scholars. In "The Movement for the Restoration of the Ten Commandments of God One Decade On," John Walliss's aim is to revisit the case of the MRTCG. He particularly discusses the subsequent commentary that has been produced in order to see whether a firmer series of answers can be obtained as to the reasons behind the murder suicides.

During the last ten years, dubbed as "the Age of the War on Terror," terrorism, or more specifically "suicide terrorism," has almost exclusively has been attributed by the media and by some intellectuals to denote Muslims' predisposition to terrorism. However, there have been numerous incidents of terrorism in the same period perpetrated by non-Muslims highlighting the cultural diversity of terrorism. In "A Sociological Analysis of Muslim Terrorism," Jan A. Ali explores suicide terrorism not as a religio-cultural but a sociological phenomenon. Ali looks at some of the pivotal causes and consequences of it using social categorization theory and Bourdieu's concept of *habitus* as tools of analysis, and argues that Muslim suicide terrorism is a response to the negative consequences of the crisis of modernity.

Glorification of warriors who sacrifice their lives to inflict harm or to defeat the enemy has been a recurrent feature of heroic tales for many centuries, so why we are filled with such revulsion against "suicide" attacks? In "So Costly a Sacrifice Upon the Altar of Freedom," Mattias Gardell examines suicide attacks as resistance strategy, examining how the method is perceived in the environments from which the players come, mainly from Palestine, where Gardell conducted field studies during the second Intifada. What drives a person to use their life as a weapon? Why are people horrified more at a suicide attack that causes dozens of deaths over a bomb attack that takes many more lives?

Since the 1960s, several thousand people have died in suicides intended as sacrifices. Violence against the self can appear in the form of suicide bombing, where the perpetrator aims to extinguish the life of as many people as possible by giving up their own. In contrast, there are self-killings that do not aim to harm anybody else. These are the fast-unto-death suicides where a person vows not to eat until a certain demand is fulfilled, and self-immolation, a protest suicide—by means of fire or otherwise—in service of a political or ideological goal. Self-immolation is not an ordinary suicide or self-destructive act, but has a religious dimension in Buddhism since one's own body is seen as a gift for a greater cause. In "Burning Buddhists: Self-Immolation as Political Protest," Katarina Plank highlights the specific relevant Buddhist ritual and textual heritage in her analysis of the recent wave of self-immolations in Tibet. She incorporates this act into a wider Buddhist set of practices called "gift of the body." The first political sacrifices made in the 1960s were intended to save Buddhism at a time when it was perceived as being threatened in South Vietnam; later, the focus shifted towards bringing an end to the Vietnam War. As a result, their sacrifices were addressed to Vietnamese politicians and to the global community. Nearly fifty years later, a new wave of self-immolations have occurred in Tibet—with previously no tradition of self-immolation—and this time, the fiery suicides by Tibetan monks and former monks can be seen as an expression of the nationalist struggle for a free Tibet. People who die in hunger strikes or protest suicides often leave behind letters for publication after death; since the 1980s, suicide bombers have recorded "martyrdom videos" in which they read aloud their last will and testament and sometimes are subsequently filmed perpetrating their attack. In "Dying to Tell: Media Orchestration of Politically Motivated Suicide," Lorenz Graitl asks what is the audience urged to do? How is violence against oneself and/or others justified? What is the underlying logic? What function do these spectacular representations serve?

Falun Gong, or Falun Dafa, is a religious movement that arose from the Qigong boom of the 1990s. It first rippled through the consciousness of western media when adherents surrounded the seat of the Chinese government and staged a peaceful mass protest. After the movement was outlawed in 1999, there has been a propaganda war between Falun Gong adherents and the Chinese government, both claiming the other guilty of atrocities and conspiratorial plots. In 2001, five Falun Gong protesters set themselves ablaze in Tiananmen Square resulting in the death of two; Falun Gong spokespeople subsequently claimed that the Chinese government had staged the suicides. In "Death by Whose Hand? Falun Gong and Suicide," Helen Farley examines the complex relationship between Falun Gong and the Chinese government, exploring the reality behind the claims and counterclaims in relation to the former's stated opposition to suicide. This will be contrasted with other Falun Gong writings which encourage adherents to refuse medical treatment and medication in order to rid themselves of *karma*.

Ever since Jonestown, part of the "cult" stereotype has been that NRMs are volatile groups, ready to commit group suicide at the drop of a hat. The assumption that the Branch Davidian community was a potential Jonestown may or may not have contributed to the initial ill-advised ATF raid. But, following the fiery holocaust set in motion by the FBI raid 51 days later, defenders of these agencies' actions uniformly portrayed the Davidians as having been a "suicide group." In "The Mount Carmel Holocaust: Suicide or Execution?," James R. Lewis presents an overview of the Davidian community, focusing particular attention on evidence that the group was not inclined to suicide. Rather, the Davidians were victims of law enforcement malfeasance.

As the central storyteller in and of American life, television has played a profound role in the maintenance and dissemination of the cult stereotype. By emphasizing these stereotypical features, television shows firmly situate cults as abnormal and dangerous entities on the American religious landscape. Many of these televised portrayals include issues of cult violence, specifically suicide. In "Rescripting the Past: Suicide Cults on Television," Lynn S. Neal analyzes how fictional American television shows from *South Park* to *CSI* have depicted the relationship between cults and suicide. In addition to episode analysis, this chapter addresses the role that popular culture plays in perpetuating anti-cult ideas and attitudes.

In "Why Muslims Kill Themselves on Film: From Girard's Victimage Mechanism to a Radical Constructivist Explanation," Christopher Hartney takes a methodological approach to representations of suicide on film that is situated between a Girardian victimage approach on one side, and a radical constructivist approach on the other. With thematics on cinema and suicide identified in this section of the chapter, the chapter demonstrates how such thematics are developed or distorted when Muslim characters are introduced to the screen. The four small case studies in this section include analysis of recent examples, including Peter Berg's Hollywood film *The Kingdom* and Stephen Gaghan's *Syriana*.

References

Cavanaugh, William T. (2009). *The Myth of Religious Violence: Secular Ideology and the Roots of Modern Conflict*. New York: Oxford University Press.

Richardson, Louise (2006). *What Terrorists Want: Understanding the Terrorist Threat*. London: John Murray.

Part I
Historical Suicide Cults

Chapter 1

The Sicarii Suicide on Masada and the Foundation of a National Myth[1]

Nachman Ben-Yehuda

Introduction

During the first century AD, the Roman Empire controlled the province of Judea. A series of incapable and corrupt Roman governors created a significant degree of resentment and unrest that erupted in 66 AD in what is now known as the Jewish "Great Revolt." In essence, this revolt challenged directly Roman control and hegemony in the province and in the region indirectly. The Romans reacted with an iron fist. A few Roman legions advanced from the north to the south crushing fortresses and suppressing resistance. Eventually, the Roman Imperial army placed a siege system around Jerusalem and in 70 AD conquered and destroyed the city, as well as burning to the ground the second Jewish Temple. While this was in fact the end of the revolt, three fortresses remained defiant: Herodion, Macherus, and Masada. In what can be easily described as a mopping-up operation, the Roman army set on conquering and suppressing these three fortresses. Masada was the last. Following a siege, on the 15th of Xanticus 73 AD, the Roman tenth legion ("Fretensis") breached the walls of Masada. That was the end of Masada and of the "Great Revolt."

Historical Reality According to Josephus Flavius vs. the Myth

There are two versions about what took place at Masada in 73 AD. The historical version is provided by first-century historian Josephus Flavius; the second version is a product of the early twentieth century and is essentially a myth. While there is some overlap between the two, and while some elements of Josephus's original and historical version do appear in the mythical version, they differ on almost all

[1] This chapter is based on Ben-Yehuda (1995; 2002; and 2009).

the important points. Understanding the political, social, and scientific context of this transformation requires that we acquire a basic understanding of these two very different narratives.

The Historical Narrative: Background and Josephus

The Great Revolt ended as colossal failure, and in disastrous large-scale bloodshed, the agonized death of thousands of Jews at the hands of the Imperial Roman army, and the enslavement of thousands more. The fall of Masada, probably in 73 AD, was the last chapter in that doomed revolt. The Masada mythical narrative (Ben-Yehuda 1995; Paine 1994; Shargel 1979; Zerubavel 1995) is a direct remnant of that period. No real understanding of some of the basic elements of modern Jewish Israeli culture—certainly issues of national and personal identity—can be attained without understanding this tragic and heroic period.

There is only one historical source available on Masada: the writings of Josephus Flavius. Josephus mentions that Justus from Tiberias wrote a historical narrative of the Jewish war, but no copies of this work have survived. Josephus thus becomes the exclusive "baseline" for understanding what happened.

Joseph Ben-Matityahu, later known as Josephus Flavius, was born in Jerusalem in 37 AD to a priestly family. He notes that he was not an enthusiastic supporter of the Great Revolt; however, when it actually began, at around 66 AD, he became commander of the Galilee, responsible for its defense. In 67 AD, the Galilee fortress Jotapata (Yodfat) fell. A few survivors, including Josephus, considered suicide. Josephus managed to fool the Romans and he and one other survivor remained alive. Instead of killing one another, Josephus persuaded the other person to surrender to the Romans. Clearly a skillfully persuasive man, when Josephus met Vespasian, the Roman commander of the forces that had conquered Jotapata, he managed to form an interesting relationship with him. Among other things, Josephus supposedly prophesied to Vespasian that he would become emperor of Rome; and indeed, Titus Flavius Vespasian did become emperor, ruling between 69 and 79 AD. Josephus traveled to Rome where he assumed a Roman name, and became a Roman citizen and an official historian. The question regarding Josephus's Jewish identity in Rome (or whatever was left of it, if any) remains open.

Josephus's history of the Jewish War was probably influenced by a complicated set of interests. Many Jews viewed him as a traitor and turncoat. As historian to the Romans, he had to write a history that would satisfy his masters. As a Jew, he had to cope with some uneasy issues of identity as well as the obvious necessity of justifying his own actions. Nothing is thus too simple when it comes to Josephus.

Josephus was not physically present during the Roman siege of Masada, and his account of the events there is probably based on the reports (*commentarii*) and/or diaries written by the Roman military officers who had taken part in the siege of Masada. We should use Josephus's account cautiously, straying from his text only if there are compelling reasons to do so. For example, his citation of Ben-Yair's last two speeches needs to be taken with caution because he was not there and the invention of the tape recorder lay more than a thousand years in the future. Still, he knew the culture intimately and could have surmised the expressions of which such speeches could consist.

Without Josephus, virtually all our knowledge of the period and the relevant events would disappear; there would "be" no Masada. Without Josephus, "the history of the last two centuries of the Second Commonwealth could be reduced to a few pages—and a good part of that would be legendary" (Aberbach 1985: 25). I thus take Josephus's text as an historical baseline. The likelihood that Josephus lied to and cheated his Roman masters as well as those who were actually involved in the events, and fabricated a siege that never was, people who never existed, or an event that never took place, does not seem very high. Josephus's account was written very close to the events and it is the exclusive description of those fateful events. Historically speaking, it is the only detailed "truth" we have about the Jewish Great Revolt and Masada. The accuracy or validity of Josephus's writings is *not* being judged, tested or challenged here.

Masada: The Site

Masada is a mountain fortress nearly 100 kilometers southeast of Jerusalem (Livne 1986). The mountain's name and fortress in Hebrew is METZADA, literally a fort, fortress, or stronghold. The Greek transliteration of METZADA is "Masada" (Simchoni 1923: 513). Masada is a spectacular site. The doomed fortress is located near the Dead Sea, in the middle of a harsh and desolate terrain, with difficult access. If one stands atop the big, barren and serene yellowish plateau facing the silent, harsh, moon-like landscape, the cold desert breeze of early morning conjures up a near-mystical atmosphere, evoking a very eerie feeling. There almost seems to be a sort of a metaphysical presence on the top of the mountain.

The extraordinary site and atmosphere conspire to provoke a powerfully suggestive state of mind. The narrative of the doomed Great Revolt of the Jews, and the tragic death of the rebels, seem somehow to be in full harmony with the harsh and desolate terrain in the midst of which looms the desolate mountain-top fortress. The bleak physical environment of Masada seems to echo the historical narrative about the bloody revolt that ended in so much destruction.

The Historical Narrative[2]

One may perhaps begin by dating the Great Revolt to the year 6 AD, when the Romans sought to carry out a census in the province of Judea. One of the main opponents of the census was Yehuda of Gamla (also identified as Yehuda of the Galilee) who, with Zadok Haprushi, kindled the fire of resistance. They developed and promulgated the "fourth philosophy." The first three philosophies were those espoused by the Essenes, the Sadducees, and the Pharisees, respectively. The "fourth philosophy" emphasized the value of freedom, and its adherents felt allegiance only to God. While Yehuda was probably killed by the Romans, the "fourth philosophy" did not die. It continued to spread throughout the land, probably becoming the ideology of a group of Jewish fundamentalist rebels known as the Sicarii, identified with the aspiration to be free of, and totally opposed to, the rule of the Roman Empire (Feldman 1984: 655–67).

We first find the term "Sicarii" mentioned by Josephus in connection with events that took place between 52 and 62 AD. "Sicarii" derives from *sica*, referring to a small dagger which the Sicarii supposedly carried beneath their robes and which they used to attack and assassinate those whom they viewed as their opponents in Jerusalem, especially during holy days. Their tactics included intimidation and threats of violence against their political and ideological opponents and they were involved in indiscriminate terror activities, including political assassinations. Such was their killing of Yonatan Ben-Hanan, the former high priest of Jerusalem. They also kidnapped hostages whom they exchanged for their own people who had been captured by the Romans. Josephus describes that the Sicarii's attitude to local inhabitants who were not overtly hostile to Roman rule as "if they had been their enemies ... by plundering them of what they had, by driving away their cattle, and by setting fire to their houses" (Josephus 1981: 598).

Headed by Manahem, the Sicarii captured Masada and its armaments in 66 AD. They then headed to Jerusalem where they used the weapons to conquer the upper city.[3] They set fire to the house of Hanania the high priest and burned

[2] References to Josephus Flavius are to *The Complete Works of Josephus*, by Josephus Flavius, translated into English by William Whiston (Grand Rapids, MI: Kregel Publications, 1981).

[3] Josephus does not provide a clear or consistent account of the events leading to this capture (1981: 491). For example, it is unclear whether Manahem's men left a garrison there, and whether upon their return to Masada, Eleazar Ben-Yair and his men had to recapture it. Josephus states

the central archives where legal and commercial documents, deeds, and notes were kept. They also killed some Jews and surrendered Roman soldiers. These acts helped to mark the beginning of the Great Revolt and to further divide the Jewish population into "zealots" and "moderates."

As Manahem was killed by those opposing the Sicarii, he was replaced by Eleazar Ben-Yair, a relative of Manahem, and a "descendant from ... Judas who had persuaded ... Jews ... not to submit to the taxation" (ibid.: 598), who headed the Sicarii's escape to Masada. Josephus states that Ben-Yair "acted the part of a tyrant at Masada" taking the role of "commander" of the "Sicarii" (ibid.: 9, 492).

After the fall of Jerusalem, Lucilius Bassus was sent to Judea as legate and continued to suppress the remnants of the Jewish Great Revolt, taking the fortress of Herodion and later laying siege to Macherus, where fierce battles raged until that fortress surrendered. Following these successes, Bassus marched to the forest of Jarden where refugees from Jerusalem and Macherus were hiding. In the ensuing battle, all the Jews in the Jarden forest were killed (ibid.: 595–7). When Lucilius Bassus died,[4] Flavius Silva succeeded him as procurator of Judea (ibid.: 598). Realizing that "all the rest of the country was subdued in this war, and that there was but one only stronghold that was still in rebellion, he got all his army[5] together that lay in different places, and made an expedition against it. This fortress was called Masada" (ibid.: 598). The siege of Masada was thus not laid immediately after the fall of Jerusalem in the summer of 70 AD.

While Josephus is at times vague in his identification of people in particular places, when he describes the siege on Masada his use of the word "Sicarii" is very consistent, perhaps the most consistent in his book (see Dvir 1966). For example: "There was a fortress of very great strength not far from Jerusalem ... It is called Masada. Those that were called Sicarii had taken possession of it formerly" (Josephus 1981: 537).

The Roman army constructed a circumvallation wall around Masada to prevent the besieged from escaping. A siege ramp leading up to Masada on the eastern side of the mountain was erected as well. The Roman soldiers used their battering ram/s on the ramp to pound at the wall around Masada, breaching and destroying part of it. The Sicarii in the stronghold hastily built another wall, this time a soft one made of wood and earth filling, which could absorb the ramming energy of the war machines without yielding. The Roman soldiers set fire to

---

that "he [Eleazar Ben-Yair] and his Sicarii got possession of the fortress [Masada] by treachery" (ibid.: 599). See also Horsley and Hanson (1985: 212), Cotton and Geiger (1989: 1–24) and Cotton and Preiss (1990).

4 Possibly at the end of 72 AD (Simchoni 1923: 512).

5 Josephus probably meant the Tenth Legion ("Fretensis").

the second wall and destroyed it as well, undoubtedly signaling the end for the Sicarii in Masada (Netzer 1991). The their choices were clear. They could (a) try to escape, (b) fight to the inevitable end, (c) surrender, or (d) commit collective suicide. The first choice may have been seen by them as hopeless. Alternative (c) meant slavery for the women and children and painful and humiliating deaths for the men. Of the 967 people on Masada only a few hundred were probably capable of fighting, most of the rest being women and children; this may have reduced the appeal of option (b). Eleazar Ben-Yair opted for option (d). He addressed the besieged population in two speeches convincing them to accept this option. The Sicarii killed one another and themselves.

The account provided by Josephus does not mention the role of the women and children in the decision. Because the hesitations following Ben-Yair's first speech are attributed to the "soldiers," it seems safe to assume that the decisions were probably made by men from the dominant social category on Masada (Sicarii), and that the men killed everyone. The Sicarii left no choice for any would-be defaulters and the seven survivors—two women and five children—had to save themselves by hiding: "Yet, was there an ancient woman, and another who was of kin to Eleazar ... with five children, who had concealed themselves in caverns under ground ... and were hidden there when the rest were intent upon the slaughter of one another. These others were nine hundred and sixty in number ... ." Josephus's description of the hidden survivors obviously hints at an element of coercion. When the Romans entered Masada, "the women heard this noise and came out of their underground cavern, and informed the Romans what had been done, as it was done; and ... described ... what was said and what was done, and the manner of it.." (Josephus 1981: 603).

The Roman breach of the wall and the collective suicide took place on the evening and night of the 15th of Nisan 73 AD.[6] When the Romans entered Masada the next day, they were met with utter silence.

The Main Components of the Masada Historical Narrative

Josephus's account contains the following components:

1. Masada was part of a failed revolt against the Roman conquerors. The fall of Masada was only the death blow in the much larger suppression of

---

6 Josephus does not state in which year Masada fell. Most researchers assume it was 73 AD (Jones 1974; Stern 1989: 370, n. 17; Cotton and Geiger 1989: 21–4; Cotton 1989).

that revolt. Josephus implies that only a few minority groups of fanatics drew the Jews into the hopeless rebellion. Some researchers (for example, Menachem Stern's works) tend to reject this implication, asserting that the revolt was both popular and widespread. Unfortunately for the Jews at the time, the military picture was bleak. The Roman Empire of the first century AD was at the peak of its power, extending from Britain to Mesopotamia and controlling nearly thirty well-armed, amply provisioned and battle-ready legions: awesome military might for those days. At the time of the Great Revolt, the Roman Consular Legate in Syria was considered most important because of the threat of military challenge from the southeastern flank of the Roman Empire. He had four legions at his disposal, as well as the three legions stationed in Egypt and others that could be—and were—brought from elsewhere. The logic and justification of attempting to challenge that kind of military might are not easily discernible, especially without the benefit of having at least some political and military alliances.

2. During this period, the local Jewish population was divided among several different ideological groups. In his discussion of Masada, Josephus consistently and repeatedly uses the term "Sicarii" to describe the Jewish rebels there (Feldman 1984: 655–67; Horsley and Hanson 1985; Stern 1973).
3. Sicarii forces took control of Masada by force in 66 AD, before the beginning of the Great Revolt (Josephus 1981: 491).
4. The Sicarii in Jerusalem were involved in so much violence against Jews and others that they were forced to leave the city for Masada long before the Roman siege began. While one cannot rule out the remote possibility that non-Sicarii were amongst those trapped on top of Masada, Josephus's account does not support this interpretation. Moreover, the Sicarii were clearly the hegemonic and dominant group there.
5. Josephus mentions that when Simon the son of Giora wanted to join the Sicarii on top of Masada, they: "came to those robbers who had seized upon Masada ... only permitted him to come with the women he brought with him into the lower part of the fortress, while they dwelt in the upper part" (ibid.: 541). Evidently, the Sicarii were not too hospitable to non-Sicarii.
6. The Sicarii in Masada raided nearby villages. One brutal raid took place when:

> They came down by night, without being discovered ... overran a small city called Engaddi ... they prevented ... citizens that could have stopped them ... arm

> themselves and fight them. They... dispersed... and cast them out of the city. As for such that could not run away, being women and children, they slew of them above seven hundred. (ibid.: 537).

Afterwards, the Sicarii raiders carried the food supplies from Ein Gedi to Masada.

7. Josephus does not state the length of the siege on Masada; hence different time frames have been suggested. Evidently, the siege did *not* begin immediately after the destruction of Jerusalem in 70 AD. First, Herodion and Macherus were conquered, then Bassus died and was replaced by Flavius Silva, who had to gather his forces and only then launched the final attack on Masada. Researchers concur that the siege and fall of Masada only took a few months, probably from the winter of 72–73 AD until the following spring, a matter of a few months or weeks (Feldman 1984: 789–90). In fact, Roth's most impressive, meticulous and credible study states:

> All in all, a nine week siege is the likely maximum, a four week siege the likely minimum, and a siege of seven weeks the most probable length for the siege of Masada. Postulating a siege of some seven weeks fits in well with the date given by Josephus for the fall of the fortress, whatever calendar is being used. (1995: 109)

This conclusion is supported by Gill's (1993) work, which suggests that the massive siege ramp on the western slope is based on a huge natural spur. If this is so, then the Roman army did not construct the ramp from the bottom of the mountain, but only added the actual ramp on top of that natural spur—a significantly less strenuous effort than previously assumed.

8. Josephus's accounts of the sieges of Jerusalem and Macherus include courageous and fierce fights and raids by the defenders against the Romans. His account of Masada includes no mention of defensive forays at all. No serious anti-Roman military challenges seem to have occurred in Masada. Josephus had an obvious interest to note Jewish heroism because it meant the even greater heroism of the Roman army that conquered them. His failure to mention any impressive resistance by the Sicarii in Masada is not insignificant. True, the topography of Masada would have made such assaults difficult, but not impossible. Thus, while there were battles around Jerusalem (and Yodfat, and Macherus), consisting of skirmishes, raids, and forays, no such activities are projected about the Roman siege of Masada. In other words, there really was no "battle" over Masada; the

Roman military effort was less pronounced than the engineering effort, but even that was not extraordinary by Roman standards.

The puzzling omission of any mention of battles around Masada should be considered in conjunction with three additional pieces of information.

(a) Josephus states that the forces headed by Simon the son of Giora joined the "robbers who had seized upon Masada" and that both forces "ravaged and destroyed the country … about Masada" (Josephus 1981: 541; Horsley and Hanson 1985: 214). The "robbers" on Masada, however, would not join Simon's forces for "greater things," because they were used to living in Masada and "were afraid of going far from that which was their hiding place." Simon and his men did not share this fear and continued their battles, eventually ending their careers in the besieged city of Jerusalem, where they fought the Romans (as well as rival Jewish factions, including the Zealots). Simon was captured by the Romans, brought to Rome and killed there.

This piece of information strengthens the impression of the lack of a "fighting spirit" among the rebels on Masada, reinforced by what did *not* happen: the fighting forces on Masada *could* have killed the non-fighting personnel and then gone out to do battle against the Romans to the bitter end. But rather than choose this alternative, they killed one another. Interestingly enough, hundreds of years later, Joseippon (1981) changed the Masada narrative to precisely this scenario. Indeed, Zeitlin (1967: 262) and Hoenig (1970: 14; 1972: 112) point out that the Sicarii did not fight.

History provides many instances of heroic fights "to the last" (Philip 1994, Perrett 1991, Perrett 1995). One example is the last stand of Leonidas and his three hundred Spartans at the pass of Thermopylae in 480 BC. Even using a strictly Jewish analogy, when the Sicarii were faced with the choice, they selected suicide rather than follow the example of Biblical Samson, who took his enemies with him into death. The attribution of a "last stand" status to Masada's Sicarii assumes a particular type of heroism, in which one *fights* to the end or, if death is inevitable, one tries to inflict as much damage on the enemy as possible: "The concept of men selling their lives as dearly as possible forms an honorable part of most national histories and also the basis of much military tradition" (Perrett 1991: 7). Josephus's Masada most certainly does not qualify as a "last stand," and indeed cannot be one.

(b) Josephus notes that after the Romans entered Masada and discovered the dead bodies, they "could [do no other] than wonder at the courage of their [the Sicarii's] resolution, and at the immovable contempt of death which so great a number of them had shown, when they went through with such an

action ..." (Josephus 1981: 603). The resolve and courage of the Sicarii in committing collective suicide apparently elicited Roman respect and wonder. But, the analytic leap from "respect" to "heroism" is *not* made by Josephus, but rather socially constructed. Indeed, Josephus describes the suicidal Sicarii as "Miserable men indeed they were!" (ibid.).

(c) Magness's work implies that if "battles" were waged around Masada, they may have been confined to the last stage of the siege only. Magness refers to "the mystery of the absence of projectile points at Masada remains" (Magness 1992: 66). Describing the possible late phase of the siege, she states:

> Under covering artillery fire, the Roman forces dragged the battering ram up the ramp and broke through the wall ... The Roman auxiliary archers added covering fire to that of the machines as the forces ascended the ramp. The Zealots certainly returned the fire with everything at their command, including bows and arrows manufactured during the last days of the siege of Masada .... (Magness 1992: 67)

The major weight of the siege and battle for Masada may have been carried out not by the more prestigious units of the Roman Tenth Legion, but by the much less prestigious *auxiliari* troops:

> The soft arrowheads from Masada indicate that there was a major contingent of *auxiliari* troops at Masada and/or that the Zealots had armed themselves in the manner of auxiliaries, with bows and arrows ... Strangely, the excavators seem to have found no projectile points of the kind that would have been shot by legionaries from torsion bows ... [i]n contrast to the situation in Gamla ...where numerous projectile points were uncovered. (ibid.: 64).

One is thus left with the unavoidable conclusion that there simply is no evidence for significant resistance of the "last-stand" type around Masada.

The overall impression, then, is that the Sicarii on Masada, so adept at raiding nearby villages, were not particularly talented fighters and, in fact, avoided battle. Perhaps they never believed that the Roman army could reach them and thus did not think that they had to fight. As it became clear that the end was approaching, they may have hastily put together some sort of defense, but if so, it was too little and too late. Eventually they did not "fight to the end," preferring suicide instead. If this deduction is valid, then the resulting conclusion is inevitable: the history of the Roman siege on Masada does not convey a particularly heroic picture.

9. Josephus "quotes" at length the two speeches made by Eleazar Ben-Yair that were required to persuade 960 people on Masada to commit suicide. The implication is that the Jewish Sicarii on Masada were at first reluctant to take their own lives.
10. Seven people survived the collective suicide. This is an important point, because the details of that last night on Masada were provided by one of the women survivors.

Thus, when we look at the main components of Josephus Flavius's narrative of the Great Revolt and of Masada, no portrait of heroism on Masada emerges. On the contrary, the narrative relates the story of a hopeless (and questionable) rebellion, of its majestic failure and the destruction of the Second Temple and of Jerusalem, of large-scale massacres of the Jews, of different factions of Jews fighting one another, of an act of collective suicide (hardly a positive act in Judaism) by a group of terrorists and assassins whose "fighting spirit" was suspect.

From the Roman military perspective, the Masada campaign against the Sicarii must have been an insignificant action after a major war in Judea; a sort of "mopping-up" operation, something which had to be done, but which did not involve anything special in terms of military strategy or effort. Another item of information may add credibility to the above conjecture. Two almost identical ancient Roman inscriptions from 81 AD were found in Urbs Salvia (in northern Italy, south of Ancona) in the late 1950s. The inscriptions describe the career of L. Flavius Silva Nonius Bassus. No mention of Masada can be found in the inscriptions (perhaps none should be expected).[7] It is stated that Flavius Silva was in charge of the "provinciae Iudaeae," and that during his career he commanded two Roman legions.

The question that cannot be evaded is how could the unsavory story that emerges from Josephus's narrative become such a positive symbol of heroism? Obviously, the mythical narrative which projects tremendous heroism had to be socially constructed and diffused, because it is totally absent from the original historical narrative.

[7] See *Annee Epigraphique* (1969–70), section 183; Pauly-Wissowa, *Paulys Realincyclopdie Der Classischen Altertums-Wissenschaft*, Supplementband 14 (Munchen 1974), 121–2, entry 181. I am very grateful to Shmuel Sermoneta-Gertel from the Department of Classical Studies at the Hebrew University who helped me with this issue.

The Masada Mythical Narrative

The Masada mythical narrative began to develop among the Jewish population of British-mandate Palestine in the early decades of the twentieth century, but accumulated momentum in the 1920s and had crystallized by the early 1940s. Although the entire Masada mythical narrative comprises a narrative with a trip to and climb up Masada—that is, a cognitive, physical, and emotional experience—we may easily delineate the cognitive aspect.

The Masada mythical narrative can be found in many school textbooks, history books, guidebooks, and pamphlets, and a large variety of other publications in Israel. Consciousness-raising trips to Masada involved schools and youth movements, and thousands of new recruits to the Israeli military were marched to Masada to swearing-in ceremonies. The myth may be said to have evolved from a critical stance towards Josephus Flavius as historian. This critical view typically remolds such problematic issues as the identity of the Masada rebels, the massacre at Ein Gedi, the "battle" at Masada, the duration of the Roman siege, the suicide, and the survivors.

What is the Masada mythical narrative?

If we take the many different sources of where the Masada myth appears (Ben-Yehuda 1995) and summarize them, then the essence of the Masada mythical narrative may be sketched briefly as follows:

The leaders of the popular Great Revolt were Zealots, adherents of one of the Jewish ideological trends of the period. The imperial Roman army crushed the revolt, conquered and destroyed Jerusalem together with the Second Temple of the Jews. The Zealots who survived the siege and destruction of the city escaped to the fortress of Masada, a stronghold difficult to reach atop a mountain near the Dead Sea. From there, the Zealots harassed the Romans and created such a threat that the Romans decided to make the tremendous military effort required to destroy Masada. Consequently, the Romans gathered their army, made the long and arduous march through the Judean desert and reached Masada. There, they surrounded the fortress and put it under siege. After three years of heroic battle by the few Zealots against the huge Roman army, the Zealots on Masada realized that their situation was hopeless. They faced a grim future: either be killed by the Romans, or become slaves. Eleazar Ben-Yair, the commander, addressed his followers and persuaded them all that they had to die as free men. They thus decided to kill themselves, a heroic and liberating death, rather than become wretched slaves. When the Roman soldiers entered Masada, they found only silence and dead bodies.

Masada has thus become a symbol for a heroic "last stand." In the words of the famous Israeli chief-of-staff and politician Moshe Dayan (1983: 21): "Today, we can point only to the fact that Masada has become a symbol of heroism and of liberty for the Jewish people to whom it says: Fight to death rather than surrender; Prefer death to bondage and loss of freedom."

Clearly, the popular, widespread Masada mythical narrative has some elements of truth in it, but in the main, it is significantly different from what Josephus tells us. It takes a long, complex, and at some points unclear, historical sequence and reduces it to a simple and straightforward heroic narrative, characterized by a few clear themes. It emphasizes that a small group of heroes who had survived the battle of Jerusalem chose to continue the fight against the Romans to the bitter end rather than surrender.

The Masada mythical narrative is thus constructed by transforming a tragic historical event into a heroic fable. The hapless revolt is transformed into a heroic war. The questionable collective suicide on Masada is transformed into a brave last stand of the few against the many. The myth is thus based on the following points:

1. The rebels/Zealots/freedom fighters on Masada were few.
2. They were soldiers who engaged in a "battle."
3. The Sicarii are seldom mentioned. "Zealots" may sound better than the negative connotation of "Sicarii." Although Josephus does not refer to the "Zealots" in positive terms, the myth-makers managed to associate "Zealots" with such feelings as "Zeal for freedom" and thus to paint the "Zealots" in positive terms. No such exercise was (or could be) performed for the "Sicarii." The mythologizers ignored Josephus, who in at least one place (pp. 598–9) included the "Zealots" among the brutal "villains" whose zeal for virtue was a sham.
4. The massacres in Ein Gedi (and elsewhere) disappear.
5. The people on Masada had come from Jerusalem, the last defenders of the city.
6. The siege of Masada was a protracted one (three years).
7. The suicide is "undone," that is, repressed or explained away as a "no-choice" situation.
8. Masada is frequently portrayed as a rebel base for "operations" against the Romans.

9. Eleazar Ben-Yair's two speeches are telescoped into one, eliminating the hesitancy of the Sicarii to take one another's lives. Heroes do not hesitate.
10. The seven hiding survivors of Masada typically disappear.

The result is the construction of a powerful, persuasive and consistently heroic tale. When it is told within a walking trip to Masada a cognitive and physical effect is achieved.

Dating the creation of the myth

The Masada mythical narrative played a crucial role in the crystallization of a new individual and collective identity for Israeli Jews between the early 1940s and the late 1960s. The return of Jews to Palestine, with the explicit political goal of creating a Jewish homeland, is typically dated to the 1880s. Secular Zionist Jews, both before and after the proclamation of statehood in 1948, doubtless craved tales of Jewish heroism, and creating the Masada mythical narrative most certainly served some very important functions for them.

Why was there such a need? During the British Mandate period, the Zionist movement pushed hard for the return of the Jews to their ancient homeland. In British-controlled Palestine itself, it was clear that the Arabs did not welcome the returning Jews and that an Arab nationalist movement was developing. The local *Yishuv* (Jewish community in pre-state Palestine) and its leaders not only had to contend with this, but also with anti-Semitic stereotypes of Jews as non-combatants, passive, money-changers, and so on. During those fateful years, there was clearly an urgent need for new, nationalistic Jewish symbols of heroism, and the Masada mythical narrative came into being almost naturally.

The need for heroic Jewish symbols was magnified tremendously in the 1930s and 1940s, as the dangerous specter of fascism loomed over Europe and the Nazi threat became increasingly manifest. Between 1940 and 1942, the "Plan for the North" (popularly known as "The Masada Plan") crystallized among the Jewish leadership. It was a direct result of the fear instilled in the *Hagana* (the biggest and most significant pre-state Jewish underground organization in Palestine) by the successes of Rommel's Afrika Korps in North Africa in 1941. In early 1942, the danger of a Nazi German invasion of Palestine seemed a very real threat. The basic idea of the plan was to concentrate the *Yishuv* into a huge fortified locality around Mount Carmel and Haifa (the evacuation of women and children—perhaps to Cyprus—was considered). The plan assumed a perimeter covering an area of about 200 square kilometers from where it was believed the fight against the Germans could be continued for as long as possible (see Ben-Yehuda 1995: 131–8).

During those early years, a few influential moral entrepreneurs and memory agents made it their goal to create and disseminate the Masada mythical narrative, especially Joseph Klosner, and, perhaps the most dynamic of them all, Shmaria Guttman. Differences existed among them. For example, while Klosner referred to the "Sicarii" in heroic terms, Guttman hid the "Sicarii." By structuring the basic theme of the Masada mythical narrative, they provided an important building block of a new identity for secular Jews in Palestine. Since Simchoni's excellent 1923 translation of Josephus was available, the myth-makers could utilize this new translation for their purposes by playing with the text (Ben-Yehuda 1995).

The story of Masada was embraced by youth movements, the pre-State Jewish underground organizations, and later the Israeli Army, and the Israeli educational system as *the* symbol of Jewish heroism. The Masada mythical narrative was constructed, delivered, and accepted as an authentic story of supreme heroism in the service of a genuine and justified cause. The narrative emphasized the pride and courage of the Jews, fighting for their liberty and their land. This heroic narrative not only created a 2,000-year-old link, but also kept it alive. The physical symbol of this connection was located in a harsh environment, which had changed only slightly since 73 AD, and which provided the narrative with a very powerful element of credibility. In a period in which the new Jewish settlers in Palestine (and later Israel) were encouraged to tour the country, Masada became a preferred site.

Yigael Yadin's excavations of Masada in 1963–65 were actually the last chapter in the crystallization of the Masada mythical narrative. These excavations provided a scientific buttress for a national and popular myth, and it is for this reason that the excavations created so much political and social interest in Israel.

The Masada mythical narrative was disseminated by almost all available cultural means of expression imaginable. First, Masada was a major ingredient in the socialization processes of all five major secular Jewish youth movements in Palestine and Israel, but to a much lesser degree for the two religious movements. Secondly, the three major pre-State Jewish underground groups used Masada explicitly in their symbols and socialization processes. Likewise, the Israeli Army used Masada as both a symbol and a site at which new soldiers were sworn in after (or during) boot camp. Fourth, elementary and high school texts, as well as general history texts and encyclopedias, propounded the myth. Fifth, the Masada mythical narrative appeared in travel guides and became part of the standard repertoire of local tour guides, eventually also encompassing the physical location as the site for ceremonies and cultural events. Sixth, both inside and outside Israel, the myth figured in poetry and prose, plays and films, music, and the plastic arts. Finally, the printed and electronic media devoted space and time to transmit the myth.

The transformation of the doomed revolt and mass suicide on top of Masada to a modern national myth of heroism was complete by the 1960s. This myth served as a cultural code that amplified patriotic values, helped to define the symbolic-moral boundaries of the new Israeli-ness, and was a building block in the emerging new personal and collective identity of many Israelis.

References

Aberbach, Moses (1985). "Josephus and His Critics: A Reassessment," *Midstream*, 31(5): 25–9.

Ben-Yehuda, Nachman (1995). *The Masada Myth*. Madison, WI: University of Wisconsin Press.

— (2002). *Sacrificing Truth: archaeology and the myth of Masada*. Amherst, NY: Prometheus Books.

— (2009). "The history, myth, and science of Masada. The making of an historical ethnography," in *Ethnographies Revisited: Constructing theory in the field*, eds. William Shaffir, Antony Puddephatt and Steven Kleinknecht. London and New York: Routledge, pp. 331–45.

Cotton, Hanna M. (1989). "The date of the Fall of Masada: The Evidence of the Masada Papyri," *Zeitschrift fur Papyrologie und Epigraphik*, 78: 157–62.

— and Joseph Geiger (1989). "The Latin and Greek Documents," in *MASADA II. The Yigael Yadin Excavations 1963–1965. Final Report*, eds. Joseph Aviram, Gideon Foerster and Ehud Netzer. Jerusalem: Israel Exploration Society and the Hebrew University of Jerusalem.

— and Yehonatan Preiss (1990). "Who Conquered Masada in 66 A.D. and who occupied it until it fell?" *Zion* 55: 449–54.

Dvir, Yehuda (1966). "The Ideological Face of the Heroes of Masada," *Hauma*, 4(15): 327–46.

Feldman, Louis H. (1984). *Josephus and Modern Scholarship (1937–1980)*. New York and Berlin: Walter de Gruyter.

Gill, Dan (1993). "A Natural Spur at Masada," *Nature*, 364(6438): 569–70.

Hawkes, C. (1929). "The Roman Siege of Masada," *Antiquity*, III: 195–213.

Hoenig, Sidney B. (1970). "The Sicarii in Masada: Glory or infamy?" *Tradition*, 11(1): 5–30.

— (1972). "Historic Masada and the *Halakhah*," *Tradition*, 13(2): 100–116.

Horsley, Richard A. and John S. Hanson (1985). *Bandits, Prophets, and Messiahs: Popular Movements at the Time of Jesus*. San Francisco, CA: Harper and Row.

Jones, C.P. (1974). "Review (of Eck's book)," *American Journal of Philology*, 95: 89–90.

Josephus, Flavius (1981). *The Complete Works of Josephus*, trans. William Whiston. Grand Rapids, MI: Kregel Publications.

Joseippon [Josephus Gorionides] (1981 edn.), ed. with intro., commentary, and notes David Flusser. Jerusalem: The Bialik Institute (in Hebrew).

Livne, Micha (1986). *Last Fortress. The Story of Masada and its People*. Tel Aviv: Ministry of Defense.

Luttwak, Edward N. (1976). *The Grand Strategy of The Roman Empire, from the First Century to the Third*. London and Baltimore, MD: Johns Hopkins University Press.

Magness, Jodi (1992). "Masada: Arms and the Man," *Biblical Archaeology Review*, 18(4): 58–67.

Netzer, E. (1991). *Masada III: the Yigael Yadin excavations 1963–1965 Final Reports: the buildings, stratigraphy and architecture*. Jerusalem: Israel Exploration Society and the Hebrew University of Jerusalem.

Paine, Robert (1994). "Masada: A History Of A Memory," *History and Anthropology* 6(4): 371–409.

Perrett, Bryan (1991). *Last Stand! Famous Battles Against the Odds*. London: Arms and Armour Press.

Philip, Craig (1994). *Last Stands: Famous Battles Against the Odds*. London: Grange Books.

Richmond, I.A. (1962). "The Roman Siege-Works of Masada, Israel," *The Journal of Roman Studies* LII: 142–55.

Roth, Jonathan (1995). "The Length of the Siege of Masada," *Scripta Classica Israelica* 14: 87–110.

Shargel, Baila R. (1979). "The Evolution of the Masada Myth," *Judaism* 28: 357–71.

Shatzman, Israel (1993). "The Roman Siege On Masada," in *The Story of Masada: Discoveries from the Excavations*, ed. Gila Hurvitz. Jerusalem: Hebrew University; Antiquities Authority; the Society for Studying Eretz Israel and Its Antiquities, pp. 105–20.

Simchoni, Y.N. (1970 [1923]). "Notes and Explanations" to the Hebrew translation (from Greek) of Joseph Ben-Matityahu (Josephus Flavius), *The History of the Wars of the Jews With the Romans*. Tel Aviv: Masada (in Hebrew), pp. 409–520.

Spero, Shubert (1970). "In Defense of the Defenders of Masada," *Tradition* 11(1): 31–43.

Stern, Menachem (1973). "Zealots," in the *Encyclopaedia Judaica*, Year Book 1973, pp. 135–51.

— (1989). "The Suicide of Eleazar Ben Yair and his Men in Masada and the 'Fourth Philosophy,'" *Zion*, 4(47): 367–97 (in Hebrew).

Yadin, Yigael (1966). *Masada: Herod's fortress and the zealots' last stand.* London: Weidenfeld and Nicolson.

Zeitlin, Solomon (1965). "Masada and the Sicarii," *Jewish Quarterly Review* 55: 299–317.

— (1967). "The Sicarii and Masada, "*Jewish Quarterly Review* 57: 251–70.

Zerubavel, Yael (1995). *Recovered Roots. Collective Memory and the Making of Israeli National Tradition*, Chicago, IL: University of Chicago Press.

Chapter 2

Religious Mass Suicide Before Jonestown: The Russian Old Believers

Thomas Robbins

Introduction

Over a period of several decades in late seventeenth- and early eighteenth-century Russia, tens of thousands of "Old Believers" committed suicide, generally by self-immolation. Most of the suicides were not individual acts but transpired in the context of catastrophic collective events at hermitages or monasteries. In several instances, the number of persons who perished at a burned-out settlement far exceeded the number of deaths at Jonestown. Convergences with the Peoples Temple holocaust include a general climate of apocalyptic excitation; a sectarian Manichean outlook which perceived absolute evil triumphant in the world, and in which "political" themes became more prominent over time, and a conviction of imminent armed assault by hostile forces. Both the Old Believers and the Peoples Temple experienced difficulties in resolving the tension between the impulse to violently confront a demonic state and the desire to develop a communal refuge where they could live according to their faith. Marked divergences include the degree of actual persecution, and the post-holocaust survival and growth of Old Believers.

Although much has been written about the mass suicide of members of the Peoples Temple community at Jonestown in Guyana in November, 1978, very little of the literature has entailed a comparative analysis focusing on other incidents involving collective suicide events resembling the tragic events at Jonestown.[1] Contemporary American "cults" have been the primary referent

[1] During the preparation of this chapter the author was not aware of any other scholarly work which ventured a comparison between the Jonestown tragedy and mass suicides among the "Old Believers" in late seventeenth-century Russia. While this article was in press, the author was sent an insightful conference paper by David Chidester, "Religious Suicide: Death and Classification at Jonestown" which had been presented to the annual meeting of the American Academy of Religion, in Dallas, Texas, in 1983. Chidester's description of the events leading up

for comparisons and prophetic extrapolations of the "lessons of Jonestown" (Seigelman and Conway 1979, Yanoff 1984). The diversity of the groups which have been subsumed under the "cult" label may vitiate the heuristic value of these warnings, even when a subcategory of "destructive cults" is specified. Numerous authoritarian, communal, and "totalistic" spiritual movements have not become involved in spectacular large-scale violence. The deviant and authoritarian practices related to life in Jonestown prior to the final holocaust are common to numerous world-rejecting sects (Hall 1981), such that the characteristic features of these movements cannot be viewed as predictive of mass suicide, although they may perhaps be necessary conditions. On the other hand, an exclusive focus on contemporary American phenomena holds constant some of the contextual factors which a cross-cultural or historical inquiry might explore.

It is noteworthy that there are certain historical episodes which bear some similarity to the events at Jonestown. This present exploratory chapter hardly represents an exhaustive analysis of either the Jonestown tragedy or any other historical episode, nor is any decisive predictive formula attempted. It is hoped that this chapter will serve as a stimulant to subsequent investigations of historical episodes of collective self-extinction which will have an explicit or implicit comparative focus. This chapter will examine one such episode and draw some suggestive parallels with the Jonestown tragedy.

The Old Believers

During the final decades of the seventeenth century, in Russia at least 20,000 men and women burned themselves to death. On a smaller scale, this practice continued until the mid-nineteenth century. Most of the suicides were not individual actions but rather were part of collective events transpiring at a monastery or peasant community linked to the schismatic "Old Believer" movement. One of the earlier instances in 1679 involved an expedition of soldiers sent to destroy a hermitage by the Berezorka river where Old Believers were said to have gathered and gone into a state of religious ecstasy. Troops were sent to take the leaders into custody, but the sectarians were warned of the approaching soldiers. "When the soldiers arrived," writes historian George Vernadsky, "they found only smouldering ruins; the Old Believers had burned

to the Russian suicides is less extensive than the present account, and his theoretical framework, though quite incisive, is very different from the present writer's exploratory focus. "Religious Mass Suicide Before Jonestown: The Russian Old Believers" was first published in *Sociological Analysis* 47(1986): 1–20.

the buildings and themselves. Seventeen hundred men and women died in the holocaust" (Vernadsky 1961: 710).

In the following sections, we will give a short review of the Great Schism in the Russian Orthodox Church and the facts leading up to the wave of mass suicide events in the late seventeenth century. We will then summarize Cherniavsky's discussion of the evolving "political theology" (1970) of the Old Believers and its relationship to their descent into apocalyptic despair. We will then develop tentative parallels with the Jonestown episode as analyzed by Naipaul (1980) and Hall (1981).

The Great Schism

The Great Dissent or *Raskol* began in the reign of Tsar Alexis, who appointed Nikon to be Orthodox Patriarch of Moscow. During the years 1652–54, Nikon decreed changes in ritual and liturgy involving the sign of the cross (to be made with three fingers instead of the traditional two), the number and manner of prostrations, the Hallelujah glorification, and texts for services. Nikon's reforms represented "resolute measures to make Russian practice conform with the usage of the Greek and Ukrainian churches of his day" (Crummey 1970: 4).[2] Supported by the tsar, Nikon forced through his reforms in a series of church councils during 1654–56 at which persisting clerical opponents of his measures were condemned. In 1656, a handful of priests led by archpriest Avvakum were disciplined and exiled. These "Old Believers" affirmed that

> The Muskovite Church was right and could never sin in word, customs or writings, for the Church was sacred and nothing in its practice or doctrine could be suppressed or altered ... They regarded any modification of the church service as a sin which obstructed the way to salvation. (Zenkovsky 1957b: 42)

Who were the dissenters? Murvar notes that the *Raskolniki*

> ... directly originated from the monastic institutions of the official state church. Organized monasticism in its totality violently opposed the changes planned by Nikon and by the tsars. The chief organizers and propagandists of resistance and the subsequent

[2] Ultimately, Nikon's revisionism may have reflected the transformation of the expanding Tsarist state from "a purely Great Russian state" to an "All-Russian Empire", Zenkovsky, (1957b: 37–58). Old Believer self-immolations were on a far larger scale.

> emergent sects were respectable leaders of the monks, including the abbots of famous monasteries. They were convinced that they were defending the only true traditionalistic Orthodox values and were willing to fight to martyrdom. (Murvar 1975)

The monks welcomed the opportunity to liberate themselves from the Orthodox hierarchy (which basically accepted the Nikonian reforms) and to exercise innovative personal charisma.

As it grew, the *Raskol* attracted large numbers of peasants, for whom religious restorationism arguably became a symbolic expression of popular antipathy to the consolidation of serfdom and the bureaucratic centralization of the tsarist state. The Nikonian revisions of tradition also had an intrinsic significance for illiterate peasants for whom "ritual gesture and doctrine were inseparable," such that arbitrary liturgical changes "might well seem to subvert the Orthodox faith itself (Crummey 1970: 9).

The Kapitons

The recruitment of common folk to the *Raskol* was enhanced by the fact that, "in the middle decades of the seventeenth century, the cultural atmosphere of Russia was charged with tension born of apocalyptic expectations" (ibid.: 7). This apocalyptic milieu will be discussed later and compared with the American milieu of 1970s and '80s. For now it must be noted that the apocalyptic mood in Russia found expression in a sect led by the ascetic hermit, Kapiton, which affirmed that "the end of the world was at hand and that Antichrist already ruled the world" (ibid.: 7). Kapiton urged his followers to prepare for the end through prayer, fasting, and other ascetic practices. However, some Kapitonists felt that this was not sufficient: "they longed to follow the example of the saints of the early church and suffer martyrdom for their faith ... Small groups of the sect's members quenched their thirst for martyrdom by burning themselves to death in 1665 and 1666 in scattered locations of northern Russia" (ibid. 45). Suicidal Kapitons referred to their immolative apotheosis as "purification by fire" (Vernadsky 1969: 698). Subsequent Old Believer self-immolations were on a far larger scale but they may have been influenced by the earlier *Kapitonovshchina*.

Old Believer Ups and Downs

A key feature of the history of the Old Believer movement prior to the largest wave of suicides in the late 1680s and early 1690s was a series of events whereby at certain points, political conditions appeared favorable for a restoration of the old practices to the Orthodox Church; however, each time defeat and repression was somehow extricated from what had seemed to be the gaping jaws of victory. Continually tantalized and then frustrated, the Old Believers became increasingly volatile and apocalyptic.

Patriarch Nikon, an ecclesiastical supremacist, fell out with the tsar and the boyars and, after 1658, ceased to exercise his patriarchal functions. Irritated by Nikon's interference in state affairs, some of the boyars began to patronize the Old Believers. The exiled Avvakum returned to Moscow and was received by Tsar Alexis. But Avvakum also tended to emphasize the importance of having the state guided by religious authorities, and the boyars "came to believe that Avvakum, given the chance, would be even more unmanageable, and more dangerous to the interests of the state as they understood them, than Nikon" (ibid.: 594). Avvakum was arrested and re-exiled in 1664. A council of bishops in 1666–67 formally deposed Nikon but also sanctioned the Nikonian reforms and anathematized the dissidents.

In 1669, three noblewomen who had joined the Old Believers were imprisoned and starved and other leading adherents were executed. At this time, government troops had been besieging the Solovokii Monastery, an Old Believer stronghold, for several years. In 1657, the monks had refused to use reformed service texts sent by the patriarch. In 1666, the opposition of the militant monks "flared into open revolt" and they declared that they were willing to suffer rather than cross themselves with three fingers, which evoked "the seal of Antichrist" (Crummey 1970: 18–19). The government intervened in 1667 and the siege of the monastery lasted eight years, during which the resisters became increasingly radicalized. They were reported to be welcoming fleeing survivors of the failed revolt of Stepan Razin. In 1673, they formally resolved not to pray for the tsar: "Gradually the political elements in the revolt achieved increasing prominence until, in the last stages, it became a hopeless protest against the legitimacy and effective power of the Russian government" (ibid.: 21). After the fall of the monastery in 1676, the soldiers "slaughtered all but fourteen of the approximately two hundred defenders and put the cloister to the sack" (ibid.: 20). But the monks who escaped became militant leaders and missionaries.

A few days after the fall of the monastery, Tsar Alexis died. He was succeeded by his sickly son Feodor, whose government exiled Matveev, a "westernizing" statesman and opponent of the Old Believers: "For a moment, the Old Believers had hopes that the wheel of history was turning and that the government would take a more conciliatory attitude toward them. These hopes did not materialize" (ibid.: 709). Tsar Feodor, whose tutor had been an anti-Old Believer polemicist, kept up the pressure: "Desperation spread among the adherents of the true faith.

They felt that the old kingdom of Antichrist was about to come. The trends developing among the Old Believers worried even Avvakum" (ibid.: 709). It was in this context that the mass suicide event, which we have previously described, took place at the Berezorka River hermitage, where soldiers discovered smoldering ruins and 1,700 corpses (ibid.: 710). But worse was yet to come!

The Revolt of the Streltsy

Avvakum urged his colleagues to pray for Tsar Feodor and hoped that he might be persuaded to return to the old ways. However, another leader, Abbot Dosifei, was determined to resort to force. He planned a demonstration among some sympathetic *streltsy* (Moscow garrison troops) and "consulted Avvakum about his plan." The latter approved, "'Act for the love of God, but move with prudence'" (ibid.: 710–11). There was an abortive Moscow conspiracy in January 1681, after which "It was decided to strengthen the punitive measures against the Old Believers" (ibid.: 711). Avvakum and three colleagues were burned at the stake on April 4, 1682.

But meanwhile Feodor had died in February, 1682. The succession was disputed between two half-brothers: 16-year-old Ivan, who was sickly and mentally deficient, and robust 10-year-old Peter. Their elder sister Sophia exploited discontent among the *streltsy*, who stormed the palace, slaughtered Matveev (who had been returned to power by the supporters of Peter) and other notables, and installed Sophia as regent. Prince Knovansky, who appeared sympathetic to the Old Believers, was appointed commander of the *streltsy*.

The *streltsy* now presented a "petition" which initially pleaded for tolerance for the old practices, but "the plea for toleration quickly turned into a demand for religious restoration" (Cherniavsky 1970: 157). Sophia was forced to sponsor a public debate on the Nikonian reforms, at which, "the Old Believers' chief spokesman, Nikita 'pustosviat' ('the bigot') treated the patriarch and Sophia herself with contemptuous disrespect and made abundantly clear that his party would be content with nothing else than a complete return to the pre-Nikonian ritual" (Crummey 1970: 22). Sophia perceived that implicit in this position was stigmatization of her father, Tsar Alexis, and her brother, Tsar Feodor, as heretics. She angrily expressed herself to this effect and stormed out of the meeting. Not long afterwards some loyalist *streltsy* arrested "the bigot," who was beheaded for *lese-majeste.* Subsequently, Sophia mobilized a detachment of gentry cavalry, which overpowered Prince Khovansky's *streltsy* guard and executed Khovansky and others.

The events of the *streltsy* revolt set the stage for intensified persecution and alienation. The crisis of 1682

> … showed that the Old Believers were prepared to support any rebellion that offered hope for the restoration of the old faith … there could be no doubt that the Old Believers were a threat to tranquillity of the state as well as the Church. Sophia understandably became their implacable enemy. (Crummey 1970: 40)

The Great Wave of Immolations

Severe new regulations against the Old Believers were promulgated by Sophia's government in 1684. Suspected heretics were to be tortured and heretics refusing to recant would be burned at the stake. The movement now went underground; many fled to Poland or sought refuge in remote regions of Russia, which were also favored because of "the dissenters' own desire to avoid all contact with the world," which was seen to have "become contaminated by the presence of Antichrist and the spread of the 'Nikonian heresies', and was forever lost for the Orthodox faith" (Zenkovsky 1957b: 51). At the time,

> Apocalyptic moods now spread among the persecuted members of the true faith. The coming of Antichrist and the end of the world was imminent. In their religious ecstasy, many of the Old Believers sought the solution of their plight in self-immolation … It is estimated that between 1784 and 1691 no less than twenty thousand men and women burned themselves. (Vernadsky 1969: 716)

In addition,

> The actual mass suicides seem to have generally arisen when armed intervention against a settlement of dissidents appeared to be on the verge of success. The besieged would set fire to buildings in which they had previously strategically placed flammable materials, such that in each of several major incidents 1000–2500 would perish.[3] In some (but not all) cases the attacks by soldiers on Old Believer strongholds which led to mass suicides were deliberately provoked by Old Believers, who seized monasteries and church buildings to force the authorities to send a military force against them so they could be martyred. Martyrdom was sought because it was believed that the

[3] Crummey states that "according to Old Believer traditions," 1,500 to "several" thousand persons perished in each of the three incidents he reports, although he reports other incidents where all the inhabitants of a settlement perished but no numbers are given (Crummey 1970: 39–57).

> apocalypse was imminent and could be hastened by confrontation and purifying immolation. The urge of passive suffering was complimented by a desire, a hunger to fight back against those who had destroyed true religion. Real social and economic grievances of a local nature intensified this spirit of resistance. (Crummey 1970: 51)

But the majority of Old Believers and the leaders opposed such extreme acts. Abbot Dosifei refused to pray for the suicide victims. In 1816, his disciple, Evfrosin, published a tract, "Refutation of the Newly Invented System of Suicide." Subsequently the volume of suicides declined but did not totally cease until 1860 (Cherniavsky 1970). "Time was on the side of the moderates" as the world failed to end on predicted dates: "The leaders of Old Belief came to see that they would simply have to adjust to continued existence in Antichrist's world." Moreover, as the extremist pro-suicide believers killed themselves, they "left the field to the moderates" (Crummey 1970: 56).

Under Peter the Great, some of the laws against Old Believers were relaxed, although they were expected to pay a double poll tax. Under the leadership of the Denisov brothers, a flourishing center of traditionalist spiritual culture developed in a settlement on the Vyg River. Mining and other economic ventures were pursued profitably and there was even some collaboration with Peter's regime on certain building projects: "The policy of Peter's government gave the more moderate Old Believers an opportunity to separate themselves from Russian society and build the institutions through which they would preserve the faith" (Crummey 1970: 51)[4]

Under the Empress Anna, in the 1730s, there was again a threat of persecution. Apocalyptic sentiments were renewed and Old Believers debated among themselves whether the person or merely the spirit of Antichrist was rampant in the state, and by implication, whether believers could justifiably pray for the tsar, and thus be safe from persecution (Cherniavsky 1970). The movement splintered into dozens of sects. But it also grew, and religious restorationism became a basic element in a crystallizing counterculture of anti-tsar and agrarian protest.

---

[4] Crummey notes that, unlike Sophia (whom Peter overthrew in 1687), "Through most of his reign, Peter I attempted to distinguish between those adherents of Old Belief who openly opposed his regime and those whose primary concern was the preservation of the old faith. The distinction cut the ground from under the militant position, for few Old Believers were prepared to kill themselves until agents of Antichrist actively persecuted them in some way" (1970: 56–7).

Apocalypticism and Political Theology

What led the Old Believers to apocalyptic despair and suicidal frenzy? Vicious persecution was a crucial factor but it cannot explain everything. First, the fierce persecution must be explained. Secondly, the dissidents were themselves confronting the established Church in a context of minimal church-state separation, but additionally in terms of their own provocative behavior and their determination to recapture control of the Church and extirpate Nikonian heresy.

It is important to realize that freedom of worship for the schismatics and toleration for religious pluralism and non-conformity were hardly the real concern of the early Old Believers. Avvakum and his followers, as well as Nikon and his supporters, believed in One True Church which must inspire and permeate the state. All of the contending parties affirmed an absolute unity of church and state. The problematic for the Avvakumists was therefore not whether they would be "left alone," but whether they could capture the state and thereby undo the impious Nikonian reforms. The Old Believer dissent was thus rather politicized from the outset.

To the Old Believers, the Nikonian revisionism implied a condemnation of the Russian past which undercut the legitimacy of the whole conceptual foundation of orthodox universalism. The past councils and tsars could not have evoked the doctrine of "Moscow The Third Rome," which was also accepted by the Nikonians (Crummey 1970). The Third Rome doctrine affirmed that

> Moscow was the spiritual capital of Christianity and that her unique and exclusive orthodoxy was historically proven and divinely confirmed. And, as the third Rome was also the last, this meant that Muscovite Orthodoxy was the only currency of the economy of salvation. If Moscow were to fall from grace, betray the faith as had the first two Romes, it would mean not only the fall of Moscow as a state, as divine punishment, but the end of the whole world; a fourth Rome there could not be, and Moscow's fall would signify the end of the possibility of salvation for all men, and the coming of the last days. (ibid.: 146)

In this context, what conclusion would have been drawn from the tsar and the patriarch's persistence in impious innovations which implicitly denied the holy Muskovite past? "There was only one general conclusion possible: if Moscow, the Third Rome, had instituted religious changes which required the condemnation of itself in its own past, then Moscow had accepted heresy—and the end was at hand (Crummey 1970: 148). "The end" meant the apocalypse: the end of the world subsequent to the second coming of Christ, which it itself preceded by the *reign of Antichrist*!

The conclusion began to surface that Alexis and Nikon were a part of Antichrist, in terms of the apocalyptic vision, a "horn" of Antichrist-as-beast. This was hard to accept, for

> ... nothing could more surely mean the end of the world than the Orthodox Tsar as a horn of Antichrist. But it made sense, particularly after 1658, when Nikon was gone and the reforms were nonetheless maintained ... In other words, the conclusion had to be drawn that the apostasy of the tsar was not an accident, temporary and random, but part of an irrevocable divine and satanic process. (ibid.: 149)

This notion was cabalistically convenient since the demonic number 666 was reflected in the revisionist council of 1666–67. It is noteworthy, however, that many Old Believers including Avvakum himself drew back from acknowledging that the total end of everything was nigh: "he preferred to emphasize that only the spirit of Antichrist was present – that is, apostasy ... was not final as long as men were willing to hold out against it" (ibid.: 149). But as the attempts to restore the old faith failed, the mood became increasingly apocalyptic.

It was this apocalyptic mood which prepared the more extreme devotees for suicide. The actual suicides were generally precipitated by real or anticipated armed assaults. Their persecution, though vicious, was not entirely arbitrary, and the subversive quality of what Cherniavsky calls the "political theology" of the Old Believers was not the sole impetus to the persecutions. The movement was gaining sympathy from "large sections of the population whose motives were not merely religious but social and political ... The Old Believers' opposition to authority was potentially the nucleus of a widespread revolutionary movement" (Vernadsky 1969: 696).

To conclude this section, the Old Believer mass suicides appear to be related to the strange interweaving of political and religious elements in their movement. Imprisoned in the Third Rome mystique and the orthodox assumptions about the theocratic role of the tsar, the Old Believers were pushed to elevate their opposition to Nikonian reforms to the level of subversive political theology, and ultimately to entertain extreme apocalyptic notions which implied the hopelessness of the world situation dominated by Antichrist. Moods of both apocalyptic despair and political truculence were intensified by a sequence of ups and downs whereby at various points the Old Believers seemed about to regain control of church policy only to have their stimulated hopes dashed. Meanwhile their heresy was spreading and its politically subversive quality was enhanced by the interface of Old Believer religious restorationism and various currents of social, economic, and political protest. Intensified deadly persecution ensued, which further heightened apocalyptic frenzy and suicidal despair and exaltation.

A feedback process of "deviance amplification" (Wallis 1977) or interaction between escalating persecution and intensifying alienation and deviant protest is clearly evident and culminated in a great wave of mass suicides. However, subsequent "re-amplification" under Peter the Great allowed the development of a prosperous settlement on the Vyg River (Crummey 1970, Zenkovsky 1957a).[5]

Comparative Analysis

There are a number of interesting parallels as well as some marked divergences between the experience of the Old Believers and that of the Peoples Temple in Guyana. The primary areas of partial convergence involve first, the deepening of a sectarian mood of apocalyptic pessimism and perceived worldly triumph of evil, which develops in the context of a general apocalyptic cultural climate; and secondly, the difficulty experienced by each movement in resolving the duality of a religious-utopian communal sanctuary; that is, each movement appears to have become more volatile as its *political anti-state elements became more prominent*. Before considering these elements, however, some preliminary lesser comparisons must be ventured.

The Old Believer movement was larger than the Peoples Temple and much more widespread, which was one reason why it survived its mass suicides. Although its initial leaders were clerical-monastic, it picked up a vast amount of support from downtrodden peasants. Similarly, the Peoples Temple, unlike most other (largely middle-class) American "cults" of the 1970s, had a rank-and-file base of poor (urban minority) participants led by a more educated cleric and middle-class colleagues.

---

5 The process whereby the alienation and the apocalyptic frenzy of the Old Believers was intensified partly in response to enhanced persecution, itself aggravated by the increasing militancy and political activism of the Old Believers, is susceptible to analysis in terms of the escalation-feedback model of "deviance amplification"(Wilkins 1964), which Wallis has applied to the conflicts between the Church of Scientology and the British and Australian governments. This model might also be explored with regard to the history of the Peoples Temple in its final years as opposition to the Temple intensified and was magnified by Jim Jones in fantasy and then further escalated in response to more extreme Temple practices. However, the formal applicability of the model to both cases may obscure the vast difference in the intensity of opposition to the Old Believers compared to the Peoples Temple. The model may also fail to take into account contextual factors such as the apocalyptic milieu, tsarist despotism, and the "Third Rome" premises.

Only a minority of Old Believers and Old Believer settlements were involved in mass suicide events. Likewise, Peoples Temple communities in California were not affected. Presumably the impact of the charisma and putative psychopathology of Jim Jones (Lifton 1979) made the difference. The leaders of those Old Believer groups which engaged in provocations to elicit a military confrontation tended to be peasants like Ivanov or radicalized former Solovetsku monks like Ignatii (Crummey 1970).

There are allegations by "moderate" Old Believers such as Evfrosin that many of the martyrdoms were involuntary because of manipulative and coercive processes within the doomed communities (ibid.: 55–6). Likewise it is believed that some of the victims of Jonestown were actually murdered or threatened with murder, while even the "genuine suicides" allegedly transpired in a manipulative context.

As we have seen, the Avvakumist leaders tended to come from the established monasteries. Similarly, Jim Jones had been a Disciples of Christ minister. Thus, Melton argues that the Peoples Temple, unlike many current "cults," was not really a "new religion," but rather represented a degenerated church, an occasional phenomenon which entails a charismatic clergyman leading a congregation in an increasingly violent, authoritarian, divisive, or otherwise morally deviant direction (Melton 1985). There may be a violent denouement, after which the movement generally disappears. The Old Believers, however, *survived their spectacular mass suicides*, grew and diversified, and gradually achieved a measure of toleration (Crummey 1970). Here the contrast with the Peoples Temple is striking.

The Persecution Factor

Persecution, or rather opposition and a perceived threat of intervention from state authorities, were significant precipitating factors for the actual suicidal events with respect to both the Jonestown and the Old Believer holocausts. But here too it is the contrast which is particularly striking. The Old Believers were officially criminalized and threatened with death and torture. In contrast, Jim Jones has phantasies of CIA mercenaries or other sinister forces stalking Jonestown in the Guyana jungles. Jones used visions of persecution to strengthen his hold over his flock. He hired attorney Mark Lane to investigate conspiracies against the Peoples Temple and Lane dutifully reported a "coordinated campaign" to destroy the Temple that involved a number of federal agencies including the CIA, the IRS, and so on. Yet Jones and his devotees were better able to believe these fantastic tales because the Temple did possess actual documentary evidence of FBI and police infiltration of radical black militant groups involving agents provocateurs (Hall 1981).

Intervention against the Temple *was* slowly escalating. Naipaul argues that the Concerned Relatives and defectors share some responsibility for the final denouement. They knew about the "white nights" of suicide rehearsal, and yet they insisted on a spectacular expedition led by a congressman which would put Jones' back to the wall: "Their hysteria goaded it to extinction ... They feared [mass suicide] ... and yet, by their words and actions, they helped create the conditions in which it could take place" (Naipaul 1980; 156).

Jones and his opponents viewed each other as demonic: "On both sides the battle raged out of control" (Naipaul 1980). The advent of Congressman Ryan was perceived by Jones as the forerunner of more decisive intervention, which was seen as an immediate certainty after Jones had ascertained that devotees had gone to kill Congressman Ryan at the local airport. Thus, both the Jones's followers and the suicidal Old Believers *were certain that the immediate alternative to suicide was falling into the hands of hostile interventionist forces representing absolute evil.*

Persecution of the Old Believers was more tangible and vicious, but the contrast should not be exaggerated. The brutal edicts of Sophia's regime could not be totally enforced in such a big country. Remote sanctuary for dissidents was possible, but some Old Believers, convinced that the Last Days were at hand, devalued safe sanctuary and sought martyrdom through overt rebellion. The real influence of the persecution factor was in shaping devotees' perceptions of the (demonic) state, which, "applied specific pressures to the Old Believers and elicited from them the specific responses which formed the foundation of their political practice" (Crummey 1970: xiii).

Apocalyptic Climates

Beyond the ambiguous factor of persecution, one striking convergence appears to entail a climate of apocalyptic expectation. In the case of both the Old Believers and the Peoples Temple, sectarian apocalyptic visions developed in the context of *broader cultural and subcultural climates of apocalyptic expectation.*

The apocalyptic mood in Russia can be dated as early as 1644, when the government's printing office published the *Book of Cyrill*, a collection of Ukranian and South Slavic apocalyptic writings, which sold—incredibly for its period—500 copies in one month. Apocalyptic thought is associated with the Kapitonists, who expected an imminent apocalypse and who are linked to the earliest pre-Old Believer instances of self-immolation: "By the 1640s then, there was a certain mood or ideology of insecurity, of rejection, in which men associated the evil they were rejecting or fleeing from, with the Tsar. And the ideology of the early Raskol intersected with, if it did not draw upon, this mood" (Cherniavsky 1970: 152–3)." Cherniavsky notes that the reforming Patriarch Nikon, after his break with Tsar Alexis in 1658, became apocalyptic and

> … began to sound very much like Avvakum … Nikon's logic paralleled that of Kapiton and Avvakum within a general apocalyptic mood. The end of the world was near, and the responsibility for this cataclysm lay with the Tsar, whose power was spreading into new areas or was no longer legitimate in areas where it had once prevailed. (Ibid.: 155)

The dissidents' apocalyptic political theology focused rather exclusively on Antichrist and was not concerned with subsequent developments such as the Second Coming of Christ.

American Apocalypticism

A similar theme of apocalyptic world rejection can be seen in the United States, in both the ideology of the Peoples Temple and the general cultural milieu of the late 1960s through to the present: "The apocalyptic mentality is very strong today in American society at large. The invention of the atomic bomb began the current apocalyptic mood, and one of several more recent manifestations of it is the powerful concern with pollution of the environment" (Enroth et al. 1972: 182). According to Robert Lifton (1985), the nuclear "imagery of extinction" had encouraged a surge of apocalyptic and cultic movements expressing a "symbolization of immortality." The apocalypticism of the radical counter-culture of the late 1960s and early '70s expressed the view that American government and society is beyond reformation and must be destroyed and supplanted by something new.

By the late 1970s, the radical counter-culture had faded; however, sociologist William Martin recently described the "growing interest in apocalyptic prophecy" and the thematizing of the "last days" by television evangelists such as Oral Roberts, Jerry Falwell, Pat Robertson, and Rex Humbard, as well as by best-selling works such as Hal Lindsey's *The Late Great Planet Earth* (first published in 1970), which has sold over 15 million copies: "No hard data are available, but millions of American evangelicals apparently believe that within the present generation … Jesus will return to lay the groundwork for a glorious thousand-year reign on earth" (Martin 1982: 30).

The return of Christ is to be preceded by the reign of Antichrist (Great Tribulation), who is expected to gain prominence by military victory over evil forces in the Middle East. Antichrist will be worshipped by a religion organized by the miracle-working False Prophet. During the Tribulation, a world government under Antichrist

> … will seek total control over humanity by requiring that every person wear a mark or a number (probably 666—the designated 'Mark of the Beast', Revelation 13:16–18) in order to buy or sell. Those who refuse to accept this Mark of the Beast will be slain or will risk starvation because they cannot buy food. Those who accept it will burn forever in Hell. (ibid.: 32).

In many quarters, the focus seems to be directed primarily to the nuances of the advent of Antichrist rather than the actual Second Coming and post-apocalyptic bliss. The rise of computers, credit cards, and gargantuan shopping malls and supermarkets have been seen as foreshadowing the 666 commercial-control system, as the rise of "cults," gay rights, the mental health movement, ecumenism and the United Nations has been perceived as anticipating the machinations of Antichrist's World Government and the False Prophets' depraved anti-religion. Contemporary crises in the Mideast, the nuclear menace, Russian aggression and other traumas have appeared to demonstrate that "pieces of the puzzle are falling into place," and the shape of the imminent fulfillment of apocalyptic prophecy is becoming visible. Martin notes the speculation in the 1970s that Henry Kissinger might be Antichrist and that the Trilateral Commission and the Council on Foreign Relations were "mighty engines of the one-world Antichrist conspiracy" (ibid.: 35–6).

The Apocalypticism of Jim Jones

Contemporary apocalypticism is not entirely associated with the political "right." A strident radical counter-cultural apocalypticism flourished in the late 1960s and early 1970s and partly converged with some variants of contemporary Christian tribulationism in its preoccupation with the environing reign of evil. Demonic evocations of "Amerika" were featured in the left-wing apocalypticism of the radical counter-culture and various quasi-Marxist and black militant sects.

"Jim Jones" notes Shiva Naipul, "built his movement on the debris of the sixties: on its frustrations, failures and apostasies" (Naipaul 1980: 293). As Jones relocated his movement in San Francisco and subsequently moved to Guyana, the radical counter-culture, the anti-war protest, and even the broad agitation against racism was winding down. But, as a tide of fervent sentiment and activism recedes, it often leaves frenzied little pools and eddies. Some of the people caught up in the flamboyant counter-culture and the exotic "hippie" scene ultimately joined relatively authoritarian and structured communal "cults." Some counter-culturalists and radical "New Left" activists ended up involved in violent paramilitary groups such as the later Weathermen or the Symbionese Liberation Army.

As the Peoples Temple, originally an evangelical church group with an anti-racist social activist record, evolved, Jones picked up and sharpened certain themes of radical protest which he extrapolated in an increasingly apocalyptic and pessimistic direction: "He and the Temple aristocracy assiduously unearthed every reference to the Ku Klux Klan and the Nazis that they could find and constructed out of them a vision of unavoidable genocidal doom" (ibid.: 308). "Jones tortured his black followers with nightmare visions of fascist takeover and genocidal doom" (ibid.: 288). He dealt in radically dualistic evocations of an absolutely evil and doomed America. A Nazi takeover was imminent and only the Temple were aware of the threat and were standing up to it. Growing economic distress and social unrest would enable a right-wing demagogue to seize power. Hitlerian genocidal policies were going to be repeated. In California, "The Peoples Temple would stage mock lynchings of blacks by the Ku Klux Klan as a form of political theatre" (Hall 1981: 183). Black members were persuaded that if they did not go with Jones to Guyana, they would surely "end up in concentration camps where they would be killed" (Krause et al. 1979: 188).

But the Peoples Temple was hardly the exclusive locus of this kind of apocalypticism. On the very day—November 18, 1978—of the Jonestown holocaust, Huey Newton, the former Black Panther leader, was giving a speech to a group of students in Boston. "'We the people' he was telling those students, 'are threatened with genocide because racism and fascism are rampant in the country and throughout the world'" (Naipaul 1980: 288). For over a decade, black agitators such as Malcolm X and George Jones had talked of an emerging American Fascism and the possibility of the white ruling class accepting a Hitleresque genocidal solution to deepening racial conflict.

A distinctly Manichean and pessimistic apocalypticism thus characterized the evolving radicalism of the Peoples Temple, which paralleled the broader radical and "anti-racist" ideological milieu. But the convergence of Jones' apocalypticism and the environing apocalypticism is not merely a matter of the frenzy of certain radical left and black militant activists. "Jim Jones was as much a Protestant fundamentalist as he was a 'Marxist,'" argues Naipaul, "The traditions, atmosphere and techniques of Protestant fundamentalism were all present in the Peoples Temple," and they can also be found in the more extreme late 1970s ecological agitation (Naipaul 1980: 294). The content of different movements' prophecies may vary but there is a vital convergence of form and imagination. There is a similar obsession with evil, sin and images of apocalyptic destruction, a similar impulse to divide humanity into the few saved and the many damned, and a similar persuasive tactic based on evoking anxiety.

Jones' prophecy converged with that of the tribulationists in terms of a vision of an imminent holocaust amidst a triumph of evil and corruption in the world. Our present troubles defy solution. America is doomed! Yet, the Christian tribulationists are at least certain of post-apocalyptic bliss in which the faithful will participate. Jones was vague on this score. According to John Hall:

> Jones' prophecy was far more radical than those of contemporary Adventist groups: he focused on imminent apocalyptic disaster rather than on Christ's millennial salvation, and his eschatology, therefore, had to resolve a choice between apocalyptic struggle with "the beast" or collective flight to establish a post-apocalyptic kingdom of the elect. Until the end, the Peoples Temple was directed toward the latter possibility. (Hall 1981: 175)

The conflict between the need to create an insulated communal refuge where the faithful could be safe from the demonic environment and live according to the truth and the impulse to militantly confront demonic authorities bedeviled both the Peoples Temple and the Old Believers, and will be discussed below. To conclude this section, however, a qualification must be entered.

The apocalyptic mood of Russia preceded the *Raskol*; nevertheless, the Old Believers and the great reaction against the Nikonian reforms were instrumental in spreading and deepening the apocalyptic mood in Russia and crystallizing an ongoing insurrectionary counter-culture of religious restorationism and agrarian protest. In contrast, Jonestown appears to have been a dead end and may have marked the *climax* of radical counter-cultural apocalypticism in the United States.

Political Confrontation and Religious Sanctuary

The most important similarity between Jonestown and the Old Believer suicides entails a pattern of interweaving political and religious elements in each movement and its situation such that *strident confrontation or perceived confrontation with an overpowering enemy undermined the precarious coexistence with the dominant authorities which even radical world-rejecting sects usually work out.*

Analysis of the Jonestown Trauma

An important analysis of the Peoples Temple movement and the Jonestown Massacre was published by sociologist John Hall in 1981. In many ways, the characteristics of the Peoples Temple Community at Jonestown correspond to the model of what Hall calls an *other-worldly sect*, which

> ... is a utopian communal group that subscribes to a comprehensive set of beliefs based on an apocalyptic interpretation of current history as we know it. It is to be replaced by a community of the elect—those who live according to revelation of God's will ... In this millennial Kingdom, those closest to God come to rule ... typically a preeminent prophet or Messiah, who is legitimated by charisma or tradition, calls the shots in a theocratic organization of God's chosen people. (Hall 1981: 173–4)[6]

Other-worldly sects have existed throughout history, generally without mass suicide events. Thus disciplinary practices and authoritarian, collectivist life-process at Jonestown are not really unusual from a historical perspective. Given the widespread occurrence of other-worldly sects,

> ... the other-worldly features of Jonestown are insufficient in themselves to explain the bizarre fate of its participants. If we are to understand the unique turn of events at Jonestown, we must look at certain distinctive features of the Peoples Temple—traits that make it unusual among other-worldly sects—we must try to comprehend the subjective meanings of these features for some of Jonestown's participants. (ibid.: 180)

According to Hall, other-worldly sects tend to develop a de facto *modus vivendi* with the environing state and society, which they believe to be totally depraved and doomed. The believers conclude that they can more or less ignore the evil society, from which they may be geographically isolated, or which is viewed as unwilling or unable to crush the community of the true faith. Given this assumption, the movement is less likely to act in a manner to provoke the putatively collapsing society. The chaos of the disintegrating and depraved culture impinge on the utopian community or "holy remnant," which is "saved" and thus under divine protection or some other sheltering umbrella.

---

6 In my view, Hall's use of the term "other-worldly" is misleading, as it implies a supernaturalist, theist, or transcendental-mystical outlook. What Hall is really pointing to is a utopian-sectarian pattern involving a stable communal enclave legitimated in terms of a "post-apocalyptic" mystique, which devalues the inevitability of priority of active confrontation with an evil and perhaps doomed environing society.

Hall's analysis of Jonestown stresses the strange interweaving of political and "other-worldly" sectarian elements in the outlook of Jim Jones and his followers. Their Manichean political orientation undercut the consolidation of an "other-worldly sanctuary," or sacred heaven-on-earth retreat which is fundamental to the survival and stability of other-worldly sects. The latter "promise the grace of a theocracy in which followers can sometimes really escape the 'living hell' of society-at-large. Many of Reverend Jones' followers seem to have joined the Peoples Temple with this in mind" (ibid.: 186). However the radical ideology of the movement, the acute concern over defectors, and the evocation of a "conspiracy" allegedly forming around the defectors and involving the US government and the CIA, produced in the minds of the leader and his faithful a *sense of persecution which was too immediate and pressing to be compatible with consolidation of a stable sectarian enclave*:

> Rather than successfully proclaiming the post-apocalyptic sanctuary, Jones was reduced to declaiming a web of "evil" powers in which he was ensnared and to searching with chiliastic expectation for the imminent cataclysm that would announce the beginning of the Kingdom of righteousness. (ibid.: 186)

Thus, Jones had not really built a "post-apocalyptic heavenly plateau" for his followers. Was Jonestown the Promised Land? This was becoming uncertain:

> Jones did not entirely trust the Guyanese government, and he was considering seeking final asylum in Cuba or the Soviet Union. Whereas other-worldly sects typically assert that heaven is at hand, Jones could only hold it out as a future goal—one that became more and more elusive as the forces of persecution tracked him to Guyana.

Hope was running out because, as Jones saw it, he was fighting an "evil and conspiratorial world that could not tolerate a living example of a racially integrated American Utopia" (ibid.: 186).

Although it shared many qualities with an other-worldly sect, the Peoples Temple is depicted in Hall's analysis as existing on the boundary between an other-worldly sect and a "warring sect." The latter defines itself as "fighting a decisive Manichean struggle with the forces of evil. Such a struggle seems almost inevitable when political rather than religious themes of apocalypse are stressed" (ibid.: 186–7). Violent political groups including revolutionary and "terrorist" groups are warring sects. Frequently, Jones and his associates acted within the militant frame of reference of a warring sect; for example, they surrounded the settlement with armed guards and staged mock CIA attacks on Jonestown. Lifton (1968) notes that revolutionaries engage in a quest for "immortality." Other-worldly sectarians short-circuit this quest in a way by the fiat of *asserting* their immortality—posting the timeless heavenly plateau that exists *beyond* history as the basis of their everyday lives. But under the persistent eyes of external critics and because "Jones himself exploited such 'persecution' to increase his social control, he could not sustain the illusion of other-worldly community" (ibid.: 187).

The growing intensity of the conspiratorial anti-imperialistic and anti-racist elements in the Peoples Temple's worldview diminished the viability of the movement as a world-rejecting sect. By emphasizing the persecution of his group by an omnipotent conspiracy, Jones undermined the feeling of autonomy and insulation vital to stabilizing its identity. Yet the movement could not become an authentic warring sect, since it clearly could not envision itself gaining a victory over a "conspiracy" which was increasingly conceptualized as *all-powerful*. With "revolutionary immortality" and sectarian "post-apocalyptic" immortality closed off, the immortality of exemplary mass sacrifice became the only form of immortality available:

> Mass suicide bridged the divergent threads of meaningful existence at Jonestown—those of political revolution and religious salvation. It was an awesome vehicle for a powerful statement of collective solidarity by the true believers among the people of Jonestown—they would rather die together than have their lives together subjected to gradual decimation and dishonour at the hands of authorities regarded as illegitimate. (ibid.: 188)

Similarly, what Zenkovsky calls the "psychology of martyrdom" among Old Believers, propelled thousands "to burn themselves rather than submit to the state, which they now considered possessed by Antichrist" (Zenkovsky 1963: 40).

Comparison with the Old Believers

The Peoples Temple, in Hall's analysis, could not resolve the antinomy of seeking a safe refuge from a putatively vicious society and stridently confronting the authorities, who were perceived as reaching out powerful tentacles to crush their refuge such that confrontation was unavoidable. There is some convergence with Crummey's analysis of the Old Believer mass suicides.

Many of the adherents encapsulated their hatred of everything new and oppressive in Russian life in the apocalyptic symbol of Antichrist. The symbol and the mood it expressed demanded resistance to the state and the official

Church—the instruments of Antichrist. For in both symbolic and practical terms, the faithful were not to submit to his power.

The logic of this position, then, led the Old Believers to a confrontation of the power of the imperial government. The overwhelming weight of their adversary, however, posed an agonizing problem of strategy. How could the faithful best make a stand against the legions of Antichrist? (Crummey 1970: 210).

The belief that the Last Days were at hand conferred a premium on confrontation. If the end of the world was at hand, then, "there was no need for concern about the continuance of the true faith. It was, therefore, justifiable for the faithful to strike a satisfy blow at the enemy and meet their inevitable fate, sword in hand" (ibid.: 220).[7]

Among both the suicidal Old Believers and Jones's followers, belief in an imminent apocalyptic demiurge devalued the idea of a permanent sectarian refuge as an essential base to conserve or propagate the true faith. In both cases, mass suicide really arose as a final affirmation of non-submission to an authority which was perceived as absolutely evil but absolutely powerful in the (doomed) world. In both cases, *the possibility of an insulated sanctuary was relinquished in behalf of a final violent confrontation*, although surviving Old Believers ultimately opted, under new leaders and a more tolerant tsar, for communal sanctuary at the Vyg River settlement.

One further point: both the Peoples Temple and the Old Believers combined political-revolutionary and world-rejecting sectarian tendencies. As both movements evolved, the former elements became increasingly prominent. This was particularly striking in the case of the Peoples Temple, whose leader, a Protestant minister, eventually renounced theism. Although the Avvakumist dissent was somewhat political from the outset, nevertheless, the Old Believers became increasingly politically activist and insurgent over a period of roughly thirty years and became increasingly obsessed with the state and tsar as demonic forces.

Professor Hall's analysis thus directs our attention to movements which uneasily combine "political" and "religious" elements within an apocalyptic

---

[7] According to Crummey, the Old Believers had three options: armed revolt, flight to some hidden refuge, or "construction of fortress communities that would rally and shelter the defenders of the old faith." Mass suicides arose as an aspect of the first option when "rebellion blended with mass suicide, and also as an outcome when flight did not avail and some hitherto hidden community was detected and assaulted. The third option seemed attractive "when it became clear that Antichrist's reign would continue into the indefinite future"; however, "the arm of the state was long" and the leaders of the Vyg community "had no choice but to reach a modus vivendi with the imperial Government" (Crummey 1970: 19–21), which, under Peter I, was prepared to relax its persecution somewhat. Thus, sectarians finally attained Hall's "post-apocalyptic plateau."

framework. The Unification movement, whose "messianic prophecy ... is defined in political terms" (Robbins and Anthony 1984: 18) represents one controversial group which fits this specification. On the other hand, the Unificationist mood is hardly one of pessimistic despair (Anthony and Robbins 1982). Perhaps a greater volatility can be found in the emerging "cults of the 1980s" (Levin and Alan 1985), which recruit from urban minorities who do not feel part of the economic recovery and patriotic revitalization. Groups such as MOVE (Quinn 1985) do indeed seem to court violent confrontations while simultaneously directing some effort to a somewhat contradictory attempt to develop a utopian communal rage.

Conclusion

An exploratory comparison has been ventured between the sixteenth-century Old Believer mass suicides and the more recent Jonestown deaths of over 900 devotees of the Peoples Temple. Striking parallels as well as significant differences have been found. The basic convergence involves a continual intensification of a mood of pessimistic apocalypticism and despairing conviction of the triumph of evil in a doomed world. This sectarian conviction is related to a generally apocalyptic mood in the broader culture and/or in an inter-movement subculture. A second partial convergence entails a gradual intensification of political and anti-statist elements in the ideology of what was originally primarily a religious movement or protest, such that the impulse stridently to confront dominant authorities and to perceive these authorities as demonic and conspiring to actively crush the movement undermined the possibility of a de facto *modus vivendi* with the state. In such an accommodation, an alienated sect attains a "post-apocalyptic sanctuary" in which devotees can in their view operationalize spiritual and communal perfection while being tolerated or benignly neglected by the putatively depraved and doomed society. Such a refuge was eventually crystallized by the Old Believers at the Vyg settlement.

There was a significant divergence, however, in the way the sequence of deepening alienation-persecution or "deviance amplification" worked itself out with respect to each group. The Old Believers suffered extreme persecution, which, however, was at least aggravated by their own strident confrontation of the regime through their increasing political activism and their growing connections with other dangerous forces of social and political protest. The deadly persecution of the Peoples Temple, however, was large *fantasised* by Jones and colleagues, although there *was* increasing opposition to the movement and pressure for some sort of intervention. The strident confrontationist tendency of the Peoples Temple manifested itself in "paranoid" phantasies of conspiratorial persecution, which rather than an actual threat of physical coercion, drove the leader and his colleagues to frenzy and despair. It is also notable that, unlike the Peoples Temple, the Old Believers survived their mass deaths, and in the Vyg community they found what Hall would call their "post-apocalyptic plateau."[8]

References

Anthony, Dick, and Thomas Robbins (1982). "Spiritual Innovation and the Crisis of American Civil Religion," *Daedalus* 111(1): 215–34.

Cherniavsky, Michael (1970). "The Old Believers and the New Religion," in *The Structure of Russian History*, ed. idem. New York: Random House, pp. 140–88.

Crummey, Robert O. (1970). *The Old Believers and the World of Antichrist: The Vyg Community and the Russian State 1694–1855*. Madison: University of Wisconsin Press.

Dodds, E.R. (1965). *Pagan and Christian in an Age of Anxiety: Some Aspects of Religious Experience from Marcus Aurelius to Constantine*. New York: Norton.

Enroth, Ronald, Edward E. Ericson, and C. Breckinridge Peters (1972). *The Jesus People: Old-Time Religion in the Age of Aquarius*. Grand Rapids, MI: Erdmans.

Hall, John (1981). "The Apocalypse at Jonestown," in *In Gods We Trust: New Patterns of Religious Pluralism in America*, eds. Thomas Robbins and Dick Anthony. New Brunswick, NJ: Transaction Publishers, pp. 171–90.

[8] The Old Believer suicides must ultimately be seen in cultural context. Murvar sees both the Avvakumists and the Kapitons as part of a distinctly Russian tradition of dissident messianic absolutism which includes the later "revolutionary messianism" of the nineteenth-century populists and the twentieth-century Bolsheviks. But the suicides of the Old Believers can also be seen as reflecting an older tradition beginning with "voluntary" martyrdoms among Christians during the Roman persecutions, E.R. Dodds, *Pagan and Christian in an Age of Anxiety: Some Aspects of Religious Experience from Marcus Aurelius to Constantine* (New York: Norton, 1965). And continuing in Byzantine times when, in the reign of Justinian, the persecuted Phygrian Montanists "locked themselves into churches and burned themselves to death rather than fall into the hands of their fellow Christians, (ibid.: 67). The image of Christ-on-the-cross may be seen to suggest a sacrificial, life-relinquishing response to persecution whereby martyrs imitate the passion of Christ. This imagery, which surely influenced the Old Believers, may also have meant something to Reverend Jim Jones.

Krause, Charles, Laurence Stern, and Richard Harwood (1979). *Guyana Massacre: The Eye Witness Account*. New York: Berkeley Books.
Levin, Jack, and James Alan (1985). "Cults: A Response to Alienation," *USA Today*, May 16.
Lifton, Robert (1968). *Revolutionary Immortality: Mao Tse-Tung and the Chinese Cultural Revolution*. New York: Vintage.
— (1979). "The Appeal of the Death Trip," *New York Times Magazine*, January 7.
— (1985). "Cult Processes, Religious Totalism and Civil Liberties," in *Cults, Culture, and the Law: Perspectives on the New Religions*, eds. Thomas Robbins, William Shepherd, and James McBride. Chico, CA: Scholars Press, pp. 59–70.
Martin, William (1982). "Waiting for the End," *Atlantic Monthly*, June.
Melton, J. Gordon (1985). "Violence and the Cults," *Nebraska Humanist* 8(2): 51–60.
Murvar, Vatro (1975). "Toward a sociological theory of religious movements," *Journal for the Scientific Study of Religion* (1975): 229–56.
Naipaul, Shiva (1980). *Journey to Nowhere: A New World Tragedy*. New York: Simon and Schuster.
Quinn, Jim (1985). "The Bombed in West Philly," *Village Voice*, May 28.
Robbins, Thomas, and Dick Anthony (1984). "The Unification Church," *The Ecumenist* September–October: 88–92.
Siegelman, Jim, and Flo Conway (1979). "Still Jonestown Runs On" (Op. Ed.), *New York Times*, November 15.
Vernadsky, George (1969). *The Tsardom of Moscow*, Vol. 5. New Haven, CT: Yale University Press.
Wallis, Roy (1977). *The Road to Total Freedom*. New York: Columbia University Press.
Wilkins, Leslie (1964). *Social Deviance*. London: Tavistock.
Yanoff, Morris (1984). "Some Lessons from Jonestown" (Op. Ed.), *Chicago Tribune*, November 18.
Zenkovsky, Serge A. (1957a). "The Ideological World of the Denisov Brothers," *Harvard Slavic Studies* 3: 49–66.
— (1957b). "The Russian Church Schism: Its Background and Repercussions," *Russian Review* 16(4): 37–58.
Zenkovsky, Vasily V. (1963). "The Spirit of Russian Orthodoxy," *Russian Review* 22(1): 38–55.

Part II
Contemporary Suicide Cults

Chapter 3

Purification, Illumination, and Death: The Murder-Suicides of the Order of the Solar Temple

Henrik Bogdan

> We leave this Earth to rediscover, with all clarity and in all freedom, a Dimension of Truth and the Absolute, far from the hypocrisies and the oppression of this world, to realize the seed of our future Generation
>
> —Transit to the Future

> Death is the same for us all.
> It is how we leave Life that makes the difference.
> You must be able to die to the profane world
> In order to be born again to the Cosmic World.
>
> —Ritual for the Donning of the Talar and the Cross

Introduction

The Order of the Solar Temple (*Ordre du Temple Solaire*, or OTS), is usually referred to as one of the "Big Five," that is, together with Peoples Temple, the Branch Davidians, Aum Shinrikyo, and the Heaven's Gate the most well-known New Religious Movements that are connected to the use of violence (see, for example, Lewis 2011). The first murders committed by the OTS occurred on September 30, 1994, when a three-month-old baby (Christopher Emmanuel) was killed, together with his parents, who were ex-members of the group.[1] A wooden stake had been driven through his heart, as the OTS leaders apparently believed that the baby was none other than the Antichrist. Four days later, on October 4, five persons were stabbed to death at the villa of the group's leader,

[1] This chapter is based on Bogdan (2006) and Bogdan (2011).

Joseph Di Mambro, and the villa was destroyed by fire. Another fire started at 1:00 AM on October 5 at an OTS center in Ferme des Rochettes, in the canton of Fribourg, Switzerland. The authorities later discovered 23 bodies, some of which had been shot, while others had been suffocated by plastic bags placed over their heads. A few hours later, three additional vacation chalets at Les Granges sur Salvan, in the canton of Valais, were set on fire, and another 25 bodies were found, including those of the leaders of the Solar Temple, Joseph Di Mambro and Luc Jouret. The 53 victims (not counting the three homicides committed on September 30) were divided into three different categories.

The first category, consisting of 15 members who were referred to as the "Awakened," belonged to the inner circle of Di Mambro and his right-hand man, Luc Jouret. This inner group of members committed suicide by taking poison. The second category, the "Immortals," who formed the majority of the dead members (30 people), were either shot or smothered. The eight members of the final category were labeled as "traitors" and were found murdered. In one of the four letters or "Testaments" that were sent out to 60 journalists, scholars, and government officials at the time of the fiery end of the OTS, it was explained that the authors of the Testaments saw themselves as the "judges appointed by a Superior Order," which in the esoteric worldview of the OTS meant that the so-called "Hidden" or "Cosmic Masters" had appointed them to this task:

> Those who have breached our Code of Honor are considered traitors, they have suffered and will suffer the punishment they deserve for the ages of the ages.
> All is accomplished according to the mandates of Immanent Justice. We hereby affirm that we are in truth, the judges appointed by a Superior Order.
> In view of the present irreversible situation, We, the Servants of the Rose+Croix, strongly reaffirm that we are not part of this world and that we are perfectly aware of the coordinates of our Origins and our Future. (Lewis 2006: 178)

These initial murder-suicides were followed over a year later, on December 16, 1995, by another group suicide in the southeast of France, near Grenoble, where members of the OTS from France and Switzerland had gathered in a forest. Most of the 16 members who were found dead, had been drugged, shot to death, and then placed in a circle, while two remaining members had poured gasoline over the bodies, set them on fire, and then committed suicide. The violence did not end here, however. Fifteen months later, on the vernal equinox (March 20, 1997), five remaining members committed suicide in Quebec, Canada. In sum, the violence of the Solar Temple led to the death of 77 individuals in Canada, France, and Switzerland between September 30, 1994, and March 20, 1997.

Naturally, the murder-suicides of the Solar Temple raise a number of important questions about the relationship between religion and violence in general, and new religious movements and violence in particular. Why did the leadership of the OTS turn to violence to solve the problems the group was facing? What sorts of problems *did* the group face? What caused many of the members to obey Di Mambro and Jouret and either murder their fellow members or commit suicide? What motivated the remaining members to commit suicide in 1995 and 1997 in order to follow the others? While the anti-cult movement and the press have usually provided simplified explanations (for example, brainwashing) for the violence of the OTS, scholars have argued that one must take into account the complexities of the case and to eschew single-factor theories. In this chapter, I first give an overview of the Solar Temple and then discuss a number of theories that have been put forward to explain the violence of the OTS.

The History, Teachings, and Organizational Structure of the OTS

After having been a member of various esoteric and initiatory societies, including the Ancient and Mystical Order Rosae Crucis (AMORC) in France between 1956 and the late 1960s, Joseph Di Mambro (b. 1924) founded an esoteric group called the Centre for the Preparation of the New Age in 1973. This group would later assume a variety of names over the years, of which Order of the Solar Temple would become the most well-known name in the Anglophone world after the murder-suicides committed in 1994. After having established its headquarters in Geneva, Switzerland, in 1978, the movement developed into a highly active organization with two distinctive sides. On the outside, the activities centered on public lectures and workshops on topics common to the French-speaking esoteric and New Age scenes. The movement's public appeal was enhanced by the recruitment of the Belgian homeopathic physician, Luc Jouret, who apparently was a charismatic speaker who easily caught the attention of his audience. Jouret would soon find himself in a leading position in the organization, second only to Di Mambro himself. These public lectures and workshops functioned as front organizations and recruiting grounds for the inner workings of the organization. On the inside, the organization was structured as a traditional esoteric initiatory society, with an hierarchical structure divided into various degrees through which the members progressed by undergoing secret rites of initiation.

A common characteristic of many new religious movements is that their organizational structure is in more or less constant change, and in that respect the Order of the Solar Temple was no exception. Introvigne has described the various layers of the organization as a "Chinese box" system (Introvigne 1995: 274). The outer shell consisted (at least for some time) of the semi-public Amenta Club (which later changed its name to Atlanta), in which Jouret, as mentioned, lectured on New Age topics such as homeopathy, naturopathy, and ecology. This outer shell worked as a recruiting ground for members to the inner and semi-secret Archédia Clubs, which were established in 1984. According to Introvigne, in this layer of the organization, one could "find a definite ritual and an actual initiation ceremony, with a set of symbols taken from the Masonic-Templar efforts of Jacques Breyer" (ibid.: 274). The third and central layer of the organization, to which only the most trusted members of the Archédia Clubs were invited, was the secret International Order of Chivalry Solar Tradition (founded in 1984), which later changed its name to the Order of the Solar Temple. To further complicate matters, a fourth organization existed: the Golden Way Foundation (previously called La Pyramide), founded by Di Mambro, which served as the parent organization of the Amenta and Archédia clubs. The order was quite successful in French-speaking countries but failed to establish itself in the English-speaking world, particularly in the United States and Australia. In the English-speaking world, the order was known by at least two names: the Order of the Solar Temple and the Hermetica Fraternitas Templi Universali. Compared to other Rosicrucian and Templar organizations, the Solar Temple was a comparatively small organization. At its height in 1989, the order had a total of 442 members: 90 in Switzerland, 187 in France, 53 in Martinique, 16 in the United States, 86 in Canada, and 10 in Spain (Mayer 1996: 54).

From the early 1990s, the OTS went through several crises, which included the defection of several members, including members of the inner core, and even Di Mambro's own son. Some of these former members would criticize the OTS in public and the movement was quickly branded as a cult by the media. Around the same time, Canadian authorities began to investigate the OTS and it was in particular charges of possession of illegal weapons that led the movement's premises in Quebec to be raided in 1993. Clearly, the news coverage and the police investigations were interpreted by the leadership of the movement as not only a conspiracy against the OTS, but also as symptomatic of the Kali Yuga, or dark age, in which society is increasingly becoming corrupt and degraded. In one of the so-called Testaments, titled "To Lovers of Justice," it was stated at the outset:

> Let the events which have entertained the Canadian press during the past several months permit everyone to recognize that everywhere in the world politicians, financiers and judicial officials have delighted in scorning democracy, squandering

> public resources, [and] manipulating, through the intermediary of a mass media hungry for scandals and sensationalist events, whole crowds of people which they themselves have rendered totally passive and unconscious. (Lewis 2006: 183–4)

The text then proceeds to list eleven points to illustrate how the media and the authorities had acted, with "cynicism and cowardice," in this "scandal" (ibid.: 186). The events, in combination with other factors (discussed below), triggered a chain of events that lead to the "transit," that is, the murder-suicides mentioned at the beginning of this chapter. The decision to make the transit was announced in one of the Testaments:

> We, the servants of the Rose+Croix, considering the urgency of the present situation, affirm:
> that we refuse to participate in systems set up by this decadent humanity;
> that we have planned, in full state of consciousness, without any fanaticism, our transit which has nothing to do with suicide in the human sense of the term;
> that according to a degree emanating from the Great White Lodge of Sirius, we have closed and voluntarily blown up all the sanctuaries of the Secret Lodges so that they will not be desecrated by impostors or by the ignorant;
> that, from the Planes where we will work from now on and by a just law of magnetism, we will be in the position of calling back the last Servants capable of hearing this last message. (Ibid.: 178)

As self-professed servants of the R+C—that is, the Rosicrucian Order—the worldview of the Solar Temple was firmly rooted in western esotericism and, more specifically, in neo-Templarism, twentieth-century Rosicrucianism, and the New Age movement. Western esotericism is a scholarly construct that covers numerous currents that share a family resemblance and can be described as a form of holistic spirituality characterized by resistance to the dominance of either pure rationality or doctrinal faith. Instead, the importance of the individual effort to gain spiritual knowledge, or *gnosis*, is often emphasized.

Furthermore, esoteric discourses are often connected to secrecy and rejected knowledge.[2] This *gnosis* is not limited to intellectual or rational knowledge but is based on experiential knowledge that is unconstrained by the limits of the intellect. The path to *gnosis* is often believed to pass through self-knowledge

---

[2] Discussions concerning the definition of western esotericism are ongoing. For the most significant recent works on the subject, see Hanegraaff (2012; 2013), and von Stuckrad (2010).

since humankind is seen as a microcosm of the universe—the macrocosm. Human beings are created in the image of God and therefore reflect the whole of creation. The created universe is usually regarded as an emanation of the godhead, and since humans are perceived as a microcosm of the macrocosm, the esotericist believes that the godhead can be found within people. The quest for self-knowledge is thus also a quest for the divine aspect of existence, just as knowledge about the godhead is of necessity knowledge about us. The holistic understanding of the universe to be found within western esotericism is based on the idea that the entire universe is alive and traversed by a network of sympathies and antipathies that link everything in nature (Faivre 1994: 10). The network, which is often referred to as mystical links, constitutes the theoretical basis of esoteric "sciences," such as astrology and ritual magic.

The Templar tradition of which the Solar Temple was part is a modern interpretation and reconstruction of the medieval Knights Templar, founded early in the twelfth century as a military monastic order whose chief object was to protect pilgrims traveling in the Holy Land, then known as "Outremer." The Order of Knights Templar was disbanded by Philip IV, "the Fair," (1268–1314) and Pope Clement V (1264–1314) in the first decade of the fourteenth century. In 1310, 54 Knights Templar were burned at the stake, and, according to Introvigne (1995: 279), the first 53 OTS deaths were intended to mimic these fiery deaths (a Swiss ex-member, Thierry Huguenin, managed to escape before being killed, thereby frustrating the plan to reach the full complement of 54 deaths). According to a Masonic legend, the Templars survived in the Highlands of Scotland and later reappeared in public as the Order of Freemasons. The first person to present this theory of continuation in public was Chevalier Michael Ramsay (1686–1743), a Scot who lived as an expatriate in Paris. In a famous oration given at a lodge in 1737, he claimed that the Order of Freemasonry was founded in the Holy Land by medieval crusaders. Although he did not explicitly identify the crusaders as Knights Templar, the connection was certainly made by the Freemasons. Soon enough, perhaps as early as 1737, Masonic Templar degrees appeared (Bogdan 2007: 95–100). During the second half of the eighteenth century, templar degrees flourished on the Masonic scene, but soon the Masonic supremacy over the Templar degrees began to be questioned. If Freemasonry is nothing but the medieval Knights Templar in modern form, then why should Freemasonry be required at all if one wanted to be a modern Templar? As Massimo Introvigne has shown in great detail, the origins of independent neo-Templarism can be traced to Bernard-Raymond Fabré-Palaprat (1773–1838), who in 1805 proclaimed himself Grand Master of the Templar Order. During the 1950s, French esotericist Jacques Breyer and later Raymond Bernard revived the Templar tradition, and by 1980 more than a hundred rival Templar orders existed across a wide spectrum, ranging from social clubs to organizations that indulge in sexual magic (Introvigne 1995: 267–73).

To the members of the Solar Temple, death was a transition, a notion that Di Mambro had most likely acquired during his time in the Ancient and Mystical Order Rosæ Crucis (AMORC), which was founded by H. Spencer Lewis (1883–1939) in 1915 and quickly became the largest Rosicrucian group in the world. According to one source, the AMORC may now have as many as 250,000 members (Barrett 2001: 357). The highly eclectic teachings of the organization have a firm foundation in occultist spirituality. Death is seen as a transition in which the physical body (which is subject to change and decay) becomes separated from the soul. According to H. Spencer Lewis, "the soul of man, or the divine essence which animates him is the only part of man which is not subject to the law of change" (Lewis 1941: 238). The soul is thus eternal and not limited by the death of the physical body. These sentiments were later echoed in the rituals of the Solar Temple (Bogdan 2006).

The Order of the Solar Temple was organized as a Masonic initiatory society with a strict hierarchy divided into different degrees. As in Craft Freemasonry, the Solar Temple had three degrees: Frères du Parvis, Chevaliers de l'Alliance, and Frères des Temps Anciens (Brothers of the Court, Knights of the Alliance, and Brothers of the Former Times, respectively). It is unclear whether these three degrees made up the Solar Temple or constituted an even more secret, inner group. At least one source suggests that in 1990 the Rule of the Solar Temple "described an order under the absolute authority of a secret inner group called the Synarchy of the Temple," which consisted of the aforementioned three degrees (Hall and Schuyler 1997: 294). In order to attain these degrees, members had to undergo a rite of initiation for each level. The number and titles of the officiants in the initiation rituals varied, and it is thus impossible to give a clear picture of how the local "sanctuaries" were organized. In the "Dubbing of a Knight" ritual of the OTS, nine officiants were mentioned: priest, deacon, ritual master, maître, chaplain, sentinel, master of ceremonies, guardian, and escorts.

The practice of rituals appears to have been the core activity of the Solar Temple. These rituals seem to have been highly elaborate and suggestive and were often enhanced by the use of opera music, visual effects, and possibly hallucinogenic drugs (Palmer 1996: 306). The visual effects included simulated lightning, in which apparitions of the masters appeared and objects such as the Holy Grail materialized (Mayer 1999: 217). The rituals of the Solar Temple can be divided into two categories: magical/mystical ceremonies and rites of initiation. The first category allegedly included sex magic practices (Introvigne 1995: 276), in which couples practiced "sperm drinking" (Palmer 1996: 311). The extent to which such practices actually occurred is, however, unclear. The second category of rituals, rites of initiation, appears to have been the central activity carried out by the OTS. According to Susan J. Palmer, the Solar Temple constructed "special underground sanctuaries which were concealed behind false walls and reached by secret passages, requiring the ritual descent of 22 steps" (ibid.: 311). She does not explain what the 22 steps refer to, but, given the esoteric context, they probably allude to the 22 paths on the kabbalistic Tree of Life. As discussed below, the surviving rituals of initiation of the OTS provide us with invaluable information for the understanding of the ritualistic and symbolic interpretations of life and death and of the esoteric worldview of the movement.

Explaining the Murder-Suicides

Scholarly literature on violence and the new religious movements often center on the four well-known cases of the 1990s (the OTS, Branch Davidians, Aum Shinrikyo, and Heaven's Gate), as well as the Peoples Temple murder-suicides at Jonestown in 1978. Based on these cases, a number of theories have attempted to explain the use of violence. Although these cases differ in several significant aspects, the tendency has been to focus on the similarities in order to find common denominators that might explain the violent ends of these groups. Chief among these common denominators are a millennial/apocalyptic ideology, a high-demand organization, isolation from the surrounding society, and a charismatic leadership.

The millennial/apocalyptic ideology denominator signifies an end-of-days expectation, which in the case of violent groups is connected to a fierce condemnation of the existing social order. The apocalyptic view of history is combined with a radically dualistic worldview, in which the group is identified with the "good" side, while society, understood in its widest sense, is identified with the "evil" side. Identification with the good side affords a group with a cosmic purpose in the sense that its members perceive themselves as chosen by God for a specific task. However, millennialism and apocalypticism are not restricted to violent new religious movements but are integrated parts of many Christian traditions. In order to differentiate between the millennialism of more violence-oriented groups and traditional millennialism, Catherine Wessinger distinguishes between progressive and catastrophic millennialism. Common to these two types is the belief in collective salvation that may be earthly and allegiance to a "principle whose authority is greater than the authority of civil law" (Wessinger 2000a: 8). Progressive millennialism is the belief that humans, under the guidance of divine agents, can progressively build the millennial kingdom in harmony and peace, while catastrophic millennialism presupposes that the millennial kingdom will be accomplished by an apocalyptic catastrophe orchestrated by God or some other superhuman agent. The catastrophe will destroy the current evil social order and lead to the subsequent salvation of the elect. According to Wessinger, the Order of the Solar Temple adhered to a catastrophic millennialism expressed in New Age terminology. The basic premise of the New Age movement (in *sensu stricto*) is that humankind is about to make a spiritual evolutionary leap forward as we enter the Age of Aquarius. The transition from the Age of Pisces to the Age of Aquarius is generally considered in the New Age movement as a positive step and is often viewed as connected with a transition from a dualistic form of thought (as exemplified by ancient religions such as Christianity) to a monistic form of thought. However, the Solar Temple took a highly pessimistic view of the evolution of consciousness and stressed that evolution "had reached its end on Earth." Wessinger argues that as a result of internal weaknesses and the simultaneous experience of cultural opposition, the leaders of the Solar Temple developed a pessimistic theology that justified a transit in order to escape the imminent cataclysm on earth (Wessinger 2000b: 223–4). Catastrophic millennialism is made evident in a number of passages of the so-called Testaments, four short texts that were sent to various scholars and the media at the time of the murder-suicides in October 1994 with the aim of justifying the members' last actions. One of these texts, "Transit to the Future," states the following:

> The race is heading irreversibly toward its own destruction. All of nature is turning against those who have abused it, who have corrupted and desecrated it on every level. Man will pay heavy tribute for he remains no less than the only one responsible for it.
>
> Awaiting favorable conditions for a possible Return, we will not participate in the annihilation of the human kingdom, no more than we will allow our bodies to be dissolved by the alchemical slowness of Nature, because we don't want to run the risk of their being soiled by madmen and maniacs. (Lewis 2006: 183)

Catastrophic millennialism is expressed even more forcefully in the second testament, titled "To All Those Who Can Still Understand the Voice of Wisdom … We Address This Last Message":

> The current chaos leads man inescapably to face the failure of his Destiny. In the course of time, the cycles have followed one another in accordance with precise rhythms and laws. Different civilizations disappeared in the course of cataclysms that were destructive but regenerative, nonetheless none of these reached a level of decadence such as ours.
> Subjected to the devastating effects of individual and collective egocentricity, marked by a total ignorance of the Laws of the Spirit and Life, this civilization will no longer escape sudden self-destruction. (Ibid.: 177)

In seeking to understand the violence enacted by groups such as the Solar Temple, the importance these groups attached to millennialism has been stressed by numerous authors (for example, Robbins and Palmer 1997; Daniels 1999; Bromley and Melton 2002), as well as by Wessinger, in her volume *How the Millennium Comes Violently: From Jonestown to Heaven's Gate* (2000a), and the edited collection *Millennialism, Persecution, and Violence: Historical Cases* (2000b). However, millennialism (or even catastrophic millennialism) is not seen as the sole reason that groups such as the Solar Temple become violent. As already mentioned, Wessinger stressed the importance of internal weaknesses and the simultaneous experience of cultural opposition that the OTS exhibited prior to the transits. In a similar manner, Hall, Schuyler, and Trinh stress in *Apocalypse Observed: Religious Movements and Violence in North America, Europe, and Japan* that focusing only on millennialism might lead one to overlook the importance of the "apocalyptic tensions between the established social order and countercultural religious movements" (Hall, Schuyler, and Trinh 2000: 3). In the case of the Solar Temple, though, the external opposition did not pose any imminent threat, and it is argued instead that "the mystical apocalypse of deathly transcendence" was the primary impetus to the violence of the Solar Temple (ibid.). Likewise, John Walliss argues in *Apocalyptic Trajectories: Millenarianism and Violence in the Contemporary World* (2004) that what triggered the leaders of the OTS to abandon their belief in survivalism and instead to adopt an apocalyptic worldview that emphasized the necessity of escaping from earth was the experience of cultural opposition—viewed as persecution—in combination with the crumbling of the charismatic authority of Di Mambro and Jouret, caused by various internal factors. Introvigne and Mayer, in line with the aforementioned scholars, argue that four factors might explain the OTS tragedy, namely, predisposing apocalyptic ideology, perception of external opposition, internal dissent and apostasy, and the crumbling charismatic authority of the leader (Introvigne and Mayer 2002: 178–83).

There has, however, been some criticism of the primacy of millennialism/apocalypticism in explaining the violent end of the Solar Temple and of the fact that discussion has lumped together the murder-suicides of the Solar Temple and Jonestown, the ATF/FBI raid on the Mount Carmel community, the Tokyo subway poison-gas attack by Aum Shinrikyo, and the Heaven's Gate suicides. James R. Lewis has questioned the often-assumed connection between violent movements (for example, the OTS), millennialism, and external provocation in an essay with the telling title "The Solar Temple 'Transits': Beyond the Millennialist Hypothesis" (2005); he instead focuses on internal factors, especially the failing health of the leader of the OTS, Di Mambro. Lewis argues that Di Mambro not only had a grandiose self-image (a common enough feature in many new religious movements) but also developed strategies of legitimacy that created an organization in which members had to be totally committed and in which dissenting views were not tolerated. Di Mambro was perceptive enough to realize that he lacked the necessary charisma to control the members directly, so he isolated himself from the majority of them, thereby creating an air of mystique and authority around himself. Direct dealings with the members on a day-to-day basis were transferred to the more charismatic and younger Luc Jouret, something that Di Mambro apparently later regretted as he grew increasingly paranoid. Furthermore, Di Mambro based his authority to a large extent on the fact that he was perceived as the sole source of communication with the "Cosmic Masters," who guided the Solar Temple. This would prove to be an unstable foundation for his authority when members began asking for proof that the Cosmic Masters existed. These factors led to the crumbling of Di Mambro's charisma and legitimacy.

More important, however, was Di Mambro's failing health. Apparently, Di Mambro was suffering from kidney failure, incontinence, and severe diabetes and believed he also had cancer. According to Lewis, the failing health of the leader is an essential factor in our understanding of "suicide cults." By distinguishing the three groups that imploded in suicide—Peoples Temple, the Solar Temple, and Heaven's Gate—from the other violent new religious movements such as Aum Shinrikyo and the Branch Davidians, Lewis stresses that these groups shared the fact that their leaders (Di Mambro, Marshall Applewhite, and Jim Jones) believed they were seriously ill or even dying—something that set them apart from Koresh and Asahara. Based on his analysis of Peoples Temple, the Solar Temple, and Heaven's Gate, Lewis presents a list of traits that are essential characteristics of a suicide group:

1. Absolute intolerance of dissenting views.
2. Members must be totally committed.
3. Exaggerated paranoia about external threats.
4. Leader isolates him/herself or the entire group from the non-believing world.
5. Leader's health is failing—in a major way, not just a transitory sickness; or, alternately, the leader believes he or she is dying.
6. There is no successor and no steps are being taken to provide a successor; or, alternately, succession plans have been frustrated.
7. The group is either stagnant or declining, with no realistic hopes for future expansion. (Lewis 2005: 311)

Peter Åkerbäck (2008), a Swedish historian of religions, agrees with Lewis that it is problematic to view violent new religious movements as constituting a particular category by themselves, since this approach emphasizes their similarities while downplaying their differences. While focusing on the suicide groups (the Solar Temple, Peoples Temple, and Heaven's Gate) in his discussion of previous research, as exemplified by John R. Hall, Catherine Wessinger, and John Walliss, Åkerbäck argues that even though these scholars emphasize the groups' religious ideology—especially an apocalyptic and millenarian worldview—their research is problematic from two perspectives. First, their discussions of the movements' apocalyptic worldviews are often too general in character. The analyses are superficial in the sense that they deal only with basic and general assumptions about apocalyptic and dualistic worldviews without actually discussing in detail the ideology of the movements themselves. Secondly, Hall, Wessinger, and Walliss attempt to understand the context of and reasons for the groups' collective suicides and overlook their religious foundation. Åkerbäck emphasizes that, as a consequence, parts of their ideologies have been neglected, while others have been highlighted. He argues that previous scholars have emphasized the groups' similarities while minimizing the differences in their ideologies. In fact, according to Åkerbäck, the reality is the converse: these groups are characterized not so much by their similarities as by the *differences* in their ideologies.

Åkerbäck describes these differences as an *ideology of opposition*, a *temporary ideology*, and an *ideology of metamorphosis*. The first category, the ideology of opposition, describes the ideology of the Peoples Temple, in which apostolic socialism was seen as an antithesis to capitalism. The temporary ideology is connected to the Solar Temple, whose ideology was based on the notion of a select few individuals who represented the temple, manifested throughout history, and assisted humankind in its spiritual evolution. After the mission had been accomplished, the group would withdraw and advance to a higher spiritual level. Åkerbäck uses the ideology of metamorphosis to denote the ideology of Heaven's Gate, which centered on reaching a level above human. These three forms of ideology give witness to three highly different forms of worldview and soteriology, and thus one is forced to question the often-assumed similarities of these groups' ideologies and their import to the understanding of the subsequent collective suicides.

In "Death as Initiation: The Order of the Solar Temple and Rituals of Initiation" (2006), I have taken a somewhat different approach to the murder-suicides of the OTS. The role of the leaders of a "suicide cult" is undoubtedly of particular importance in trying to understand the motivating factors for extreme groups like the Solar Temple. However, at the same time such a focus runs the risk of avoiding the question of what motivated the members to follow their leaders into death. Strategies of authority notwithstanding, suicide must appear as a plausible option for the members in order for them to carry out such a drastic action. In the case of the Solar Temple, I have argued that a close reading of the rituals of initiation and the esoteric context of the movement can afford us with at least a partial key to understanding why the members (at least some of them) chose to join the transit. Through the rituals, it is possible to understand the symbolic universe of the members and thus to place the transit within a frame of reference. The practice of rituals of initiation was central to the Solar Temple, and members progressed higher up in the hierarchy by undergoing them. A central theme in these rituals is the notion of purification, which was connected with the element of fire. The idea of spiritual purification was also connected to death symbolism, which is a common theme in many western rituals of initiation, such as the Master Mason degree of Freemasonry. However, in the case of the OTS, this was connected to a neo-gnostic dualism in which the material body was seen as less important than the spiritual self. The highly ritualistic circumstances of the murder-suicides and the fact that all traces of the Solar Temple were to be erased by fire indicate that the murder-suicides were seen as a final ritual of initiation, a rite of passage that led from the profane world to the spiritually pure world of another planet. The following extract from one of the rituals of initiation (Ritual for the Donning of the Talar and the Cross) found at the OTS headquarters in Switzerland gives an idea of the content and symbolism of these rituals of initiation:

> Death is the same for us all./It is how we leave Life that makes the difference.
>
> But always remember/that Death is an illusion./In fact,/It is only another aspect of Life.

> At this Station, let me tell you/that you must also consider Life/as ephemeral as smoke passing by,/or a cloud drifting overhead,/and all its glory/is like a flower in the meadow/which unfolds in the morning and dies at eventide.
> In the world of illusions,/all must pass away.
> Everyone must one day confront/The great problem of Death/which alone gives meaning to Life./You must be able to die to the profane world/in order to be born again to the Cosmic World.
> Therefore, let the quality and the wholeness of Life/compensate for its shortness./ You, wishing to be a Knight of the Temple,/Do not think of living according to Cosmic Good.
> And since nothing is more uncertain/than the hour of Death ... prepare yourself each day to be FREE/to leave this Earth/and to continue/on a parallel Invisible plane,/free from all human and terrestrial chains/which keep you prisoner of yourself. (Bogdan 2006: 150)

Conclusion

The murder-suicides of the Order of the Solar Temple stand out as one of the very few examples of a western esoteric group that turned violent. The ritual purification of the soul strived for in the initiatory system of the Order, neo-Templar notions of chivalry and self-sacrifice, and Rosicrucian beliefs in the importance of secret societies and Hidden Masters, in combination with New Age notions of an evolutionary leap forward for humankind as we enter the Age of Aquarius, formed the basic components of the esoteric worldview of the Solar Temple. In contrast to other violent new religious movements—apart from Aum Shinrikyo—the members of the Solar Temple were not marginalized members of society. On the contrary, the members of the OTS were generally well-integrated into society, well-connected politically and socially, and affluent.

To sum up, the various hypotheses for the murder-suicides of the Solar Temple often emphasize catastrophic millennialism in combination with factors such as perception of external opposition, internal dissent and apostasy, and the crumbling charismatic authority of the leader. Furthermore, the explanations of violence offered by scholars are often reached by a comparison with other violent new religious movements, especially the well-known cases from the 1990s (the Branch Davidians, Aum Shinrikyo, and Heaven's Gate), together with the Peoples Temple murder-suicides at Jonestown in 1978. This comparative approach has, however, been criticized for its tendency to focus on the similarities of these different groups, while to a large extent ignoring their differences. A final criticism has involved the assumption that millennialism is essential to our understanding contemporary violent groups.

References

Åkerbäck, Peter (2008). *De obeständiga religionerna: Om kollektiva självmord och frälsning i Peoples Temple, Ordre du Temple Solaire, och Heaven's Gate.* Stockholm: Stockholms universitet.

Barrett, David V. (2001). *The New Believers: A Survey of Sects, Cults, and Alternative Religions*. London: Cassell.

Bogdan, Henrik (2006). "Death as Initiation: The Order of the Solar Temple and Rituals of Initiation," in *The Order of the Solar Temple: The Temple of Death*, ed. James R. Lewis. London: Ashgate, pp. 133–53.

— (2007). *Western Esotericism and Rituals of Initiation*. Albany: State University of New York Press.

— (2011). "Explaining the Murder-Suicides of the Order of the Solar Temple: A Survey of Hypotheses," in *Violence and New Religious Movements*, ed. James R. Lewis. New York: Oxford University Press, pp. 133–45.

Bromley, David G., and J. Gordon Melton, eds. (2002). *Cults, Religion, and Violence*. New York: Cambridge University Press.

Daniels, Ted, ed. (1999). *A Doomsday Reader: Prophets, Predictors, and Hucksters of Salvation*. New York: New York University Press.

Faivre, Antoine (1994). *Access to Western Esotericism*. Albany: State University of New York Press.

Hall, John R., and Philip Schuyler (1997). "The Mystical Apocalypse of the Solar Temple," in *Millennium, Messiahs, and Mayhem: Contemporary Apocalyptic Movements*, eds. Thomas Robbins and Susan J. Palmer. New York: Routledge, pp. 285–311.

— (1998). "Apostasy, Apocalypse, and Religious Violence: An Exploratory Comparison of Peoples Temple, the Branch Davidians, and the Solar Temple," in *The Politics of Religious Apostasy*, ed. David G. Bromley. Westport, CT: Praeger, pp. 141–70.

—, and Sylvaine Trinh (2000). *Apocalypse Observed: Religious Movements and Violence in North America, Europe, and Japan*. New York: Routledge.

Hanegraaff, Wouter J. (1998). *New Age Spirituality and Western Culture: Esotericism in the Mirror of Secular Thought*. Albany: State University of New York Press.

— (2012). *Esotericism and the Academy: Rejected Knowledge in Western Culture*. Cambridge: Cambridge University Press.
— (2013). *Western Esotericism: A Guide for the Perplexed*. London: Continuum.
Introvigne, Massimo (1995). "Ordeal by Fire: The Tragedy of the Solar Temple," *Religion* 25: 267–83.
— (1999). "Unde dérive vers l'homicide et le suicide l'Ordre du Temple Solaire," in *Sectes et démocratie*, eds. Françoise Champion and Martine Cohen. Paris: Editions du Seuil, pp. 300–313.
— (2000). "The Magic of Death: The Suicides of the Solar Temple," in *Millennialism, Persecution, and Violence: Historical Cases*, ed. Catherine Wessinger. Syracuse, NY: Syracuse University Press, pp. 138–57.
—, and Jean-François Mayer (2002). "Occult Masters and the Temple of Doom: The Fiery End of the Solar Temple," in *Cults, Religion, and Violence*, eds. David G. Bromley and J. Gordon Melton. New York: Cambridge University Press, pp. 170–88.
Lewis, James R. (2003). *Legitimating New Religions*. New Brunswick, NJ: Rutgers University Press.
— (2005). "The Solar Temple 'Transits': Beyond the Millennialist Hypothesis," in *Controversial New Religions*, eds. James R. Lewis and Jesper Aagaard Petersen. New York: Oxford University Press.
—, ed. (2006). *The Order of the Solar Temple: The Temple of Death*. London: Ashgate.
—, ed. (2011). *Violence and New Religious Movements*. New York: Oxford University Press.
Lewis, Spencer H. (1941 [1929]). *Rosicrucian Questions and Answers with Complete History of the Rosicrucian Order*. San Jose, CA: Rosicrucian Press.
Mayer, Jean-François (1996). *Les mythes du Temple Solaire*. Geneva: Georg Editeur.
— (1999). "Les chevaliers de l'Apocalypse: L'Ordre du Temple Solaire et ses adeptes," in *Sectes et démocratie*, eds. Françoise Champion and Martine Cohen. Paris: Editions du Seuil, pp. 205–23.
Palmer, Susan J. (1996). "Purity and Danger in the Solar Temple," *Journal of Contemporary Religion* 1(3): 303–18.
Robbins, Thomas, and Susan J. Palmer, eds. (1997). *Millennium, Messiahs, and Mayhem: Contemporary Apocalyptic Movements*. New York: Routledge.
von Stuckrad, Kocku (2010). *Locations of Knowledge in Medieval and Early Modern Europe: Esoteric Discourse and Western Identities*. Leiden: Brill Academic Publishers.

Walliss, John (2004). *Apocalyptic Trajectories: Millenarianism and Violence in the Contemporary World*. New York: Lang.

Wessinger, Catherine (2000a). *How the Millennium Comes Violently: From Jonestown to Heaven's Gate*. New York: Seven Bridges.

—, ed. (2000b). *Millennialism, Persecution, & Violence: Historical Cases*. Syracuse, NY: Syracuse University Press.

Chapter 4

Rhetoric, Revolution, and Resistance in Jonestown, Guyana[1]

Rebecca Moore

Introduction

A complete understanding of all the factors contributing to the deaths of 918 people in Jonestown, Guyana in November 1978 may forever elude us. Nevertheless, an important factor often overlooked is the radical rhetoric that dominated black activism in the fifteen years preceding the mass deaths. A discourse asserting the positive need to fight, and even to die, for the cause infused Peoples Temple at least by the late 1960s in northern California. It permeated daily life in Jonestown, especially when Jim Jones, the group's leader, arrived in mid-1977 to make his permanent home in the community.

This discourse was framed in the language of martyrdom. Given the times in which the Temple arose, when political murders in the US seemed commonplace, this rhetorical move was eminently rational. Huey Newton, a Black Panther leader, called the militant activism of the era "revolutionary suicide," in recognition of his belief that "the revolutionary must always be prepared to face death" (Newton 1973: 7). Jim Jones re-interpreted revolutionary suicide to mean actual suicide, rather than suicidal actions. He viewed mass death as a form of resistance, in which a strong protest was made through the lives, and bodies, of those courageous enough to take the step.

The question of whether Jones's followers fully understood or completely accepted his perspective, however, continues to haunt considerations of the deaths in Jonestown. This chapter addresses several issues that persistently demand attention. First, it considers the explicit threats that members of Peoples Temple made concerning mass suicide, before turning to initial news accounts of Jonestown, and the reasons the media initially reported them as mass suicide.

---

1 An earlier version of this chapter was published as Rebecca Moore, "Rhetoric, Revolution, and Resistance in Jonestown, Guyana," *Journal of Religion and Violence*, 1(3) (2013): 303–21.

It then examines the ongoing debate regarding the nature of the deaths: did adults voluntarily kill themselves? How should we characterize the deaths of the children? The chapter locates this analysis within a broader discussion of the social stigma associated with suicide. Finally, it compares the revolutionary rhetoric used by Black Power movements in the US with the language used by Peoples Temple. The discourse of both movements emphasizes a willingness to die fighting persecution and repression, and reveals an expectation that this will happen. The chapter argues that the members of Peoples Temple saw themselves as true martyrs in the cause of African-American liberation.

The Threat of Mass Suicide

It seemed to come as no surprise that more than nine hundred Americans living in Jonestown, a communal agricultural project in Guyana, committed mass suicide on November 18, 1978. Members of Peoples Temple, a new religious movement headquartered in San Francisco, had made ominous threats throughout 1978. An oppositional group called the Concerned Relatives—comprised of ex-members and relatives of members of Peoples Temple—filed an "Accusation of Human Rights Violations" in April 1978, in which the first complaint referred to suicide. The "Accusation" quoted a letter that Temple member Pam Moton had written the previous month to members of the United States Congress, which stated that "I can say without hesitation that we are devoted to a decision that it is better even to die than to be constantly harassed from one continent to the next" ("Accusation of Human Rights Violations" 1978). Additional evidence in the "Accusation" came from Yolanda Crawford, a former member of the Temple who had recently returned from Jonestown. Crawford said that "I heard Jim Jones say, 'If anyone tries to start anything, we are ready and prepared to die for our cause'" ("Affidavit of Yolanda D. A. Crawford" 1978).

Peoples Temple's response to the publicity generated by the "Accusation" was not reassuring. In a press release dictated from Jonestown via shortwave radio to Temple members in San Francisco, Harriet Tropp stated, "it would seem that *any* person with *any* integrity or courage would have *no* trouble understanding such a position." She went on to quote Martin Luther King's statement in support of ultimate commitment: "we must develop the quiet courage of dying for a cause." Tropp concluded by saying that the people of Jonestown would "defend the integrity of our community" by dying if necessary, though that was not their purpose (Tropp 1978).

Rather than backing down, the Concerned Relatives gained new ammunition in their battle a month later. In May 1978, Deborah Layton Blakey, a Jonestown defector, issued a sworn statement upon her return to the US titled "Re the Threat and Possibility of Mass Suicide by Members of the People's Temple." Blakey reported occasions on which mass suicide was discussed, although she recounted only a single instance of a suicide drill occurring in the five months she lived in Jonestown. At that time, the group was told that the situation was hopeless, and that it was better to die for the glory of socialism than to be tortured by the mercenaries who were coming. Everyone, including the children, lined up and drank a small cup of what they had been told was a poison that would kill them in 45 minutes. Jones "warned us that the time was not far off when it would become necessary for us to die by our own hands" (Blakey 1978).The accounts of Blakey and other members of the Concerned Relatives persuaded Leo Ryan, a member of Congress from California, to travel to Jonestown in November 1978 to investigate the charges. As he was leaving the agricultural project, he and three reporters, along with a departing Jonestown resident, were shot dead at a nearby airstrip by a few young men from Jonestown. Shortly thereafter, the community of nine hundred gathered in the central area of the project, where almost all of them either ingested poison, were injected with poison, or, in the case of infants and children, had the poison squirted down their mouths. Only two—Jim Jones and my sister Annie Moore—died of gunshot wounds.

Murder or Suicide?

Initial accounts of the deaths that occurred in Jonestown characterized them as suicides, with the earliest appearing in the pre-dawn hours of November 19, when a CIA memo reported "mass suicides" ("The NOIWON Notation" 1978). News coverage during the first week followed the lead given by government sources, as indicated by the second-level headline in the *New York Times* of November 20: "Troops Find Bodies—Mass Suicide Is Indicated After Attack on Americans in Which 5 Were Slain" (Associated Press 1978). The next day: "400 Are Found Dead In Mass Suicide By Cult." The third-level head for the same article stated that "Parents Reported to Give Children Poison Before Dying Beside Them" (Nordheimer 1978a). By November 24, however, the deaths were described for the first time as "mass suicide and killings," although the headline called it the "Sect's Suicide Rite" (Nordheimer 1978b), a description that continued to appear in headlines. Three days later, on November 27, reporter Jon Nordheimer, who had written daily articles for the *Times*, termed it the "mass murder-suicide," and other writers soon described the deaths as "killings and suicides." Eventually these specific descriptors were replaced by "massacre" and "tragedy," terms that reflected the writers' attitude toward the deaths.

The mass suicide description was never accurate, of course, since the three hundred infants and children could not choose to die in any meaningful sense. Nevertheless, early eyewitness accounts indicated that most adults voluntarily took the poison. An audiotape made at the time revealed that only a single person, Christine Miller, verbally dissented, and she was shouted down by the crowd (Audiotape Q042 1978). Odell Rhodes, who escaped from Jonestown on November 18, has consistently stated that most died willingly (Feinsod 1981). Stanley Clayton, who fled during the deaths, initially reported only a single person resisting, but later claimed that a number of others resisted (Wooden 1981). Dr Leslie Mootoo, the Guyana government pathologist who investigated the deaths, observed injection marks on the upper arms of at least seventy adults, and questioned whether these individuals died voluntarily. A number of writers (for example, Hougan 1999) have characterized the deaths as murder as a result of Dr Mootoo's testimony.

The 2006 edition of *the jonestown report* featured a forum titled "Was It Murder or Suicide?" to which a dozen writers, myself included, contributed ("Was It Murder or Suicide" 2006). Some authors argued strongly that it was murder, because Jonestown residents did not seriously intend to kill themselves; nor did they have any choice in the matter. As Josef Dieckman writes, "There was only one option: death. The only 'choice' they were offered was whether that death would be by their own hand or by someone else's. That's not choice, that's murder" (Dieckman 2006).

However we may understand the nature of the deaths in Jonestown, we cannot escape the fact that events of the last day were carefully organized and rehearsed a number of times. My own two sisters, Carolyn Layton and Annie Moore, are implicated in the planning process. Carolyn wrote to Jim Jones an "Analysis of Future Prospects" in which she asked: "If we make a stand or decide to die how are we going to do it? ... How will we have the knowledge to know now is the time to go ahead and do it? Do you give everyone pills?" (Layton 2005).

Annie submitted various ways to kill people, proposing exhaust fumes or poisoning the water or food supply. In a note to Jim Jones, she wrote, "I never thought people would line up to be killed but actually think a select group would have to kill the majority of the people secretly, without the people knowing it." She thought that beheading would be "terrorizing," and argued that the main reason for suicide was to assure the safety of the children, who might be hurt if the residents of Jonestown violently resisted any attacks (Moore n.d.).

Even conceding that the death of a child of five months or five years could not be considered a suicide, the following question remains: how did the parents who killed their children in Jonestown view their own actions? We may look to similar historical instances of parents killing children for an answer. The male Jews at Masada slew their wives and children with their knives before they killed themselves as the Roman army advanced. Chaja Kubrzanska and Basia Binsztein of the village of Jedwabne, Poland, drowned their children and then killed themselves in a nearby pond rather than let the Nazis take them ("The Testimony of Szmul Wasersztein" 1945). Terrified civilians on the island of Saipan threw their children over a cliff into the Pacific Ocean, and jumped in afterwards, to avoid torture by invading American troops, which they believed would occur if they were captured ("Victory in the Pacific" n.d.). Should we consider these deaths, including those of the children at Jonestown, as acts of murder if the parents believed they were sacrificing their children to avoid a fate worse than death?

The people of Jonestown had discussed this possibility openly. On April 12, 1978, during one of the regularly held emergency drills, residents announce their willingness to take the lives of their own children rather than leave them for the fascists. Jones elaborates, saying that they are already prepared to be "genuinely compassionate" in the case of such an emergency. If the child were over the age of 11, "she would take up a cutlass and fight till she was dead, unless it came to an overwhelming invasion, and then we would gently put them to sleep" (Audiotape Q637 1978)

I believe that we should consider the children's deaths in Jonestown, just as we view them at Masada, Jedwabne, and Saipan: parents did indeed kill their children, but they did not murder them. A literary example makes this same point. The character Sethe in Toni Morrison's novel *Beloved* has been brutalized by slave owners, and to prevent her daughter Beloved from facing the same doom, Sethe cuts her daughter's throat. "She had to be safe," says Sethe, and I put her where she would be ... I'll explain to her, even though I don't have to. Why I did it. How if I hadn't killed she would have died and that is something I could not bear to happen to her" (Morrison 1988: 200).

The Stigma of Suicide

The question of when suicide should more appropriately be called murder is not new. Suicide itself carries negative moral freight, with most people in the US saying it is "morally wrong" (Saad 2011). But according to the French sociologist Emile Durkheim, suicide is a neutral term that should be "applied to all cases of death resulting directly or indirectly from a positive or negative act of the victim himself, which he knows will produce this result" (Durkheim 1951: 44; original text appears in italics). Durkheim then uses the word "suicide" to describe a range of behaviors, which include what he calls "altruistic suicide," as in the case of soldiers fighting in a lost cause, Jains abstaining from all food, and Christian martyrs dying for their faith. He also identifies a type of obligatory altruistic suicide, such as *sati*, the centuries-old practice, now outlawed, in which Hindu widows throw themselves upon the funeral pyres of their husbands, and *hara-kiri*, in which disgraced Japanese men disembowel themselves to save their families from dishonor.

Some philosophers and theologians have challenged Durkheim. R.G. Frey (1978), R.B. Brandt (1975), and others, seem to consider all forms of self-destruction to be suicide. In contrast, William Tolhurst rejects the view that "mere foreknowledge that one's death will result from one's actions is a sufficient condition for suicide" (Tolhurst 1990: 77). He gives examples of "altruistically motivated self-caused deaths" which he claims are not suicides, such as the pilot who guides a disabled plane away from a populated area, knowing he will die in the consequent crash. According to Tolhurst, these examples are different from other instances of actual altruistic suicides, such as the Buddhist monk who immolates himself to protest a war. What Tolhurst is trying to do is to "reconsider the moral status of suicide," by saying that "it seems clear that suicide is not selfish and blameworthy by definition" (ibid.: 84).

In contrast, Suzanne Stern-Gillet contends that rhetorically it is necessary to consider "different *manners of viewing* a person's death" (Stern-Gillet 1990: 93; original emphasis). She is concerned that Durkheim broadens the definition of suicide to include the self-sacrifice of Socrates, Jesus, and Bobby Sands, the IRA prisoner who died during a hunger strike. The central issue for Stern-Gillet is the question of who is truly responsible for the individual's death: Athens or Socrates? Pilate or Jesus? Margaret Thatcher or Bobby Sands? She concludes:

> To call X a suicide amounts, among other things, to ascribing X the moral responsibility (and sometimes, but not always, the blame) for X's death. To call X a martyr amounts, amongst other things, to ascribing the moral responsibility (and, usually, the blame) for X's death to someone else (usually a government, an institution, or an organization) (Ibid.: 99–100; original text appears in italics).

In other words, the concept of suicide indicates responsibility for the death. In Stern-Gillet's view, to say that someone is "forced to commit suicide" negates the meaning of suicide.

These arguments counter Durkheim's (failed) effort to de-stigmatize the concept of suicide. The word itself bears judgment against the individual doing it, and the act carries a stigma which explains our efforts to differentiate between types of self-caused deaths. Immanuel Kant was opposed to suicide in all circumstances, yet allows it by another name: "It is no suicide to risk one's life against one's enemies, and even to sacrifice it, in order to preserve one's duties toward oneself" (quoted in Brandt 1975: 64).

Commenting upon the view that one can sacrifice one's life to save one's humanity, John Donnelly adds, "But this can in no way be construed as an act of suicide" (Donnelly 1978: 103). Even in daily life, we use euphemisms concerning biomedical end-of-life decisions which might be called suicide: letting nature take its course, withdrawing life-sustaining treatment, and so on (Szasz 1999: 6).

Religious acts of self-sacrifice are rarely called suicide, except in the case of contemporary suicide bombers. (It is important to note that Muslim supporters consider these individuals as martyrs, the same way that Christians view those who sought death for the glory of God in the Roman arena). While most mainline religions today condemn suicide, they also continue to provide the justification, or "invitation," in Margaret Battin's words, for death: reunion with the deceased, release of the soul, self-sacrifice, martyrdom and avoidance of sin, death and the attainment of the highest spiritual state (Battin 1995: 57–74).

This discussion does not resolve the debate over whether the deaths in Jonestown were suicides or murders, but it does illuminate the problems inherent in identifying those deaths as "mass suicide." Deaths that occur within a religious or political setting, in which the actors see themselves participating in a larger drama on a world stage, cannot be reduced, or trivialized, by one epithet or another. Thus the deaths in Jonestown defy easy categorization.

Narratives of Revolution and Sacrifice

The term adopted by the Jonestown community both before and on that fateful day—"revolutionary suicide"—provides the best description of the cultural and emotional context that existed in Jonestown. Civil rebellions and antiwar protests in America's cities provided the backdrop for the rapid expansion of the Temple from rural northern California in the late 1960s to urban San Francisco and Los Angeles in the early to mid-1970s. In addition, anti-colonial movements sweeping throughout Africa and Asia, and the establishment of socialist governments in Latin American countries, created a global awareness that African Americans were part of a larger struggle for justice and equality.

The emigration to Guyana, a cooperative socialist republic, solidified the commitment that Temple members had to the global struggle for freedom. They saw themselves as comrades-in-arms in the great fight against capitalism.

The specter of violent death at the hands of agents of the state was an ever-present reality for 1960s radicals. This could be seen in the murders of black leaders, civil rights workers, and student protestors, as well as in the deaths of hundreds in the civil rebellions that swept through American cities during that decade. Coupled with the loss of thousands of American soldiers in Vietnam, not to mention millions of Vietnamese, death loomed large in all sectors of society. While radical rhetoric may have exaggerated the extent of the crisis, social activists nonetheless could see that the apparatus of government clamped down harshly when its interests were challenged.

This repression engendered a revolutionary narrative that emphasized resistance to oppression, even at the cost of one's life. We find appeals both to armed struggle and to sacrificial death in speeches, newspapers, essays, sermons, poetry, literature, and drama. An eerily prescient poem titled "Revolution!!" by Richard W. Thomas describes a collective death for a cause, concluding: "We shall die properly, all at once!" (Thomas 1968: 196).

Many additional examples of the revolutionary narrative that African-American writers employed in the 1960s appears in the 1968 anthology *Black Fire*. An essay by Calvin C. Hernton titled "Dynamite Growing out of Their Skulls" predicts that African Americans will explode in violence, while whites "will be at a complete loss to understand why so many black people have gone mad." The essay concludes that "nothing will stop the blacks except to kill them" (Hernton 1968: 78, 104). Another illustration of the radical narrative is the one-act play *Black-Ice*, in which a group of radicals kidnap a congressman and hold him hostage in exchange for the release of a prisoner on death row. The plot is foiled, three of the schemers are killed as they attempt to escape, and a woman is left with the congressman, who begs for his life:

> CONGRESSMAN: All of you will go free.
> MARTHA: How can you promise that? You're just a Congressman.
> CONGRESSMAN: You'd be surprised at the power a Congressman has. We run this country.

At the end of the play, Martha shoots the congressman. The last line is: "You didn't die very well!" (Patterson 1968: 564, 565).

The clearest and most militant articulation of the priorities and programs of Black Power came from the Black Panthers. Founded in 1966 in Oakland,

California, the Black Panther Party (originally the Black Panther Party for Self-Defense) directly challenged police brutality against African Americans. In contrast to the practice of nonviolent resistance, the Panthers encouraged armed resistance, especially against the police who carried out state-sponsored oppression of African Americans and other people of color. They argued that "all Black and oppressed people should be armed for self-defense of our homes and communities against these fascist police forces" ("March 1972 Platform" 1972). This provocative stance led to lethal showdowns between the Panthers and the police, which in turn fed the belief that death was just around the corner.

Huey P. Newton, co-founder of the Black Panthers, served three years in prison on charges of killing a police officer and wounding another, before winning an appeal and being released from San Quentin in 1970. His theory of revolutionary suicide, and his persona as persecuted political figure, served as the model for discourse in Peoples Temple. In the essay "Revolutionary Suicide," Newton writes "Although I risk the likelihood of death, there is at least the possibility, if not probability, of changing intolerable conditions" (Newton 1973: 5). He contrasts "reactionary suicide"—what he calls the self-murder of those who are crushed by reactionary forces—with revolutionary suicide, in which "we must move against these forces, even at the risk of death" (ibid.: 5). Newton then goes on to cite a number of revolutionaries, such as Che Guevara, Fidel Castro, and Mikhail Bakunin, who argued that revolutionaries are essentially doomed men. He compares the 1960s radicals with the American colonists, the dispossessed of the French Revolution, the Russians of 1917, the Jews of Warsaw, and other heroic radicals. These revolutionaries were not suicidal, nor did they actively seek death, yet they knew that their lives were at stake.

In an interview with the official organ of the African National Congress of South Africa, the liberation group in that country in 1970, Newton describes the program of the Panthers as one of armed struggle. "We have hooked up with the people who are rising up all over the world with arms, because we feel that only with the power of the gun will the bourgeoisie be destroyed and the world transformed" (Newton 1995: 198). His eulogy for Jonathan Jackson and William Christmas, who were killed in a shoot-out in the Marin County Courthouse in 1970, includes the statement: "If the penalty for the quest for freedom is death, then by death we escape to freedom" (ibid.: 221). He concludes the eulogy for another Black Panther who was shot and killed, with the words: "Samuel Napier was a servant of the people; he gave the supreme gift to the people. So therefore Samuel Napier was the Supreme Servant of the people" (ibid.: 230). Newton's concept of revolutionary suicide thus required dying in battle.

Revolutionary Suicide in Peoples Temple

While the fiery rhetoric of Newton, the Black Panthers, and those in the Black Power movement may appear overblown and self-aggrandizing today, it is vital to remember that activists at the time believed they were engaged in a life-and-death struggle. Documents obtained under the Freedom of Information Act and other public records suggest that this belief was not mere paranoia (Jones 1988). The members of Peoples Temple used the same language, since it was an African-American political-religious group also responding to the social turmoil raging in the US in the 1960s and 1970s. Duchess Harris and Adam John Waterman argue that many Temple members deliberately utilized Black Power rhetoric "because it was an available and appealing syntax of revolutionary social and political change" (Harris and Waterman 2004: 105). Perhaps more to the point, African Americans comprised between 80 and 90 percent of the membership of the Temple in California, and accounted for 70 percent of those who died in Jonestown. Black Power was not empty rhetoric for Temple members.

Jim Jones expounded a political message that radicalized the young and exhorted a social gospel message that offered spiritual hope to the elderly. The Temple offered "survival programs" (ibid.: 106) such as health services for senior citizens and welfare advocacy for poor people. Members also volunteered as activists in a variety of political movements that included protesting the Bakke decision by the US Supreme Court, which rejected the principle of affirmative action; joining the California Coalition against the Death Penalty, and participating in a Gay Rights rally. The Temple sponsored anti-colonial events, such as the 1976 African Liberation Day celebration, which hosted speakers from liberation movements from the US and abroad. Members circulated petitions against the incarceration of South Africa's Nelson Mandela, and refugees from the military coup in Chile, such as Orlando Letelier and Laura Allende, spoke at the Temple.

Jones himself was "an obscure socialist thinker, blending elements of atheism, Christianity, Marxism, Leninism, Maoism, and Third World revolutionary rhetoric into a complicated brew of political sentiments" (ibid.: 106). Audiotapes recovered from Jonestown feature Jones reading news from *Pravda*, a Soviet newspaper, and Tass, the Soviet news agency, about liberation movements from around the world (the head of Tass and his wife actually visited Jonestown on April 15, 1978). In the news from November 6, 1978, Jones reported on protests in the Arab world against the Camp David Peace Agreement, the handover of power from the Rhodesian government to black majority rule, the decision in the Philippines to release those detained under martial law, and trade talks between China and Thailand (Audiotape Q169 1978).

Peoples Forum, the newspaper of the Peoples Temple, also printed news of radical leaders and events. The first issue, published in April 1976, highlighted Dennis Banks, the co-founder of the American Indian Movement who was fighting extradition proceedings to South Dakota in connection with the Wounded Knee uprising of 1973. An article on intimidation against the Temple from the December 1976 edition focused on spies identified at a talk given at the Temple by civil rights activist Unita Blackwell Wright. "This country must be maintained on the road to social democracy," the article reads. "It is beginning to appear that our corporate state has gotten out of touch with the needs of its people." It concludes with a warning to all those attempting to:

> ... circumvent the Constitutional guarantees of freedom of speech, religion, and assembly, that we will not stand idly by while these freedoms are smothered ... We would be prepared to do so even if it meant our death, because we firmly believe that liberty is worth that price ("Intimidation Won't Succeed" 1976: 2).

A review of *Peoples Forum*, audiotape transcripts, and other primary-source documents reveals that the discourse of Peoples Temple was neither as cogent, coherent, or radical as that of the Black Panthers or other Black Power movements. The willingness to die, however, is marked, as can be seen in the above quotation. Six months after my sister Annie Moore joined the Temple in 1972, she wrote a letter in which she stated: "I want to be in on changing the world to be a better place and I would give my life for it" (Moore 1986: 94). In her last letter to me in October 1978, Annie described various conspiracies against the group that had been uncovered. "What's interesting," she wrote, "is that it is all coming out before we are all dead, not the case with JFK, RFK, and MLK" (ibid.: 282).

The notion of suicide was not explicitly discussed by the residents of Jonestown until September 1977, when they believed they were under attack. Tim Carter, who escaped on November 18 the following year, wrote that Jim Jones claimed that the situation was so dire that they needed to commit suicide in order to prevent the fascists from killing the people. Jones called for a vote, but only two people supported the suicide option; in a second vote the next day, three more joined the two. All were female leaders of the Temple (Carter 2006). Nevertheless, when Jones spoke to the Deputy Prime Minister of Guyana via shortwave radio, he reversed the outcome: all but two supported "a vote that we would rather die than return to the United States." The two dissenters, he added, thought they might be able to bring about revolutionary change in the US (Audiotape Q800 1977).

A journal kept by Temple member Edith Roller and an audiotape recording indicate that revolutionary suicide was unambiguously and repeatedly discussed at a community meeting on February 16, 1978. (This may have been the discussion Deborah Layton referred to in her affidavit of June 1978, following her defection). Roller wrote that Jim Jones had said the political situation in Guyana was dangerous and that alternatives needed to be explored. Many residents proposed moving to Africa, and Roller publicly recommended "that instead of revolutionary suicide (which had been suggested), we seek to send our young people to some African country where they could be used in a revolutionary cause" (Roller 1978). Other people who spoke that night agreed, arguing that they should take a stand and fiercely resist any attacks, but Jones maintained that revolutionary suicide was preferable to being taken prisoner, becoming a slave, or returning to the United States. "There's no way to make any moral sense out of further fighting," he said, "because it'd be maybe black people having to kill black people that they'd use to come after us, and we would lose our moral impact" (Audiotape Q642 1978). At the end of the discussion, Jones announced that there was no alternative to revolutionary suicide, and ordered residents to line up to take what they believed was poison.

Discussions of revolutionary suicide intensified throughout 1978. Julia Scheeres maintains that "night after night, Jones held his death vote" (Scheeres 2011: 127). Some time between November 1977 and June 1978, residents were asked to write down what they would do in a final "white night." Their responses veered from the sincere to the fanciful:

> Rose O. Sharon: I have given my life to you. [I] Don't care about my life.
> Thom Bogue: What I would do if I was sent to kill someone, I would have a vessel of nitroglycerin along with a full screen spark strike, then I would walk up to [a] person and pull the string and blow me and the person up. And if I were caught along the way I would put out a do-or-die threat. If you get in my path or try to stop me, I will blow you up ... .
> Shirley Baisy: I can give my life, my children['s] life or any member of my family. I don't think we were put here to live forever. ("What I Would Do ... " n.d.).

We know that Thom Bogue's declaration, at the least, was fraudulent as he tried to escape from Jonestown many times, and did in fact survive on November 18, 1978 by leaving with Congressman Ryan.

Whatever their private thoughts might have been, residents affirmed their commitment to die on a tape made at the end of that summer. The statements clearly are made for posterity, as several speakers allude to the future and those who will listen to the tape. Although they do not agree on a single definition of revolutionary suicide, they do admit that death is the only way out. Some want to die to prove that they laid down their lives for something worthwhile; some would rather die than live any other place in the world; some want to make a statement in support of the communism practiced in Jonestown; some are dying in solidarity with other freedom fighters around the world, and some are just tired of running. The declaration of Liane Harris perhaps rings most true of those made that night:

> I wanted to say that if I can't participate in this liberation struggle here in Guyana—where all the people here in Jonestown are free, they have lots of food, everyone has housing, the children are blooming and growing with education where they are learning everything they can. This is the only place where I found freedom—and if I can't have it here, I'd rather be dead. (Harris 1978)

Liane was not in Jonestown on November 18, but instead died in the bathroom of the Temple headquarters in Georgetown, Guyana, along with her mother and two siblings.

The tape made on the last day as the deaths are occurring includes Jim Jones' pronouncement that they were not destroying themselves, but rather were committing revolutionary suicide:

> One thousand people who said, we don't like the way the world is. [Tape edit] Take some. [Tape edit] Take our life from us. We laid it down. We got tired. [Tape edit] We didn't commit suicide, we committed an act of revolutionary suicide protesting the conditions of an inhumane world. (Audiotape Q042 1978)

Just as Huey Newton differentiated between reactionary suicide and revolutionary suicide, Jim Jones distinguished self-destructive suicide from revolutionary suicide. He condemned suicide, saying, "It's *immoral* to commit suicide for selfish reasons. It's *hostile*. It's an act of vengeance to do it" (Audiotape Q8331978, italics in transcript). He claimed that a suicide would be reincarnated for 10,000 years. In contrast, revolutionary suicide was an unselfish act intended to resist the evils of capitalism.

Conclusion

Members of Peoples Temple were immersed in the rhetoric of revolution. Resistance shaped the discourse they used to describe America, the Babylon of racism and capitalism. (Members and Jones referred to the US as Babylon, for example, Audiotapes Q182 1978, Q217 1978, Q673 1977, and Q933 1977). The group addressed two fronts to oppose these evils. First, they worked for social justice in the urban areas of San Francisco and, to a lesser extent, Los Angeles. Secondly, they created an alternative society in Guyana in which the problems of America's economic and political system no longer existed. The mean streets of the ghetto—with their drugs, addiction, crime, alcoholism, juvenile delinquency, and other ills—were left far behind.

Self-sacrifice was required to participate in the struggle. This self-denial encompassed not only martyrdom at the hands of the oppressors, but also self-murder, if the death promoted a larger cause or purpose. In the case of Jonestown, the deaths served as a blow by the powerless against the powerful. Joost Meerloo's description of the honor code among the Japanese who once required *hara-kiri* to save a family from disgrace resonates with the resistance seen in Jonestown. According to Meerloo, such death is a self-justification, a purification, and a recovery of lost honor: "It also meant a silent, honorable revenge on those so high in the governmental hierarchy that they, according to the code, could not be attacked directly without the aggressor losing respect and self-respect" (Meerloo 1962: 53).

Unlike their contemporaries, the people of Jonestown ultimately rejected armed aggression. They turned the violence upon themselves, thereby proving the righteousness of the cause for which they died: "The 'suicide' says: 'I was right after all; I shall teach you a lesson by my death'" (ibid.: 54). Thus, the revolutionary suicide of Jonestown was the best weapon that the weak could use against the strong. The people maintained their integrity by dying what they hoped would be a noble death in a cause greater than themselves.

References[2]

"Accusation of Human Rights Violations by Rev. James Warren Jones Against Our Children and Relatives at the Peoples Temple Jungle Encampment

[2] Note: The website Alternative Considerations of Jonestown and Peoples Temple is shortened to Alternative Considerations throughout.

in Guyana, South America" (1978). *Alternative Considerations.* Accessed January 28, 2014. At <http://jonestown.sdsu.edu/?page_id=13081>.

"Affidavit of Yolanda D. A. Crawford Showing the Teachings and Practices of Rev. James Warren Jones in Guyana, South America" (1978). *Alternative Considerations.* Accessed January 28, 2014. At <http://jonestown.sdsu.edu/?page_id=13085>.

Associated Press (1978). "Guyana Official Reports 300 Dead At Religious Sect's Jungle Temple," *New York Times*, November 20.

Audiotape Q042 (1978). *Alternative Considerations.* Accessed January 28, 2014. At <http://jonestown.sdsu.edu/?page_id=29084>.

Audiotape Q169 (1978). *Alternative Considerations.* Accessed January 28, 2014. At <http://jonestown.sdsu.edu/?page_id=27352>.

Audiotape Q182 (1978). *Alternative Considerations.* Accessed January 28, 2014. At <http://jonestown.sdsu.edu/?page_id=27358>.

Audiotape Q217 (1978). *Alternative Considerations.* Accessed January 28, 2014. At <http://jonestown.sdsu.edu/?page_id=27380>.

Audiotape Q637 (1978). *Alternative Considerations.* Accessed January 28, 2014. At <http://jonestown.sdsu.edu/?page_id=27509>.

Audiotape Q642 (1978). *Alternative Considerations.* Accessed January 28, 2014. At <http://jonestown.sdsu.edu/?page_id=27514>.

Audiotape Q673 (1977). *Alternative Considerations.* Accessed January 28, 2014. At <http://jonestown.sdsu.edu/?page_id=27528>.

Audiotape Q800 (1977). *Alternative Considerations.* Accessed January 28, 2014. At <http://jonestown.sdsu.edu/?page_id=27589>.

Audiotape Q833 (1978). *Alternative Considerations.* Accessed January 28, 2014. At <http://jonestown.sdsu.edu/?page_id=27599>.

Audiotape Q933 (1977). *Alternative Considerations.* Accessed January 28, 2014. At <http://jonestown.sdsu.edu/?page_id=27619>.

Battin, Margaret Pabst (1995). *Ethical Issues in Suicide*. Englewood Cliffs, NJ: Prentice-Hall.

Blakey, Deborah Layton (1978). "Affidavit Re the Threat and the Possibility of Mass Suicide by Members of the People's Temple." FBI document RYMUR 89-4286-B-2-d-3. *Alternative Considerations.* Accessed January 28, 2014. At <http://jonestown.sdsu.edu/?page_id=13072>.

Brandt, R.B. (1975). "The Morality and Rationality of Suicide," in *A Handbook for the Study of Suicide*, ed. Seymour Perlin. New York: Oxford University Press, pp. 61–76.

Carter, Tim (2006). "Murder or Suicide: What I Saw," *the jonestown report*, 8. *Alternative Considerations*. Accessed January 28, 2014. At <http://jonestown.sdsu.edu/?page_id=31976>.

Dieckman, Josef (2006). "Murder vs. Suicide: What the Numbers Show," *the jonestown report*, 8. *Alternative Considerations*. Accessed January 28, 2014. At <http://jonestown.sdsu.edu/?page_id=31969>.

Donnelly, John (1978). "Suicide and Rationality," in *Language, Metaphysics, and Death*, ed. John Donnelly. New York: Fordham University Press, pp. 88–105.

Durkheim, Emile (1951). *Suicide: A Study in Sociology*, trans. John A. Spaulding and George Simpson. New York: The Free Press.

Feinsod, Ethan (1981). *Awake in a Nightmare: Jonestown: The Only Eyewitness Account*. New York: W.W. Norton.

Frey, R.G. (1978). "Did Socrates Commit Suicide?" *Philosophy*, 53: 106–8.

Harris, Duchess and Adam John Waterman (2004). "To Die for the Peoples Temple: Religion and Revolution after Black Power," in *Peoples Temple and Black Religion in America*, eds. Rebecca Moore, Anthony B. Pinn, and Mary R. Sawyer. Bloomington and Indianapolis: Indiana University Press, pp. 103–22.

Harris, Liane (1978). "Statement." Audiotape Q245. *Alternative Considerations*. Accessed January 28, 2014. At <http://jonestown.sdsu.edu/?page_id=27394>.

Hernton, Calvin C. (1968). "Dynamite Growing out of Their Skulls," in *Black Fire: An Anthology of Afro-American Writing*, eds. Leroi Jones and Larry Neal. New York: Morrow, pp. 78–104.

Hougan, Jim (1999). "The Secret Life of Jim Jones: A Parapolitical Fugue," *Lobster* 37: 2–20; also at *Alternative Considerations*. Accessed January 28, 2014. At <http://jonestown.sdsu.edu/?page_id=16572>.

"Intimidation Won't Succeed" (1976). *Peoples Forum* 1, December.

Jones, Charles E. (1988). "The Political Repression of the Black Panther Party 1966–1971: The Case of the Oakland Bay Area," *Journal of Black Studies* 18: 415–34.

Layton, Carolyn (2005). "Analysis of Future Prospects," in *Dear People: Remembering Jonestown*, ed. Denice Stephenson. San Francisco and Berkeley, CA: California Historical Society and Heyday Books, pp. 105–6; also on *Alternative Considerations*. Accessed January 28, 2014. At <http://jonestown.sdsu.edu/?page_id=13115>.

"March 1972 Platform" (1972). *The Black Panther Party Research Project*. Accessed August 1, 2013. At <http://www.stanford.edu/group/blackpanthers/history.shtml>.

Meerloo, Joost A.M. (1962). *Suicide and Mass Suicide*. New York and London: Grune and Stratton.

Moore, Annie (n.d.). "Letter to Jim Jones." FBI document RYMUR 89-4286-223-EE-1-M77. *Alternative Considerations*. Accessed January 28, 2014. At <http://jonestown.sdsu.edu/wp-content/uploads/2013/10/EE1-K-M.pdf>.

Moore, Rebecca (1986). *The Jonestown Letters: Correspondence of the Moore Family 1970–1985*. Lewiston, NY: Edwin Mellen Press.

Morrison, Toni (1988). *Beloved*. New York: Penguin.

Newton, Huey P. (1973). *Revolutionary Suicide*. New York: Writers and Readers Publishing.

— (1995 [1972]). *To Die for the People: The Writings of Huey P. Newton*, ed. Toni Morrison. New York: Writers and Readers Publishing.

"The NOIWON Notation" (1978). *Alternative Considerations*. Accessed January 28, 2014. At <http://jonestown.sdsu.edu/?page_id=13678>.

Nordheimer, Jon (1978a). "400 Are Found Dead In Mass Suicide By Cult; Hundreds More Missing From Guyana Camp," *New York Times*, November 21.

— (1978b). "Guyanese Comb Jungle Fruitlessly for Survivors of Sect's Suicide Rite," *New York Times*, November 24.

Patterson, Charles (1968). "Black-Ice," in *Black Fire: An Anthology of Afro-American Writing*, eds. Leroi Jones and Larry Neal. New York: Morrow, pp. 559–65.

Roller, Edith (1978). "Journals," February 16. *Alternative Considerations*. Accessed January 28, 2014. At <http://jonestown.sdsu.edu/?page_id=35693>.

Saad, Lydia (2011). "Doctor-Assisted Suicide Is Moral Issue Dividing Americans Most," Gallup Poll, 31 May. Accessed August 1, 2013. At <http://www.gallup.com/poll/147842/Doctor-Assisted-Suicide-Moral-Issue-Dividing-Americans.aspx>.

Scheeres, Julia (2011). *A Thousand Lives: The Untold Story of Hope, Deception, and Survival at Jonestown*. New York: Free Press.

Stern-Gillet, Suzanne (1990). "The Rhetoric of Suicide," in *Suicide: Right or Wrong?*, ed. John Donnelly. Buffalo, NY: Prometheus Books, pp. 93–103.

Szasz, Thomas (1999). *Fatal Freedom: The Ethics and Politics of Suicide*. Westport, CT: Praeger.

"The Testimony of Szmul Wasersztein, one of the seven Jewish survivors, about the murder of the Jews in Jedwabne, 5 April 1945," *The Righteous Among the Nations*, Yad Vashem. Accessed August 1, 2013. At <http://www1.yadvashem.org/yv/en/righteous/stories/related/wasersztein_testimony.asp>.

Thomas, Richard W. (1968). "Revolution!!" in *Black Fire: An Anthology of Afro-American Writing*, eds. Leroi Jones and Larry Neal. New York: Morrow, p. 196.

Tolhurst, William E. (1990). "Suicide, Self-Sacrifice, and Coercion," in *Suicide: Right or Wrong?*, ed. John Donnelly. Buffalo, NY: Prometheus Books, pp. 77–92.

Tropp, Harriet (1978). Audiotape Q736. *Alternative Considerations*. Accessed January 28, 2014. At <http://jonestown.sdsu.edu/?page_id=27569>. *Alternative Considerations*. Text of press release also at <http://jonestown.sdsu.edu/?page_id=18455>.

"Victory in the Pacific" (n.d.). *American Experience*. Accessed August 1, 2013. At <http://www.pbs.org/wgbh/americanexperience/features/biography/pacific-koyu-shiroma>.

"Was It Murder or Suicide: A Forum" (2006). *the jonestown report*, 8. *Alternative Considerations*. Accessed January 28, 2014. At <http://jonestown.sdsu.edu/?page_id=31981>.

"What I Would Do If There Was A Final White Night" (n.d.). FBI files RYMUR 89-4286-c-5-a, pp. 1–29. *Alternative Considerations*. Accessed January 28, 2014. At <http://jonestown.sdsu.edu/?page_id=13126>.

Wooden, Kenneth (1981). *The Children of Jonestown*. New York: McGraw-Hill.

Chapter 5

Individual Suicide and the End of the World: Destruction and Transformation in UFO and Alien-Based Religions

Carole M. Cusack

Introduction[1]

UFO and alien-based religions emerged after World War II, drawing upon the "materialist" sightings of flying saucers by Kenneth Arnold and the Roswell Incident in 1947 (Partridge 2005: 170–71), and the "spiritual" concept of Ascended Masters from the Theosophical Society tradition (founded 1875), which was extended to include extra-terrestrials, after the dead, Tibetan lamas, and other sources of wisdom transcending the knowledge of living humans (Chryssides 2011: 7–8). This syncretistic blend of conspiracist, political, and religious beliefs permeated mainstream society via the popular narratives of science fiction, novels, and films. The influential "alien messiah" film *The Day the Earth Stood Still* (1951) presented a distinctly Christian version of the message (Etherden 2005), with apocalyptic and conspiratorial themes resonating in the paranoid Cold War atmosphere of the post-war United States. World War II, in particular the bombing of Hiroshima and Nagasaki in August 1945, sharpened popular awareness of the destructive potential of technology, particularly in the area of weapons development. UFO and alien-based religions, many of which were founded in the 1950s, developed in various directions, with some groups preaching an eschatology of battle and destruction of the earth (such as the Church Universal and Triumphant, founded in 1975 but heir to the Summit Lighthouse, founded in 1958), while others envisaged a harmonious

[1] Thanks are due to my research assistant, Venetia Robertson, who helped with library searches and note-taking for this chapter, and to Don Barrett, whose encouragement has sustained me over the years.

Intergalactic Parliament in which humans participated in peaceful interactions (such as the Aetherius Society, founded in 1954) (Partridge 2005: 182–3).

From the vantage point of the twenty-first century, the most notorious movement is Heaven's Gate (formerly Human Individual Metamorphosis), led by Marshall Herff Applewhite (1931–97) and Bonnie Lu Nettles (*née* Trusdale, 1927–85) from the mid-1970s. Heaven's Gate attracted attention when 39 members committed suicide in March 1997 in Rancho Santa Fe, an affluent neighborhood in San Diego County, California. This chapter examines the apocalyptic expectations of UFO and alien-based religions, with a focus on Heaven's Gate, and argues that suicide, the willful destruction of the body and abandonment of human life, is generally understood as positive, undertaken to enable the transition to the "Next Level." Heaven's Gate was opposed to suicide *per se*, but redefined it as turning "against the Next Level when it is being offered," claiming that human bodies were mere "vessels" and "vehicles," so that the destruction of these containers was an action of little importance (Zeller 2011: 172–3). Viewed from this theological worldview, suicide births the human individual into the "Next Level," just as eschatological destruction of the Earth (or the universe), is understood as a positive transformation that births a new world, the "new Heaven and new Earth" of the New Testament's Revelation. Thus individual destruction of the body and the eschatological destruction of the world are functionally identical phenomena connected in a microcosmic-macrocosmic relationship.

Eschatology and UFO and Alien-Based Religions

Expectation of the end of the world has been a prominent motif in religions and mythologies for millennia, though the ways in which signs of the end are identified, the precise nature of the destruction envisaged, and the situation that will obtain after the apocalyptic event differ. A distinction is often drawn between the Semitic monotheisms (Judaism, Christianity, and Islam) and other religions with a linear cosmological narrative and concept of time, and those with a cyclical understanding of time, including Hinduism and Buddhism (Kranenborg 2003: 137–49). For the purposes of this chapter, this distinction is unnecessary, as both types of religion understand the end times to be followed by a re-created world, purified from the taint of the old, which may begin anew. There are a range of related technical terms that describe the end times: eschatology (from the Greek *eschaton*, "last" and "–logy," "the study of"), which refers to discourses, both religious and secular, about the end times (Landes

2011: 18); apocalypse (from the Greek, *apocalupsis*, meaning "to disclose"), which refers to revelation of the events of the end times; and millennialism and millenarianism (from the Latin *mille*, "one thousand") (*Collins Dictionaries* <http://www.collinsdictionary.com>), both referring to the Christian concept of the thousand-year rule of Christ on Earth, which may either antedate the destruction of the Earth or postdate it, depending on theological interpretation (Hunt 2001: 2). These terms are used indiscriminately, and may serve to indicate the absolute end of time and the world through total destruction, or merely the passing of some aspect of the current order deemed undesirable, or the replacement of the flawed world by a different, perfected world.

These concepts continue to be relevant to new religions due to the substantial debt that such religions owe to both the Judeo-Christian worldview and theology (Piff and Warburg 2003: 123–36), and also to the Theosophical Society's formulation of "Eastern" religions (that is, Hinduism and Buddhism) as relevant to spiritual seekers in the West, through their posited compatibility with modernity and science. The founders of Theosophy, Russian bohemian and Spiritualist medium Helena Petrovna Blavatsky (1831–91) and American Civil War veteran Colonel Henry Steel Olcott (1832–1907), paved the way for the incorporation of extraterrestrials though their acceptance of channeled beings ("Ascended Masters") as sources of wisdom. In the US, Guy Ballard (1878–1939) founded the I AM movement with his wife Edna in the 1930s (AM = "Ascended Masters"), and he extended the "hierarchy of masters [to] include Venusians" (Partridge 2005: 173). J. Gordon Melton has argued that I AM is the first UFO religion (Melton 1995: 7), but Christopher Partridge claims that it is primarily Theosophical, not UFO-logical (despite the presence of extraterrestrial Masters). What is important is that I AM provided a bridge to break-away alien-based religions like the Summit Lighthouse, founded by Mark Prophet (1918–73) in 1958 (Whitsel 2003: 7), and that the teachings of Ballard, Prophet, and others, blending Theosophical eastern themes with esoteric Christianity, set a precedent for the teachings of Applewhite and Nettles, which drew on New Age and esoteric Christianity, in the 1970s.

The contribution of popular culture to emergent UFO and alien-based religions can be assessed with reference to a variety of popular cultural media. Of central importance is the influential "alien messiah" film *The Day the Earth Stood Still* (1951). Scripted by Edmund H. North, with a score composed by Bernard Herrmann (who worked with Alfred Hitchcock), the plot featured an alien messiah, Klaatu, whose spaceship landed in Washington, DC (Wojcik 2003: 275). Klaatu's mission, assisted by the robot Gort, is to warn humanity that the possibility of nuclear war on Earth is of great concern to the citizens of other planets, who are committed to peace. While on Earth, Klaatu is befriended by a young boy named Bobby who takes him on a tour of the city. He is distressed to hear that those buried in Arlington National Cemetery have died in war and violent conflicts. He warns Professor Barnhart that Earth must become peaceful. Yet, humanity chooses to kill Klaatu, who like Jesus is resurrected on the third day. He then leaves Earth with the warning that "humanity must submit to live peacefully, being watched over by the robots [like Gort] or be destroyed" (Etherden 2005). This narrative frames UFO and alien-based theology in terms of a "messiah" who comes to "save" Earth from its own self-destructive urges, which replicates a Christian understanding of these new narratives. Its eschatological tone is undeniable: violent humans have exceeded their moral capacity by the development of nuclear weapons, and they must submit to the wise care of the advanced aliens or inevitably destroy themselves and the planet. This early case of popular culture intersecting with alternative religious beliefs and worldviews paved the way for later science-fiction texts, such as Robert A. Heinlein's novel *Stranger in a Strange Land* (1961), the title of which is itself a biblical allusion, to become scriptures for new religions. Heinlein's novel inspired the foundation of the Church of All Worlds (CAW) by Tim Zell and Lance Christie in 1962 (Cusack 2010: 53–82).[2]

The Summit Lighthouse and its successor, the Church Universal and Triumphant (CUT), represent important stages in the development of UFOlogical religions, and the apocalyptic expectations of such religions. On one level, CUT is a classic case of the failure of prophecy, as Mark Prophet's second wife Elizabeth Clare Prophet, *née* Wulf (1939–2009), CUT's leader following his death in 1973, announced the apocalypse would occur on either October 2, 1989, or March 15, 1990. In the period 1973–90, CUT—which had begun with an eschatology largely based on Alice Bailey's Arcane School, in which "the immanent earthly reappearance of Christ" was taken to signal "a collective and terrestrial salvation" (Whitsel 2003: 22)—moved to a more esoteric understanding of the coming *eschaton*, in which survivalism and stockpiling arms were strategies to prepare for a war with the Soviet Union, and an extensive system of bunkers were constructed at the group's Montana headquarters, Royal Teton Ranch. When CUT members "emerged from the organization's fallout shelters the day after a prophesied nuclear holocaust should have destroyed much of the US—many having resigned from employment

[2] CAW, it must be noted, despite its science-fiction origins, has a decidedly non-apocalyptic theology, despite its concern over ecological devastation and its clarion call to humanity to protect the Earth, Gaea, which is itself the living goddess.

and sold their possessions—"about one-third of the membership immediately severed ties with the church" (Partridge 2005: 296). The movement diminished in importance as Elizabeth Clare Prophet developed Alzheimer's Disease. After her death in 2009, the CUT teachings continued via a loose network of ex-members who established groups, and the official Church Universal and Triumphant, headquartered in Corwin Springs, Montana, which continues to expect the end times (Anon. 2008).

How religious groups coped in the face of failed apocalyptic predictions was researched by Leon Festinger, Henry Riecken, and Stanley Schachter, in their ground-breaking book *When Prophecy Fails* (1956). The Seekers, a UFO group started in the late 1940s, received messages through "Mrs Keech" (Dorothy Martin [1900–92]) from cosmic figures called the Elder Brothers, including Space Brother Sananda (formerly the historical Jesus), who predicted that flying saucers from Venus would appear in major cities around the globe and that a flood would destroy the world on December 21, 1954 (Stone 2006: 6). When the predicted apocalypse did not eventuate, Mrs Keech claimed that the planet had been spared due to the spiritual efforts of the Seekers, which generated light to counter the darkness of the present order. This appeared to be an irrational response, and an abandonment of more logical reactions to failed predictions, but Joseph F. Zygmunt has noted that:

> Millenarian movements with well-developed ideologies are in a position to meet such crises by drawing on their own ideological resources. Prophetic failures may be ideologically rationalised, explained, reinterpreted, or denied, leaving millennial hopes intact. (Zygmunt 2006: 90)

Christopher Partridge has argued that the eschatological scenarios of almost all UFO religions tend to feature themes that may result in violence. The non-mainstream nature of UFO beliefs fosters a *contra mundum* stance, and expectations that aliens in spaceships will liberate those enlightened humans and obliterate those who live contented in the corrupt world order force both a commitment to the abandonment of human life in this world, and the adoption of an attitude that it is both inevitable and acceptable that the vast majority of humanity will be destroyed (Partridge 2005: 190).

For example, the Aetherius Society, founded in 1954 by English taxi-driver George King (1919–97), advocates a benign Theosophical view of aliens as sources of wisdom. King, a "contactee" (mediumistic communicator) encountered beings including Venusian Master Aetherius, Mars Sector 6, and Master Jesus. They asked him to become the "Primary Terrestrial Channel" and participate in an Intergalactic Parliament dedicated to the pursuit of peace (Rothstein 2003: 170, 173). Aetherians practice yoga, meditation, pilgrimage to sacred mountains, and vegetarianism; still, they hold the apocalyptic belief that if their mission to bring peace and enlightenment to the Earth fails, they will be rescued from atop sacred mountains by extraterrestrials, leaving the world to perish (Anon. n.d.). Thus it is accurate to say that UFO religions share an interest in the end of the world with religions such as the Semitic monotheisms, Zoroastrianism, Hinduism and Buddhism, and that, like the apocalyptic scenarios of these "traditional" religions, UFO religions envisage the eschaton as involving the destruction of the present order and of those who are not believers. These contentions are unremarkable, but in the case of Heaven's Gate, the expectation of the apocalypse resulted in a more active approach to the transition to what Applewhite and Nettles called the "Next Level."

A Brief History of Heaven's Gate

In 1975, scholars Robert Balch and David Taylor become covert participant-observers in a UFO movement led by Marshall Herff Applewhite and Bonnie Lu Nettles, who over time were known by various names (including Bo and Peep, as shepherds of their flock, Guinea and Pig, as subjects in a "cosmic experiment," and Ti and Do), but were generally called by followers "the Two," a reference to the two witnesses of Revelation 11:3 (Balch 1995: 142–3). The prominence of this Bible verse in the Two's self-understanding was an early pointer to apocalyptic currents in their teachings. Applewhite and Nettles had met in 1972 in a Houston psychiatric hospital, where she was a nurse and he was a patient struggling with homosexual desires (Appleyard 2005: 117). Both were raised in Christian families (Applewhite's father was a Presbyterian minister), but Baptist Nettles was affiliated with the Houston Theosophical Society, practiced meditation, and was interested in channeling spirits. Applewhite was divorced when he met Nettles, and he recognized her as the "spiritual" partner he had longed for, with whom he would have an intimate but non-sexual relationship. In 1972, Nettles was a mother of four children in a troubled marriage, and she quickly decided to throw in her lot with Applewhite (Zeller 2011: 157). They briefly held classes at the Houston Christian Arts Center, but in 1973 Applewhite had a revelation that they were the two witnesses from the New Testament book of *Revelation,* and that they "would be assassinated and return ... to life three and one-half days later" (Balch 1985: 15). The "cloud" or vehicle that would take them to Heaven would be a spaceship; this event was referred to as "the Demonstration." They taught a message of eternal life in the "Next Level" that could be achieved by abandoning human attachments. This involved converts leaving jobs, homes, friends, family, and possessions (constituting a small, secular "end" of their world, and obliteration of their identity), to follow the Two.

Recruits to the movement usually joined after attending a public meeting in which Bo and Peep presented their message and took questions. Balch and Taylor, the earliest researchers on the UFO religion, characterized most of the converts as seekers, members of the "cultic milieu" (Campbell 1972: 119–36). Despite the organization of members into pairs (later known as "check partners") and "families," the orientation was individualistic. Conversation was restricted to the "Process" of tuning in to the next level, and apart "from a brief period when members tuned in together before meetings there was an absence of ritual" (Balch and Taylor 2011: 40–41). Balch has argued that Bo and Peep designed the group structure

> … to lead members through an awakening similar to their own. They put men and women together in platonic partnerships where each was expected to help the other in the overcoming process … Only by escaping the planet's spiritually poisoned atmosphere could humans expect to break the endless cycle of death and reincarnation. Once seekers reached the next level, they would become immortal androgynous beings. (Balch 1995: 143)

The majority of converts responded to the counter-cultural and alternative aspects of the teaching, although Christian ideas were prominent as well. The Two taught that spaceships seen by humans were a means of transport and communication between Heaven and Earth; the occupants of the ships were Gardeners of the Earth and the present human race was merely one crop planted by these beings; Jesus was a Next Level being who was born from a human body, died and became an immortal body, and departed Earth on a spaceship; Ti (Nettles) was more advanced in the Next Level than Do, and was equated with the Father whereas Applewhite was identified with Jesus, and that the members of the group who remained faithful were, as Applewhite put it, "not humans recruited by Ti and Do into some cult, but *rather were members of the Next Level before ever meeting them*" (Applewhite 2011: 27; original emphasis).

In late 1975, Bo and Peep withdrew into "the wilderness" for four months. At this time, there were few authority structures, and of approximately two hundred members, many departed from the Two's guidelines, particularly with regard to increased social communication, which in turn revealed disillusionment and demoralization among the ranks. When the Two returned in 1976, they took steps to prevent further departures by ceasing to recruit and telling the 88 remaining members that "all the ripe fruit had been picked so that final preparations for the harvest could begin" (Balch 1985: 22). Their authority increased as they ceased holding public meetings, moved to an isolated part of Wyoming, structured the group and the camp to maximize separation from wider society, stopped referring to "the Demonstration" as imminent (indeed, the "assassination" they were supposed to endure was re-interpreted as savage media coverage), and revealed only they could communicate with the Fathers on the Next Level. In late 1976, the group moved to Utah, and Bo and Peep sent "nineteen of the weaker members ... to Arizona with instructions to get jobs and support themselves" (ibid.: 23). Most of these people defected soon after. Patricia Goerman has argued that after the Two's return, the group entered a third phase of development, in which "overcoming human ways" was crucial, and "[t]heir lives became rigidly structured, practicing drills and exercises, wearing uniforms, and limiting their contact with others" (Goerman 2011: 61–2).

A next phase was entered in 1992, when the group re-emerged under the name Total Overcomers Anonymous. Much had occurred between 1976 and 1992: Ti (Nettles) developed cancer in the early 1980s and died in 1985, necessitating a radical rethink of the religion's theology (discussed below); the group had inherited money in the late 1980s which made it possible to abandon campsites for a more settled life, and the World Wide Web was launched in 1989. The development of Do's theology was articulated in his 1988 statement, "88 Update—The UFO Two and Their Crew," first published on the Heaven's Gate website, where it was stated that it was not copyrighted and could be reproduced. Do spoke of his relationship with Ti, provided the position statements that they had co-authored, and sketched the vagabond lifestyle of the group between 1976 and 1988, a period he referred to as "the classroom." He acknowledged that the outside world viewed the group as a "cult," and described their activities as follows:

> They experimented in all kinds of disciplines, such as wearing hoods to learn about the "conning" ways of their visual personalities, and making 12-minute checks—each person physically going to a given spot every 12 minutes to concentrate on his or her desire to serve. They were given new names with three letters in the first syllable and a common two-syllable second part ... For a while they lived on the trust fund of one of the students, but for the most part supported themselves by, as many as needed to, taking jobs outside the classroom ... All in all, the students have been in the classroom 12 years now, and their numbers are down to a few dozen. (Applewhite 2011: 26)

Do spoke of the realizations the "class" made with regard to UFOs, the nature of Jesus' resurrection (which was the actualization of a "Next Level" body), and articulated a theory of reincarnation in which human cravings that have not been overcome lead to the person being "replanted" by the "Gardener." The disposable nature of the human body was plainly stated (it is "like a suit of clothes") and the lack of distinctively human qualities of the Next Level bodies (which had neither digestive nor reproductive organs) was also stressed (ibid.: 27–8). Do spoke extensively of the temptations of Lucifer, which he identified with the New Age and "alternative" spiritual teachings, which is interesting in the light of the UFO beliefs he outlined, but points to a shift to understanding the Two's message chiefly in terms of Christianity rather than the Theosophically influenced notions to which Nettles had adhered.

Academic studies of Heaven's Gate have identified key themes in this document that point to the imminence of the end times in Do's thinking. Winston Davis argued that the members of Do's "classroom" were not brainwashed, as the popular media claimed, but rather had been trained in what he terms "religious obedience." An examination of the farewell videos left by group members and of online materials showed that Heaven's Gate regarded the common understanding of responsibility as a "pseudo-virtue." Davis argued that modern people value being responsible and code it as "conscientious, dependable, predictable, and good" but for Do it was

> ... the creation of evil space aliens ... These "discarnate Luciferians" were said to determine what is right and wrong for the populace as a whole ... "They want you to be a perfect servant to society (THEIR society—of THEIR world)" [and that] students must devote themselves to the negative ethical praxis of "overcoming" the world. (Davis 2011: 87–9)

This attitude exhibits what Michael Barkun has called "fact-fiction reversal," characteristic of "the conspiracist world" (Barkun 2003: 29).The world of Do's classroom was nothing if not paranoid and conspiracist: the only truth resided in the teachings of the Two, and the outside world, in which the majority of people lived, was deluded and in thrall to Lucifer. Applewhite and Nettles had from the earliest days phrased their demands in terms of counter-cultural values like personal transformation, individualism, and "flexibility." However, the "crew" of the Two were trained rigidly in obedience in a world where to be "flexible" meant following orders "without adding your own interpretation," and learning "to be dependent on his Older Member as that source of unlimited growth and knowledge" (Davis 2011: 94–5). That obedience, and the centrality of the Two as a source of authority, point clearly to an "end times" scenario in which obedience to the leader(s) will be a test, and will be examined in greater detail in the final section of this chapter.

By the early 1990s, the group "operated a Web design business, owned a lot of computer equipment, and attempted to propagate their message in online chatrooms and discussion forums" (Cowan 2011: 140). This was novel in the 1990s, and at the time of the group's mass suicide, much was made by the media of Heaven's Gate's strong Internet presence. On March 29, 1997, the *New York Times* published an article that quoted the well-known anti-cult activist Rick Ross, who stated that "the group that called itself Heaven's Gate was emblematic of a growing number of small, computer-connected cults that have flourished in the last decade, and particularly the last five years as the Internet has grown" (Markoff 1997). Yet, until the fateful day of the suicides, the local community, while it viewed the group as strange—their landlord and the owner of the cybercafé they frequented, Gigabytes, knew they were teetotal and celibate—otherwise found the uniformed, short-haired members "really polite," quiet, and gentle (Hoffman and Burke 1997: 34–5).

The Rancho Santa Fe Suicides, March 1997

On March 26, 1997, the bodies of 39 members of Ti and Do's UFO religion were found by authorities in Rancho Santa Fe. They had committed suicide, believing that they would complete their Human Individual Metamorphosis and ascend to the Next Level, via a spacecraft concealed by the Hale-Bopp Comet. Cause of death was the ingestion of a vodka, phenobarbital, and applesauce mix, and the members were aged between 26 and 72. Reactions to this dramatic act were mixed; the historian Richard Landes termed the mass suicide "a grotesquely literal application of this motto, and a parody of Christian Rapture apocalyptic," and argued it was due to "the interminable delay of the great event" (Landes 2011: 407); religious studies scholar James R. Lewis claimed that Applewhite desired to rejoin Nettles in the Next Level and was in failing health. Reluctant to consider a successor, Applewhite saw the Hale-Bopp Comet as "the sign he was waiting for to set in motion the final solution to his quandary" (Lewis 2003: 113). Hugh B. Urban, in contrast, noted the group's failure to sell a film script embodying their beliefs to Hollywood, as well as its stockpiling of guns and ammunition, and the fact that the Hale-Bopp Comet passed the Earth during the Christian Holy Week, which may have been significant to Applewhite (Urban 2011: 117).

Whatever the case, the press reported the suicides in a sensationalist fashion, and the ritualistic details of the discovery of the bodies of the "cult members" were circulated widely. The members of Heaven's Gate were found lying on bunk beds, wearing black shirts and trackpants, under purple shrouds. Each wore new Nike trainers and had money for the interplanetary toll in their breast pockets. They wore armbands bearing the words "Heaven's Gate Away Team," testifying to their love of the popular television series *Star Trek*. Members appear to have killed themselves in groups, with others cleaning up after them. As Benjamin E. Zeller has noted, the media "fixated on the material culture of the Heaven's Gate dead, as well as the medical histories of its members, several of whom had been surgically neutered" (Zeller 2012: 59). Revelations about the religion were not limited to the discovery that some had undergone castration; the farewell messages left online by eight of the "crew"—Drrody, Glnody, Jwnody, Lvvody, Nrrody, Slvody, Stmody and Tddody ("ody" was understood to mean "children of the Next Level")—offered further evidence of Do's teachings and the authoritarian nature of the religion.

Winston Davis analyzed these statements and concluded that Applewhite and Nettles had been "genuinely loved and respected," and commented on how the Heaven's Gate doctrines were very close to the content of traditional Christianity (Davis 2011: 99). Instead of ascending to Heaven, members would be "beamed up," as in *Star Trek*. The group's ascetic lifestyle, uniformed attire, and adoption of names for use within the religion recalled Roman Catholic and Orthodox monasticism, and the practice of voluntary castration, startling to modern western people accustomed to think of sexual fulfillment as a right and sexuality as a possible means to transcendence, merely echoed the New Testament verse, Matthew 19:12: "For there are eunuchs who were born that way, and there are eunuchs who have been made eunuchs by others—and there are those who choose to live like eunuchs for the sake of the kingdom of heaven" (*New International Version*, <http://www.biblegateway.com/passage/?search=Genesis%202:9&version=NIV>), a favorite verse of Do's. The messages posted by members expressed dependence on the leaders, and complete willingness to abandon human existence. The following extracts (cited in Davis) are representative:

> Nrrody: Ti and Do and the Next Level are my life. Without them, there is nothing—literally. Nothing else is real. [22, 2].
> Stmody: I am totally dependent on them for everything and am better off because of it. I am lost without them and only someone who doesn't know them would see this dependency as a sign of weakness. [24, 1] ...

> Glnody: I know that what Ti and Do taught is the only reality. [29, 2].
> Lvvody: Now that I was ... with my Teachers I knew I was safe—in their hands and the Next Level's safe-keeping. There was no more fear. [30, 5]. (Davis 2011: 98–9).

For members, it is evident that their life in the world was of little value, and their faith in Ti and Do's teachings made it easy for them to die when asked by their Teachers, who insisted that they "must leave *everything* of your humanness behind. This includes the ultimate sacrifice and demonstration of faith—that is, the shedding of your human body" (Zeller 2011: 172).

Of particular interest is the fact that Applewhite, when he planned the ritual suicide, took care to ensure that the right members were present at the time of the event, and that there were survivors who continued to preach the Heaven's Gate message to the world. There was a tension in Heaven's Gate between Do's authoritarianism, which manifested in somewhat creepy analogies between his followers and domestic pets, especially neutered dogs who were "preoccupied with service, preoccupied with pleasing ... waiting for one moment of attention from that human" (read "Next Level being," that is, himself), and the emphasis that was placed on freedom, which resulted in members, over time, being urged to leave if they were not absolutely committed (Davis 2011: 96). Do issued communiqués over the years urging "lost sheep" to return, and in 1991–92 made a series of satellite television broadcasts that expressed urgency regarding the imminent end times. Do declared, "It's harvest time. Harvest time means that it's time for the garden to be spaded up. It's time for a recycling of souls. It's time for some to 'graduate.' It's time for some to be 'put on ice.' It's time!" (Zeller 2011: 170). It was to be five years after that broadcast that the end time manifested, and in December 1996, Applewhite apparently sent Rio di Angelo (real name Richard Ford, also known as Nneody) from Rancho Santa Fe to witness to the religion after the event. Di Angelo has since published a book (Di Angelo 2007) about his experiences with Heaven's Gate, maintains that Do's teachings are authentic (he had never met Ti); five years later, he still considered himself the messenger of the religion (Hettena 2002).

That individual members of Heaven's Gate believed that when they killed themselves they would be taken aboard a spaceship that was hidden by the Hale-Bopp Comet is uncontroversial, as is the contention that they believed that the destruction of their human bodies was unimportant because they would then possess a "Next Level" body (Chryssides 2011: 14). Thus, individual suicide in Heaven's Gate was reinterpreted so that death at one's own hand was not abhorrent, but desirable, and the destruction of the earthly body birthed the Next Level body. These beliefs were expressed, in the videotaped farewell statements of various members, via the language of science fiction: Jwnody ended her message with "Thirty-nine to beam up!" (referring to *Star Trek*'s catchphrase "Beam me up, Scotty"), and Ollody, as Zeller has observed, "concluded his exit video by declaring that the heavenly truths 'could be accepted by humans more easily in the form of science fiction' ... explaining that the group had hoped to create a SF television series to teach their beliefs" (Zeller 2012: 68).

This model of transformation is also apparent in the religion's attitude to Earth and the purpose it served. Ti and Do consistently taught that Earth was a laboratory or experiment by the aliens "dwelling in the Kingdom of Heaven," described as a garden in which humans had been planted in order that they might grow souls. Daniel Wojcik noted that "Representatives from this Kingdom periodically make 'soul deposits' in the bodies of humans, preparing them to be transplanted to a higher evolutionary level" (Wojcik 2003: 278). Thus both humans and the Earth were creations of the aliens, and served the spiritual purpose of the inhabitants of the Kingdom. Zeller has argued that Do's increasingly apocalyptic tone from the early 1990s onward resulted from his need to reconcile two things: "the place of bodily death in salvation, and the role of Ti" (Zeller 2011: 171). Nettles had died of liver cancer in 1985. It may be hypothesized that it was expected that she would be collected by the Next Level beings prior to death, to take on her Next Level body. When this did not happen, Do's apocalyptic tone shifted to focus on the idea that the human body would have to be disposed of (that is, one would have to die) before the Next Level body could be achieved.

But what of the Earth, the garden in which humans are planted, and of those living upon the planet who had not accepted Ti and Do's preaching? Despite Applewhite's greater focus upon Christianity, his eschatological model for the unenlightened and the laboratory in which they live appeared to be reincarnation-based (as indeed was his model for human individuals). In 1988, he wrote, "this civilization, from Adam's time until now, is just one planting of Earth's true 'Gardeners'" (Applewhite 2011: 19). Members' final messages testified to the importance of Do's teaching that those humans who were not members of Heaven's Gate caused the garden of Earth to become polluted, and that the Gardeners would only plant seeds after it has been destroyed and renewed. Jnwody wrote, for example, that "The weeds have taken over the garden and truly disturbed its usefulness beyond repair—it is time for the civilisation to be recycled—'spaded under'" (Zeller 2012: 70). This suggests that Heaven's Gate correlated the suicides with destruction and renewal of the world; the two processes were therefore in a microcosmic-macrocosmic relation.

This interpretation is complicated somewhat by the fate of two surviving members of the religion who were not at the Rancho Santa Fe house at the time of the suicides: Charles Edward "Chuck" Humphrey (known as Rkkody) and Wayne Cooke (known as Jstody). In May 1997 they rented a motel room in Encinitas and tried to commit ritual suicide as their classmates had done two months earlier. George Chryssides stated that

> Cooke succeeded, while Humphrey failed. However on February 17, 1998, Humphrey was found dead in a tent near Ehrenberg, California, having placed a plastic bag over his head, with a pipe connected to a supply of carbon monoxide. He was wearing the standard black trainers and a black t-shirt bearing a patch that read "Heaven's Gate Away Team." (Chryssides 2011: 130)

These actions are determined and confirm that Humphrey and Cooke were absolutely convinced that they, too, despite having missed the spaceship arriving with the Hale-Bopp Comet, could enter the Next Level and rejoin the Two. Yet they must have been aware that the physical world had, apparently, continued as usual after the "crew" had been "beamed up." The same tensions manifest in the roles played by Rio di Angelo and other survivors into the twenty-first century; they insist on the truth of the Two's message, in the face of the apparent failure of the world to have been "spaded up" and renewed. We cannot know how this cognitive dissonance is being managed, but one explanation is Zygmunt's notion that the survivors regard themselves as the "link between the supernatural and earthly phase of the millennial drama, the bridgehead to the new future, entrusted with the responsibility of maintaining and spreading the faith until the time for complete fulfillment finally arrives" (Zygmunt 2006: 100).

Conclusion

This chapter has argued that UFO and alien-based religions emerged in a climate of fear and suspicion after World War II, and were in part a response to Cold War anxieties. These new religions, whether drawing upon the doctrines of Christianity or continuations of Theosophical movements, expounded a worldview that was eschatological and contained the possibility of violence, due to its focus on the passing-away of the tainted current order (Partridge 2005: 190). Applewhite and Nettles' UFO religion, Heaven's Gate, while not founded until the 1970s and having distinct and original teachings, reproduced many of the apocalyptic motifs of both previous UFO religions and conservative

Christianity. These included the Kingdom of Heaven, the figure of Jesus, and the role of extraterrestrials as the saviors of humanity. After the death of Nettles in 1985, it has been argued that Do needed to re-frame his theology to understand why no spaceship came for her before she died, and his commitment to the abandonment of human-ness was extended to include the active shedding of the body via suicide, which was a process that would coincide with the "spading up" of the Earth by its alien Gardeners, in preparation for the planting of a new type of human. The relationship of these two expected events—the mass suicide (which was enacted, thus not counting as an example of failed prophecy) and the "spading up" of the Earth (which did not occur and thus may be perceived as failed prophecy)—was one of microcosm and macrocosm, in that suicide would birth the Next Level body for the individual, and the process of "spading up" would result in the planting of new crops in the purified, weeded "garden."

References

Anon. (n.d.). "The Holy Mountains of the World," *The Aetherius Society*. Accessed January 20, 2012. At <http://www.aetherius.org/index.cfm?app=content&SectionID=79&PageID=35>.

Anon. (2008). "Church Goes Online, Keeps Bunker Ready," *Billings Gazette*, December 1. Accessed December 21, 2012. At <http://billingsgazette.com/news/state-and-regional/montana/article_32f3da6c-79f3-5db2-b8e8-ce49fa1dac2f.html>.

Applewhite, Marshall Herff (2011). "'88 Update – The UFO Two and Their Crew,'" in *Heaven's Gate: Postmodernity and Popular Culture in a Suicide Group*, ed. George D. Chryssides. Farnham and Burlington, VT: Ashgate, pp. 17–35.

Appleyard, Bryan (2005). *Aliens: Why They Are Here*. New York: Scribner.

Balch, Robert (1985). "'When the Light Goes Out, Darkness Comes': A Study of Defection from a Totalistic Cult," in *Religious Movements: Genesis, Exodus, Numbers*, ed. Rodney Stark. New York: Paragon House, pp. 11–63.

— (1995). "Waiting For the Ships: Disillusionment and the Revitalization of Faith in Bo and Peep's UFO Cult," in *The Gods Have Landed: New Religions From Other Worlds*, ed. James R. Lewis. Albany, NY: State University of New York Press, pp. 137–66.

— and David Taylor (2011). "Seekers and Saucers: The Role of the Cultic Milieu in Joining a UFO Cult," in *Heaven's Gate: Postmodernity and Popular Culture in a Suicide Group*, ed. George D. Chryssides. Farnham and Burlington, VT: Ashgate, pp. 37–52.

Barkun, Michael (2003). *A Culture of Conspiracy: Apocalyptic Visions in Contemporary America*. London: University of California Press.

Campbell, Colin (1972). "The Cult, the Cultic Milieu, and Secularization," *A Sociological Yearbook of Religion in Britain* 5: 119–36.

Chryssides, George D. (2011). "Approaching Heaven's Gate," in *Heaven's Gate: Postmodernity and Popular Culture in a Suicide Group*, ed. George D. Chryssides. Farnham and Burlington, VT: Ashgate, pp. 1–15.

Collins Dictionaries. Accessed December 21, 2012. At <http://www.collinsdictionary.com>.

Cowan, Douglas E. (2011). "'A Sometimes Mysterious Place': Heaven's Gate and the Manufactured Crisis of the Internet," in *Heaven's Gate: Postmodernity and Popular Culture in a Suicide Group*, ed. George D. Chryssides. Farnham and Burlington, VT: Ashgate, pp. 139–54.

Cusack, Carole M. (2010). *Invented Religions: Imagination, Fiction and Faith*. Farnham and Burlington, VT: Ashgate.

Davis, Winston (2011). "Heaven's Gate: A Study of Religious Obedience," in *Heaven's Gate: Postmodernity and Popular Culture in a Suicide Group*, ed. George D. Chryssides. Farnham and Burlington, VT: Ashgate , pp. 77–104.

Di Angelo, Rio (2007). *Beyond the Human Mind: The Soul Evolution of Heaven's Gate*. Beverly Hills, CA: Rio Di Angelo.

Etherden, Matthew (2005). "*The Day the Earth Stood Still*: 1950s Sci-Fi, Religion and the Alien Messiah," *Journal of Religion and Film* 9(2) <www.unomaha.edu/jrf/Vol9No2/EtherdenEarthStill.htm> accessed December 10, 2009.

Goerman, Patricia. (2011). "Heaven's Gate: The Dawning of a New Religious Movement," in *Heaven's Gate: Postmodernity and Popular Culture in a Suicide Group*, ed. George D. Chryssides. Farnham and Burlington, VT: Ashgate, pp. 57–76.

Hettena, Seth (2002). "Heaven' s Gate Survivor Keeps Faith," *Associated Press*, March 26. Accessed December 21, 2012. At <http://www.rickross.com/reference/heavensgate/gate38.html>.

Hoffman, Bill and Cathy Burke (1997). *Heaven's Gate: Cult Suicide in San Diego*. New York: HarperPaperbacks.

Hunt, Stephen (2001). "Introduction: The Christian Millennium—An Enduring Theme," in *Christian Millenarianism: From the Early Church to Waco*, ed Stephen Hunt. London: Hurst & Company, pp. 1–11.

Kranenborg, Reender (2003). "Hindu Eschatology Within Modern Western Religiosity," in *New Religions in a Postmodern World*, eds. Mikael Rothstein and Reender Kranenborg. Aarhus: Aarhus University Press, pp. 137–49.

Landes, Richard (2011). *Heaven on Earth: The Varieties of Millennial Experience.* New York: Oxford University Press.

Lewis, James R. (2003). "Legitimating Suicide: Heaven's Gate and New Age Ideology," in *UFO Religions*, ed. Christopher Partridge. London and New York: Routledge, pp. 103–28.

Markoff, John (1997). "To The Gullible, Net Offers Many Traps," *New York Times*, March 28. Accessed December 12, 2012. At <http://www.nytimes.com/1997/03/28/us/to-gullible-net-offers-many-traps.html?ref=heavensgate>.

Melton, J Gordon (1995). "The Contactees: A Survey," in *The Gods Have Landed: New Religions From Other Worlds*, ed. James R. Lewis. Albany. NY: State University of New York Press, pp. 1–14.

New International Version. BibleGateway.com. Accessed December 19, 2012. At <http://www.biblegateway.com/passage/?search=Genesis%20 2:9&version=NIV>.

Partridge, Christopher (2005). *The Re-Enchantment of the West*, Volume II. London and New York: T. & T. Clark.

Piff, David and Margit Warburg (2003). "Millennial Catastrophe in Popular Bahai'i Lore," in *New Religions in a Postmodern World*, eds. Mikael Rothstein and Reender Kranenborg. Aarhus: Aarhus University Press, pp. 123–36.

Rothstein, Mikael (2003). "Hagiography and Text in the Aetherius Society: Aspects of the Social Construction of a Religious Leader," in *New Religions in a Postmodern World*, eds. Mikael Rothstein and Reender Kranenborg. Aarhus: Aarhus University Press, pp. 165–93.

Stone, Jon R. (2006). "Introduction," in *Expecting Armageddon: Essential Readings in Failed Prophecy*, ed. Jon R. Stone. London and New York: Routledge, pp. 1–30.

Urban, Hugh B. (2011). "The Devil at Heaven's Gate: Rethinking the Study of Religion in the Age of Cyberspace," in *Heaven's Gate: Postmodernity and Popular Culture in a Suicide Group*, ed. George D. Chryssides. Farnham and Burlington, VT: Ashgate, pp. 105–38.

Whitsel, Brad C. (2003). *The Church Universal and Triumphant: Elizabeth Clare Prophet's Apocalyptic Movement*. Syracuse, NY: Syracuse University Press.

Wojcik, Daniel (2003). "Apocalyptic and Millenarian Aspects of American Ufoism," in *UFO Religions*, ed. Christopher Partridge. London and New York: Routledge, pp. 274–300.

Zeller, Benjamin E. (2011). "Scaling Heaven's Gate: Individualism and Salvation in a New Religious Movement," in *Heaven's Gate: Postmodernity and Popular Culture in a Suicide Group*, ed. George D. Chryssides. Farnham and Burlington, VT: Ashgate, pp. 155–81.

Zeller, Benjamin E. (2012). "Heaven's Gate, Science Fiction Religions and Popular American Culture," in *Handbook of Hyper-real Religions*, ed. Adam Possamai. Leiden and Boston, MA: Brill, pp. 59–84.

Zygmunt, Joseph F. (2006). "When Prophecies Fail: A Theoretical Perspective on the Comparative Evidence," in *Expecting Armageddon: Essential Readings in Failed Prophecy*, ed. Jon R. Stone. London and New York: Routledge, pp. 87–104.

Chapter 6

Apocalypse in Uganda: The Movement for the Restoration of the Ten Commandments of God One Decade On

John Walliss

Introduction

On the morning of March 17, 2000, in Kanungu, Uganda, several hundred members of the Movement for the Restoration of the Ten Commandments of God (hereafter MRTCG) died when a massive explosion ripped through their church.[1] All those not killed in the initial explosion died in the subsequent fire, their potential escape routes—the church's windows and doors—being boarded up and nailed shut. According to eyewitnesses, in the week or so prior to their deaths, members had sold their possessions "at throw away prices" or even burned them in anticipation of what one member referred to in a letter to his wife as "the closure of the 'ARK'" that would precede the time when "*the wrath of the Almighty God the creator is let down on to non-repentants*" (UHRC 2002: 6.3, 2.6, original emphasis). Members also settled outstanding debts and engaged in frantic efforts to persuade their loved ones and lapsed members to travel to Kanungu, telling them "that the Blessed Holy Mary would appear to deliver a special message between 16 and 18 March 2000" (ibid.: 6.3). On March 16, members had a "last supper" at which they consumed, among other items, three

1 As with much of the story of the MRTCG, there is even disagreement about the exact numbers who died in the fire. The Ugandan Human Rights Commission Report (2002) lists the number as "over 500" while a list based on Kabale Diocese records lists 597 (Kabazzi-Kisirinya, Nkurunziza, and Banura 2000: 97–112). More recent estimates by Jean-Francois Mayer (2011) and Richard Vokes (2009) put the numbers who died at 311 and 400 respectively. Moreover, as Mayer observes, even were we to know the exact numbers who died in the church, the possibility of more graves remaining undiscovered cannot be ruled out.

cows that were slaughtered for the occasion. At midnight, one of the leaders, Joseph Kibwetere, deposited a number of documents, including the MRTCG's Certificates of Registration, land title and its book *A Timely Message from Heaven: The End of the Present Times* with the police at Kanungu, before joining his followers in prayers and the singing of hymns in their church in preparation for the prophesied divine visitation (Bagumisiriza 2005).

In the initial aftermath of the fire, both the Ugandan police and the global media were quick to label the incident as a "collective suicide." Even before detailed information emerged, the media were drawing parallels between the deaths in Uganda and other recent collective "cult suicides." News programs and newspapers featured interviews with a variety of self-styled "cult experts," who offered typically anti-cult interpretations of the incident. However, as the Ugandan police investigations continued, this interpretation changed. Between March 20 and end of April, the police discovered several hundred more bodies at various properties belonging to the MRTCG, all showing signs of having met a violent end.[2] What had initially begun as an investigation into an apparent collective suicide had, by the end of April, been transformed into a murder investigation, with warrants being issued for the arrest of the MRTCG's leaders on multiple murder charges. Although explanations evoking the specters of Jonestown, Waco and the like were still espoused in some quarters, in the months following the fire a new theory emerged: that the murder-suicides were the response to a crisis within the MRTCG precipitated by a prophetic disconfirmation in late 1999. Following the apparent failure of a prophecy that the world would end on December 31, it was claimed, significant numbers of members began to be openly critical of the MRTCG leadership, demanding the return of monies they had donated. In addition, several key members of the Movement defected. Faced with this crisis, and being either unwilling or unable to refund their dissatisfied followers, the MRTCG leadership allegedly set about liquidating opponents before engineering their own and their followers' deaths, or, according to some, fleeing the country with the money.

---

[2] Again, the figures for the number of those who died in these locations are approximate: 153 in Buhunga (Rutooma); 81 (after which the police stopped counting) in Rushojwa (Mitooma); 74 at the house of one of the Movement's leaders, Dominic Kataribaabo, in Rugazi (Bunyaruguru); 55 in Buziga (Makindye), and 331 in Karengye (Kanungu).

The Movement for the Restoration of the Ten Commandments of God

The origin of the MRTCG can be traced back to an 'epidemic' of reported visions of the Virgin and Jesus that swept through Catholic circles in southern Uganda throughout the 1980s (Introvigne 2000; Mayer 2001). Yet several, often contradictory, accounts exist concerning its initial development (Walliss 2004: Ch. 6; Vokes 2009: Chs. 4–6). If we are to believe the account left behind by the MRTCG itself in its book, *A Timely Message: The End of the Present Times* (MRTCG 1996), the Movement developed out of the visions of several individuals: most notably Credonia Mwerinde (b. 1952), Angelina Migisha (b. 1947), Ursula Komuhangi (b. 1968), and Joseph Kibwetere (b. 1932). In the spring of 1981, it is claimed, Mwerinde began to experience visions of the Virgin Mary and Jesus. Mwerinde kept these visions secret until nine years later, when she received another vision instructing her to "take these messages to all of the people we send you to without discriminating [against] anybody, without taking sides or being selfish" (ibid.: 1).

According to Mwerinde, the Virgin informed her that she had returned "to save the world" from destruction. The Virgin went on to say that God was angry that the Ten Commandments were being broken by humanity and had in His anger decided to "destroy them." The Virgin pleaded with Him to allow her and Jesus to return to earth in order to command humanity to repent and obey the Ten Commandments before it was too late. God responded:

> You cannot manage them. They are spoilt. I sent them my only son, Jesus Christ, who taught them, counseled them, cured their sickness, made their cripples walk, restored sight to the blind and made the dumb speak. Instead of being grateful to him for all this, they made him suffer; instead of becoming righteous, they killed him. Let me deal with them as they deserve and give them what they merit. (ibid.: 2)

The Virgin, however, prostrated herself before Him, asking for the chance to save a few thousand souls from destruction. Jesus, Mwerinde claimed, implored his father to allow her to return to earth and undertake the mission. Moved by these requests, God gave both of them His permission to spread word to the world, telling them "If only a few repent, it is those only that I will forgive, if they are many, so many will be saved; even if one repents alone, he will also be forgiven" (ibid.: 3).

In the nine years between Mwerinde's initial apparition and the one instructing her to take the Virgin's message to the world, several others who went to become central figures in the MRTCG reported similar messages. In the spring of 1984,

Joseph Kibwetere, a former primary school teacher and politician, claimed that he had received a message from the Virgin and Jesus, instructing him "to repent, to completely reject all my sins, to pray more and to mortify myself" (ibid.: 21). If Kibwetere did so, he would be sent to his "neighbors to teach them to restore the Ten Commandments of the Lord God which they have abandoned" (ibid.: 21). Three days later, Mwerinde's sister, Angelina Migisha, who had similarly received visions of the Virgin and Jesus since childhood but had, like Mwerinde, kept silent about them, reported an apparition in which the Virgin informed her that she had been chosen "to be a model for the Nation of Uganda in Restoring the Ten Commandments of God" (ibid.: 119). Migisha also claimed that Jesus had informed her that he and his mother had selected twelve *entumwa* or apostles, whose "mandate and vocation" was to bring people back to the Ten Commandments. Finally, in June 1989, a few weeks after Mwerinde claimed to have received her instructions to spread the Virgin's message, Migisha's daughter, Ursula Komuhangi, is said to have received an identical message, instructing her to spread the message amongst "all categories of people but especially to your fellow youths," who were, the vision claimed, especially guilty of abandoning the Fourth, Fifth and Sixth Commandments (ibid.: 34).

Subsequently based in Kibwetere's home, Mwerinde attracted a number of followers (in some accounts approximately two hundred people), including several local priests. Notable amongst these was Father Dominic Kataribaabo who became the third leader of the MRTCG, and also the chief author of the Movement's literature. Over a period of years, however, serious frictions developed within the household, not least because of Mwerinde's erratic, and sometimes violent, behavior. According to accounts subsequently provided by Kibwetere's family, Mwerinde would claim to receive messages from the Virgin via telephones hidden in cups and plates, informing her that, for example, Kibwetere should take his children out of school, or that he should sell possessions to feed his household. According to one of Kibwetere's daughters, Edith, on one occasion, Mwerinde announced that the Virgin had told her that a sacrifice was needed immediately and that all Kibwetere's children under five should be killed (Burke 2000). They also allege that Mwerinde beat followers and mistreated family members by, for example, denying them food or medical attention, claiming that she was following the instructions of the Virgin.

Consequently, in 1992, one of Kibwetere's sons attempted to force the Movement from the property. The Movement, now numbering around 250, subsequently settled on a piece of land near Kanungu that had been bequeathed to Mwerinde by her father upon his death the previous year. The Movement called the site *Ishayuuriro rya Maria* ("Rescue Place for the Virgin Mary") and built a settlement, comprising of a house for the leaders, separate dormitories for male and female members, a boarding school, two guest houses, kitchens, stores, a shrine, a cemetery, a poultry project, and a dairy farm with thirty Friesian cows. Several centers were also established in other towns (Banura, Tuhirirwe and Begumanya 2000).

Although media coverage referred to it pejoratively as a "cult," strictly speaking the MRTCG is best conceptualized as a Catholic sect. As Mayer observes, in general terms, the MRTCG "cannot be separated from a wider religious milieu of popular Catholicism in Uganda" and represents a form of "selective traditionalism" (Mayer 2001: 2011). While it rejected some of the reforms of the Second Vatican Council, such as communion in the hand rather than on the tongue and the practice of General Absolution, it nevertheless, unlike some Catholic schismatic groups (cf. Cuneo 1999), accepted the Pope as the legitimate head of the Church. One theme to emerge from the MRTCG's literature was "Christ Jesus and the Blessed Virgin Mary say they did not bring a new religion but they came to revive what had been abandoned" (MRTCG 1996: 17).

Such concerns, along with descriptions of the apocalyptic fate awaiting the unrepentant, are expressed vividly in *A Timely Message to the World*. The first three chapters (approximately a quarter of the book) relate descriptions of Mwerinde's, Kibwetere's, and Komuhangi's visions and outline in obsessive detail the ways in which humanity has been tempted by Satan away from the Ten Commandments, and some of the ways this situation can be amended. Also described are punishments that await those who continue in sinful ways. AIDS, for example, is depicted as a punishment from God for the breaking of the Sixth Commandment. Similarly, at the end of recounting her 1989 vision, Mwerinde relates a vision of hell in which

> The people who are in hell are crying; they are burning but they cannot get to ashes instead they remain alive but with unimaginable misery and agony ... You find in hell people of all colors, of all races, languages, the small and the great, the learned and the unlearned, short and tall, the rich and the poor, people with high social standing, everyone who failed to observe the Commandments is in this place. The hell fire does not discriminate between persons. (Ibid.: 20).

The path to heaven, however, was not straightforward, and Mwerinde warned how "those going to heaven are few" (ibid.: 20). Those who wished to earn their place must follow a life of piety and strict asceticism reminiscent of monastic rules. Members were expected to refrain from sex and were enjoined not to speak, aside from when praying or singing hymns. They also, again akin to monastic rules, followed a rigid timetable of prayer, fasting, and ascetic behavior. Mondays, Wednesdays and Fridays were days of fasting, beginning at 3AM with prayers called "The Way of the Cross." At 5AM, members would sleep, rising at 7AM to work until 1 p.m. They would then attend another hour-long prayer session, after which there was one hour's free time. Following this, they would work until supper at 8 p.m. Their day would then end with night prayers from 11 p.m. until midnight. Members were also prohibited from wearing ordinary clothes, and were required to wear robes. Neophytes, for example, wore black, while green was worn by those "who had seen the commandments," and green and white was worn by "those who were ready to die in the ark." Members of all degrees also wore two rosaries around their neck, facing forwards and backwards, and carried a third in the hands. On occasions, a fourth would also be worn under the garments (Banura, Tuhirirwe and Begumanya 2000: 26–30).

Although conditions were undoubtedly harsh, they were more palatable than the apocalyptic fate prophesied for those who rejected the Ten Commandments. *A Timely Message* describes this fate, during what it terms the "Period of Chastisement" and the subsequent "Three Days of Darkness" in shocking and vivid detail. During this time, it is claimed, "there will be great tribulation upon all the people such that has never before been experienced by any person since the creation of the world" (MRTCG 1996: 46). The world will be racked by natural disasters such as hailstones, "hurricanes of fire," snow, tornados, lightning, floods, storms, earthquakes, whirlwinds, and "disturbance of the soil." Rivers and lakes will turn to blood, become poisonous, or simply dry up, while "clouds will fall from their position and hit the people, some will die, those who survive will remain miserable" (ibid.: 50). Women will give birth to animals, and animals will give birth to human infants. There will be fatal accidents involving cars and aeroplanes, as well as civil disorder, with religious denominations and nations fighting amongst each other, and families fighting amongst themselves.

Famine will strike, with crops being destroyed by locusts. Cattle will be either destroyed by adverse weather conditions or die from disease. Meat from slaughtered cattle will be poisonous, and cows will either not give milk, or give milk that is undrinkable. Other foods, especially alcohol, will turn to poison. The result will be cannibalism, with the strong eating the weak, and parents eating their own offspring or the offspring of others. "Fierce animals" and "frightening beings that are partly man and partly animal" will also wander the earth, "hunting for the person who has not got the Ten Commandments" (ibid.: 53, 48). Domestic animals, which "are already possessed by the devil," will become poisonous so as to kill their masters. Devils will emerge from the underworld 'to harass people' and work "signs and wonders" so that "The people who will not have the Ten Commandments will accept the signs as coming from God" (ibid.: 47, 51).

At the end of the Period of Chastisement, it is claimed, several signs will appear to "mark the end of this generation" (ibid.: 59). First, a huge bird of prey with "claws similar to those of an eagle and ... a crest on its head which was similar to that of a cock" will take up a position from which it is visible by the whole world. Next a "large crucifix" will appear that will make "all the earth tremble"(ibid.: 58). Finally, 'a sound like that of a trumpet or bugle resounding like the sound of a bell' will be heard, followed a period of silence across the world, until "three holy ones of God" appear to command that "THOSE OF YOU WHO HAVE BEEN REDEEMED, GO TO TAKE UP YOUR PLACES!" (ibid.: 58, 59: original emphasis; cf. Matthew 24:31). Three days of darkness will follow, during which the penitent will go into buildings—referred to as "Arks" or "Ships"—to wait:

> They were ordered to shut all the doors and not to open anything at all, All activities such as eating, praying ... should take place inside for three days. Anything that remained outside in the dark turned into devil. These devils lamented and cried for three days after which they were thrown into hell. (Ibid.: 58)

At the end of this period, only a quarter of the world's population ("the redeemed") will survive to inherit the world. Drawing on the final chapter of the Revelation of St John (Revelation 21:1–2), *A Timely Message* describes how "I saw a new earth come down from heaven. This new earth contained every good thing of every type that pertains to the spiritual and the material well being of the human person. The new earth is very beautiful and it has plenty of light" (ibid.: 67).

Death and the underworld will be vanquished and Satan, in fetters, will no longer be able to tempt the redeemed, who will be given "new knowledge, new bodies and new material things that will be very beautiful" (ibid.: 54). "The new earth will be connected with Heaven," and there will be constant visitation of people coming to earth from Heaven (ibid.: 60, 68). Indeed, Uganda itself will become "the New Israel, the second Israel," which will in turn convert all other nations (ibid.: 60).

Accounting for the Murder-suicides

A decade on, there is still a great deal that we do not know about what transpired within the MRTCG in the spring of 2000. There was no detailed forensic examination of the scene or the bodies, that in many cases had been exhumed by inmates from a local prison using makeshift implements and were quickly reburied (Mayer 2011; Twesigye 2010). Uncertainty hovers over the numbers who died, with sources giving different figures. The possibility that further bodies lie undiscovered can also not be ruled out (UHRC 2002: 1).[3] It is unlikely that this situation will improve; the Judicial Commission of Inquiry set up by the Ugandan government in December 2000 never received funding and so never met, and in March 2009, the Ugandan police decided to "temporarily shelve" its investigation (Atuhaire 2005; Mubangizi 2009; Bogere 2009).

In the initial stages of the police investigation, fraud was quickly highlighted as the most likely motivation for the murder-suicides. Officials within the Ugandan police quoted by the BBC, for example, stated they saw no purpose to the murders "unless the intention of the sect leaders was to take money from their followers" (BBC Online 2000, March 28). According to this theory, the Movement's leaders had never been (or were no longer) sincere, but, rather, were intent on relieving credulous followers of their possessions. It is claimed this plan was derailed when, following the failure of a prophecy that the world would end on 31 December 1999 (itself possibly an attempt to obtain more money from followers), significant numbers of the membership openly criticized the leaders, demanding the return of their money and property that they had donated.[4] Consequently, the leadership (possibly with the assistance of a few selected members or possibly hitmen from the Congo or Rwanda [Bwire 2007]) began to murder hundreds of dissidents, burying them in mass graves subsequently discovered by the police. Finally, the leaders set a date on which they engineered what to all intents and purposes appeared to be a collective suicide in order to kill the remainder of the members and cover their departure with their ill-gotten gains.[5]

---

[3] See footnote 1. Additionally, Twesigye (2010: 39), for example, speculates that if the government had continued exhuming the bodies, the number of dead "would have exceeded 3,000."

[4] The UHRC report, for example, notes how, early in 2000, there are "stories of increased discontent among followers in regard to the restoration/recovery of their properties" (UHRC 2002: 6.1). Similar views were also expressed by members interviewed for a UK Channel 4 documentary on the MRTCG (Channel 4 2000) and in several of the accounts reproduced in Bagumisiriza (2005). See particularly the accounts of Mrs Rukanyangira (pp. 26–9) and Peter Ahimbisibwe (pp. 32–5).

[5] One eyewitness, for example, later claimed to have seen both Mwerinde and Kibwetere sneaking out of the MRTCG's compound late on the evening before the fire "carrying small suitcases" (Hammer 2000). Similarly, another witness, one Baguma Gaston, interviewed for the Channel 4 documentary claimed to have seen Mwerinde on the morning of the fire, driving away from the church to the north in a car with several of her relatives and an unknown man (Channel 4 2000; Bagumisiriza 2005: 51). For a similar account, see Nkurunziza (2007). This

A variation on this theory posits that the MRTCG leadership first predicted the end of the world for the end of 1992, and then the end of 1995, before finally settling on 31 December 1999. When the final date came and passed without incident, dissent began to grow (Atuhaire 2003: Ch. 6). The leadership took steps to quell this, however, by shifting the date forward. In an unpublished letter to a local newspaper written in January 2000, for example, Kibwetere claimed that

> ... my boss Jesus Christ, has appeared to me and given me a message to all of you that there are some people arguing over the message that this generation ends on 1/1/2000. On the contrary, the generation ends at the end of the year 2000 and no other year will follow. (Quoted in Vokes 2009: 6)

In early March 2000, Mwerinde provided more precise information, telling members that the Virgin had appeared to her and told her that the world would end on March 17 (Bwire 2007: 120). This raised the spirits of some, although other members were not convinced and demanded a return of their donations, a situation that clearly threatened the Movement's financial viability and continued existence (Atuhaire 2003: Ch. 6). Others became openly disloyal, broke their vows of silence, and began to question the authority of Mwerinde and the other leaders. In an attempt to placate them, "Credonia promised that the Blessed Virgin Mary would refund the money from the sale of the members' properties." She also "asked her priests to record the names of those followers who were discontented" (UHRC 2002: 6.1). Those who submitted complaints were, according to witnesses, called to a meeting with the MRTCG leaders and never seen again. Those who asked where these individuals had gone were told that they had been transferred to another of the MRTCG's properties or "that the Virgin had taken them to Heaven" (Atuhaire 2003: 85). Having thus "weeded out" the dissenters, the MRTCG leaders then began to plan for a collective suicide of the faithful.

---

theory has never truly gone away despite there being little corroborating evidence to support them (Bagumisiriza 2005, Mayer 2011). In May 2003, it was reported that Kibwetere had undergone plastic surgery to hide his identity and was living in Israel (Odong 2003) and a recent (March 2011) Ugandan press article concluded that "it is unclear whether Kibwetere and Mwerinde died in the fire" and that the police "arrest warrants still stand" (Sempogo 2011). Vokes (2009: 215) also quotes a rumor, told to him "by a very high ranking official in Kampala," that Mwerinde had survived and had fled to Belgium a few weeks after the fire, using her own passport. Kataribaabo had also, they claimed, "been tracked by the intelligence services as far as a Nairobi slum, before that trail also went cold."

The problem with both these theories is that an examination of the extant literature produced by the MRTCG shows that the prophecies concerning the end of the world related to the transition between 2000 and 2001, and not between 1999 and 2000 (Mayer 2001).[6] In *A Timely Message*, for example, it is stated that:

> When the year 2000 is completed, the year that will follow will not be year two thousand-and-one. The year that will follow shall be called Year One in a new generation that will follow the present generation; the generation that will follow will have few or many people depending on who will repent. Those who repent and come back to God are the ones that will come to Year One, of the next generation, and they will be called "the redeemed." (MRTCG 1996: 53–4)

Similarly, the MRTCG's certificate of incorporation, dated 1998, describes how one of its objectives

> ... is to notify all the people in the world to prepare themselves for the closing of this generation which is already at hand at each one's door and also to prepare for YEAR ONE of the next generation after year 2000, which will consist of people who will enter the new earth where sorrow and misery are absent. (Quoted in Mayer 2001: 206)

Indeed, according to Mayer, the MRTCG "explicitly criticized those who were predicting the end of the world for 31 December 1999" (ibid.: 207).

Yet there is a significant amount of evidence that would seem to support the claim that MRTCG members believed that something momentous would occur on or around March 17, 2000. Kibwetere, for example, is reported to have written to his family the day before the fire, asking them to carry on "with what we have been doing because we are going to perish" (Borzello 2000). Similarly, Mwerinde is said to have told a friend less than a week before the fire that "we shall be going to heaven, and you will be hearing about us on radio and reading about us in newspapers" (quoted in Mayer 2001: 208). Such views were not confined to the MRTCG leadership. One member was quoted as telling a local man that he was leaving to go to Kanungu "because our leader received a message from God that on 20 March, we will meet Jesus and Mary" (BBC Online 2000, April 2, no pagination). The parents of one woman wrote to her "saying that they were 'preparing to go to Heaven'" (BBC News Online 2000: March 21).

---

6 That said, there is some circumstantial evidence that could point to the transition from 1999 to 2000 as significant. According to Bagumisiriza (2005), the MRTCG had stopped growing food in April 1999, a situation that, while open to a variety of interpretations, could point to an imminent end of the world.

In another case, one member wrote to his wife about "the closure of the 'ARK,'" and of how "there will be no year 2001":

> As we follow directives from Heaven, we are supposed to gather in the selected area before the wrath of the Almighty God the creator is let down on to non-repentants. Keep my words on your hearts, there will never be the year 2001. Catastrophes will befall human kind and the indicators of such will be wars, crime increase such as murder, rape, robbery, etc. There will be a lot of fear among the human races! Appearance of strange animals and people will be noticed. I would request you that if you come across such, simply run and look for me. I will not fail to seek refuge for you. Whoever wanted his brother or family to perish? Do not stick to property. Simply leave it behind and run for your dear [life.] I will always pray for you, as I have nothing else I can do! May God guide you! (Quoted in UHRC 2006: 2.6)

One possible solution to this contradiction could be that, perhaps as a consequence of internal dissent, the MRTCG leadership moved the date of the apocalypse forward from 2000/2001 to March 2000. This explanation would seem to find a degree of support within *A Timely Message*, where it is stated that "The Blessed Virgin Mary ... is warning us so often that if the people persist in disobeying and displeasing God, He will shorten the period stated and will close this generation before reaching to the year 2000" (MRTCG 1996: 61). Moreover, there is a clear precedent for such a course of action in the example of Aum Shinrikyo, where, as a consequence of internal and external pressures, Asahara Shoko moved the prophesied date of destruction from the turn of the millennium, to 1997, before finally settling on 1995 (Reader 2000).

A third theory is that the MRTCG committed collective suicide in response to real or perceived external opposition, which exacerbated the pressures within the group. In an influential theory of apocalyptic violence, John Hall and his colleagues have argued that when groups holding apocalyptic ideologies encounter opposition in the outside world they may engage in either a "warring apocalypse of religious conflict" and turn violence outwards against their real or perceived opponents, or, through an act of collective suicide, undertake a "mystical apocalypse of deathly transcendence" (Hall et al. 2000; see also Bromley 2002; Wessinger 2000). Indeed, Mayer has suggested that the deaths could perhaps be understood as a form of Catholic equivalent of the Dispensationalist notion of the rapture, with the elect being taken away from the earth (in this case by an act of collective suicide) prior to the beginning of the endtime scenario (Mayer 2011).[7]

Several pieces of evidence seemingly support such a conclusion. Primarily, the Makerere University report makes reference to a general climate of opposition and disapproval directed against the MRTCG by the local Catholic Church, claiming that "when Kibwetere announced the formation of his movement, he met with strong opposition from the mainstream Catholic Church" (Banura, Tuhirirwe and Begumanya 2000: 15–16). The report goes on: "this opposition would remain throughout the existence and operations of the Movement." It also refers to how the MRTCG generated "a big controversy in the Catholic Church," and how some leaders were excommunicated and seen as "rebels." This, it is claimed, "made it unpopular even in Kanungu" to the extent that "people, especially the Catholic faithful, did not appreciate associating with an ex-communicated rebel group and they were warned by their religious leaders never to do so" (ibid.: 34). In his contribution to the volume, Banura goes so far as to claim that

> ... the scorn poured on the movement and its members together with a certain sense of isolation following the excommunication and suspension of the leaders from the mainstream Catholic Church may have led [the] leaders to found camps as locations where the movement could operate without any interference or hindrance. (Banura 2000: 50)

The role that the Catholic hierarchy played in the demise of the MRTCG is explored in detail by Emmanuel Twesigye, who argues that what he terms the groups "Marian martyrdoms" were engineered by a mentally ill Kataribaabo as "a holy means to liberate and save the Marian devotees from a hostile and perishing world ... [and thereby] transform the faithful Catholic Marian devotees into angel-like Spiritual beings" (Twesigye 2010: 13). Far from being victims of either a mass murder or fraud, he argues, members "wanted to die" (ibid.: 69). According to Twesigye, the fledgling group ran into opposition from the Mbarara Diocese, particularly Bishop John Baptist Kabuki and Bishop Paul Bakyenga, the former of whom "waged a counter moral crusade" against it (ibid.: 149; cf Vokes 2009: 110–19). In 1991, the leadership of the MRTCG was formally barred from taking communion until they renounced their prophecies and returned to orthodoxy. The priests within the group were formally interdicted by Kabuki, and forbidden to celebrate the Eucharist or hear

7 Compare with the case of Heaven's Gate: see Walliss (2004: Chapter 4). Heaven's Gate is Cusack, Chapter 5 in this volume.

confessions. Kabuki also submitted a report on Marian apparitions in the area to the Pope and discussed his findings with him during an audience. Rather than renouncing their views, the MRTCG leadership moved out of Kabuki's orbit to Kanungu. However, in 1999, Bakyenga was promoted to archbishop of the Western Catholic Province of Uganda, a position that would put Kanungu—and thereby the MRTCG—under his spiritual authority. The group also became involved in a land dispute with a local bishop, who joined Bakyenga in condemning the group and its prophecies as dangerous. Katirababo, according to Twesigye, reacted to this by sinking into "a severe and deep state of clinical depression, at the beginning of the year 2000" (Twesigye 2010: 153). In this state, he became delusional, convinced that God wanted him to sacrifice his followers "as a form of Christian martyrdom, and as a means to redeem and deliver them from the Catholic Church that had rejected them." Kibwetere and Mwerinde ("who were also very depressed and probably suicidal"—ibid.: 153) confirmed that this was God's will, and in the spring of that year the leadership began to "martyr" their followers.

The MRTCG would also appear to have been the victim of a degree of local opposition, although largely in its initial years. A document produced by the leadership in May 1995 provides examples of what it saw as 'persecutions' beginning in the early 1990s. These included an incident in June 1990 where, during Sunday worship, "a team of persecutors ... closed all the outlets and started beating us and hurt us," an attempt in December 1992 by parishioners from another church to demolish *Ishayuuriro rya Maria*, as well as a raid by an armed group in October 1993 who, after forcing the group from the compound, looted or destroyed what remained. Such was their fear that the MRTCG only returned to the compound a year or so later (Mayer 2011). The group had also fallen foul of the police and local authorities, although the most potentially damaging of these—the arrest of Credonia Mwerinde, Angelina Migisha, and others for "making house-to-house visitations and spreading religious ideas which the local councils thought were strange and dangerous," as well as "allegedly recruiting and training guerrillas to fight and overthrow the government of Uganda"—was over a decade prior to the March 2000 fire (Bagumisiriza 2005: 78). In 1994, the local Resident District Commissioner (RDC) also wrote an official letter to the Ugandan president highlighting his concerns about the MRTCG, calling for it to be officially investigated (Twesigye 2010: 81). In November 1998, the school that the MRTCG had established at *Ishayuuriro rya Maria* was closed down indefinitely by the local district administration for "engaging in acts that violated the Constitution of the Republic of Uganda, the Local Government

Act and the Public Health regulations." However, it continued to operate and to receive government funding until March 2000 (UHRC 2002: 5.1).

It is unclear, however, what role, if any, this opposition played in precipitating the March 2000 conflagration. Atuhaire acknowledges the existence of opposition but claims it had little effect, and that any complaints made against the MRTCG were not investigated by the authorities, who, citing religious freedom and observing that the MRTCG was a registered non-governmental organization (NGO), responded with indifference (cf. Bagumisiriza 2005: 13). Equally, Twesigye claims that little was done at the local level in response to the RDC's 1994 letter because the Assistant District Commissioner (ADC), Rev. Richard Mutazindwa, was, he alleges, "friendly to the Marian Movement leaders," writing an opposing report and supporting the group's application to be recognized as an NGO. Such claims are echoed by the UHRC report, which states that the leaders of the MRTCG "deliberately kept as close as possible to Government officials, especially the local leaders," by, for example, establishing camps near police posts, participating in community activities, paying graduated taxes and rents promptly, and voting "overwhelmingly" for the ruling National Resistance Movement in both the 1996 presidential and parliamentary elections and the 1997–98 local council elections (UHRC 2002: 5.7). The UHRC report further claims that the MRTCG also sought to influence local leaders through bribery; allegedly offering on one occasion "a very big envelope" to an official who had refused to support its registration as an NGO (ibid.). Indeed, the MRTCG had organized a "grand party" for March 18, 2000 in order to bid farewell to the outgoing ADC, Rev. Richard Mutazindwa, and welcome his successor (Banura 2000).[8]

It is, of course, possible that the dissent that allegedly developed within the MRTCG in early 2000 created a sense of paranoia within its leadership that resulted in the slightest outside criticism being perceived as persecution. There would appear to be some indirect evidence to support this possibility. In one message from the Virgin reproduced by Atuhaire dating from April 1998, members are informed that "in the year two thousand (AD 2000), you will encounter further persecution when you increase on your development." They are then instructed:

[8] See also the testimony of several individuals quoted in Bagumisiriza (2005); local security personnel (pp. 35–6), "a business woman in Kanungu Trading Center" (around p. 64) and Mrs Rukanyangira (around p. 27).

> ... when you realize that the battles have approached you, *you should take your important documents for custody with those responsible for the security, that is, the nearest police.* Then you should start to clear the way for your souls. But you should not be afraid; those who preceded you experienced the same: Do you think that God had ignored the martyrs? (Quoted in Atuhaire 2003: 109; emphasis added)

As this is what did take place, it could be speculated that, at the very least, the MRTCG's leadership felt a sense of persecution, perhaps brought on by a combination of internal pressures and the possibility of an official investigation.

A more recent theory that diverges radically from the preceding is provided by Richard Vokes in his volume *The Ghosts of Kanungu*. Vokes argues the MRTCG initially did not emphasize a specific date for the end of the world, but only began to do so after it was exposed to other Marian organizations in the mid-1990s, primarily through Katiribaabo. Rather than an attempt to flee external opposition or silence unruly members, Vokes argues, the March 2000 conflagration was the result of the MRTCG leadership's interpretation of apocalyptic ideas within the global Marian movement in the late 1990s. He asserts that the claim that members wanted their possessions returned in response to prophetic failure encounters several problems:

> ... women were *not* handing over their property in expectation of the end of the world, but instead, in response to the serious misfortunes they were experiencing in the here and now. Moreover, at least some of these women would have joined the Movement sometime *before* it had developed a millenarian outlook (given that this shift was a later development). It is therefore unlikely that millenarianism could have been part of these women's initial decision to join ... given that most of these women had only turned to the MRTC[G] in the first place out of desperation with the sect representing some sort of "option of last resort," it is difficult to imagine that they would have then later concluded that they probably were better-off on their own, after all. (Vokes 2009: 195)

However, without doubt the most radical aspect of Vokes' thesis revolves around his analysis of the March 2000 murder-suicides themselves. Again rejecting the dominant interpretation, he claims, based on an interview with a former leading member of the group who departed prior to the fire, that those whose bodies were subsequently found after the fire had not been murdered in the early months of 2000, but had in fact died during a malaria outbreak in the region two years beforehand. The damage to the bodies, such as broken necks, that were interpreted by the police and media as evidence of foul play, was rather caused during exhumation. He speculates that those who died in the actual fire itself had been poisoned by a small number of members prior to the explosion and had therefore died (relatively) willingly rather than being murdered. Thus rather than seeing the MRTCG's dramatic denouement as the final stage in a process of mass murder which had begun as a reaction to dissent, Vokes, to some extent echoing Twesigye, would have us believe that it was instead a willing collective suicide inspired by interpretations of global Marian predictions to which the group had been exposed for the better part of a decade.

Conclusion

Over a decade since the March 2000 conflagration, we are in the curious position of knowing more than we did, but finding that much of what we know is contradictory and/or based on evidence that either ambiguous or non-existent. It is unlikely that a definitive answer to what happened in around Kanungu in the spring of 2000 will emerge. Were the Ugandan police to re-open their investigation, much, if not all, of the forensic evidence that would form the basis of their investigation has been either unwittingly contaminated or destroyed during the initial investigation, or subsequently lost. We cannot be certain of basic facts, such as how many died at the properties owned by the group or, beyond obviously being burned to a cinder, how they died. While many accounts point to prophetic failure in 1999, if not before, no material produced by the group (at least that is extant) supports this view. Equally, any account that points to external opposition playing a role in the MRTCG's dramatic denouement must square this with the support it apparently enjoyed, possibly as a result of bribery and corruption, from local authorities. While Twesigye's account of the role played by the local Catholic Church in pushing the group's leadership towards an act of collective suicide is interesting, his argument contains a number of internal contradictions. Equally, questions could be raised about the reliability of Vokes's respondent; a man who, if other accounts are to be believed, could have played a role in the murders themselves. That said, of all the accounts of what happened in Kanungu in the spring of 2000, I personally find Vokes's most convincing for several reasons, not least the quality of fieldwork on which it is based. Crucially, he answers the question of why, if the MRTCG had claimed the world was going to end in the transition from 1999 to 2000, there is no evidence of this in the group's documents. Put simply, there was no 1999/2000 prophecy; the key date for the group was the shift from 2000 to 2001 at the latest. The views of pathologists and an expert on fire investigations, albeit relying on video evidence, are also noteworthy for questioning the *doxa* that the bodies typically believed to have been murdered in the spring of 2000 may have died some years before and of natural causes. However, as he acknowledges, even his account "is both partial and contingent" (Vokes 2009: 213), and could be challenged by new evidence.

Bibliography

Atuhaire, Bernard (2003). *The Uganda Cult Tragedy: A Private Investigation*. London: Janus Publishing Company.

— (2005). "Who Cares About Kanungu?," *New Vision*, March 17. Accessed July 30, 2013. At <www.religionnewsblog.com/10596/who-cares-about-kanungu>.

Bagumisiriza, Narcisio (2005). *The Kanungu Tragedy March 17th 2000, and Details of Related Discoveries: The Movement for the Restoration of the Ten Commandments of God*. Kabale, Uganda: Kabale Diocese.

Banura, Gerard (2000). "A Critical Evaluation of the Kanungu Tragedy," *The Kanungu Cult-Saga: Suicide, Murder or Salvation?*, eds. S. Kabazzi-Kisirinya, D.R.K. Nkurunziza, and Gerard Banura. Uganda: Department of Religious Studies, Makerere University, pp. 47–59.

—, C. Tuhirirwe and J. Begumanya (2000). "Kanungu Research Team's Report," in *The Kanungu Cult-Saga: Suicide, Murder or Salvation?*, eds. S. Kabazzi-Kisirinya, D.R.K. Nkurunziza, and Gerard Banura. Uganda: Department of Religious Studies, Makerere University, pp. 12–46.

BBC News Online (March 21, 2000). "Ugandan Cult Murder Suspicions Grow." Accessed July 30, 2013. At <http://news.bbc.co.uk/1/hi/world/africa/685864.stm>.

BBC News Online (March 28, 2000). "Fraud Suspicion in Cult Killings." Accessed July 30, 2013. At <http://news.bbc.co.uk/1/hi/world/africa/693078.stm>

BBC News Online (April 2, 2000). "Uganda Mourns its Dead." Accessed July 30, 2013. At <http://news.bbc.co.uk/1/hi/world/africa/698326.stm>

Bogere, Hussein (2009). "Police Calls of Kibwetere Hunt," *The Observer*, March 26. Accessed July 30, 2013. At <http://www.observer.ug/index.php?option=com_content&task=view&id=2665&Itemid=59>.

Borzello, Anna (2000). "A Party, Prayers, Then Mass Suicide," March 20. Accessed July 30, 2013. At <http://www.theguardian.com/world/2000/mar/20/3>.

Bromley, David G. (2002). "Dramatic Denouements," in *Cults, Religion and Violence*, eds. Bromley, David G. and J. Gordon Melton. Cambridge: Cambridge University Press, pp. 11–41.

Burke, Jason (2000). "Beyond Belief," *The Observer*, April 30. Accessed July 30, 2013. At <http://www.theguardian.com/theobserver/2000/apr/30/features.magazine47>.

Bwire, Robert (2007). *Ashes of Faith: A Doomsday Cult's Orchestration of Mass Murder in Africa*. Amsterdam: Frontier Publishing.

Channel 4 (2000). *Witness: The Cult That Couldn't Stop Killing*.

Cuneo, Michael W. (1999). *The Smoke of Satan: Conservative and Traditionalist Dissent in Contemporary American Catholicism*. Baltimore, MD: Johns Hopkins University Press.

Hall, John R., Schuyler, Philip D. and Sylvaine Trinh (2000). *Apocalypse Observed: Religious Movements and Violence in North America, Europe and Japan*. London: Routledge.

Hammer, Joshua (2000). "An Apocalyptic Mystery: The end of the world was delayed, so a cult leader took matters into his own hands," *Newsweek*, 135(14) (April 3): 46–7.

Introvigne, Massimo (2000). "Tragedy in Uganda: The Restoration of the Ten Commandments of God, a Post-Catholic Movement," April 5. Accessed July 30, 2013. At <www.cesnur.org/2002/uganda.htm>.

Kabazzi-Kisirinya, S., D.R.K. Nkurunziza, and Gerard Banura eds. (2000). *The Kanungu Cult-Saga: Suicide, Murder or Salvation?*. Uganda: Department of Religious Studies, Makerere University.

Mayer, Jean-François (2001). "Fieldnotes: The Movement for the Restoration of the Ten Commandments of God," *Nova Religio* 5(1): 203–10.

— (2011). "'There Will Follow a New Generation and a New Earth': From Apocalyptic Hopes to Destruction in the Movement for the Restoration of the Ten Commandments of God," in *Violence and New Religious Movements*, ed. James R. Lewis. Oxford: Oxford University Press, pp. 191–214.

MRTCG (The Movement for the Restoration of the Ten Commandments of God) (1996). *A Timely Message from Heaven: The End of the Present Times*. Rukungiri, Uganda: The Movement for the Restoration of the Ten Commandments of God.

Mubangizi, Michael (2009). "Fire in the Name of God," *The Observer*, March 26. Accessed July 30, 2013. At <http://www.observer.ug/index.php?option=com_content&task=view&id=2667&Itemid=59>.

Nkurunziza, Andrew (2007). "I Narrowly Survived the Kanungu Inferno," *The Monitor*, April 9. Accessed 1 April 2014. At <http://allafrica.com/stories/200703150867.html>.

Odong, James (2003). "Kibwetere in Israel, MPs Told," *New Vision*, Kampala, May 8: 4.

Reader, Ian (2000). *Religious Violence in Contemporary Japan: The Case of Aum Shinrikyo*. London: Routledge.

Sempogo, Herbert (2011). "No Arrests 11 Years After Kanungu Massacre," *New Vision*, March 16. Accessed July 30, 2013. At <www.newvision.co.ug/PA/8/13/749327>.

Twesigye, Emmanuel K. (2010). *Religion, Politics and Cults in East Africa: God's Warriors and Mary's Saints*. New York: Peter Lang.

UHRC (Ugandan Human Rights Commission) (2002). *The Kanungu Massacre: The Movement for the Restoration of the Ten Commandments of God Indicted*. Uganda: Uganda Human Rights Commission.

Vokes, Richard (2009). *Ghosts of Kanungu: Fertility, Secrecy, and Exchange in the Lakes of East Africa*. Woodbridge, Suffolk: James Currey.

Walliss, John (2004). *Apocalyptic Trajectories: Millenarianism and Violence in the Contemporary World*. Oxford: Peter Lang.

Wessinger, Catherine (2000). *How the Millennium Comes Violently: From Jonestown to Heaven's Gate*. London: Seven Bridges Press.

Part III
Social-Political Suicides

Chapter 7

A Sociological Analysis of Muslim Terrorism

Jan A. Ali

Introduction

This chapter seeks to provide a modest contribution to the understanding of terrorism. It explores, in particular, "Muslim suicide terrorism" not as a religious but as a sociological phenomenon. It locates terrorism in the context of crisis situation of the modern world and seeks to situate Muslim suicide terrorism as a religious response to the consequences of European colonialism and crisis in society. Many so-called terrorists are not passive objects of social, economic, and political forces, or puppets, but are instead educated and innovative international actors who have developed well worked-out methodologies to put their plans into action and to achieve political goals.

Pierre Bourdieu's concept of habitus (1977) offers a useful way of understanding the ways in which the environments in which Muslim suicide terrorists are raised and cultural and material influences shape their disposition to act, their means of interpreting the world, and ultimately how they express themselves politically. This chapter attempts to redefine the contours of Muslim suicide terrorism by removing it from its surrogate abode in Islam to its rightful domicile in the postcolonial situation in which many Muslims live. It presents Muslim suicide terrorism as a habitus that is responsible for structuring political comportment and action. The attempt is to understand why terrorism occurs in the Muslim context and seeks to demonstrate that what we are dealing with today is a general habitus of Muslim suicide terrorism induced by the crisis situation in society directly afflicting many Muslims. I argue that Muslim suicide terrorism is a response to the consequences of colonialism and the crisis or negative consequences of modernity; economic deprivation, social injustice, inequality, political turmoil, and so on.

Definition

The term "terrorism" has its origin in the word *terror*, which has a Latin origin meaning "to frighten." It is perhaps for this reason that terrorism is often used interchangeably with the term "terror," obscuring the possibility of a more precise, tangible, and meaningful explanatory definition of the term. Also, terrorism is a term that is politically and emotionally charged (Hoffman 2006). At the same time, it is not immutable: "Separating the tactics of terror from the concept of terrorism is necessary but difficult" (Mahan and Griset 2008: 3). These factors make the task of defining terrorism in any precise way enormously difficult (Wardlaw 1989). Yet the definition of terrorism is imperative simply because it has important ramifications. For instance, organizing global counter-terrorism operations necessitates common agreement among those involved over rules and procedures (Deflem 2006). Prosecution, surveillance, prehearing incarcerations, and imprisonment under terrorism law similarly demands properly worked out definition.

Sue Mahan and Pamala L. Griset describe terrorism as "an ideological and political concept" (2008: 3). In terms of terrorism as a political concept, Hoffman asserts that "Terrorism, in the most widely accepted contemporary usage of the term is fundamentally and inherently political" (2006: 2). Politics is about power struggle, therefore, any definition is likely to spark emotive and hostile disputation. Terrorism derives its meaning from a broader philosophy to which an individual or a group subscribes.

In light of this, if a person shares the philosophical viewpoint of terrorists, he or she is a terrorist and if a person disagrees with such a view, he or she is not a terrorist (Cooper 2001). Is terrorism simply a matter of personal viewpoint? A vast majority of people would agree that fundamental values—for example, justice and freedom—are worth protecting and fighting for, even if one must sacrifice their own life in the process. In a sense then, "one person's terrorist is another person's freedom fighter" (Crenshaw 2001; Lodge 1982; Velter and Perlstein 1991). Oppressive governments describe those who resist them as terrorists. However, those who use violence to overpower the same governments consider themselves "freedom fighters." Hoffman (2006) observes that most, if not all, terrorist organizations understand themselves as freedom fighters. If politics and ideology could be separated from the definition, it would hardly matter who is terrorizing whom. However, this is not actually the case, and as Cooper (2001) suggests, terrorism must be defined by the character of the act itself.

So why, then, is terrorism so difficult to define? Hoffman (2006) says this is because the meaning of terrorism changes so frequently that there is no way of holding onto one meaning forever or for a prolonged period of time. Cooper (2001: 881) says that it is due to the fact that "there has never been, since the topic began to command serious attention, some golden age in which terrorism was easy to define." Additionally many violent acts such as war, riot, organized crime, or even a common assault, may easily fall under some definitions of terrorism. Even damage to property that does not jeopardize life is ordinarily perceived as a crime of nonviolent nature. However, for critics of so-called "eco-terrorists" such as the Earth Liberation Front and Animal Liberation Front (Kushner 2003), property damage is viewed as an act of violence and terrorism.

Walter Laqueur claims that "more than a hundred definitions have been offered" (1999: 5), including a number of his own, and says that terrorism is difficult to define because "there is not one but many different terrorisms" (ibid.: 46). Schmid and Jongman (1988) found 109 definitions in their well-known review in the late 1980s and Andrew Silke (2004) asserts that this figure had doubled by 2004.

Any definition of terrorism must include individual motivation, social environmental factors, and political purpose. So this discussion relies on Hoffman's definitional model, which distinguishes certain pivotal characteristics of terrorism and leads to some understanding of the concept. Terrorism is:

- ineluctably political in aims and motives;
- violent—or, equally important, threatens violence;
- designed to have far-reaching psychological repercussions beyond the immediate victim, or target;
- conducted either by an organization with an identifiable chain of command, or
- conspiratorial cell structure (whose members wear no uniform or identifying insignia), or by individuals or a small collection of individuals directly influenced, motivated, or
- inspired by the ideological aims or example of some existent terrorist movement and/or its leaders , and
- perpetrated by a subnational group or non-state entity. (Hoffman 2006: 40)

Origins of Terrorism

It has been argued that terrorism began in first century Judea during the Jewish rebellion against Roman occupation (66–73 CE) (Kushner 2003; Hoffman

2006; Mahan and Griset 2008). One faction of the rebels called "Sicarii" were named for a short carved dagger (*sica*) which they used to slit the throats of both Romans and members of the Jewish establishment in public. They were part of a group known as Zealots (from Greek *zelos*, meaning strong spirit) who stood against Roman occupation of Judea.

During the French Revolution, the Jacobin Club led by Maximilien Robespierre, which rose to power in France in 1792, enforced a *régime de la terreur* commonly known in English as the "Reign of Terror" (June 1793–July 1794). This is a potent example of state terrorism executed to advance the objectives of a revolutionary movement. Although the Reign of Terror was enforced by the Jacobin-dominated government of the day, when the Jacobins lost power, "terrorist" became a term of abuse. The Jacobin Club's actions were the first to be described as terrorism in the modern world by British philosopher Edmund Burke (Mahan and Griset 2008). This is apparently an early example of the term being used in its contemporary sense.

In the twentieth century, terrorism became the trademark of numerous political movements from both sides of the political spectrum. Technological advancements such as automatic, chemical, biological, and nuclear weapons, and miniature electrically detonated explosives, provided terrorists with new modes of causing death. The development of air transportation facilitated new techniques, methods, and opportunities. Terrorism was almost an official policy in authoritarian states such Nazi Germany during the reign of Adolf Hitler, the Soviet Union when Stalin was in power, China during Mao Zedong's leadership, and Cambodia under Pol Pot.

In the late twentieth and early twenty-first centuries, some of the most extreme groups involved in terrorism had an innovative religious ideology—for instance, HAMAS (Harakat al-Muqawama al-Islamia or Islamic Resistance Movement), Hezbollah (Party of God), and al-Qaeda (Arabic for "The Base") in the Middle East. Some of these groups, including the LTTE (Liberation Tigers of Tamil Eelam) in Sri Lanka, espoused the method of suicide bombing or suicide terrorism, in which the bomber would try to cause destruction to an important economic, military, political, or iconic object by detonating a bomb strapped on his or her body. For Muslims, the proclivity to commit acts of terrorism originated from new religious cosmology and ideology. As we will see, ideology plays a key role.

Ideology

There is a long tradition in social science generally and in political science in particular which argues that the ideological factor is an important determinant of violent mobilization (Gurr 1970; Lichbach 1989; Muller and Seligson 1987). Although there is no Islamic scriptural support for terrorism, the ideology of Muslim suicide terrorism is developed from a complex interpretation of the concept of *jihad* (struggle), which is complex and multidimensional, but the common understanding of it is that it is a struggle against any "evil."

Transnational jihadist ideology asserts that western states and societies are inimical to Islam. Jihadists see Islam and the Christian West in a conflictual relationship. They often trace this as far back as the Crusades and portray their enemy as violent and call for defensive combat against them. Hence, framing the combat as a defensive reaction against evil makes those engaged in this process appear to be victims rather than aggressors and consequently gives their cause a religious tone towards which all good Muslims are persuasively ushered.

Jihadists have an articulated ideology and a definitive plan. They generally work with a keen sense of the need for change on individual and social levels. The individual, they believe, needs to be properly socialized into the Jihadists' version of the Islamic worldview and the community should be re-molded to espouse and project Islamic values into the political, economic, and social structures of society. Islam is used, and some may say abused, to reinforce group norms and to institute moral sanctions for individual behavior. It is used to provide universal goals and values, which in turn offer a sense of community (*ummah*).

This makes jihadism an attempt to re-establish an Islamic order, albeit the Jihadists' version of it. Muslims governed by the *shariah* (Islamic law), a society in which justice, moral purity, peace, and prosperity prevail, can be achieved through an Islamic polity (Guazzone 1995). Moral purity, therefore, is the key aspect of Jihadist ideology. Untainted morality is achievable, for the Jihadist movements, not through rationality but through serious observance of the *shariah* and by living in an Islamic state governed by Islamic principles (Moussalli 1999). Islam is *din wa-dawlah* (religion and state) precisely because morality is absolute. Thus, Jihadist ideology conceives of Islam as an all-encompassing system embodying social, economic, political, and spiritual aspects of life in one complete and holistic order (ibid.).

Founded upon this ideology, Muslim suicide terrorism is political terrorism or political in nature. If we place the Muslim experience in the context of European colonialism and in the crisis situation of the Muslim world, a much clearer picture emerges that explains some of the motives and rationales behind

Muslim terrorist activities in recent years. Before we do this, however, let us examine Bourdieu's *A Theory of Practice* (1977) and his pivotal concept of habitus to provide the overall discussion with some theoretical context.

Pierre Bourdieu's Theoretical Framework

Bourdieu's theoretical project is a vital contribution to the analysis and explication of "social influences," especially of what people do and why they do it, and how their social actions contribute to the reproduction of those very influences (Rey 2007: 40). Social influences explain how Muslim suicide terrorists come to perceive and understand their social world, how they shape their disposition to act, and how they choose to express themselves politically. Bourdieu focused on constructing a critical sociology that explained power relationships generated and regenerated out of cultural resources, processes, and institutions (Swartz 1997: 52). For Bourdieu, power is not an independent sphere but is, rather, located at the center of social life. Culture is viewed by Bourdieu as an expression of power, and not necessarily without political content. Bourdieu sees sociology as a powerful analytical tool capable of "producing awareness of those mechanisms that make life painful, even unlivable" and of "bringing contradictions to light" (Bourdieu 1999: 629). "Symbolic violence" is a key concept in *A Theory of Practice*, which refers to the norms and values espoused by dominant social actors in the society, "naturalized" as self-evident "truth" and accepted as such by the dominated populace. This power is both visible and invisible in the social sphere. Bourdieu's *Theory of Practice* (1977) reveals a set of diverse modalities of power as they are negotiated through cultural tools at the social level and at the level of individual choice, affecting the temperament to engage in political action and assume a political identity. The practice, therefore, is the outcome of different habitual configurations and dispositions (habitus) accompanied by resources (capital) and ignited by social settings or social conditions (fields) (Crossley 2001: 96). The interaction between capital and fields and hegemonic subjects that shape individual experience often have indirect effect with which they may not consciously identify, yet which inform their insights and worldview (habitus).

The habitus may be seen as the quiescent part in the construction and expression of identity that ultimately shapes practice and action. Habitus assists the disposition to assume and practice a particular identity. For Muslim suicide terrorists, it may be suggested that identities are constructed in relation to these practices in fields of resistance.

Habitus

Habitus denotes people's ability to presuppose the mindset and actions needed within specific social settings or fields to better understand, in the present case, Muslim suicide terrorism. It is habitus and its connection with the field and the capital treasured by the field that establishes what a person is capable of doing or achieving. It is a common set of learned and embodied temperaments and knowledge of the world, built out of both objective structures and individual biography.

The term "habitus" is related to the words "habit" and "habitual." It denotes an inclination towards a particular way of behaving—ingrained in our bodies as well as our intellects, normally at the subconscious level. Habitus is second nature:

> Habitus tends to shape individual action so that existing opportunity structures are perpetuated. Chances of success or failure are internalised and then transformed into individual aspirations or expectations; these are in turn externalised in action that reproduce the objective structure of life chances. (Swartz 1997: 103).

According to Bourdieu (1977: 8 and 95), habitus refers to "generative principles of distinct and distinctive practices" that are directly connected to being immersed in different social and cultural norms which work together as a fusion of force between "the intrinsic and relational characteristics of a position" and "a unitary set of choices of persons, goods, practices." Drawing attention to his idea of the collective embodiment of processes, Bourdieu explains that the principles, norms, values, and common rituals and practices in everyday social living are embodied "beyond the grasp of consciousness," and that the body as a vessel of memory is composed in a way that is "capable of instilling a whole cosmology, an ethic, a metaphysic, a political philosophy" (ibid.: 94):

> ... the habitus is the product of the work of inculcation and appropriation necessary in order for those products of collective history, the objective structures, (e.g. language, economy etc.) to succeed in reproducing themselves more or less completely, in the forms of durable dispositions. (Ibid.: 85).

Bourdieu explains how practice (agency) is connected to capital and field (structure) through habitus. In *Distinction* (1984: 110), Bourdieu demonstrates this figuratively by the following formula: (Habitus x Capital) + Field = Practice.

Put differently, what people do in society (action) is *practice*, which occurs in a variety of interrelated ways in the *fields*—sub-spaces in society or the social world—that together make up society. What people do amounts to personal pursuit of different possessions (*capital*); whether these are symbolic or "real" depends on the *fields* in which their *practice* takes place. Perhaps what makes Bourdieu's concept of habitus important for an analysis of Muslim suicide terrorism is his challenge to connect microsystem variables such as framing and cognitive schemes to macropower structures.

Muslim Colonial Experience

In the last 150 years or so, the conditions for terrorism were incubating in Muslim responses to the challenges and experiences generated by western influence and intrusion. European conquests of Muslim territories, which began in the sixteenth century, overwhelmed Muslim societies with new western technologies, methods of economic management, political systems, and ideology (Bagader 1994). The advent of colonialism broke up the established Islamic political order, particularly that of the Mughal dynasties and the Safavid and Ottoman Empires, which had remained intact for centuries, and contested traditional beliefs and norms, thus causing a major crisis of Islamic authority and Muslim identity (ibid.). Under western influence and colonial rule, modernity "found its way" into the *dar al-Islam* (abode of Islam), bringing sweeping changes in the Muslim world (Rahman 1982; Esposito 1983; Hunter 1988). The processes of secularization, urbanization, and modernization, undermined and challenged old myths, doctrines, institutions, social structures, and social relationships. As a result, Muslims and Muslim societies underwent radical socio-economic, cultural, and political reorganization, reshuffles, and changes (Rahman 1982).

To counter the domination of European colonial powers and secure its survival, the Islamic religion took on a political dimension in the twentieth century in the *dar al-Islam*, inspiring anti-colonial and nationalist movements. Many Muslim states adopted the political, economic, and educational institutions of the western states that had colonized them. They experimented with liberal nationalism, socialism, and Marxist communism but without success: "Problems of authoritarianism, legitimacy, and political participation continued to plague most Muslim countries" (Esposito 1983: 12).

Despite the majority of Muslim states embracing modernization and national development after independence, in general, social and economic conditions did not improve for ordinary Muslims (Hunter 1988). Many continued to experience poverty, social inequality, and injustice. Living standards for most ordinary Muslims barely changed. A general mood of decline and stagnation continued and the vast majority of Muslims finally realized that "the paradigm of modernisation and the political elites associated with it have failed to avert the Islamic world's decline and end its state of political and economic dependency" (ibid.: xii). By uprooting old social and political institutions and patterns of relationships, whether based on tradition or religion, material modernity created a void. The newly created social and political forces and other new demands did not properly cater for or offer appropriate channels of expression: "The result for the majority of people has been a growing feeling of psychological, social, and political alienation and disorientation" (ibid.: xiii).

The development of Muslim terrorism as a significant political phenomenon can be understood from this perspective. That is, many Muslims felt a strong sense of being socially, economically, and politically eclipsed and deprived of the benefits of modernization. Muslim terrorism, therefore, is a struggle against the forces "hostile" to religion and aspects of traditional and religious life. Muslim terrorists who subscribe to this ideological approach see terrorism as the last hope for bringing about religiously practical and acceptable changes in their societies. For these terrorists, the recovery of Islamic glory is the solution to currently existing problems or more broadly to the crisis of modernity.

Economic and Material Deprivation

Some studies (Atran 2005; Baregu 2002) posit that there is no correlation between economic and material deprivation—that is, poverty—and terrorism, whilst others (Berman 2002; Gutierrez 2002; Richmond 2003) concede a strong link. The South Korean Nobel Peace Prize laureate Kim Dae-Jung acknowledged in 2001 that poverty breeds terrorism, and his view was echoed subsequently by other members of the exclusive group of Nobel Peace Prize winners (Jai 2001). Laura D'Andrea Tyson, former chief of the Presidential Council of Economic Advisors under the Clinton administration and dean of the Hass School of Business at the University of California at Berkeley, suggested a Marshall Plan to combat political despotism and eradication of poverty because she saw poverty and hopelessness in poor remote parts of the world were perfect breeding grounds for a network of terrorism bent on wreaking havoc and mass destruction (Tyson 2001). Hudson posits that "terrorists in much of the developing world tend to be drawn from the lower sections of society. The rank-and-file of Arab terrorist organizations include substantial numbers of poor people, many of them homeless refugees" (1999: 50). Krueger and Maleckova (2002) in their study of Hezbollah militants in Lebanon found a statistical link between poverty and terrorism, in that poverty had a strong negative effect on the possibility of some members of the Lebanese community becoming Hezbollah militants, or, more precisely, a 30 per cent increase in poverty led to a 15 percent rise in Hezbollah militant recruitment. Li and Schaub (2004: 236) posit that "a primary cause of transnational terrorism is underdevelopment and poverty ... Poor economic conditions create 'terrorist breeding' grounds, where disaffected populations turn to transnational terrorist activities as a solution to their problems."

The impact of limited economic opportunity has a multiplier effect, which links with the attraction to militancy and terrorism. In Muslim countries, a strong cultural expectation exists for young men. Employment for young men forms a conduit to independence enabling them to purchase their own homes, get married and raise families. With social breakdowns and economic crises, many young men and even women are unable to achieve this, and therefore are forced into long-term or even permanent "social cadetship." This experience is not unique to young men in the Muslim world; young men in other poor countries suffer similar experiences. When the transition into adult independence seems unachievable for many young people and when they feel most vulnerable, terrorist organizations appear, offering solutions. The appeal of terrorism or terrorist organizations then is not only about economic independence or class position in the Marxist sense, but is associated with status in Weberian sense, connected to the importance of lifestyle, participation in consumer culture, and a sense of social freedom and well-being.

Though terrorism is a heterogeneous phenomenon, there is something that brings different terrorists and terrorist groups together, and that is their dissatisfaction with prevailing economic conditions, particularly poverty. The clearest evidence of the economic causes of terrorism or terrorism linked to economic issues in society, particularly poverty and socio-economic inequality, can be found in the recent work of Mutlu Koseli (2010) in Turkey. Koseli posits that it can be inferred from his study that Turkish provinces with a high percentage of poor populations have more terrorist incidents, when compared with more equal or even privileged provinces. He says that "In sum, it appears from the findings of this study that poverty and the conditions leading to such poverty are related to the support and spread of terrorism in the provinces of Turkey" (Koseli 2010: 159).

Another indicator of terrorism Koseli identifies in his study that is worth mentioning is education, which of course directly involves and affects young people who appear most prominently as terrorists. Koseli observes that when inequalities in education between provinces in Turkey rise, so do the incidents of terrorism. He notes that "It can be inferred from the results of this study that unequal distribution of education service is contributing to the support and spread of terrorism in the provinces of Turkey" (ibid.).

Poverty and lack of education among other factors, either independently or in conjunction with each other, in Turkey, and presumably elsewhere, are indicators which reveal that unequal distribution of government resources in society has a "real" connection with terrorism. One simple reason for this is that unequal distribution of government resources is seen, particularly in the underprivileged sector of society, as unfair and unjust. In this regard, Baregu (2002) and Gutierrez (2002) note that perception of injustice emanating from governmental failure is one of the prime motivations for terrorism.

There is no doubt that a correlation exists between economic and material depravation and terrorism. This can be further understood by looking at Durkheim's (1951) concept of anomic suicide. Anomic suicide is the consequence of an unexpected and sudden change in the social standing of an individual. The change produces a new set of circumstances or a situation to which the individual is powerless to react. Take, for instance, sudden economic crises, a series of investment failures, or strings of resource busts (when the regulatory ability of the government and key institutions in society weakens and individual "feelings" are left unattended), suicide levels rise.

Consequently,

> ... a kind of *declassement* occurs, suddenly thrusting certain individuals into a situation inferior to the one they occupied hitherto. They must therefore lower their demands, restrain their wants, learn greater self-control ... they are not adjusted to the condition imposed on them and find its very prospect intolerable; thus they experience sufferings which detach them from a reduced existence even before they have tried it. (Durkheim, quoted in Lukes 1975: 210)

It is critical to note, however, that individuals respond differently to crisis situations and not everyone afflicted by a reduced standard of living and poverty resorts to anomic suicide. It is, however, clear that one way in which individuals respond to their economic malaise or woes is anomic suicide or, in the Muslim context, "suicide terrorism."

The Crisis of Modernity

A factor other than economic that helps to explain terrorism is the crisis of modernity. It is being argued that the catalysts for Muslim terrorism are the negative consequences of the process of modernization, or the crisis of modernity. Modern political elites have been unsuccessful in preventing the Muslim world's decline and stopping its political and economic dependency on the West. In this connection, Hunter explains:

> Thus, while material modernity has tended to disintegrate old sociopolitical institutions and patterns of relationships, it has not replaced them with new ones ... The result for the majority of people ... psychological, social, and political alienation ... These feelings ... propelled ... to seek some sense of stability and continuity by reverting to their traditional way of life. (Hunter 1988: xiii)

In a sense then, modernization has been largely unsuccessful in creating a just foundation for world societies and overcoming the social ills that have plagued humanity.

Similarly, Keyder argues that when Muslims failed to benefit from capitalism and modernization, they turned their backs on them and turned to "a community-building movement, seeking to keep the noxious effects of the market, which is identified with secularist immorality, out of the community of believers" (1986: 13). These real or perceived failures have provided the catalyst for many Muslims to join terrorist organizations.

Ted Gurr asserts that both small and large-scale studies on causes of terrorism reveal that it does not occur in a specific or prescribed place, but anywhere at any time. It is, however, true that terrorism has commonly been seen as occurring more "in developing societies rather than in the poorest countries or in the developed West and is especially likely to emerge in societies characterized by rapid modernization and lack of political rights" (Gurr 2006: 86). Butko argues that Islamist

> ... movements have arisen in reaction to attempts at rapid development and modernization which have not fulfilled the expectations of a majority of their populations. Urbanization, higher education and the perception of relative material deprivation have led to feelings of alienation, frustration, and hence, a growing sense of powerlessness. (Butko 2004: 33).

Muslim terrorism is thus viewed as a response to the prevailing conditions in the modern epoch. Muslim terrorism is undeniably the result of poor political and economic circumstances associated with the process of modernization in many Muslim countries.

Rising unemployment, the increasing divide between rich and poor, and lack of opportunities for young men and women in terms of employment and education all contribute to a crisis situation in society. Tessler asserts that Muslims "regard their problems as grounded in existing patterns of political economy, and they accordingly attribute much of the responsibility for their plight to the political regimes by which they are governed" (1997: 93).

The failure of their own governments and precarious local conditions turn Muslims towards terrorism. Sidahmed and Ehteshami argue that the constant failure of the states to meet people's social needs in the face of rising economic problems and a "combination of ... factors create[d] fertile ground for the growth of the Islamist forces" (1996: 7).

Mendelsohn argues that Islamists believe that the "disjoining" of religion and science as part of the process of secularization have effectively removed all restraints against what may be described in Islamist circles as the harmful forces of modern science and technology. Created by God to operate in perfect harmony to control nature, the Enlightenment project and subsequent secularization process have inappropriately introduced rivalry between science and religion, adversely impacting nature. Islamists have emerged as "the restorers of the lost harmony" (Mendelsohn 1993: 24).

In Rajaee's argument, Muslim terrorism can be seen as a response "to the *consequences* of modernity—to its political (i.e., colonialism), educational (i.e., new school systems and modern institutions of learning), and ideological (i.e., the ideologies of nationalism, democracy, and socialism) by-products" (1993: 103, original emphasis). Like Rajaee, Roy argues that the Islamist cause is a modern phenomenon and a socio-religious response "of anti-colonialism, of anti-imperialism, which today has simply become anti-Westernism" (Roy 2001: 4).

Social conditions resulting from widespread conflicts which are characterized by oppressive policies and practices, discrimination, injustice, and inequality that cause extensive physical, economic, social, and cultural dislocations, weaken and even destroy the social ties that cement the structure of society, thus creating feelings of humiliation, uprootedness, isolation, bitterness, and vengeance, in some quarters. Such conditions constitute in part the crisis of modernity and are conducive to the rise of suicide terrorism, whereby some Muslims are willing to sacrifice their lives for a "greater good," such as the honorable political existence of their community.

Social dissolution, particularly in contemporary Muslim societies, helps us discern that Muslim suicide terrorism is related to the disintegration of social groups where individuals feel disenfranchised and their ties to society and the stability of social relations within the society are all weakened if not destroyed. The high degree of social disintegration, normlessness, social isolation, disenfranchisement, discrimination, and repression in society leads some Muslims to suicide terrorism. Under the weight of the crisis of modernity, Muslims' weak social integration leads them to extreme isolation or "social detachment" which precludes them from seeking support from family and the religious community to cope with difficulties. As a response, Muslims resort to suicide terrorism, not as an easy way out of a life of misery, but to make a political statement and as an act of unselfishness sacrifice where the goal is for the sake of the community. Muslim suicide terrorists believe that this is the supreme sacrifice and a cause for "greater good" and not a "suicide" for the purpose of achieving social prestige, public praise, and recognition.

Conclusion

Muslim suicide terrorism always manifests in public acts. What is important to note is that suicide bombers who work with each other in groups must also be motivated to achieve a collective goal, thereby engaging in or fulfilling a cause that is much larger and higher than the individual. Evidence such as video recordings and written testimonies of "Muslim martyrs" (*shahid*s) often reveal altruistic motivation behind suicide bombing. The prevalence of joint missions or group strikes and the presence of Muslim-martyr video recordings and written testimonies, such as those left by members of the Hezbollah movement in Palestine (Dabbagh 2005), prove that a vast majority of acts of suicide terrorism are either in part or in full motivated by a shared purpose, and are not merely a reflection of personal grievance and sorrow (Pape 2005; Dabbagh 2005).

Most Muslim terrorist groups engaged in suicide missions or bombings are intimately intertwined with their respective societies because of their pursuit of political objectives which much of the society support, given the prevailing poor socio-economic and political conditions. From the perspective of Muslim terrorist groups or organizations, suicide attacks are necessary because of the existence of imbalance in military muscle between the state and themselves but, more importantly, attacks will exert greater pressure on the enemy. Put differently, suicide attacks are constructed around the idea of altruism, not as an end in themselves but as a vehicle for accomplishing the greater good of the collective.

People who have suffered hardship and crises for a prolonged period of time at the hands of a formidable enemy in the end react to perceived and real inferiority by lending support for suicide missions. Suicide attacks are a vehicle for people to vent their anger and express their feelings of disempowerment, uprootedness, dispossession, hopelessness, resentment, and injustice. Such attacks represent a confrontation between a subordinate group and the ruling authorities in which the former deliberately uses any resources at its disposal against an existing order it perceives as illegitimate.

Muslim terrorist campaigns are a form of resistance and should be seen as such. This resistance is directed toward the dominant class exercising power in the society. Thus Foucault's concepts of power and resistance are handy for understanding Muslim suicide terrorism. For Foucault, power is the ability to bring about social change. The difference between "resistance" and "power" is linked to the "subject-position" of the subject that employs its ability to generate social change. The hegemonic subject is the dominant group that exercises power, whereas the counter-hegemonic subject is the underclass that resists.

For Foucault, behavioral options for a subject are regulated by the "subject-position" of that actor in the organization of power. A subject selects tactics from a pre-existing collection of mechanisms. In the case of Muslim suicide terrorists, it could be suggested that they select resistance from a composite of tactics available to counter-hegemonic subjects. Their agency is restricted as is their choice of tactics.

Whenever there is power, there is always resistance. This is a widely acknowledged fact. Based on this understanding of the power-resistance dynamic, resistance is a natural response to those in power, for example HAMAS's resistance to Israel and Fateh, and the resistance of Fateh and Israel to HAMAS. Each subject in this network of power sees itself as a counter-hegemonic subject resisting the hegemonic subject. Resistance is an altruistic mechanism that seeks to change the power balance in the social world and bring about positive social change.

When aggrieved Muslim communities collectively share a sense of inequality, the situation quickly generates a sense of moral outrage, and consequently provides the motivation and justification for violence. How this violence is learnt then becomes critical in understanding Muslim suicide terrorist campaigns. Habitus enables us to understand that Muslim suicide terrorists have entered a new national and global situation produced by modernization and development. In these new settings, they are not only acquiring new knowledge and a new habitus, but are also attempting to revive parts of the old habitus.

Members of a social group (in this case, the in-group constituted by terrorists) place great emphasis on their socially shared standards—norms and values that distinguish them from the out-group—and they develop a unique habitus. In-groups such as Hezbollah and Al-Qaeda have their own rituals, practices, and ideologies. Members not only need to learn them but also practice them. Practices such as combat training in the context of suicide missions become critical. Potential bombers undergo training, for instance, to act normal in a crowd whilst having a bomb strapped to their bodies. They undergo intensive training and programming through attending lectures delivered by senior members, reviewing videos and written testimonies of past bombers, examining infrastructures and buildings for potential targets, body conditioning and disciplining, and target practice. Most importantly, they undergo intense psychological conditioning/indoctrination—which is the most critical part of developing a "terrorist habitus." *Undergoing these processes enables terrorists to acquire a particular outlook on the world and develop a unique disposition*. These rituals of terrorism training separate the members from others and from other groups. They have their own categories, assumptions, and criteria to use to make sense of their own activities and the world as well as to measure others. Once the rituals and practices become internalized, they form the habitus, a second nature. Hence, blowing up oneself takes place "naturally," as part of their acquired habitus.

Habitus can thus be seen making sense of the emergence of terrorist organizations and the practice of suicide violence. Muslims join terrorist organizations to become part of a solid group with distinct identity and undertake certain rituals, practices, and training within it to develop a habitus of self-destruction. The concept of "habitus" and its links with other important concepts of "field" and "capital" provides a powerful theoretical structure. The terrorist habitus shapes political action and infuses it with meaning as part of the development of identity. Muslim suicide terrorism is a collective Muslim experiential response to the consequences of colonialism and the crisis of modernity. The terrorist subculture is a habitus that develops over a period of time as part of the pursuit of *capital* in the *field* and eventually embodies the *agency* that becomes the *practice*.

References

Atran, S. (2005). *Genesis and Future of Suicide Terrorism*. Accessed July 6, 2012. At <http://www.interdisciplines.org/terrorism/papers/1/23/4>.

Bagader, A. (1994). "Contemporary Islamic Movements in the Arab World," in *Islam, Globalization and Postmodernity*, eds. A. Ahmed and H Donnan. London: Routledge and Kegan Paul, pp. 114–26.

Baregu, M. (2002). "Beyond September 11: Structural Causes of Behavioral Consequences of International Terrorism," in *Response to Terrorism: What Role for the United Nations*? ed. International Peace Academy. New York: Chadbourne and Parke.

Berman, E. (2002). *Hamas, Taliban and the Jewish Underground: An Economist's View of Radical Religious Militia.* Accessed July 6, 2012. At <http://dss.ucsd.edu/~elib/tamir.pdf>.

Bourdieu, P. (1977). *Outline of a Theory of Practice*, trans. Richard Nice. Cambridge: Cambridge University Press.

— (1984). *Distinction: A Social Critique of the Judgement of Taste.* London: Routledge and Kegan Paul.

— (1999). "Postscript," in *The Weight of The World: Social Suffering in Contemporary Society*, eds. P. Bourdieu et al. Stanford, CA: Stanford University Press.

— and Wacquant, L. (1992). *An Invitation to Reflexive Sociology*. Chicago, IL: University of Chicago Press.

Bourge, C. (2002). "Terrorism Not From Poverty", *United Press International.* Accessed July 6, 2012. At <http://www.upi.com/inc/view.php?StoryID=11022002-041550-1870r>.

Butko, T. (2004). "Unity through Opposition: Islam as an Instrument of Radical Political Change," *Middle East Review of International Affairs*, 8(4): 33–48.

Cooper, H. (2001). "Terrorism: The Problem of Definition Revisited," *American Behavioral Scientist*, 44(6): 881–93.

Crenshaw, M. (ed.) (1995 and 2001 edns.). *Terrorism in Context.* University Park: Pennsylvania State University Press.

Crossley, N. (2001). *The Social Body: Habit, Identity and Desire.* London and Thousand Oaks, CA: Sage Publications.

Dabbagh, N. (2005). *Suicide in Palestine: Narratives of Despair*. Northampton, MA: Olive Branch Press.

Deflem, M. (2006). "Global Rule of Law or Global Rule of Law Enforcement? International Police Cooperation and Counterterrorism," *Annals of the American Academy of Political and Social Science*, 630: 240–51.

Durkheim, E. (1951). *Suicide: A Study in Sociology*, trans. John Spaulding and George Simpson. London: Routledge and Kegan Paul.

Esposito, J. (1983). 'Introduction: Islam and Muslim Politics," in *Voices of Resurgent Islam*, ed. J. Esposito. Oxford: Oxford University Press, pp. 3–15.

Guazzone, L (ed.) (1995). *The Islamist Dilemma: The Political Role of Islamist Movement in the Contemporary Arab World.* Reading: Ithaca Press.

Gurr, T. (1970). *Why Men Rebel.* Princeton, NJ: Princeton University Press.

— (2006). "Economic Factors," in *The Roots of Terrorism*, ed. Louise Richardson. London and New York: Routledge, pp. 85–101.

Gutierrez, F. (2002). "Terrorism and Inequality," in *Responding to Terrorism: What Role For the United Nations*? ed. International Peace Academy. New York: Chadbourne and Parke.

Hoffman, B. (2006). *Inside Terrorism*, rev. edn. New York: Columbia University Press.

Hudson, R. (1999). *The Sociology and Psychology of Terrorism: Who Becomes A Terrorist and Why*? A Report Prepared Under An Interagency Agreement by the Federal Research Division. Washington, DC: The Library of Congress.

Hunter, S. (1988). "Introduction," in *The Politics of Islamic Revivalism: Diversity and Unity*, ed. S. Hunter. Bloomington: Indiana University Press, pp. ix–xv.

Jai, J. (2001). "Getting at the Roots of Terrorism," *The Christian Science Monitor*, December 10.

Keyder, C. (1986). "The Rise and Decline of National Economies in the Periphery," *Review of Middle East Studies*, 8: 3–14.

Koseli, M. (2010). *Poverty, Inequality and Terrorism Relationship in Turkey: An Analytical Approach to Root Causes of Terrorism.* Dudweiler Landstr: VDM.

Krueger, A. and J. Maleckova (2002). "The Economics and the Education of Suicide Bombers," *The New Republic*, June: 27–33.

Kushner, H. (2003). *Encyclopedia of Terrorism.* London: Sage.

Laqueur, W. (1999). *The New Terrorism: Fanaticism and the Arms of Mass Destruction.* New York: Oxford University Press.

Li, Q. and D. Schaub (2004). "Economic Globalization and Transnational Terrorism," *Journal of Conflict Resolution*, 48(2): 230–58.

Lichbach, M. (1989). "An Evaluation of 'Does Economic Inequality Breed Political Conflict?' Studies," *World Politics* 41(4): 431–70.

Lodge, J. (1982). "Terrorism and Europe: Some General Considerations," in *The Threat of Terrorism*, ed. J. Lodge. Boulder, CO: Westview Press, p. 150.

Lukes, S. (1975). *Emile Durkheim, His Life and Work: A Historical and Critical Study.* Harmondsworth: Penguin Books.

Mahan, S. and P. Griset (2008). *Terrorism in Perspective*, 2nd edn. Los Angeles, CA: Sage.

Mendelsohn, E. (1993). "Religious Fundamentalism and the Sciences," in *Fundamentalisms and Society: The Fundamentalism Project*, eds. M. Marty and R. Appleby. Chicago, IL: University of Chicago Press, pp. 23–41.

Moussalli, A. (1999). *Moderate and Radical Islamic Fundamentalism*. Gainesville: University Press of Florida.

Muller, E. and M. Seligson (1987). "Inequality and Insurgency," *American Political Science Review*, 81(2): 425–52.

Pape, R. (2005). *Dying to Win: The Strategic Logic of Suicide Terrorism*. New York: Random House.

Rahman, F. (1982). *Islam and Modernity: Transformation of an Intellectual Tradition*. Chicago, IL: University of Chicago Press.

Rajaee, F. (1993). "Islam and Modernity: The Reconstruction of an Alternative Shiite Islamic Worldview in Iran," in *Fundamentalisms and Society: The Fundamentalism Project*, eds. M. Marty and R. Appleby. Chicago, IL: University of Chicago Press, pp. 103–25.

Rey, T. (2007). *Bourdieu on Religion: Imposing Faith and Legitimacy*. London: Equinox.

Richmond, O. (2003). "Realizing Hegemony? Symbolic Terrorism and the Roots of Conflict," *Studies in Conflict and Terrorism*, 26(4): 289–309.

Roy, O. (1994). *The Failure of Political Islam*. London: I.B. Tauris.

— (2001). *The Failure of Political Islam*, trans. Carol Volk. Cambridge, MA: Harvard University Press.

Schmid, A. and A. Jongman (1988). *Political Terrorism*, 2nd edn. Oxford: North-Holland Publishing Company.

Sidahmed, A. and A. Ehteshami (1996). "Introduction," in *Islamic Fundamentalism*, eds. A. Sidahmed and A. Ehteshami. Boulder, CO: Westview Press, pp. 1–15.

Silke, A. (2004). "An Introduction to Terrorism Research," in *Research on Terrorism: Tends, Achievements and Failures*, ed. Andrew Silke. London: Frank Cass, pp. 1–29.

Swartz, D. (1997). *Culture and Power: The Sociology of Pierre Bourdieu*. Chicago, IL: University of Chicago Press.

Tessler, M. (1997). "The Origins of Popular Support for Islamist Movements: A Political Economy Analysis," in *Islam, Democracy and the State in North Africa*, ed. J. Entelis. Indianapolis: Indiana University Press, pp. 93–126.

Tyson, L. (2001). "It's Time to Step up the Global War on Poverty," *Business Week*, December 3.

Velter, H. and G. Perlstein (1991). *Perspective on Terrorism*. California: Wadsworth Press.

Wardlaw, G. (1989). *Political Terrorism*. New York: Cambridge University Press.

Chapter 8

So Costly a Sacrifice Upon the Altar of Freedom: Human Bombs, Suicide Attacks, and Patriotic Heroes

Mattias Gardell

Introduction

In the biblical story of Samson (Judges 13–16), the hero commits mass murder by killing himself. The Israelites had lived under Philistine rule for forty years when God caused a barren women to give birth to a national liberator. "The boy is to be a Nazirite, dedicated to God from the womb" said the angel. "He will take the lead in delivering Israel from the hands of the Philistines." Bestowed by God with supernatural strength, Samson performs daring deeds, such as killing a lion with his bare hands, burning down the Philistines' grain stores, olive groves and vineyards, and slaying a thousand enemies with the jawbone of an ass. Eventually, Samson's mistress Delilah made him reveal the secret of his strength: his head had never been shaved. One night when Samson was asleep, Delilah let someone shave off his hair. Samson's eyes were gouged out, and he was brought to Gaza in shackles. Bound to a pair of supporting pillars in a temple before the Philistine nobles and thousands of spectators, Samson prayed to God that he would regain his power to get revenge on the Philistines. "Let me die with the Philistines," said Samson, and he pulled the pillars together with such force that the house collapsed on the rulers and all the people who were gathered there. "Thus he was able to kill many more Philistines when he died than while he lived."

The story of Samson and Delilah, with its themes of heroism, love, betrayal, and self-sacrifice, has fascinated people throughout history. Samson's story has been portrayed in art, theatre, opera, film, and literature. In modern evangelical tradition, Samson is exemplary. For example, the Evangelical *Brobyggarna* (Bridge Builders) hail Samson as a "heroic freedom fighter," "famous for his superhuman physical strength, resourcefulness and many accomplishments in his fight against the Philistines" (Brobyggarna 2008). In rabbinic literature, Samson embodies the Lord's power, the righteous avenger. In secular Israeli nationalist discourse, Samson is a personification of Jewish strength, the male warrior hero who is willing to sacrifice his life for Israel's victory. The "Samson Option" became the name of Israel's secret nuclear weapons program that began in the mid-1960s (Hersh 1991). David Ben-Gurion, Shimon Peres, and Moshe Dayan regarded nuclear weapons as a last resort: like Samson, they would take the enemy with them in death. Israel's willingness to act as Samson if attacked was hailed by popular apocalypticist Hal Lindsey: "Israel will not allow itself to be destroyed as a weakling, and certainly will not die alone, even if it has to destroy itself to nuke the Middle East" (Lindsey 2007).

Glorification of the male warrior who sacrifices his life to inflict defeat on the enemy has been a recurring feature of heroic tales for many centuries. So, why are we filled with such horror by the modern "suicide bomber" figure? Comparing empirical data collected mainly in Palestine during the second Intifada, this chapter on suicide attacks as a resistance strategy reflects on this issue. Why are we more horrified by a suicide attack that leaves dozens dead, than we are by a drone attack that takes many more lives?

Life as a Weapon

Conventionally, the study of modern suicide attacks begins with the Japanese kamikaze pilot who made his debut in 1944, during the final year of World War II. Inspired by ultra-nationalist patriotism, samurai ideals of *bushido* ("the warrior's way") and the machine's prominent role in modernity's ideology of technology, hundreds of Japanese young men formally volunteered their bodies in order to become living missiles and to guide their bomb-equipped fighter planes or submarines against the US Navy's aircraft carriers and destroyers (Axell and Kase 2004). *Kamikaze* means "divine wind," and alludes to the legendary typhoon that overturned Kublai Khan's invasion attempt in 1281, by sinking his huge fleet, and all its crew. Read as evidence of the nation's unique position in the eyes of the divine, the story was re-actualized in Japanese nationalist discourse before the looming US invasion when the kamikaze units were formed. The official designation was *shinpū tokubetsu kōgeki tai* (神风特别攻擊队, "special attack unit, the divine wind"). The signs for 'divine wind', 神风, can be read in Chinese (*shinpū*), as did the Japanese Imperial administration, or in Japanese (*kamikaze*), which eventually became the term that was universally recognized. In postwar Japan, the pilots who were part of this special attack unit are hailed as patriots who voluntarily gave their lives to the country's defense. There are statues of kamikaze pilots in various Japanese cities, and war museums, including Kanoya, and the old military airport in Chiran. The pilots' heroic narratives are articulated in Japanese novels, manga stories, poetry and motion pictures, such as the 1993 blockbuster *Gekkou no Natsu* ("Summer of the Moonlight Sonata"), and the 2001 epic *Hotaru* ("Firefly"). In Japanese youth culture, the term "kamikaze" has "cool" connotations (c.f. "bad" in English). "*Kamikaze*" is the name of a strong alcoholic drink made with vodka, orange liqueur, syrup and sugar; *Kamikaze* is the name of a popular rock fanzine, and the term is used in marketing strategies by companies that sell extreme sports products such as fast motorcycles.

In Western parlance, a kamikaze pilot is a "suicide pilot," a brainwashed robot rather than a hero, and figuratively the term is used for fanatical people who recklessly engage in impossible enterprises or ill-conceived projects that are doomed to fail. For example, the Christian evangelist who went to Afghanistan to convert the Taliban to Christianity was called the "kamikaze missionary" (Gunnarson 2007).

Significantly, the terms "kamikaze pilots" or "suicide pilots" are not employed for the American pilots who carried out similar actions during World War II. Nor are these pilots mentioned in the history of modern suicide attacks. Yet, the Japanese kamikaze pilots were *preceded* by American pilots, who used their lives and planes as weapons, including in the defense of the US colony of the Philippines, in December 1941. For example, on December 8, 1941, Captain Colin P. Kelly sacrificed his life by intentionally guiding his bomber right into a Japanese warship, an act for which he was posthumously awarded the Distinguished Service Cross. Kelly was not considered a suicide pilot, but rather a true American hero whose legend was magnified after death. There is a Colin P. Kelly Memorial in Madison, Florida, a Colin P. Kelly Street in San Francisco, a Colin Kelly Middle School in Eugene, Oregon, a Colin P. Kelly Highway and Colin P. Kelly Post Office in Florida, and the US Navy named one of their vessels USS *Colin P Kelly*. There are Kelly portraits in oil, his statue stands at an American air base in the Philippines, and his exemplary deed is retold in comics, including an issue of *True Comics* used in US schools and military education.

There are other heroic tales, including that of Lieutenant Colonel Jimmy Doolittle, who played a key role in the *Payback Mission*, a death-defying attack on Tokyo in April 1942, from which none of the participants thought they would escape alive. The story is retold in the sentimental commemorative website *Home of Heroes* (homeofheroes.com 1999): Japan had won sweeping victories against the US military in Hawaii, Guam, and the Philippines. President Franklin D. Roosevelt reasoned that a spectacular operation was needed to prove that the

Japanese were not invincible. Why not an attack against Tokyo? Although it would not have any immediate military value, Roosevelt thought the symbolic, psychological gain would be invaluable. A select group of aviators, who were perfectly aware of the fact that the fuel would not be sufficient to return to the US airbase if they managed to reach the mission's target, was secretly trained and led by Doolittle. "I don't intend to be taken prisoners," said Doolittle. "I'm 45 years old and have lived a full life. If my 'plane is crippled beyond any possibility of fighting or escape, I'm going to have my crew bail out and then I'm going to dive my B-25 into the best military target I can find."

The operation was successful, but at the cost of all the planes. Three airmen died. Eight were captured and faced a Japanese military trial. Returning planes ran out of fuel and crashed over China. Roosevelt did not want to reveal how the attack was planned, and announced to the world that the avenging heroes had come from Shangri-La, the mythical paradise in the Himalayas. A US aircraft carrier was named the USS *Shangri-La* in honor of the event; those who died during the attack received the Distinguished Flying Cross, and the story has been retold in more or less embroidered Hollywood productions, such as *Thirty Seconds Over Tokyo* (1944) with Spencer Tracy as Doolittle, and *Pearl Harbor* (2001), featuring Alec Baldwin as Doolittle.

For the purpose of this chapter, the most significant difference is neither the number of death-defying pilots (there were far more Japanese), nor the fact that many of the pilots survived (as also happened to Japanese pilots), or that the actions were remembered as patriotic heroism rather than irrational suicide attacks (as indexed in both Japanese and US military history). Rather, it is the fact that it is the American, and not the Japanese, nationalist narrative that generally has been accepted as sound, which points to the victor's ability to objectify historiography as history.

Following World War II, the history of suicide missions continues in various armed conflicts and political contexts. Before 1980, the method was unusual, though not unknown. Robert A. Pape (2003, 2006) lists 188 suicide attacks between 1983—when Hezbollah carried out the spectacular attacks on French and US military bases in southern Lebanon—and the first years of the second Intifada, 2000–01. The secular Tamil Tigers' elite unit, the Black Tigers, carried out the most attacks—75 of the 188—as part of the armed struggle for Tamil independence in Sri Lanka. Other parties to employ the tactic include: the armed wing of the Kurdish secular-nationalist *Partiya Karkerên Kurdistan* (PKK); Chechen rebels against Russia; Iranian soldiers who braved Iraqi troops and minefields in the 1980s; the vanguard *jihadis* who engaged the United States and Saudi Arabia in the mid-1990s; Kashmiri separatists, and militant

Islamists who fought the regimes in Algeria and Egypt in the 1990s. Propelled in part by the attention to the method paid by globalized media, suicide attacks became a global fashion after the millennium, embraced by individuals and movements in Algeria, Afghanistan, Chechnya, Egypt, England, Iraq, Israel, Kashmir, Morocco, Pakistan, Palestine, Philippines, Spain, the United States, and Uzbekistan, including the coordinated attacks on the World Trade Center and the Pentagon on September 11, 2001, which remain the most spectacular (Pedahzur 2005; Pape 2006; Gambetta 2006; Reuter 2004; Hafez 2007).

Noticeably, the method has not been monopolized by any particular category of people but used by Americans, Japanese, Tamils, Kurds, Muslims, Christians, Hindus, Buddhists, secularists, socialists, separatists, and ultra-nationalists: typically as a last resort against an enemy perceived as militarily superior. This also applies to the American airmen who chose to use their planes as weapons against the Japanese. The attacks came at a time when the US military lost battle after battle to the Japanese, who then appeared militarily superior. When war fortunes turned and the Japanese were forced to retreat, American suicide attacks ended in favor of other methods of killing. Conversely, Japanese kamikaze pilots were not deployed until 1944, during the final phase of the war when Japan was being bombed and American occupation was at their doorstep.

Martyrs, Terrorists, and Invested Knowledge

Palestinian suicide attacks/martyr operations differ from their predecessors in at least two significant respects. Unlike the American, Japanese, and Iranian soldiers, Palestinian martyrs were not backed by a state. In Palestine, there are no well-funded cinematic industries to make epic war films that could move the public to tears over the heroic warriors' sacrifices for the nation. There are no finances to build war museums, or even to cast magnificent statues. Marketers of the daring deeds must make do with home-produced videos, printed martyr posters to adorn the walls along local streets, and medallions with martyrs' pictures and names to hang on a necklace. Unlike the Tamil Tigers, Hezbollah and the PKK, Palestine martyrs of the second Intifada were not trained guerrilla soldiers, nor part of a special command unit or even a militia. Rather, they were civilians who acted independently or, more commonly, had volunteered as martyrs to the command of the armed wing of some Palestinian faction, who then assisted with funding and logistics, and took credit for the operation.

All social knowledge is interested, contextual, and situational. Few contemporary fields of political knowledge have such a diversity of stakeholders who have so much invested in the truth-claims generated from each perspective, as the Palestine–Israel conflict. The very naming of a specific act or event depend on from where the speaker is talking, which means that a similar action can be labeled differently, according to who is talking and who the actor is. Let me exemplify. In the prelude to the summer war of 2006, an Israeli soldier was captured by Palestinian forces on June 25. The incident was condemned immediately by the then Swedish Foreign Minister Jan Eliasson (2006): "Kidnappings of this kind can never be accepted." The day before, on June 24, two Palestinian soldiers had been captured by Israeli military, without Eliasson responding. Of course, only a state with resources to legal violence may "arrest" an offender, which links the usage of the terms to the root of the conflict: since the UN Partition Plan of 1947 for Palestine to establish two independent states in the area, only Israel has yet been recognized. However, as Israel's occupation of the Palestinian territories is illegal, and sovereignty under international law is vested in the population under occupation, the Israeli forces only exert authority in the Occupied Territories as a trustee of the sovereign, and cannot legally act as a sovereign state, and "arrest" Palestinians who exert their legal right to resist the occupation (Ben-Naftali et al. 2005). Yet, mainstream Western media uncritically tend to detach the terms "arresting" and "kidnapping" from their legal context when applied to the Israel–Palestine conflict. Israelis "arrest" Palestinians, while Palestinians "kidnap" Israelis. The reverse seems unthinkable: when do we hear of Israelis who "kidnap" Palestinians, or Palestinians "arresting" Israelis? This may explain why Eliasson did not repeat his principled stance—that kidnappings can never be tolerated as a legitimate political means—when four days later, on June 29, the Israeli military raided Palestinian cities and abducted twenty Palestinian MPs, including eight ministers in the newly elected Palestinian administration. How would Eliasson have assessed the event if the actors of the scenario had been reversed: if the Palestinian National Authority had ordered an armed raid into Israel to abduct members of the Knesset?

This logic affects and complicates the conversation about the kind of armed resistance we are discussing. The concepts "suicide attacks" and "martyrdom operations" are not neutral or objective, but products of opposing political perspectives. The terms thus carry a bias, and the fact that consumers of Western media are more accustomed to the term Palestinian "suicide attack" than "martyr operation" is in itself noteworthy. Attempting to get around this problem, in this chapter I will frequently resort to the stylistically clumsy formula of "suicide bombings/martyrdom operations," sometimes reversing the order, or opting for the less burdened neologism "human bomb." When, mainly for stylistic reasons, I choose to use the term "suicide bombing" or "martyr operation," I urge the reader to keep in mind that one person's suicide bomber may be another's martyr, and vice versa: one person's self-sacrificing hero may be the other's horrifying suicide terrorist.

Suicide Attacks/Martyr Operations under the First and Second Intifada

The wave of Palestinian martyrdom operations during the second Intifada was preceded by a smaller series of suicide bombings between 1994 and 1997. It commenced following the American-Jewish settler Baruch Goldstein's suicide attack/martyr operation in Hebron, February 25, 1994. Goldstein entered the crowded Ibrahimi Mosque in the morning during the month of Ramadan and shot dead 29 Palestinians before he was overpowered and beaten to death. Following this, Hamas and Islamic Jihad claimed responsibility for a series of attacks, formulated as a "response" to Israeli aggression, to which the Israeli military "answered" in an escalating spiral of mutual "counterattacks" (Tamimi 2007: 159ff, Reuter 2004). In Beyt Lid, outside Tel Aviv, on April 4, 1994, 19-year-old Ali Imawi pulled out his Uzi and shot into a military bus. One soldier died and three were wounded. Like Goldstein, Ali had no chance to get away and his bullet-riddled body was displayed on newscasts. A few months later, Ali's childhood friend Hisham approached an Israeli checkpoint on a bomb-equipped bike. As revenge for Ali and the murder of Hani al-Abid, the Palestinian leader whom the Israeli military killed in revenge for Ali's attack, Hisham set off the bomb and took three Israeli soldiers with him in death (Andoni 1997).

In total, there were 16 Palestinian suicide attacks/martyrdom operations between 1994 and 1997, including car bombs, bicycle bombs, and body bombs, which claimed at least 162 lives (Pape 2003). The attacks carried out during this period were, according to Palestinian polls, quite unpopular. Less than one in five, or 18 percent of Palestinian respondents, supported the method. This can be contrasted with Palestinian public opinion during the second Intifada, when over a hundred suicide attacks claimed more than five hundred lives, and two thousand more were injured. According to polls from the first year of the second Intifada, the figures were reversed: four-fifths, or about 80 percent of the respondents gave the attacks their support. Attitudes towards martyrdom operations/suicide bombings in the mid-1990s and early 2000s had thus shifted diametrically (Reuter 2004: 184).

A possible explanation for the shift in public opinion may be found in the changed political context. During the mid-1990s, a majority of Palestinians believed that the 1993 Oslo Treaty would result in a two-state solution and lasting peace. However, Palestinians grew gradually disenchanted with the prospects of the future as Israel colonized more and more Palestinian land instead of dismantling settlements. Close to 90 percent of the territory that, under the United Nations Partition Plan of 1947, should have been divided between two states (one Jewish-Israeli and one Arab-Palestinian), were now under Israeli control. Palestine was fragmented into a scattered archipelago, with 220 mini-reserves or micro-homelands functioning as isolated enclaves surrounded by Israeli-controlled territory. The occupied West Bank was divided into three areas: Zones A, B, and C. In Zone A, which represented less than 3 percent of the West Bank, the Palestinian Authority controlled everything except water, security, and borders, which were controlled by Israel. In Zone B, which represented more than 14 percent of the territory, a joint rule was established between the Israeli occupying power and the Palestinian Authority, with the exception of water, security and border crossings, which were controlled by the Israeli authorities. Zone C, which accounted for over 72 percent of the territory, was controlled by the Israelis (RWB 2003; B'Tselem 1999; Gahrton 2008; Said 2001, 1995, 1996). Peace talks dealt with the transferring of small percentages of territory from one zone to another, but did not touch on the main issues of the conflict, such as ending the occupation, Palestinians' right to national independence in a sovereign state, the status of Jerusalem, and the refugees' right of return.

Israel allowed the Palestinian Authority to gain control over Ramallah and Jericho, but introduced a ban on Palestinians traveling without a permit between the Palestinian-controlled areas, passing between Zones A, B and C, between separated locations within a single zone, between the West Bank and Gaza, and no Palestinians were allowed to visit Jerusalem. A far-reaching network of military checkpoints and fortified borders enforced the prohibitions on Palestinians moving between Palestinian cities inside the occupied territory. To Palestinians, the result was claustrophobic. To visit relatives, see friends, bring goods to market, harvest crops, get to university, get to the hospital, and commute between home and work became impossible or extremely time-consuming. The building of a Palestinian infrastructure was prevented, unemployment grew and the Palestinian enclaves became dependent on foreign aid, which in turn was dependent on Israeli goodwill in permitting the movement of goods to and from the Palestinian mini-enclaves. The outside world saw perhaps only a small amount of this. Many believed that it was only a matter of time before a Palestinian state would be declared. The overall situation created tension, and frustration in the Palestinian community, which was released in the second Intifada, which began in September 2000.

The popular uprising aiming at "shaking off" (*intifada*) the Israeli occupation involved general strikes, demonstrations, boycotts, armed attacks, and Palestinian youth challenging with slingshots and stones Israeli soldiers in their tanks and armored vehicles. Israel sought to overcome the insurgency through military interventions, targeted assassinations, arrests, and curfews. When the anti-colonial uprising did not show signs of ceasing, the Israeli military's Operation Defensive Shield was initiated in the spring of 2002 with a series of massive military assaults on Palestinian towns and villages. The presidential residence, along with government buildings, office complexes, shopping centers, residential neighborhoods, theaters, community centers, schools, small businesses, and industries, were literally reduced to rubble by tanks, attack aircraft, helicopters, bulldozers, missiles, rockets, and invasion forces. Israel is one of the world's strongest, best-equipped, and best-trained military powers. The Palestinian militias, with their handguns and homemade rockets, were fighting a losing battle. According to the Israeli human rights organization B'Tselem (2008), between September 2000 and September 2008, the Israeli military killed 4,828 Palestinians, including 954 children, 2,229 non-combatants, and 871 people whose role as combatants (for example, those who threw stones) is debatable. During the same period, 1,061 Israelis were killed, including 123 children and 726 civilians, a category that encompasses settlers, armed or unarmed. About half of the Israeli victims were killed in Palestinian suicide attacks.

Hence, suicide attacks/martyrdom operations were at the time one of the most lethal methods of Palestinian resistance. One reason is the absence of militarily advanced weapons in a battle against an militarily well-equipped enemy. As one of the Palestinian resistance fighters I talked with in Nablus in February 2003, put it:

> The Israelis are afraid of our martyrs. But we can swap: give us your Apaches [attack helicopters], F-16s [attack aircraft], Merkavas [tanks] and APCs [armored vehicles] and you can get our stones, slingshots and explosive belts. Then we can hunt your children, demolish your cities and make the world to feel sorry for us when you blow yourselves in the air.

The prevailing media representation is of Palestinian suicide attacks carried out by frustrated young male Islamists from the underclass. This image stands in sharp contradiction to the empirical data I collected during field studies in the West Bank in 2002 and 2003. This material includes 207 people who used their lives as weapons, either as human bombs or by conducting attacks with other weapons, without viable prospects of escaping alive. The dominant age group was 20–29 years, with the larger portion being older than 25. The age group of 30–39 years was larger (29 individuals) than the under-20 bracket (21 individuals). Nine people were between 40 and 49 years, and five people were 50 years or older. Although most were men, there are six women in the data. It is difficult to determine what percentage were Islamists, but some guidance can be found using the organizations that took credit for the attack. Nearly half of the attacks were carried out with the support of Hamas or Islamic Jihad, the remainder were secular, socialist, or nationalist, national liberation organizations. The attacks were carried out not only by men or women from the lower classes, but by people of every possible class background. Judged from letters and testimonies left behind, a majority of 72 percent cast their action in terms of national liberation, or personal retaliation (17 percent). Most subjects who sacrificed their lives had a relative or friend killed by the Israeli military, or had witnessed a fatal Israeli military attack, which had made the occupation personal.

These findings are consistent with other research. Robert J. Brym and Bader Ajaj (2006) investigated the background and rationale for 138 suicide attacks between 2000 and 2005. They narrowly defined this category as attacks with explosives, but no firearms or vehicles. They found that 82 percent of the attacks were reactive, that is, explicitly cast as a "response" to an Israeli aggression. In terms of personal motives, messages left by 101 of the subjects were dominated by nationalist themes, usually phrased as retaliation for Israeli aggression against Palestine (46 percent). This was followed in numbers by personal retribution for the murder of a relative or friend (23 percent), while religious motivations were only expressed in 2 percent of messages. In terms of official statements announced by the organizations that claimed responsibility for the attacks, nationalism again dominated (37 percent), followed by retaliation for Israeli attacks against the organization or its representatives (22 percent). Only 7 percent claimed religious motives.

In the Palestinian culture of resistance, martyrs who chose to sacrifice their life were attributed a heroic status. News of a deed, broadcast through television, radio, newspapers, and weblogs, attracted a wide audience. Homemade video productions with the dead martyr's farewell greetings, ghastly scenes showing the bloody remains of Palestinian victims of Israeli military assaults, slain children, crying mothers, and demolished houses, followed by news clips from television detailing the lethal outcome of the martyr's attack on the enemy, were sold in local video stores. Creative filmmakers composed "best of" martyr operations, sometimes with themes such as martyrs from specific areas or cities, or martyrs from individual national liberation organizations. Heroic tales were constructed, often including details about how a particular operation occurred; how the brave—alone or in pairs—crossed the Israeli border, how they disguised themselves, and how they managed to get through into enemy territory and achieve their goal. These narratives became part of contemporary folklore. Martyr posters in chromatic colors were plastered on the walls of the city. Portraits of the sacrificing warrior heroes were depicted against backdrops of killed Palestinian children, Israeli military, the Al-Aqsa Mosque, or the general havoc of the martyrdom operation. Other themes included the martyr's portrait inserted in romanticized scenes of nature's beauty, with horses galloping in green pastures, lush vegetation, rivers, and beaches. The motif of the sea had a particular impact in Nablus. From the rooftops and surrounding hills of Nablus, one could see the ocean; so close, yet impossible to reach as it was on the other side of the border in what is now Israel. The sea could be seen, but never felt: it beckoned alongside freedom. A martyr operation received extra attention in the martyr's village or hometown. Armed militiamen fired salutes of respect, the street in which the martyr lived may be renamed in his honor by local graffiti artists, medallions with the hero's portrait were sold out quickly, and worn with sad pride by relatives and friends. Relatives, neighbors, and representatives of the city's important families and political factions came to give their homage and condolences.

Taken together, the news reports, martyr posters, videos, and medallions, heroic tales, lyrics, and graffiti, mourning rituals, and salutes of respect, provided new potential martyrs with information of what would happen if they chose to sacrifice their lives in the asymmetrical war of national resistance. In the confrontation with a militarily superior enemy, martyr operations provided a concrete opportunity for those who desired to *do* something. It was a method that obviously terrorized the dominant power, a path for the brave who wanted to inscribe their names in the annals of national liberation. As the principal of a school in Ramallah put it: "As a living person here, you're nothing. As a dead person you can become a hero, at least for a moment" (Reuter 2004: 167). During this particular time, the Palestinian militias did not need to seek for recruits as they had the pick of the crop. Palestinians volunteered to such an extent that the militias had to refuse most of the hopeful prospects. "People, including young people, need to feel respected," stressed Eyad el Sarraj, Palestinian psychiatrist in Gaza:

> They want status within their society. Today the martyr is glorified. The martyr for them is the power of the people, the power to take revenge on behalf of the victims. They have all these romantic notions. They see the martyr as courageously sacrificing himself or herself for the sake of everyone, as a symbol of the struggle for freedom, because this is what these people are fighting for. (2002)

Their Suicide Terrorists, Our Heroes

To give one's life for the lives of others and for the sake of freedom has long been one of humanity's most noble acts. In a letter written in 1864 to Mrs. Lydia Bixby of Boston, who lost five sons in the Civil War, Abraham Lincoln wrote the famous words: "I pray that our Heavenly Father may assuage the anguish of your bereavement, and leave you only the cherished memory of the loved and lost, and the solemn pride that must be yours to have laid so costly a sacrifice upon the altar of freedom." The final words are carved in relief on the statue of Lady Columbia at the National Memorial Cemetery of the Pacific in Honolulu, dedicated to the soldiers who sacrificed their lives for the nation during World War II, Korea, and Vietnam, and one of Hawaii's more popular tourist attractions with millions of visitors each year. Here, Lincoln's words speak to the dead heroes and their families: "The genuine pride you must feel at having made such a costly sacrifice on the altar of freedom." Lincoln's Bixby letter is key to Steven Spielberg's war epic *Saving Private Ryan* (1998), where a group of US soldiers led by Captain John H. Miller (Tom Hanks) go deep behind German lines in Normandy to bring home Private James Ryan (Matt Damon), who has lost all his brothers in World War II. When the soldiers—after gruesome hardships and severe losses—finally find Ryan, he is with a decimated squad that has been tasked with defending a bridge from the approaching Germans. He refuses to return home: "You can tell my mother that when you found me, I was with the only brothers I had left. And that there was no way I was deserting them. I think she'd understand that." Realizing that Ryan will not leave the bridge, the rescue team joins Ryan and his men in the unequal struggle against the Germans. When air support finally arrives, all but Ryan and Miller have died. "James, earn this," says a shot, bleeding and dying Miller to Ryan a moment before he too dies, "earn it." While the narrator reads Lincoln's letter, the film shifts from past to present. An aged Ryan walks slowly through the memorial cemetery's rows of white crosses alongside his wife, children, and grandchildren who symbolize the Americans who could live thanks to the patriotic soldiers' sacrifices. Ryan kneels before the cross that bears Miller's name. "Every day I think about what you said to me that day on the bridge." Ryan whispered, his voice trembling. "I tried to live my life the best that I could. I hope that was enough. I hope that, at least in your eyes, I've earned what all of you have done for me." Ryan gets up on his feet, stands back and salutes. He turns, moving slowly towards his family, and the film fades out into a giant American flag proudly flying in the wind as testimony to all those who sacrificed their lives on the altar of freedom. *Saving Private Ryan* was nominated for eleven Oscars and became the blockbuster of 1998, collecting $480 million globally in its first year of release. Spielberg's epic is only one of many films that portray the male warrior hero who sacrifices his life for the greater good. The theme recurs in *Band of Brothers*, *300*, *Armageddon*, *Independence Day*, *Inglourious Basterds*, and other war epics that won a worldwide audience of beating hearts, not only in the US, but also in Palestine. In light of the long tradition of these films, it seems strange that we do not recognize the Palestinians who put their precious sacrifice on the altar of freedom in the same way. Why is that?

In an open letter to George W. Bush, former Lebanese Prime Minister Selim el-Hoss asked, "Those deplorable suicidal operations which you brand as terrorism, have they not ever for a moment prompted you to ask yourself the question: why would a young boy or girl be willing to sacrifice himself or herself with utter peace of mind and full determination?" Can it really be that we do not understand? A Hezbollah member interviewed by anthropologist Ghassan Hage (2003) during fieldwork in southern Lebanon could not possibly imagine that this was the case:

> The Americans pretend not to understand the suicide bombers and consider them evil. But I am sure they do. As usual, they are hypocrites. What is so strange about saying: "I am not going to let you rob me of all my humanity and all my will?" What is so strange about saying: "I'd rather kill you on my own terms and kill myself with you rather than be led to my death like a sheep on your own terms?" I know that the Americans fully understand this because this is exactly what they were celebrating about the guy who downed the Philadelphia flight on September 11, the one where the hijackers failed to hit their target. Isn't that exactly what he must have said when he decided to kill himself and everyone else by bringing the plane down? Didn't he say to those hijacking him: "I'd rather kill you on my own terms and kill myself with you rather than be led to my death like a sheep on your own terms?"

This Hezbollah member referred to the fourth suicide attack on September 11, when a number of the passengers on Flight 93 banded to fight the hijackers. This caused the plane, which was probably on the way to the White House or Capitol Hill, to crash outside Shanksville, Pennsylvania, killing the hijackers and all other passengers. As Susan Faludi (2008: 69) notes, this incident was perfect for mythmaking, due to the facts of what actually happened being so scant. In a "ferocious assault," *Newsweek* wrote, a "band of patriots came together to defy death and save a symbol of freedom." In *Heroes: 50 Stories of the American Spirit*, Lenore Skomal (2002: 12) states that "as much as the terrorists had meticulously planned their suicide mission, they could never have foreseen the problems they'd encounter trying to maintain control on a flight carrying what you have to concede was God's All-Star Team." Congress instituted the Honoring the Passengers and Crew of United Flight 93 Act to award medals of honor to the heroes who sacrificed their lives to inflicting defeat upon an enemy. A national memorial was built on the site where the plane crashed, and Newark Airport, from where Flight 93 took off, was renamed Newark Liberty Airport. Although we cannot determine exactly what happened during the drama onboard of Flight 93 with absolute certainty, we can note that the passengers who braved the hijackers are said to have performed a suicide attack under another name: they were patriots who sacrificed their lives on the altar of freedom. To the Hezbollah member, the analogy between the hijacked plane and occupied Palestine was as obvious as his amazement that Americans did not seem to recognize as heroes the Palestinian braves who sacrificed their lives to attack the occupying power that has taken control of their country and threatened to completely devastate their nation.

Hereby, we have returned to the issue raised in the introduction: the horror we feel in the face of the suicide bomber figure. Why do we seem to become more upset by a suicide attack that ends ten lives than by an airborne bomb attack that ends hundreds of lives? It cannot reasonably be because the act is directed against civilians. Civilian casualties are not a prerequisite for a suicide attack; they can be strictly directed at military targets and still keep the same name. Conversely, history shows that airborne bombardier attacks do not only kill soldiers, but may well harvest civilian lives. While a suicide attack might kill ten people in a pizzeria, an airborne bomb attack may kill as many in the pizzeria and reduce the whole city block to rubble without arousing the same amount of horror. If it is not about civilian casualties, why are the former seen as a terrifying barbarian, and the latter a distinguished man of honor, a war hero?

As detailed by Edward Said (1978), the Orientalist knowledge tradition produces the Oriental as a distinct species by "nature" set apart from universal man. The essentialized dichotomy of them and us, East and West, Muslims and normal people, recurs in a series of opposites in which the "us" of the speaking subject is given meaning by being contrasted to an imagined "them"—irrational/rational, barbarian/civilized, underdeveloped/developed, despotic/democratic, unfree/free—in a multiplicative chain of binary oppositions. Although Islam has been one of Europe's many religions for more than thirteen hundred years, and Muslims have been active contributors to the history we call "Western," the doctrine of essentialized difference makes it possible to construe "Muslims" as a collective community "by nature" alien to and distinct from "Westerners." From this point of departure, cultural racist theories of antagonistic identities in terms of a "clash of civilization" may be formulated, in which two ontologically distinct beings are pitted against each other (Gardell 2010). Since the figure of the Oriental is not perceived of as an autonomous subject acting on high moral grounds, but as an irrational barbarian, it becomes impossible to think "hero who sacrificed his life on the altar of freedom" of a Palestinian. Conversely, it becomes impossible to think "crazy, sexually frustrated suicide terrorist" about Samson, Colin P. Kelly, Private Ryan, and the heroes of Flight 93. A Palestinian becomes a suicide bomber because he is Oriental: the value of the act is determined by the perceived nature of the actor.

"There is a world of difference between Western values and Muslim ones," declared Raphael Israeli (2003: 13) in his study of suicide terrorism: "One of the more puzzling aspects of Islamic terrorism, which has almost no parallels in other cultures, is the readiness of the perpetrators to blow themselves up in the process of destroying the enemy" (ibid.: 71), a phenomenon Israeli terms "*islamikaze*." Israeli sees the rationale as uniquely Islamic, explicable only with reference to the fact that the perpetrators are Muslims, construed as an imagined collective set apart from universal man. To these Muslims, "Paradise is unexpectedly depicted in exciting, plastic, worldly, and pleasurable terms, not in some vague spiritual entity worthy of mystics and saints of other traditions. Sex and wine, the two foremost taboos in traditional Islamic society, are exalted," Israeli claims, "as accessible and permissible in unlimited quantities" (ibid.: 88). Moreover, far from applauding the martyrs as heroes who sacrificed their lives on the altar of freedom, their families adore them because they believe that they "fulfil a societal-family ideal, by preparing the grounds in Paradise for the whole family to follow: something that makes their act bearable, not to say desirable, for their loved and loving ones." Hence, Muslims blow themselves and others into pieces in order to drink alcohol and be sexually active in heaven. Now, the most remarkable is not Israeli's thesis, but the extent to which such a remarkable thesis has gained ground in Western conversations about the suicide terrorism phenomenon, which says a lot about the current standing of cultural racist thought. How we explain the problem of suicide attacks has implications for how the phenomenon should be addressed. If the problem is perceived to stem from a political situation, there must be a political solution. If the problem is caused by sexually frustrated religious fanatics who wish to go to heaven, the security apparatus may be entrusted to protect us by eliminating the problem with extraordinary methods. Hence the Israeli Police Minister Gideon Ezra's proposal to expand collective punishment by killing all the relatives of the suicide bombers, and desecrating their remains by burying them in pig blood and pig hides (Reuter 2004: 198).

An additional explanation for the horror caused by a suicide attack concerns Western notions of civilized killing in warfare. Since the dawn of Europe's colonial expansion, Western wars in Africa, Asia, and the Americas—typically referred to in terms of civilization's war against barbarism—has been characterized by superior military technology resulting in minimal losses. In the battle of Omdurman in 1898, to take one example, British colonial troops used the portable Maxim Gun, which was the world's first fully automatic, water-cooled machine gun that could fire 500–600 rounds per minute. "The whole face of the slope became black with swarming savages," wrote war correspondent Winston Churchill, referring to the sight of Sudanese warriors marching towards the colonial army with pride, spears, and swords. There was never any danger:

> The infantry fired steadily and stolidly, without hurry or excitement, for the enemy were far away and the officers careful. Besides, the soldiers were interested in the work and took great pains. The empty cartridge-cases, tinkling to the ground, formed a small but growing heap beside each man. And all the time out on the plain on the other side bullets were shearing through flesh, smashing and splintering bone; blood spouted from terrible wounds; valiant men were struggling on through a hell of whistling metal, exploding shells, and spurting dust—suffering, despairing, dying. Such was the first phase of the battle of Omdurman. (Churchill 1902: 226)

In this battle, 22,000 Sudanese were slaughtered. The Colonial Army lost 48 men. With the exception of World War II battles against Japan, the technological upper hand of the Western military in the wars against Oriental forces has persisted. In the first Iraq war, in January 1991, the US military tested new generations of advanced long-range missiles, combat helicopters, attack aircraft, bombers, night bombers, warships, and armored vehicles against the Iraqi Army's outdated tanks, old pieces of artillery and ground troops. Up to 200,000 Iraqi soldiers and 100,000 Iraqi civilians died. The United States lost 148 men, a quarter of whom were their own troops shot in error. The other 27 states of the US-led Coalition lost a total of 89 soldiers, accidents included (Hiro 2003; Gardell 2005; Fisk 2005).

Today, the "civilized world" has reached a stage of military-technological development that makes it possible to conceive of war without personal sacrifice, and without "us" necessarily having to face its bloodier aspects. "We" kill "the other" from thousands of meters away, or from air-conditioned control rooms located hundreds of miles from the targeted site, with coffee in paper cups, in front of flashing computer screens. War is converted into computer games, which may certainly be exciting, challenging, and requiring of skill, but distanced from the realities of blood, intestines, brain matter, horror, grief, and devastation on the ground. This means that "we" have begun to imagine war in terms of clinical operations in which we run as little risk of lethal damage as a surgeon at the university hospital. Suicide attacks are diametrically opposite. The stake is exactly their own life. The method appears from this perspective as highly uncivilized, unsophisticated, retrograde, and, yes, *barbaric*. This impression is highlighted by the low-tech killing with simple explosives wrapped around the body, or homemade bombs primed in utility vehicles, bicycles, cars, old trucks without either armor or GPS, and the brutal directness of the deed in which the line of separation between killing and death collapses. There are no clinical features, no surgical precision, no spacing between the executioner and the victim. On the contrary, the remains of the perpetrator are mixed with those of the victims, a reality that seems rather remote from the control rooms and computer screens in the high-tech war where killing is separated from death.

The superiority of Western military technology in combination with discourses of Orientalism and the experience of colonial history in which the "we" of the speaking subject are always colonizing the other, creates the gap that separates "their" martyrs from "our" heroes, despite the common tradition from which we both spring. We share the same hyper-masculine romantic stories, the same heroic poetry, and the same foundational ideal that the only way to be human is to face death rather than unfreedom.

Conclusion

This common tradition means that Westerners too celebrate anti-colonial self-sacrificing heroism, at least in fiction. In the Oscar-winning *Independence Day*, a 1996 box-office success that drew in $816 million in revenue worldwide, and was widely popular in Palestine, the Earth is threatened by an alien high-tech civilization from outer space who arrive with their fleet aboard a giant mothership aiming to colonize the planet. The technologically superior colonizers destroy a number of the world's major cities, and invasion is imminent. The increasingly desperate resistance movement is coordinated by the United States, and culminates on July 4. "[O]nce again we'll be fighting for our freedom," says President Thomas J. Whitmore (Bill Pullman):

> We are fighting for our right to live. To exist. And should we win the day, the Fourth of July will no longer be known as an American holiday, but as the day the world declared

> in one voice: "We will not go quietly into the night!" We will not vanish without a fight! Today we celebrate our Independence Day!

David Levinson (Jeff Goldblum) and Steven Hiller (Will Smith) manage to plant a virus in the computer running the force-field that protects the colonial mothership. "All we can do now," says Levinson, "is to pray to God." A division of attack aircraft led by President Whitmore launches a furious counterattack. "Payback's a bitch, ain't it?" shouts pilot Russell Casse (Randy Quaid), who had previously been abused by the aliens. The resistance movement wages an unequal struggle against the colonizers' military superiority. When the aliens prepare their most advanced weapon of mass destruction by opening a hatch in the mothership, Russel Casse realizes what he must do. He glances at the photograph of his three children. "Tell my kids I love them," he says to the control room on Earth. "Good luck, buddy," says the president, who realizes what Casse is going to do. "All right, you alien assholes!" roars Casse, "Up Yours!" and drives at full speed into the opened hatch in the spacecraft. The mothership explodes into a sea of fire. Back down on earth, an officer turns to Casse's eldest son who was following the drama from the control room monitors. "What your father did was very brave. You should be proud of him." The son smiles vaguely, looking the officer steadily in the eye, and says, "I am."

References

Andoni, Lamis (1997). "Searching for answers: Gaza's Suicide Bombers," *Journal of Palestine Studies*, XXVI(4): 33–45.

Axell, Albert and Hideaki Kase (2004). *Kamikaze: Japans självmordspiloter.* Lund: Historiska Media.

Ben-Naftali, Oma, Aeyal M. Gross and Karen Michaeli (2005). "Illegal Occupation: Framing the Occupied Territory," *Berkeley Journal of International Law*, 23(3): Article 2.

Brobryggarna (2008). "Fråga pastorn! Bibelfråga: Samson och Delila, Brobyggarna Kristen församling". Accessed October 28, 2008. At <http://www.crossnet.se/kyrkor/brobyggarna/200.simson.html>.

Brym, Robert J. and Ajaj Bader (2006). "Suicide Bombings as Strategy and Interaction: The Case of the Second Intifada," *Social Forces*, 84(4).

B'Tselem (2008). "Statistics", "Fatalities". Accessed October 28, 2008. At <http://www.btselem.org/English/Statistics/Casualties.asp>.

Churchill, Winston S. (1902 [1899]). *The River War. An Account of the Reconquest of the Sudan*. London: Longman.
"Eliasson: Släpp soldaten fri" (Eliasson: Release the Soldier), *SvT*, June 28.
Faludi, Susan (2008). *The Terror Dream: Myth and Misogyny in an Insecure America*. New York: Picador.
Fisk, Robert (2005). *The Great War For Civilisation; The Conquest of the Middle East*. London: Fourth Estate.
Gahrton, Per (2008). *Palestinas frihetskamp. Historia, analys och personliga iakttagelser* (Palestine's Liberation Struggle. History, Analysis and Personal Observations). Stockholm: Carlsson.
Gambetta, Diego (ed) (2006). *Making Sense of Suicide Missions*. New York: Oxford University Press
Gardell, Mattias (2005). *Bin Laden i våra hjärtan. Gobalisering och framväxten av politisk islam* ("Bin Laden in Our Hearts": Globalization and the Rise of Political Islam). Stockholm: Leopard.
— (2008). *Tortyrens återkomst* (The Return of Torture). Stockholm: Leopard.
— (2010). *Islamofobi* (Islamphobia). Stockholm: Leopard.
Gunnarsson, Bo (2007). "'Kamikaze-missionär' mördad av talibaner" (Kamikaze Missionary Killed by Taliban), *Aftonbladet*, July 26.
Hafez, Mohammed M. (2007). *Suicide Bombers in Iraq: The Strategy and Ideology of Martyrdom*. Washington, DC: United States Institute of Peace Press.
Hage, Ghassan (2003). "'Comes a Time We Are All Enthusiasm': Understanding Palestinian Suicide Bombers in Times of Exighophobia," *Public Culture*, 15(1): 65–89.
Hersh, Seymour M. (1991). *The Samson Option. Israel's Nuclear Arsenal and American Foreign Policy*. New York: Random House.
Hiro, Dilip (2003). *Desert Shield to Desert Storm: The Second Gulf War*. Lincoln, NE: iuniverse.
Home of Heroes (2012). Accessed October 28, 2008. At<www.homeofheroes.com>.
Israeli, Raphael (2003). *Islamikaze. Manifestations of Islamic Martyrology*. London: Frank Cass.
Lindsay, Hal (2007). "The Samson Option," *Standing With Israel*, July 14.
Pape, Robert A. (2003). "The Strategic Logic of Suicide Terrorism," *The American Political Science Review*, 97(3): 343–61.
— (2006). *Dying to Win: The Strategic Logic of Suicide Terrorism*. New York: Random House.
Pedahzur, Ami (2005). *Suicide Terrorism*. Cambridge: Polity.

Philo, Greg and Mike Berry (2004). *Bad News From Israel*. London: Pluto Press.
Reuter, Christoph (2004). *My Life Is a Weapon: A Modern History of Suicide Bombing*. Princeton, NJ: Princeton University Press.
RWB (Reporters Without Borders) (2003). *Israel/Palestine: The Black Book*. London: Pluto Press.
Said, Edward (1978). *Orientalism*. New York: Pantheon Books.
— (1995). *The Politics of Dispossession: The Struggle for Palestinian Self-Determination*. New York: Vintage Books.
— (1996). *Peace And Its Discontents: Essays on Palestine in the Middle East Peace Process*. New York: Vintage Books.
— (2001). *The End of the Peace Process: Oslo and After*. New York: Vintage Books.
Sarraj, Eyad el (2002). "Suicide Bombers: Dignity, Despair, and the Need for Hope," *Journal of Palestine Studies*, 124, Summer.
Skomal, Lenore (2002). *Heroes: 50 Stories Of The American Spirit*. Philadelphia, PA: Running Press Book.
Tamimi, Azzam (2007). *Hamas. A History from Within*. Northampton, MA: Olive Branch Press.

Films

300 (2007). Zack Snyder (dir.), Warner Bros. and Legendary Pictures, 117 min.
Armageddon (1998). Michael Bay (dir.), Touchstone Pictures, 150 min.
Gekkou no Natsu (Summer of the Moonlight Sonata) (1993). Seijiro Koyama (dir.), Pony Canyon, 111 min.
Hotaru (Firefly) (2001). Yasuo Furuhata (dir.), Toei, 114 min.
Independence Day (1996). Roland Emmerich (dir.), 20th Century Fox, 145 min.
Pearl Harbor (2001). Michael Bay (dir.), Touchstone Pictures and Buena Vista International, 183 min.
Saving Private Ryan (1998). Steven Spielberg (dir.), DreamWorks and Paramount Pictures, 170 min.
Thirty Seconds over Tokyo (1944). Mervyn LeRoy (dir.), MGM, 138 min.

Other

S 1434 Honoring the Passengers and Crew of United Flight 93 Act of 2001, In the Senate of the United States, 107th Congress, 1st Session, September 19, 2001.

HR 3054 True American Heroes Act, In the House of the United States, 107th Congress, 1st Session, October 5, 2001.

Chapter 9

Burning Buddhists: Self-Immolation as Political Protest[1]

Katarina Plank

Introduction

On the morning of January 8, 2012, the Buddhist monk Sonam Wangyal, also known as Lama Sobha, prepared to end his life by self-immolation. Living at a monastery in Darlag county, Golog Tibetan Autonomous Prefecture, Qinghai (in the Tibetan area of Amdo), Lama Sobha was a well-respected and popular *tulku* (reincarnated teacher). That morning, he recorded a message to explain the purpose of his sacrifice, and put the tape in a pocket in his monk's robe. He then went to a hill where he lit incense, said prayers and distributed leaflets in which he explained that his self-sacrifice was a selfless act: not for his own glory, but for the people of Tibet and the country's future. He proceeded to the police station in Darlag and whilst outside the building is reported to have drunk kerosene and then poured the liquid over himself before setting himself on fire. Dressed in his maroon-colored monk's robe, he burned to death in front of the police station.[2]

Lama Sobha was thus the first *tulku* to sacrifice his own life in a fiery political protest. He was not, however, the first Tibetan to do so, but his suicide was one in a series of many self-immolations which began in 2009 and escalated in 2011 and 2012 to the point that even experts on Tibet were surprised by the extent of the sacrifices. Between March 2011 and November 2013, over 120 Tibetans have self-immolated, as reported by the International Campaign for Tibet.

---

1 An earlier version of this chapter was published as Katarina Plank, "Living Torches of Tibet—Religious and Political Implications of the Recent Self-Immolations," *Journal of Religion and Violence*, 1(3) (2013): 343–62.

2 The description is based on information reported by Radio Free Asia on January 9, 2012, and from the International Campaign for Tibet report, "Harrowing images and last message from Tibet of first lama to self-immolate," February 1, 2012 <https://www.savetibet.org/harrowing-images-and-last-message-from-tibet-of-first-lama-to-self-immolate>.

Although self-immolation has gained media attention, only a minority of cases have been reported in the global media.

The recent wave of self-immolations mark a new development in the Tibetan nationalist struggle, as auto-cremations have historically never been part of Tibetan culture and religion, neither as a part of devotional practices nor as political protest. How is it that the self-immolations have escalated since 2011—how were they at all possible, and what could have triggered them? Was it the Arab Spring, the revolutionary wave of demonstrations in Arab countries that began with a self-immolation in Tunisia in December 2010, that served as a model? Or did the Tibetan self-immolators draw inspiration from Vietnamese monk Thich Quang Duc, who in 1963 was the first to use auto-cremation as political protest? Were there religious connections? Could the deaths be explained by other cultural, historical, geographical or political events? Religion has been employed by researchers to help explain the self-immolations, but the responses differed as to what degree religion had explanatory value.[3] Some believe that self-immolation could not be linked to Tibetan Buddhism simply because the human torches were Tibetan monks and nuns. Shakya states: "Self-immolation as a form of protest is not intrinsically a Buddhist act any more than suicide bombing is an Islamic act. What links the current incidents to religion is that most of the Tibetans who have committed self-immolation have been monks or nuns" (Shakya 2012). However, others, such as Craig, argued that Tibetan Buddhism plays an important role in understanding how these actions are meaningful in a Tibetan context; that they can be seen as an altruistic healing practice in which the individual, by his or her actions, believes they can affect the surrounding environment and how this act can also be understood as a manifestation of a *bodhisattva* ideal, in which one's own death becomes a selfless act for the good of others (Craig 2012).

This chapter will trace the genealogy of self-immolation through the Buddhist textual and ritual heritage that led to the prototypical act of burning oneself to death as a political protest—the auto-cremation of the Vietnamese Buddhist monk Thich Quang Duc in 1963—and how this in turn has inspired others to use self-immolation for political purposes. Self-immolations appear clustered in time and space, and this important aspect makes it relevant to include self-immolation when discussing suicide cults, even though the act in itself is usually individual and not collective.

---

[3] In the spring of 2012, a special issue of the online journal *Cultural Anthropology* was compiled in which self-immolation was discussed by researchers on Tibet from various scientific disciplines. Refer to this issue for more detailed comments. See McGranahan and Litzinger (2012).

This chapter is based on secondary sources, principally reports from journalists and exile Tibetan networks. Since access to primary sources (in the form of interviews with surviving self-immolators and eyewitnesses) is lacking, the chapter focuses on contextualizing self-immolations in Tibet by analyzing Lama Sobha's posthumous message, and tracking the specific Buddhist elements that have historically contributed to the use of auto-cremation as a political protest.

Self-immolation: Sacrificing One's Own Body for a Greater Cause

Lama Sobha's auto-cremation contains several elements typical of political self-immolation: a sacrifice of oneself through suicide for a greater cause, public display, and an action that has no intention of harming anyone else. Self-immolation as political protest has a distinct religious character, since it is the body that is sacrificed. An important aspect that distinguishes self-immolations from other political suicides is that the intentional killing of oneself is done without harming others. This non-violent aspect differentiates self-immolations from other political suicides. Unlike suicide bombers, whose bodies become weapons, self-immolators do not inflict physical or material harm on people or buildings (Biggs 2005: 173). As an act of protest, self-immolations aim to be public in at least one of two ways: the act occurs in a public place where it is witnessed by onlookers, or a message is left behind addressed to politicians or to the public (ibid.: 175).

Self-immolation has religious connotations, as "immolate" means sacrifice and, according to the *Concise Oxford Dictionary of English Etymology*, it originates from the Latin word *immolatus* (past participle of *immolare* "to sprinkle with sacrificial meal", from *in-* (upon) and *mola* (meal). Immolation is thus an act of sacrificial offering, and self-immolation therefore means a sacrificial offering of oneself. Since the 1960s, the term "self-immolation" has had political overtones. Above all, it has come to be associated with death by fire after the Vietnamese monk Thich Quang Duc set himself alight during the Vietnam War (see below in the section "The Prototype of Auto-cremation as Political Protest—the Death of Thich Quang Duc"). Yet self-immolation does not necessarily include a fiery death; Biggs's (2005) thorough analysis of reported self-immolations between 1963 and 2002 shows that other methods of self-sacrifice include jumping from tall buildings or ingesting poison. Benn distinguishes between auto-cremation and self-immolation, stating that the latter is a wider set of religious practices in which the body is given as a gift (Benn 2007). I follow Benn's distinction in this chapter to establish how auto-cremation is part of the wider theme of Buddhist self-immolation, mindful that distinction differs from popular conceptualizations where associations of death by fire have become linked to self-immolation.

Self-immolation as a political protest need not necessarily be a solitary act: two or more individuals can coordinate their sacrifices. Biggs notes that self-immolations are distinct actions that distinguish themselves from suicides and martyrdoms. Martyrdom may resemble self-immolation, in that death is faced voluntarily, usually at the hands of another (as in the case of the Archbishop Romero of El Salvador, who died in 1980 after denouncing military repression); however, it is not the same as suicide. Nor can the Hindu form of marital sacrifice, *sati*, in which a widow burns to death on her husband's pyre, be termed self-immolation as it lacks a collective dimension. Personal suicides often have private reasons and they are rarely carried out for a collective cause. Suicide in a cult can be a collective action, but if believers seek to achieve a more exalted existence in the afterlife instead of bringing about political change, this also cannot be included in the definition of self-immolation. Hunger strikes, however, do resemble self-immolation, even though few actually starve themselves to death (Biggs 2005: 174).

Politically motivated self-immolations are grouped in both space and time and they are more common in Buddhist and Hindu contexts. The individual's personal religiosity seems not to play a role, whereas the individual's religious affiliation does: 'What matters is the proportion of Hindus and Buddhists. Both of these are positively correlated with the rate of self-immolations, whereas the proportions of Christians and Muslims are not' (ibid.: 186). In his review of 553 politically motivated self-immolations between 1963 and 2002, Biggs found no reports of self-immolations in Africa or the Middle East. Instead, 75 per cent of Biggs' material included reports of self-immolations in Asia and, specifically, India, Vietnam, and South Korea. A quarter of the reports came from cases in Europe and North America.

The significant difference between Indic religions (Hindu, Jain, and Buddhist) and Abrahamic religions (Jewish, Christian, and Islamic), Biggs argues, can be traced both to the scriptures as well as to practices regarding the handling of dead bodies. Hindu and Buddhist texts contain several examples of self-immolations and, as will be shown, sacrifice of the body or a part of the body is an established form of devotional practice in some East Asian branches of Buddhist tradition. The treatment of dead bodies also plays an important role in understanding the differences in Abrahamic and Indic religions. Fire is a central component of death practices and burning evokes reverence among Buddhists and Hindus:

> Cremation is deeply rooted in Indic religion. By extension, death by fire seems sacred—in a way that is still utterly repugnant in the West, despite the recent importation of cremation ... Whatever the precise effect of religious tradition, the difference between the Semitic West and the Indic East remains inescapable. (Ibid.: 187)

However, it is not only cremation in itself, but also beliefs about death and what follows that have led to diametrically different practices linked to a shared eschatology. The belief in the resurrection of the dead body at the end of the world—shared by Abrahamic religions—necessitates an intact body and thus the burial of the whole body.

Self-immolation seems to be a phenomenon that comes in waves. It is more likely that an individual chooses to sacrifice him- or herself if someone else has already done so (ibid.: 188). This pattern also emerges clearly in the self-immolations in Tibet, where the burning Buddhists inspire other Buddhists to burn themselves to death.

Self-immolations in Tibet

Self-immolation as an act of political protest is a new phenomenon in Tibet, and did not occur inside the country before 2009. This fact contributed to experts on Tibet being overwhelmed by the intensity of self-immolations that has taken place since 2011. Most auto-cremators have been male, and a large proportion come from Ngaba, in the northeastern region of Tibet (and the northwestern parts of Sichuan province). Several of the self-sacrifices have been by young monks or former monks connected to the Kirti monastery in Ngaba. In addition to these young men, nuns, laymen and laywomen have also burnt themselves in political protest, as well as the *tulku*, Lama Sobha, who was in his forties (McGranahan and Litzinger 2012). A few cases of self-immolations among Tibetans in exile have also been reported. The recent political history of Tibet has contributed to Tibetans making these sacrifices, which are probably not so much an attempt to appeal to the Chinese authorities to change its policy on Tibet, as a means to inspire Tibetans to continue their nationalist struggle.

Tibet (officially the Tibet Autonomous Region) is an ancient and autonomous region in western China. The country's inaccessible location in the Himalayas resulted in little contact with the outside world. This meant that Tibet could develop into a distinctive cultural and religious community marked by the Tibetan language and Tibetan Buddhism. This changed dramatically in 1950 when the People's Republic of China sought to incorporate Tibet.

The Chinese regarded Tibet as historically part of China and argued that the country needed to be released from oppression and poverty. The incorporation of Tibet has become a highly charged issue not only in Tibet, but also worldwide and among exiled Tibetans.

The first Tibetan to burn himself in a political protest was Thubten Ngodup, an exiled Tibetan who set himself on fire in New Delhi in 1998. The protest was a reaction to Indian police interrupting a hunger strike that had continued for 50 days against Chinese rule in Tibet. When police moved the hunger strikers to hospital, Thubten Ngodup set himself alight and died from his injuries two days later, according to the biography issued by the Canada Tibet Committee. His action was not followed by more auto-cremations; it would be more than ten years before the next Tibetan set fire to himself. This time it was in the aftermath of massive worldwide protests against the Chinese occupation of Tibet, which were triggered by the news that the 2008 Olympic Games were to be held in China. This also led to demonstrations inside Tibet, the largest protests since the Dalai Lama had escaped in 1959. As a result of the repressive response from Chinese authorities, a young monk called Tapey set fire to himself after prayer ceremonies were cancelled at the Kirti monastery in Ngaba county. The Ngaba region was initially the focus for auto-cremations, with a majority of the self-immolations taking place there (30 of 50 between March 2011 and August 2012), and many of those committing suicide being either young monks or former monks at Kirti monastery, according to the International Campaign for Tibet. Ngaba is in eastern Tibet, in the traditional regions of southern Amdo and northern Kham, an area located on both sides of the Sichuan-Qinghai border. Ngaba has been affected over the past decade by resettlement programs, where Chinese authorities have forced nomads to settle in small towns, which has resulted in widespread unemployment and social problems. This may be a contributing factor that explains why so many young monastics have set themselves on fire in these areas. According to Fischer:

> it is clear that the resettlements have been profoundly disruptive to local communities in this region and have added to the already existing pressures for young people to move out of farming and herding and into small towns where employment conditions are dire and there are worsening social problems. In this context of dislocation and alienation, it is understandable that the ordained—as vanguards of an indigenous moral order—might feel the need for extraordinary measures. (Fischer 2012)

The fact that so many self-immolations have occurred suggests that Tibetans have incorporated the notion of self-sacrifice in the nationalist struggle for a free

Tibet (Shakya 2012). There is no word in Tibetan expressing a sacrifice of one's own body for political purposes, and Tibetans are seeking new ways to integrate political meanings with existing terms:

> The closest term used recently for self-immolation in the sense of an act of sacrifice is "*rang srog blos btang*" (giving up one's life), but this does not have a sense of offering oneself for a greater cause. Nor does the Tibetan term *lus sbyin*, meaning "offering of the body," which is used for the Buddha's offering of his body as alms. The offering of the self as a religious gift holds no connotation of protest or disavowal. Thus, the search for new terminology reflects the shifting nature of political discourse among Tibetans and its permeation everywhere by the global language of protest and resistance. (Ibid.)

It is difficult to discern the individual motives for self-immolation, since few of the Tibetans who set themselves alight have left messages. It is, however, apparent that auto-cremation has become a communicative tool in a repressive environment where individuals have few other options. The lack of democratic influence distinguishes, nevertheless, the Tibetan protests from most other self-immolations, which usually take place in political environments with a higher degree of democracy, and where self-sacrifice is likely to have a greater opportunity to make an impact (Biggs 2005: 187). The Tibetan auto-cremations can therefore be understood primarily as a means of communication directed to other Tibetans to inspire them further in their nationalist struggle, rather than a statement addressed to the Chinese authorities. Thus it is possible to intepret the last message of Lama Sobha, which entails both a clear political and religious motive, and where his self-sacrifice is understood in tantric terms.

Lama Sobha's Last Message

According to Tibetan exile sources such as the International Campaign for Tibet, Lama Sobha left behind a final message to explain his. After Lama Sobha's death, the recording, approximately nine minutes in length, was transcribed and translated from Tibetan into English and Chinese, and published on the Internet in order to reach a global audience. Lama Sobha's self-sacrifice is framed in a ritual setting and with a soteriological interpretation of what he wanted to convey to the audience. In his message he switches between explaining his sacrificial act and reciting prayers to ensure the Dalai Lama a long life so that he can return to Tibet. His message is addressed to all those Tibetans who live within and outside Tibet's borders; it is not a message to the Chinese authorities to end their repressive rule.

This gives his self-sacrifice a nationalistic dimension, which he reinforced by presenting his action as a continuation of previous auto-cremations and expressing his solidarity with the earlier "heroes." He calls upon his fellow Tibetans to continue building a Tibetan nation, to continue protecting the Tibetan language and its culture, and to do this by being a devout Buddhist: "It is extremely important to genuinely practise Buddhist principles in order to benefit the Tibetan cause and also to lead all sentient beings towards the path of enlightenment." The message also indicates a Buddhist interpretive framing in which Lama Sobha explains his sacrifice as a form of tantric practice. Tantra is based on the notion of correspondences between one's own body and the universe, with the idea that one's body can be used to affect the surrounding world. In the message, Lama Sobha explains how his self-sacrifice is a way to transform darkness into light for the well-being of others. By sacrificing his own body and turning it into a burning torch, he wants to create a light that reaches and affects all living beings in a positive way so that they can be reborn in the western paradise of Amida Buddha, the Pure Land, and there reach Buddhahood.

He also states that he performs prayers for the Tibetan self-burners to lead them towards a more favorable spiritual development, as he points out that many of those who sacrifice themselves seem to have acted in anger. The karma doctrine, which teaches that the intention of a person's behavior will have consequences and affect the individual even in future lives, plays a crucial role in understanding why it is important for Lama Sobha to help people who died in a state of anger. Greed, hatred, and delusion are considered to be the foundations of negative karma and thereby shape the karmic repercussions in an adverse way. It was also important for Lama Sobha to clarify the intent of his own actions: that he acts selflessly with no aspirations of personal glory, and that he dedicates the sacrifice to the Dalai Lama and other lamas who are spiritual teachers in his tradition. This is especially important, since suicide is a controversial issue among Buddhists.

Additionally, Lama Sobha frames his sacrifice in relation to a heritage that indicates that he is aware of how the practice of self-immolation is legitimized in Buddhist textual tradition. Lama Sobha makes a direct reference to a *jataka* story, a well-known and often retold story of how the future Buddha, in one of his previous lives as Prince Mahasattva, meets a tigress with five newborn cubs. The *bodhisattva* sees they are emaciated and so hungry that there is a risk they will eat each other out of desperation. In order to prevent an act of matricide and infanticide (which the doctrine of karma considers to be the most serious negative actions one can perform), Mahasattva throws himself, in an act of compassion, off a cliff offering his body as food for the tigers. By referring to this story, Lama Sobha shows that his sacrifice is linked to wider Buddhist practices where the body is seen as a gift; practices found in both textual sources and documented historical practice.

The Gift of the Body in Buddhist Literature

The tale of Prince Mahasattva is the second story in the Tibetan collection *Mdo mdzangs blun*, better known as the "Sutra of the Wise and the Foolish." The collection includes stories of Buddha's previous lives (*jataka* tales) and other people's past lives (*avadanas*). The stories tell how the *bodhisattva* was reborn either as a human being or an animal. *Jataka* stories have many themes and can be found in both Indian and Greek legendary material, especially fables, but their framing is distinctly Buddhist and as such they have been significant for both monks and laypeople throughout history. One of the stories belonging to the theme of the body as a gift concerns a hare who offers himself as food and jumps into the fire to feed a tired traveler. Another tells of King Sivi, who plucked out his own eyes to give the gift of sight to a blind man.

Jataka tales are widespread throughout Buddhist countries. Ethnographic and art historical studies have shown that the *jatakas* are extremely popular to the present day in South and South East Asia (Appleton 2010: 8–19). In Sri Lanka, a gift of the body is considered meritorious, and appeals for blood and organ donations are often framed in Buddhist idioms; both doctors and patients refer to *jataka* stories to reinforce donations requests. Donations of corneas are especially supported by the story of King Sivi, mentioned above (ibid.: 152).

The theme of giving one's body or parts thereof as a gift is thus established in the *jataka* literature, and provides a shared heritage for both Theravada and Mahayana Buddhism, the latter of which Tibetan Buddhism is a part. Here, these gifts are seen as an expression of a generosity exceeding physical limits. The *jataka* stories tell how the *bodhisattva* cultivates the perfections, *paramita*, which will lead to Buddhahood. Stories that are concerned with how the *bodhisattva* sacrifices a part or all of their body have been described collectively as *dehadana* ("gift-of-the-body") stories, by Ohnuma (1998) because they can almost always be classified as an example of the perfection of generosity or giving (*danaparamita*). *Jataka* stories do not, however, serve as the prototype for the fiery death by auto-cremation. Instead, another important East Asian Buddhist text has become the model of self-immolation by fire: the *Lotus Sutra*.

There are many theories about what led to the emergence of Mahayana Buddhism somewhere between 200 BCE and 200 CE, and today most researchers agree that the movement arose as a literary cult at a time when many new texts were added to the Buddhist canon, new texts that were considered to be the original words of the Buddha. One of the most important of these texts was the Sutra of the Lotus Blossom of the Marvelous Dharma, or as it is usually called, the *Lotus Sutra*. This text has become one of the most important texts in eastern Asia, and is an object for veneration by Buddhists throughout China, Korea, Japan and other parts of Asia. When and where the *Lotus Sutra* was composed, and in what language, is unclear, but the first Chinese translation from Sanskrit was made around 255 CE. The *Lotus Sutra* has been translated into many Asian languages including Tibetan, Hsi-Hsia, Mongol, Manchu, Korean and Japanese, and is established as an important text in world literature (Watson 1993: ix–x).

The *Lotus Sutra* contains 28 chapters, combining prose and verse, and consists of an anthology of sermons, stories and devotional manuals. In its twenty-third chapter, "Former Affairs of the Bodhisattva Medicine King," is a passage that has come to serve as a template for the practice of auto-cremation. The Bodhisattva Medicine King, in one of his previous incarnations, is taught by the Buddha Pure and Bright Excellence of Sun and Moon (*Candrasuryavimalaprabhasasri*) about the *Lotus Sutra*. This inspired the *bodhisattva* to desire Buddhahood, which was possible by cultivating austerities. Therefore, he exercised diligently for 20,000 years, reached a high meditative level, and was thus satisfied with his performance. The *bodhisattva* then wished to make a sacrifice to Buddha Pure and Bright Excellence of Sun and Moon and to the *Lotus Sutra*, which enabled him to achieve the deep meditative level. He therefore meditated, and with the power achieved through his meditative state, flowers and incense appeared, which he then offered to the Buddha. However, he regarded this offering inferior in comparison to the sacrifice of his body. The text then describes the preparations for the great sacrifice, a passage that has come to give textual legitimacy for auto-cremation:

> When he had finished making this offering, he rose from his samadhi and thought to himself: Though I have employed my supernatural powers to make this offering to the Buddha, it is not as good as making an offering of my own body.
>
> Thereupon he swallowed different perfumes ... and he also drank the fragrant oil ... and doing this for a period of twelve hundred years. Anointing his body with fragrant oil, he appeared before the Buddha Sun Moon Pure Bright Virtue, wrapped his body in heavenly jewelled robes, poured fragrant oil over his head and, calling on his transcendental powers, set fire to his body. The glow shone forth, illuminating

> worlds equal in numbers to the sands of eighty million Ganges. The Buddhas in these worlds simultaneously spoke out in praise, saying: "Excellent, excellent, good man! This is true diligence. This is what is called a true Dharma offering ... Good man, this is called the foremost donation of all." ... The body of the bodhisattva burned for twelve hundred years, and when that period of time had passed, it at last burned itself out. (Translation by Watson 1993: 282).

After this great sacrifice, the *bodhisattva* performs another offering in which he burns his forearms for 72,000 years, whereby he inspires other beings to reach perfect awakening. The chapter concludes by noting that this form of bodily offering—to burn part of one's body, or to give one's finger as a sacrifice—is not reserved only for advanced practitioners, but is a practice available to ordinary people who want to aspire to Buddhahood. However—as is noted at the same time—religious merits stemming from memorizing a single verse from the *Lotus Sutra* far exceeds any other reading or practice.

Preparations for the sacrifice, as well as the burning of the body, have left echoes in history. Some aspects of the text are especially important for understanding the theme of self-immolation. The *Lotus Sutra* describes how the sacrifice was done as a consequence of the *bodhisattva* having reached a deep meditative state, and self-immolation was understood in the text as an advanced procedure made possible by this state. The sacrifice was performed to develop and strengthen the perfections (*paramitas*) necessary to reach Buddhahood, but in this case it was not *danaparamita*, associated with selfless generosity, but the perfection of vigor (*virya*). It was also a sacrifice performed for the Buddha, in order to reach the full awakening of Buddhahood. This aspect, says Benn, is important for understanding the ultimate goal of self-immolation and why it could be said to benefit others: "By becoming a Buddha rapidly the self-immolator would soon find himself in a position to rescue sentient beings from suffering by means of a Buddha's salvific powers" (Benn 2009: 111). This approach is reflected in Lama Sobha's message when he describes his auto-cremation as a tantric practice to help release those in pain from their suffering.

The theme of giving one's body as a worthy form of practice is not unique to the *Lotus Sutra* or to the *jataka* stories. The theme is found elsewhere in Mahayana literature, and especially where the perfection of generosity (*danaparamita*) is emphasized. In one of the most influential texts in medieval China, the Treatise on the Great Perfection of Wisdom, attributed to the prominent Indian philosopher Nagarjuna (c. 150–250 CE), there is an explanation of why a *bodhisattva* must be prepared to selflessly give parts of their own body:

> What is to be understood by the fulfilment of the perfection of generosity appertaining to the body which is born from the bonds of karma? Without gaining the dharma body [*dharmakaya*] and without destroying the fetters, the bodhisattva is able to give away without reservation all his precious possessions, his head, his eyes, his marrow, his skin, his kingdom, his wealth, his wife, his children and his possessions both inner and outer. But his mind remains unmoved. (Quoted by Benn 2009: 119).

There are also other texts where auto-cremation is described, for example, the King of Samadhi Sutra, as well as in a collection of short texts *The Lotus of Compassion*, which describes in detail how the Buddha inflicts extreme violence on the body.

The theme of self-immolation was popular not only in medieval China, but also in other parts of the Buddhist world. A Burmese text in Pali which was compiled during the eleventh or twelfth century CE, Knowledge of the World (*Lokapannatti*), tells how King Ashoka wrapped his body in an oil-soaked cloth and burned it in front of a stupa containing relics of Sakyamuni. In another more recent Pali text, Birth Stories of the Ten Bodhisattvas, many stories can be found where children, heads, eyes, and so on are given as offerings (ibid.: 120–23). To sum up, it is clear that the theme of self-immolation both could be and was construed as a legitimate bodily path to complete awakening in Buddhist literature. In addition to these textual passages that describe auto-cremation and self-immolations, these themes are also documented as a part of Buddhist religious practice.

Auto-cremation as Religious Practice in Buddhist Tradition

There is evidence from various sixth-century CE sources that Chinese Buddhists burned their bodies with the *Lotus Sutra* (Jan 1965, Benn 1998, 2007, 2009). This evidence can be found in biographies about eminent monks and nuns, in popular miracle stories associated with the sutra, and in epitaphs inscribed on stone for self-immolators. The biographies of Chinese monks who had auto-cremated show that many were careful to mimic the drinking of incense and oil, as well as draping the body with oil-soaked cloth, before they burned themselves in front of a stupa or before a large audience (Benn 2009: 114). Auto-cremations were public performances and have continued to be so.

However, Benn notes that one of the Chinese terms used for self-immolation—*sheshen*, "abandoning the body"—does not always have to refer to death or self-mutilation. The term is also used to describe what was believed to happen just prior to death, before the next life began on the samsaric wheel. It could also be synonymous with abandoning everyday life and becoming a monk.

The Chinese term "abandoning the body" also includes a broad range of extreme acts (not all of which result in death):

> feeding one's body to insects; slicing one's flesh, burning one's finger or arm; burning incense on the skin; starving, slicing or drowning oneself; leaping from cliffs or trees; feeding one's body to wild animals; self-mummification (preparing for death so that the resulting corpse is impervious to decay); and of course auto-cremation. (Benn 2007: 9–10)

What historical origin then does the burning of the body actually have? Its roots probably lie in indigenous Chinese practices that are documented to have taken place long before the *Lotus Sutra* was translated. It can thus be seen as an "apocryphal practice" in Chinese Buddhism (Benn 1998), for example, indigenous Chinese medicine made use of mugwort which was ignited on the skin, and there are documented ritual auto-cremations to pray for rain. But the passages in the *Lotus Sutra*, as well as other texts, have been used to legitimize the burning of the body as part of Buddhist devotional practice. Benn summarizes:

> The *Lotus Sutra* may be a unique scripture, but the auto-cremation of Medicine King within it is by no means sui generis. The analogous cases of gifts of the body in many other forms of Buddhist literature must have convinced Chinese Buddhists that this was a perfectly orthodox form of offering, and that, furthermore, auto-cremation was an option open to the ordinary practitioner ... An appreciation of the complex interplay between text and practice in Chinese Buddhism shows that auto-cremation was far from the extreme or deviant practice that it might first appear to be, and that it possessed a logic and aesthetic that could be appreciated by the larger Buddhist community. (Benn 2009)

The burning of the body is an accepted feature of Buddhist devotion in East Asia, to this day. Auto-cremations have been documented in China and Japan in the nineteenth century (Williams 2002: 155), and the practice of sacrificing one's fingers and burning incense on the skin is still carried out in countries like China, Taiwan, Korea and Japan (Bundy et al. 1991). The ordination ritual for Chinese and Korean male and female monastics also includes burning small marks on the shaved head or the forearm, a practice ultimately derived from the example of the Medicine King (Benn 1998). The *Lotus Sutra* text not only created a template for auto-cremation by showing how and why it is performed, but when performing the act of self-immolation, the immolators also chanted the chapter on the Medicine King. The scripture was thus a kind of performative speech

(Benn 2009: 108). However, self-cremations as political protest constitutes a fairly new phenomenon.

The Prototype of Auto-cremation as Political Protest—the Death of Thich Quang Duc

Political self-immolations can be found prior to 1963. These were, however, isolated incidents that did not prompt people in other places to mimic the practice. The death of Thich Quang Duc changed this and his fiery end inspired people elsewhere in the world. This was facilitated by the new mass media opportunities (where images could be quickly reproduced in various media), as well as by the availability of flammable liquid, which made the act of burning oneself in a public political protest possible (Biggs 2005: 178).

Thich Quang Duc's suicide can be contextualized in the domestic political situation in South Vietnam. The war between North and South Vietnam began in 1959, with North Vietnam led by Ho Chi Minh and South Vietnam by Ngo Dinh Diem. Diem, as a Catholic, favored the Catholic Church, despite the fact that Buddhists represented about 80 percent of the population in South Vietnam. Catholics were given senior positions in the public sector and the military, they received preference in business contexts, and even tax reductions. Diem banned the flying of the Buddhist flag in conjunction with the May Vesak celebration (Buddha's birthday), which led the monk Thich Quang Duc to carefully prepare his suicide, together with two other monks, in an attempt to direct the attention of the international community to the oppression of Buddhists. On June 11, 1963, the trio traveled together by car to an intersection outside the Cambodian Embassy in Saigon, where they staged the auto-cremation. One monk helped Thich Quang Duc to place a cushion for him to sit on, and the other poured gasoline over him. Sixty-seven-year-old Thich Quang Duc then took a match and set himself alight. He died within minutes. In a letter he left behind, he urged Diem to sympathize with all the people of Vietnam, and to implement religious equality. He also invited the Buddhist *sangha* and lay Buddhists to demonstrate their solidarity and make sacrifices in order to protect Buddhism in Vietnam.

Though Thich Quang Duc's actions were not sanctioned by the *sangha*, his suicide had the desired effect. Diem was forced to sign a document to strengthen the position of Buddhism in the country; however, this was never actioned, leading to more tension. Protests, including marches, fasting and strikes, resulted. The auto-cremation carried out by Thich Quang Duc gained followers among male and female monastics, and subsequently they came increasingly to focus on ending the war (Topmiller 2005).

The auto-cremation of Thich Quang Duc protested against how the dharma, the teachings of the Buddha, was being oppressed and threatened. The action—even though it had not been performed for centuries in Vietnam—could be understood both culturally and religiously by other Vietnamese. A *bodhisattva* is expected to defend the dharma. Even though taking one's own life is a controversial issue for Buddhists, the doctrine of skilful means, *upaya*, permits a *bodhisattva* to take life in order to save life if done with an altruistic and pure intention. The motivation to self-sacrifice outweighs the negative karma of the deed (King 2009: 78–9).[4]

Thich Quang Duc's self-immolation in 1963 became a template for similar protest actions, and was adopted around the world, not only among Buddhists. His auto-cremation was well-orchestrated; foreign journalists and photographers had been summoned to document the self-sacrifice. Self-immolation through fire usually receives media attention, as there is a powerful visual appeal generating strong emotions. In Tibet, however, few visual documentations have reached the global media, and the Tibetan immolations must primarily be seen as a way of communicating with other Tibetans to inspire them to pursue a nationalist struggle. After the death of Lama Sobha, photographs of his charred body were disseminated on Internet forums, as well as photographs and footage of other Tibetan self-immolators, who were portrayed as heroes.

When Thich Quang Duc burned himself to death, it was to draw the international community's attention to the oppression that Buddhists were subjected to by the ruling Catholic president of South Vietnam. Media reportage of burning Buddhists in Tibet have a similar effect, to make others aware of the Tibetan experience of subjugation. This reflects two primary goals of self-immolation: appealing to bystanders and inducing sympathizers (Biggs 2005: 175). The burning body evokes strong emotions in the audience, both those close to the deed as well as global viewers who experience the event partially through newspapers, television, and the Internet. A photograph or film of a human in flames is a powerful image. For those at the scene, other strong sensations also have an effect: the smell of burnt skin and the sight of a body reduced to ashes. The act of self-immolation becomes a fiery imperative, urging bystanders and sympathizers to take action, to react, to contribute to change. Seeking publicity, Lama Sobha also set fire to himself in the sight of other Tibetans in an urban context. His taped message was reproduced on exiled Tibetan websites. Not all

---

4 See also Kelly (2011), for a discussion on altruism as a motivating factor for a *bodhisattva*.

self-immolators leave messages, which makes it impossible to know what triggers them to carry out the act and how they perceive and interpret it. The message of Lama Sobha demonstrates an awareness of self-immolation as part of Buddhist tradition, but to what degree other self-immolators make this connection is not clear. There is thus a risk of over-interpreting the religious dimension and heritage. The extent to which auto-cremations take place in one region of Tibet shows that geographical and regional political conditions are important factors for understanding these fiery self-sacrifices.

Conclusion

This chapter has tried to show the history of Buddhist and pre-Buddhist ideas and devotional practices that have turned the gift of the body and auto-cremation into an expression of political protest. Self-immolation is more common in Buddhist and Hindu cultures, but has been adopted as a form of political protest in other contexts. However, there is a significant religious and cultural divide between Abrahamic and Indic religious traditions, which is apparent when linking the frequency of auto-cremation to geography. Self-immolation through auto-cremation is rare in Christian or Muslim cultural contexts. This can partly be explained by different beliefs about death and what follows after death, and it has led to diametrically different practices of how a dead body is handled and what role cremation might play. In Abrahamic religions, it is customary to bury the entire body. This practice is linked to a shared eschatology: the belief in the resurrection of the dead at the end of the world which necessitates an intact body.

In Hindu and Buddhist contexts, however, cremations are a common occurrence, and death by fire contains a sacred and pure dimension. To sacrifice one's body or parts thereof is an established theme in religious literature and the practice of both Theravada and Mahayana Buddhist traditions, and is interpreted as pure and selfless, as well as a *bodhisattva* act whose ultimate purpose is to relieve people from suffering, or to protect the Buddhist *dharma* when it is threatened.

Self-immolation is not an ordinary suicide or self-destructive act, but has a religious dimension, since one's own body is a gift for a greater cause. Usually, auto-cremation is an individual act that is rarely a part of a collective or cultic practice. However, since one of the characteristics of self-immolation is that they occur in clusters, one event seems to inspire others to mimic the action. Those individuals who are drawn to self-immolation do not use suicide terrorism or alternative acts that may harm others: self-immolations and auto-cremations are distinctively nonviolent in character and intend no injury to either people or property. Instead, their ultimate aim is to gain reactions from onlookers and supporters, reactions that lead to a stronger moral position and the desire to take action. Auto-cremations are thus a sort of burning imperative of action. The burning Buddhists in Vietnam in the 1960s intended to save Buddhism at a time when it was perceived as being threatened in South Vietnam, and later focus shifted towards ending the Vietnam War. As a result, their sacrifices were addressed to Vietnamese politicians and to the global community. Nearly fifty years later, a new wave of self-immolations have occurred in Tibet—with previously no tradition of self-immolation—and this time, the fiery suicides by Tibetan monks and laypersons can be understood as an expression of the nationalist struggle for a free Tibet. The posthumous message from the incarnate *tulku* Lama Sobha also shows how he incorporates his sacrifice into a Tantric Buddhist context and interprets his action as a tantric practice and as a way to transform darkness into light.

References

Appleton, N. (2010). *Jataka Stories in Theravada Buddhism: Narrating the Bodhisattva Path*. Farnham and Burlington, VT: Ashgate.

Benn, J.A. (1998). "Where Text Meets Flesh: Burning the Body as an Apocryphal Practice in Chinese Buddhism," *History of Religions*, 37(4): 295–322.

— (2007). *Burning for the Buddha: Self-Immolations in Chinese Buddhism*. Honolulu: University of Hawai'i Press.

— (2009). "The Lotus Sutra and Self-Immolation," in *Readings of the Lotus Sutra*, eds. S.F. Teiser and J.I. Stone. New York: Columbia University Press, pp. 107–31.

Biggs, M. (2005). "Dying Without Killing: Self-Immolations, 1963–2002," in *Making Sense of Suicide Missions*, ed. D. Gambetta. Oxford: Oxford University Press, pp. 173–208.

Budny, P.G., P.J. Regan, P. Riley, and A.H.N. Roberts (1991). "Ritual Burns: The Buddhist Tradition," *Burns*, 17(4): 335–7.

Canada Tibet Committee (1998). "Biography of the late Thubten Ngodup". Accessed September 7, 2012. At <http://www.tibet.ca/en/newsroom/wtn/archive/old?y=1998&m=4&p=29_4>.

Central Tibetan Administration (2012). "Self-Immolator Lobsang Lozin Laid to Rest". Accessed September 7, 2012. At <www.savetibet.nethttp://tibet.

net/2012/07/19/self-immolator-lobsang-lozin-laid-to-rest-entire-region-in-mourn>.

Craig, S. (2012). "Social Suffering and Embodied Political Crises," *Cultural Anthropology. Hot Spot: Self-Immolation as Protest in Tibet*, April 10. Accessed April 2, 2014. At <http://www.culanth.org/fieldsights/97-social-suffering-and-embodied-political-crisis>.

Do, Thien (1999). "The Quest for Enlightenment and Cultural Identity: Buddhism in Contemporary Vietnam," in *Buddhism and Politics in Twentieth-century Asia*, ed. I. Harris. London: Continuum, pp. 254–84.

Fischer, A.M. (2012). "The Geopolitics of Politico-Religious Protest in Eastern Tibet', *Cultural Anthropology, Hot Spot: Self-immolation as Protest in Tibet*, April 9. Accessed April 2, 2014. At <http://www.culanth.org/fieldsights/100-the-geopolitics-of-politico-religious-protest-in-eastern-tibet>.

Gyatso, J. (2012). "Discipline and Resistance on the Tibetan Plateau," *Cultural Anthropology. Hot Spot: Self-immolation as Protest in Tibet*, April 8. Accessed April 2, 2014. At <www.culanth.org/.../96-discipline-and-resistance-on-the-tibetan-plateau>.

Hoad, T.F. (ed.) (1996). *The Concise Oxford Dictionary of English Etymology*. Oxford: Oxford University Press/Oxford Reference Online. Accessed April 2, 2014. At <http://www.oxfordreference.com/view/10.1093/acref/9780192830982.001.0001/acref-9780192830982>.

International Campaign for Tibet (2012a). "Harrowing images and last message from Tibet of first lama to self-immolate ...". Accessed July 21, 2012. At <http://www.savetibet.org/media-center/ict-news-reports/harrowing-images-and-last-message-tibet-first-lama-self-immolate>.

— (2012b). "Self Immolation Fact Sheet". Accessed September 7, 2012. At <http://www.savetibet.org/resource-center/maps-data-fact-sheets/self-immolation-fact-sheet>.

Jan, Y.-H. (1965). "Buddhist Self-Immolation in Medieval China," *History of Religions*, 4(2): 243–68.

Kelly, B.D. (2011). "Self-immolation, Suicide and Self-harm in Buddhist and Western Traditions," *Transcultural Psychiatry*, 48(3): 299–317.

Keown, D. (2012 [2004]). *A Dictionary of Buddhism*. Oxford References Online.

King, S. (2009). *Socially Engaged Buddhism*. Honolulu: University of Hawai'i Press.

McGranahan, C. and R. Litzinger (2012). "Self-immolation as Protest in Tibet," *Cultural Anthropology. Hot Spot: Self-immolation as Protest in Tibet*,

April 8. Accessed April 2, 2014. At <http://culanth.org/fieldsights/93-self-immolation-as-protest-in-tibet>.

Ohnuma, R. (1998). "The Gift of the Body and the Gift of Dharma," *History of Religions*, 37(4): 323–59.

Paldron, T.M. (2012). "Virtue and the Remaking of Suffering," *Cultural Anthropology. Hot Spot: Self-immolation as Protest in Tibet*, April 8. Accessed April 2, 2014. At <http://culanth.org/fieldsights/98-virtue-and-the-remaking-of-suffering>.

Radio Free Asia (2012). "Angry Tibetans Parade Corpse". Accessed July 21, 2012. At <http://www.rfa.org/english/news/tibet/burn-01082012101534.html>.

Sangster, L. (2012). "The Afterlife of Images," *Cultural Anthropology. Hot Spot: Self-immolation as Protest in Tibet*, April 10. Accessed April 2, 2014. At <http://culanth.org/fieldsights/114-the-afterlife-of-images>.

Shakya, T. (2012). "Transforming the Language of Protest," *Cultural Anthropology. Hot Spot: Self-immolation as Protest in Tibet*, April 8. Accessed April 2, 2014. At <http://culanth.org/fieldsights/94-transforming-the-language-of-protest>.

Sperling, E. (2012). "On the Question of Why and to What End," *Cultural Anthropology. Hot Spot: Self-immolation as Protest in Tibet*, April 9. Accessed April 2, 2014. At <http://culanth.org/fieldsights/106-on-the-questions-of-why-and-to-what-end>.

Topmiller, R. (2005). "Struggling for Peace: South Vietnamese Buddhist Women and Resistance to the Vietnam War," *Journal of Women's History*, 17(3): 133–57.

Watson, B. (1993). *The Lotus Sutra*. New York: Columbia University Press.

Williams, P. (2002). *Mahayana Buddhism: The Doctrinal Foundations*. London and New York: Routledge.

Chapter 10

Dying to Tell: Media Orchestration of Politically Motivated Suicides

Lorenz Graitl[1]

Introduction

The tragic events of September 11, 2001 sparked a wave of publications about suicide bombing, a subject that attracted little scholarly attention in the 1980s and 1990s. This led many researchers to focus on related phenomena like suicide protest, fasting-unto-death, or martyrdom in general. Given the vast amount of academic work on suicide bombings, as well as the great body of literature on suicide notes,[2] it is astonishing that there are rather few studies that deal specifically with sacrifice notes related to politically motivated suicides (Park 1994; Movahedi 1999; Park 2004; Hafez 2007; Leenaars et al. 2010). Focusing on textual representations of self-killing in the name of a higher cause, this article tries to imagine "what message it might contain" (Spivak 2004: 93) and to reconstruct its communicative logic. A suicide attacks are not only about "dying to win" (Pape 2005) and striking anywhere without recourse to an escape plan; it is also about spreading a message, thereby turning one's own death into a media weapon.

Politically Motivated Suicide: Definition and Historic Evolution

A politically motivated suicide shall be defined as deliberate self-killing[3] for the advancement of a collective cause (Biggs 2005: 173–4) accompanied by a

1 I want to thank Charisma Lee who corrected my English and various friends who translated Turkish texts for me.

2 Letters in the context of what sociologist Emile Durkheim (1952) would have called "egoistic suicide."

3 See also Mayo's (1992) definition of suicide as summarized by De Leo et al. (2006: 8). This is of course a scientific definition that does not always correspond with what the agents

request, though sometimes implicit, for response and a call to action. This can appear in the form of suicide bombing, where the perpetrator usually aims to extinguish the life of as many people as possible. Two forms of self-killing that do not aim to harm other individuals[4] include fasting-unto-death (where a person refrains from eating until a certain demand is fulfilled) and the suicide protest (by means of fire or otherwise), in service of a political or ideological goal. Such examples of self-killing can already be found in pre-modern and early modern times. In 574, the monk Tao-chi and seven of his friends fasted to their deaths in protest against anti-Buddhist measures (Jan 1965: 2). Another example can be found in 1786. Protesting Joseph II's decision to abolish several state holidays in the Austro-Hungarian Empire, a man burned himself on a funeral pyre opposite a tree where he had attached a crucifix and an image of the Virgin Mary (Osiander 1813: 184). In the late eighteenth and nineteenth centuries, the first suicide bombings could be observed, as in the Polish-Russian War of 1792, or various battles between Greece and the Ottoman Empire in the nineteenth century (Diez 1838: 412–15).[5] Until the second half of the twentieth century, there was little mutual influence between different cases of political suicide, which rarely appeared in campaigns or waves.

A global diffusion of suicide protest as a protest repertoire began in 1963 (Biggs 2005) and of suicide bombing as a military strategy in 1981 (Horowitz 2010). Both modes of action spread to dozens of countries and have been executed in every year since the initial occurrences. The rise of suicide protest can be traced back to the self-immolation of the monk Thich Quang Duc in 1963, whose spectacular suicide provoked worldwide reactions and contributed tremendously to the overthrow of the South Vietnamese regime later that year (Biggs 2005: 204–5). In the following decades, the wish to emulate Duc's model led to a widespread adoption of self-immolation, demonstrating that

attribute to their act, as a majority reject using the word "suicide."

4 Comparing different phenomena like suicide bombing and suicide protest should not be seen as a moral judgment. This chapter tries to analyze abstract commonalities of various political suicides without putting the deliberate killing of civilians by suicide bombers on a level with peaceful forms of protest like self-immolation or fasting-unto-death. It should be stressed that suicide protest encompasses diverse political currents which can be diametrically opposed, ranging from anti-Nazism to Holocaust denial.

5 Although Diez's descriptions are sometimes exaggerated and in a few cases even apocryphal, his interpretation of these deeds might be very disturbing for modern audiences. Before he describes the stories of several European suicide bombers whose victims are often Muslims he states: "Blowing yourself up in the air is a great and heroic mode of death … in which the suicide almost always also drags a large number of other individuals into death" (Diez 1838: 412, author's translation from German).

this protest repertoire can be used by almost any movement without links to a sole political current (ibid.: 182). It has been used by peace activists in South Vietnam, by Kurdish nationalists (Grojean 2008), by the Korean Worker's and Minjung Movements (Park 1994; Kim 2008; Kim 2012), as well as by upper-caste students in India who felt threatened by their government's affirmative action policy. In 1995, self-immolation was even employed by a Munich-based Holocaust denier.

Though death by fire is most common, suicide protests can be accomplished by any method: shooting, poisoning, strangulation, self-inflicted stab wounds, or jumping in front of a train. Furthermore, suicide protests can appear as isolated instances, as a series of events with interruptions, or as waves. The self-immolation in 1982 of the Turkish citizen Artin Penik in the name of all "Armenians in Turkey" (*Hürriyet* 1982) was an isolated event, expressing his rejection of an attack by ASALA[6] on Ankara Airport from just days before. In a series with interruptions, the fatal deed leads to imitations targeting the same or a similar cause, with a delay of several months, years, or decades, as in the numerous suicides connected to the Kurdish independence movement that have been taking place since 1982 (see Grojean 2008: 676–9).

Entire waves of suicide protest can be observed in India in recent years, although strangely attracting scant media attention in the West. Between January and April 2009, 25 men in Tamil Nadu (India) and the Tamil diaspora attempted and committed suicide protesting the Sri Lankan Civil War.

An even larger wave took place between November 2009 and January 2014 in the context of the Telangana Movement. Its proponents seek the bifurcation of Andhra Pradesh and the creation of an independent Telangana state within the Indian union. Their arguments for secession are not based on any ethnic or religious difference, but lie in what they see as the systematic socio-economic under-development of the region by the eastern regions of the present Andhra Pradesh state. Even though the present author has counted some 200 cases and movement partisans claim more than a thousand deaths,[7] it took the Indian government four years to finally grant the wish for a new state. This delay was also caused by the existence of the competing Samakhya Andhra Movement that vows to uphold the unity of Andhra Pradesh and has also resorted to the use of suicides, albeit in lesser number, from December 2009 until January 2010.

---

[6] The Armenian Secret Army for the Liberation of Armenia sought to avenge the Armenian genocide by attacking Turkish diplomats and institutions in various countries. ASALA's goal was to establish an independent Armenian state on the soil of Turkey.

[7] Although this is likely an exaggeration, the actual number of attempted and completed self-killings might still be in the several hundreds, making it the largest wave of suicide protests in history.

The first modern suicide bombing is widely considered to have been the attack by the Shi'ite Al-Dawa on the Iraqi embassy in Beirut in December 1981 during the Iran–Iraq War. Several attacks in Lebanon followed. Most fraught with consequences were the October 1983 twin suicide bombings against US and French barracks in which 299 people were killed with explosive-laden trucks (Pedahzur 2005: 48). The complete withdrawal of US and French troops in the succeeding months led other groups like Sri Lanka's Tamil Tigers to copy this successful model, one that has spread to over forty countries. The last decade has witnessed not only a dramatic increase in suicide attacks but also a transition. During the 1980s and 1990s, the majority of bombings were committed by nationalists both Islamic—such as Hezbollah and Hamas—and secular, such as the PKK and the Tamil Tigers. Most bombings are now perpetrated by groups that adhere to a Salafi-Jihadi ideology, like al-Qaeda or Ansar al-Sunna in Iraq.

In contrast with suicide protest and suicide bombing, a global diffusion of fasting-unto-death has yet to take place, as few are actually willing to surrender their life during self-starvation. Apart from isolated cases, fasting-unto-death is mainly connected to Irish Republicanism (most famous is the case of IRA member Bobby Sands), different (sub-) nationalisms in India, and illegal communist parties in Turkey (including the PKK).

Sacrifice Notes: What Do They Tell Us?

Previous research on "ordinary" suicide has probed for the meanings, or intentions, behind suicide notes (Ho et al. 1998). Based on the theories of ten suicidologists, Leenaars and colleagues used a list of 35 protocol sentences focusing on intra-psychic and interpersonal factors to compare 33 notes of Korean self-immolators with 33 notes of "common" suicides from the United States. The study suggests important differences between the two samples, the main difference being the "extreme suicidal mind" of the Korean immolators (Leenaars et al. 2010: 666). The authors found that 90.9 percent of the Korean immolators' notes show evidence of a "serious disorder in adjustment" (such as depression, schizophrenia, and borderline personality) and 100 percent of "murderous impulses," while the scores in the corresponding categories in the US sample were only 24.2 and 0 percent respectively (ibid.: 664). While the results of this study cannot be dismissed entirely, it is necessary to ask if such approaches do not fail to grasp several important aspects of self-chosen martyrdom. Most important is the possibility of a direct assessment of the intra-psychic condition based solely on those texts. Several factors work against this. Martyr videos and farewell letters are highly standardized and have a rather limited discourse. Political organizations can alter a text prior to death or afterwards (Grojean 2008: 597–611) or even be its actual author (Merari 2010: 134). Even though altruistic self-sacrifice might indeed, in some cases, be obscuring motivations grounded in hopelessness or egotistic reasons (Merari 2010: 267; Biggs 2005: 199), the analysis of a sacrifice note will probably not be the key to discovering other causes. If we suppose that Palestinian suicide bombers are secretly depressed and seek death for purely personal reasons, they would certainly not state that in their testaments. Sacrifice notes tell more about the way in which the author wants the audience to perceive the act rather than revealing the actual state of mind prior to the deed (Yang and Lester 2011). Using pre-defined and pre-interpreted categories as Leenaars and colleagues do also misses certain important expressive and instrumental elements in the content of sacrifice notes (Jorgensen-Earp 1987; Singh 2011).

It is extremely difficult to conduct empirical research on political suicides, since it is almost never possible to interview agents before the deed or witness the act itself. Interviews with family members might be unreliable as they glorify the entire biography or portray the person as an innocent victim manipulated by an organization. Similarly, captured suicide bombers may reinterpret their original motivations or deny their guilt. Apart from interviews, some of the few resources that are accessible to outsiders are written letters or martyr videos produced for publication after death. The present author has collected a sample of excerpts and full texts gathered mainly from digital newspaper archives and sympathizers' homepages. Instead of searching for the "true" motivation behind the act, this chapter tries to deal with sacrifice notes by asking new questions. What meaning is attributed to self-chosen death? For whom are the messages written? What is the audience urged to do?

Expressive Elements: "I am convinced we will reach victory"

Commonalities in sacrifice notes stem from mutual influence—mostly but not exclusively restricted to a regional context—as well as from the fact that they face similar communicative problems, and can thus be regarded as communicative genres (Luckmann 1989). As with notes left by "ordinary" suicides, the authors of sacrifice notes often give instructions regarding property or express love for their family and friends (Jacobs 1967; McClelland et al. 2000). However, the politically motivated sacrifice can be accepted as such only if it is represented as a legitimate and reasonable act with a positive result. In contrast to suicide notes, self-chosen death cannot be framed as self-murder or suicide but as martyrdom[8] or sacrifice, a distinction that was already observed by Halbwachs (1978 [1932]: 291–308). Thus the content of the documents is often diametrically opposed to that of suicide notes. Although Shneidman (1985: 131) defines "hopeless-helplessness" as one of the universal characteristics of all suicides, it would be difficult to find a similar expression of emotion in the testaments of suicide bombers. Jamal Sati, a member of the Lebanese Communist Party who perpetrated an attack in 1985, describes the feelings prior to his imminent death as a human bomb not as melancholic but as euphoric:

> My happiness was so great when the enemy Israeli forces were forced to retreat and withdraw from my district under the heavy blows of the Resistance ... But my happiness was even greater when the leadership of the Front agreed that I could continue participating in its operations ... and it is much more exciting that I have to perform a suicide operation. (Khoury and Mroué 2006: 189)[9]

Because Sati wants his death to be understood as martyrdom, he encourages his family to be proud of him and celebrate his actions:

> As for you, the dearest and finest mother and father in existence, my beloved brothers and sisters: my wish for you is not to mourn and wail, but rejoice and dance as you would do at my wedding, for I am the proud groom of martyrdom, and that is the happiest wedding I could hope for. (Ibid.: 189)[10]

In the case of Hamas, it is interesting to observe that the group not only regards self-inflicted death as martyrdom (as Islamic law forbids suicide), but also engages in psychological discourse, referring to scientific research about suicide bombers:

---

[8] This can also be seen in the manifesto of Anders Breivik who initially planned to die in his killing spree on Utøya and referred to his act as a "martyrdom operation." After criticizing the Protestant Church for its moderate stand on suicide, Breivik goes on to explain that a "Justiciar Knight" who faces certain death at the hands of the enemy or kills himself in an explosion will indeed be a martyr. This is allegedly sanctioned by Catholic canon law (Breivik 2011: 1345–50). In his argumentation, the anti-Muslim attacker Breivik parallels the discourse of Salafi-Jihadi groups who justify suicide bombings with an invented tradition of "martyrdom operations" that have supposedly existed since the time of the prophet Mohammed (see Elif Medya 2010).

[9] Sati recorded three different versions of his last will and testament, one of which was aired by the state-owned television station Télé-Liban (Khoury and Mroué 2006: 183).

[10] Similar appeals not to weep or to wear black have been made by Palestinian suicide bombers (Hafez 2006: 91–2) and the Black Tigers, the suicide squad of the LTTE in Sri Lanka.

> Some people have the impression that Hamas' soldiers are people who have despaired in life and want to die ... And when studies were conducted with some objectivity, results showed that most Hamas soldiers are contrary to this misleading impression. Desperate individuals cannot form a resistance movement that can bear the brunt of repeated crackdowns by the occupation for 17 years. (Ezzedeen Al-Qassam Brigades 2006)

Similarly, the British citizen Waheed Zaman, who planned to die in 2006, explicitly tries to refute the media image of suicide bombers as psychologically unstable and manipulated youngsters by implicitly referring to his status as a final-year biomedical science student in his martyr video: "I have not been brainwashed, I am educated to a very high standard. I am old enough to make my own decision" (BBC 2008).

Indeed, many authors feel obliged to ensure that their death is not assessed as an ordinary suicide, including those who do not have to deal with a religious suicide taboo. Eyüp Beyaz, a member of the Revolutionary People's Liberation Party Front in Turkey who was shot after trying to bomb the Ministry of Justice, clarifies in his final letter that he is pursuing the act *because* he overly esteems human life:

> Even though I love life very much I consciously and willingly end it, so that injustice, poverty and dependency on imperialism end and a life in dignity can be possible. My life shall be dedicated to my beloved people, my home and the radiant future of my country. It shall be dedicated to the future of our children. (Özgürlük 2007)

Colonel Rooban, a Black Air Tiger who died in 2009 when he tried to crash his plane into the Sri Lanka Air Force headquarters, expressed much the same: "I have never dreamed of wasting one's precious life; However, I feel privileged and proud that I can become a black tiger to earn respect for my people and my homeland" (TamilNet 2009c). Utterances like these unintentionally disprove Durkheim's hypothesis (1952: 221), reiterated by Stack (2004: 9), that "altruistic suicides ... occur in social groups where there is a low value placed on the individual." Additional justifications state that the voluntary surrender of one's own life is the only way. "There is no other option" (TamilNet 2009a) wrote the journalist Muthukumar, the first person who set himself ablaze to protest the war in Sri Lanka in 2009. The authors of sacrifice notes often explain the rationality of going to their deaths, confident in the triumph of their cause. An unwavering belief in success can be found in almost all of the last letters of Turks who were fasting to death. Ilginç Özkeskin, who succumbed to self-starvation in 1996, wrote: "Like the other comrades I am convinced we will reach victory.

To achieve this victory, I will fall too, like my comrades" (DHKC Information Bureau 1996). Some authors do not confine themselves to promise that they will be unequivocally triumphant, but even announce that they will become immortal after they donate their life for the cause. The motif of immortality is frequently encountered in the last letters of Turkish Communists or the above-mentioned Jamal Sati. The secular suicide bomber states that through his heroic deed he will stay alive in the memory of those who survive him: "Now, I am departing my country, in body only; I will still exist in the souls of all the honest patriots in Lebanon" (Khoury and Mroué 2006: 189).

Instrumental Elements: The Strategic Logic of Writing

Sacrifice notes not only attribute very different meanings to the transition from life to death; they are also directed to a public different from that which would read suicide notes and thus look for different responses. As representations of sacrificial acts, the notes follow the structure of sacrifice as observed by Mauss and Hubert (1981 [1899]). According to Turner (1966), this sacrificial system is an almost universal mode of symbolic communication. The act is initiated by a "sacrificer" who offers a "victim" to a godhead hoping that they will show their gratitude in return. A "sacrificer"—an individual, a family, a clan, a tribe or a nation (Mauss and Hubert 1981: 10)—is supposed to benefit from the sacrificial offering that was made. As in pre-modern martyrdom, the "sacrificer" and the "victim" merge into one in politically motivated suicide. However, the face of dying for a cause has changed since the time of Mauss and Hubert. In contrast to pre-modern religious sacrifices, the act is directed less at those who are physically present but rather towards a public that can witness it through the media. Today's acts can also be dedicated to the environment, the prevention of a nuclear catastrophe, the success of a political party, the establishment of world peace, or socialist revolution. For the sacrificer, it is no longer necessary to be part of the collective for which he intends to give his life. Politically motivated suicides differ significantly from traditional sacrifices, in that the former usually do not aim to elicit divine intervention (Biggs 2012) and focus rather on the reactions of the audience. These can vary, ranging from a small group such as the comrades of the fasting-to-death Özkeskin, to the "inhabitants of the whole world!" (Prague TV 2007) addressed by Zdenek Adamec, a young man who burned himself to death in 2003. Some draft individual letters to each audience; others speak to many different groups in a single document. Muthukumar, for example, lists several groups in both Tamil

Nadu, and Tamil Eelam [Sri Lanka], the Tamil Tigers, as well as the international community, and President Obama himself.

Target audiences can be roughly divided in three different groups, which Cook and Allison (2007: 88) have already described for martyr videos: "(1) organization members (or strong ideological supporters of the organization), (2) sympathetic publics (including potential recruits), and (3) unsympathetic publics (enemies)." Many messages are addressed to the group with which agents identify, usually defined along the lines of religion, ethnicity, nationality, or political belief. The future martyr stresses that he is dying for the group and thus unites an imagined community (Anderson 1989) in a common loss. Dying as a martyr, the author speaks from the position of an elite, reassuring the audience that they are on the right path and encouraging them to further mobilize or to focus on specific problems. The sacrifice of the martyr is meant to prove the invincibility of the group as shown in the video message of one of the LTTE's Black Tigers: "What I want to tell to you all before I leave is that there is nothing that a black tiger cannot destroy whenever there's barriers in front of our struggle" (YouTube 2008).

In messages directed to potential sympathizers in the national or world public, the author speaks from a further distance. The tone of these messages can range from friendly to accusatory. Murukathasan, a Sri Lankan Tamil, immolated himself in front of the UNO headquarters in Geneva to send a message to the world community: "This will tell you a bright message which reach your heart and minds and wake up your soul" (TamilNet 2009b). Though the international community has ignored the suffering of the Tamils, he expresses no hostility towards them. Instead, he hopes that his fiery death—intended to be a representation of the suffering of the Tamil civilians affected by war—will evoke empathy and compassion, which in return will bring the international community to intervene in the Sri Lankan Civil War.

Direct appeals can also be made to a state or population regarded as hostile or "traitors" and "collaborators" within one's own collective. Waheed Zaman's martyr video seeks to explain to US and UK publics that they, the "infidel" inhabitants, were targeted with suicide bombings as punishment for their sins against Muslims:

> You will not feel any security or peace in your lands until you [stop] [we say] interfering in the affairs of the Muslim completely. I'm warning you today so tomorrow you have no cause for complaints. Remember, as you kill us, you will be killed and as you bomb us, you will be bombed. (BBC 2008)

Such expressions of extreme hostility are found not only in the videos of suicide bombers but also in the letters of those employing suicide protest or fasting-unto-death. In his farewell letter, Artin Penik condemns the "ASALA murderers," appearing as an angel of revenge when he threatens that the group's roots will be exterminated by the Turkish nation if they do not put an immediate end to their actions (*Hürriyet* 1982).

The specific requests for response made in sacrifice notes can differ greatly and their communicative logic can be quite diverse (Graitl 2012), with some demands remaining rather vague. Alice Herz, a US anti-war protester who burned herself to death in 1965, advocated making the world a better place where humans can live in peace and dignity (Shibata 1977: 30). Other notes go beyond appeals for mobilization (Kim 2008) and have a very complex agenda. While Artin Penik pleas for ASALA to stop their violence, his death is also meant to prove that Armenians are peaceful, loyal citizens who do not sympathize with terrorist actions. Reading between the lines, Penik's self-immolation further serves to protect Armenians who had been targeted in retaliation for past ASALA attacks.

Regardless of how diverse their intentions may be, all the authors of a sacrifice note must deal with one common communicative problem: ensuring that the audience actually follows the urgent call to action. This can be achieved by giving convincing political analysis, or through emotional appeals (Jorgensen-Earp 1987; Lahiri 2013), to their audience's compassion, shame, or horror. The ultimate argument that is made remains death, however. Dying is seen a necessity without alternative by the authors; otherwise, their public outcry might not be heard: "Our words are dead until we give them life with our blood" (*The Herald* 2008, 21 November), was written in red ink by Nicky Reilly, who made a futile attempt to die as a suicide bomber in the UK in 2008.

Self-sacrifice as a Media Weapon: Success and Results

Apart from the military benefits of suicide bombings (Pape 2005; Moghadam 2008), so far there has been hardly any research on the efficiency of political suicides. Success is not easy to define and even more difficult to measure (Biggs 2005; Kim 2008). The following shall discuss the various extents to which a politically motivated suicide can be successful. The first objective requires that the message reaches the intended audience(s). For that, a message must exist in the first place. Some people may think that their actions are self-explanatory, and forego drafting a statement. In this case, the death will usually fail to be regarded as political suicide unless family or others can explain underlying motives and thus undertake the responsibility of making sense of the deed. The contents of some letters remain forever unknown due to the violent character of the suicide itself. Shortly before jumping in front of a train in the name of an independent Telangana in August 2011, 25-year-old Pottigari Ramesh had called his brother, indicating a sacrifice note in his wallet (*The Hindu* 2011). When the police recovered his body, neither wallet nor sacrifice letter could be found. Telangana politicians then alleged that the police had purposefully concealed the note, though this remains unproven. Even the absence of censorship provides no guarantee for the successful communication of intent. In fact, most sacrifice notes are only quoted in excerpts, which might nevertheless be enough to spread "the message." Artin Penik is probably the only person whose entire note was published on a newspaper's front page, in the state-owned *Hürriyet* (1982). If newspapers or television stations decline to release the content, this task must be fulfilled by a network of organization members or sympathizers.

As Smith (2008: 458) has eloquently stated: "It takes two to create a martyrdom; the actor who sacrifices life and the community that offers the title." Self-chosen death is not always rewarded with the crown of martyrdom. The social community that is addressed by the martyr-to-be may be divided in their reactions and some might regard the person as a "crackpot" (Jorgensen-Earp 1987: 91), or a terrorist. People who kill themselves for an idea or a political aim that are already very popular rarely have to deal with these problems. The birth of a martyr cannot take place without a group of martyrologists who spread his message and pledge to make sure that the sacrifice will not be in vain. Yet the group of martyrologists can unknowingly form a new interpretation of the act or deliberately set it in a new frame. In the case of the Telangana suicides, several parties compete over the appropriation of the martyrs. Furthermore, they argue about whose policy is in accordance with the wishes of the deceased.

After successfully explaining the motivation to the intended audiences and gaining as much social acceptance as possible, another difficulty is to make permanent political change and effectively obtain the goals formulated in the message. The overall societal impact may be the best index of the efficiency of a politically motivated suicide. Nevertheless, it is not always possible to prove whether and to which extent major political change is causally determined by a previous self-sacrifice. Failure is much easier to detect. Environmental activist Ulrich Baer's self-immolation in Germany in 1994 did gain media attention for a short time, but his name was quickly forgotten. As no movement claimed his legacy, and the government was not pressured to implement any policy change, the deed had hardly any result. In contrast, both the self-immolation of Artin Penik and of Muthukumar had far-reaching consequences. After Penik had burned himself in protest against the first attack by the Armenian group ASALA targeting civilians, the Turkish government eagerly accepted the sacrifice of its Armenian citizen. When state officials attended his funeral, he was acknowledged as a legitimate representative of Armenians in Turkey as was his intention. His communicative strategy to prove the patriotism of the native Armenians and their abhorrence of terrorism was thus effectively realized. At the same time, the attempt to change the tactics of the armed group utterly failed. ASALA did not desist from its violence and continued to attack civilians. The success of Penik's action was thus ambivalent. So was the self-immolation of Muthukumar in Tamil Nadu, India. His death immediately sparked mass demonstrations, strikes, and some minor violent riots, heating up the already existing anger about the war against Tamil civilians in Sri Lanka. Knowing that they could not ignore Muthukumar's immolation, the regional government offered compensation to his family, which they declined. The consequences of his action were not limited to intensifying protests as it even inspired other people to sacrifice their life as well, thus realizing the threat made against the international community in his sacrifice letter: "If you are interested in adding us to the list of Aborigines, Maya and Inca peoples, each day one of us will come in front of you and kill ourselves, as it comes in one of our myths" (TamilNet 2009a). In this way from January until April 2009, 25 more men attempted to or succeeded in killing themselves for similar demands. Despite this tremendous impact, Muthukumar could not achieve all of his objectives. The international community completely ignored his act and no country pressured Sri Lanka to stop its war. In contrast, the Turkish government conceded to demands made by Ilginç Özkeskin and eleven other hunger-strikers who died in 1996. Most significantly, it announced the cessation of transfers to Eskisehir prison where the incarcerated would have been subjected to solitary confinement. This decision was not directly influenced by the sacrifice notes of the deceased, but rather by the wish of the government to absolve itself from further controversy, as dozens of other prisoners were refusing food and facing death.

Some political suicides may go far beyond the concern that is initially uttered. Before the Buddhist monk Thich Quang Duc burned himself to death, he had written a letter to South Vietnamese President Diem asking him "to be kind and tolerant towards his people and enforce a policy of religious equality" (Joiner 1964: 918). In fact, Quang Duc's suicide—and subsequent self-immolations inspired by his act—contributed to the overthrow of the government in the November 1963 coup sanctioned by the Kennedy administration. The latter had hitherto backed the Diem regime but was not willing to face any more suicides (Biggs 2005: 204–5; Murray Yang 2011: 4).

The effects of suicide protest can also be unintentional as in the case of the Tunisian street vendor Mohammed Bouazizi in December 2010. After the police confiscated his vegetable and fruit cart (thereby taking away his means of subsistence), Bouazizi decided to self-immolate in front of the governor's office to communicate his frustration over the miserable conditions he had to live in and to shame the responsible officers. Most likely Bouazizi did not foresee the events that his suicide would trigger. Not only did he spark mass unrest that led to a quick overthrow of the Tunisian regime, he galvanized mass protests and revolutions in many African and Arab countries. Though Bouazizi did leave a Facebook message to his mother before he died, the story of his humiliation by the police—he was allegedly slapped by a female officer—attracted larger public attention because his fate was one with which many people could identify. Thus the reactions to his tragic death were not limited to public shock and outrage, but also led to the unleashing of collective frustrations in various countries, resulting in a turnover of the whole political landscape in North Africa and the Middle East.

Events initiated by political suicides can sometimes be counterproductive, causing more harm than benefit to a political movement. When five followers of Falun Gong self-immolated themselves in 2001, the Chinese government effectively used the footage of the act to discredit the movement as a cult that manipulates people into committing suicide (Biggs 2005: 205–6; Farley this volume).[11]

Conclusion

Politically motivated suicide is mainly a media weapon based on an instrumental rationality in which a person dies with the aim of effecting a major change of the political situation. Neither Durkheimian nor suicidological or psychiatric approaches do full justice to the nature of this kind of self-sacrifice. Durkheim regarded altruistic suicide as a phenomenon predominantly found in "lower societies" and explained by excessive social integration, lack of individualization, lack of intellectual development, and a disdain of the value of life (Durkheim 1952: 217–40). As Durkheim—writing in 1897—believed that all of these forces would be eradicated by ongoing modernization in the future, he predicted

---

11 A decade later, the Chinese government made a huge effort to prevent the production and distribution of any photographic or video materials of Tibetan self-immolators.

that altruistic suicide was destined for extinction (ibid.: 373). Some authors like Pape (2005: 171–98) and Stack (2004) use Durkheim's explanatory frame for present-day altruistic suicides, including suicide bombing. Even though Stack discusses some mistakes in Durkheim's theory,[12] he states "the primitive society model can be applied to countercultures and perhaps even certain subcultures in modern society that approximate primitive societies" (2004: 19). Suicide bombing, suicide protest, and fasting-unto-death are in no way archaic. In fact, they are the very result of modernization processes. Technological innovations like the stabilization and miniaturization of explosives as well as the invention of gasoline (Biggs 2005: 178) made suicide bombings and self-immolations possible. Turks fasting to death after the year 2000 made use of modern medical knowledge when they abstained from solid food but took vitamin B1 to prevent the Wernicke-Korsakoff syndrome and to extend the "communicative suffering" (Biggs 2012) up to a period of more than 300 days prior to their death. The evolution of a global media society is possibly the most important factor that enabled the rise of politically motivated suicide. Messages can be distributed in a very short time to large audiences and potentially even a global public. Media orchestrations of politically motivated suicides have always adapted to new developments. As early as the nineteenth century, letters were drafted in hopes of being distributed by news agencies (ibid.). For a long time, those who killed themselves in the name of an idea had to depend on others to report their actions. When Quang Duc died in 1963, he needed US newspapers to tell the world about his act of protest. By the mid-1980s this had changed. Secular-nationalist groups in Lebanon were the first to produce martyr videos of suicide bombers that could be aired on the same day by state-owned television stations. The protagonists now became media producers themselves and could as a consequence take more control of how their acts would be perceived. Today, videos of suicide bombers in Iraq and other countries are uploaded to the Internet, which thus serves as an alternative public outlet for Jihadi groups and others. As described earlier in this chapter, the media have also been responsible for the global diffusion of political suicides as reports on the success of certain cases caused others to emulate their model. Though many political suicides—especially suicide bombings—are collectively planned, they can also be set in motion by individuals acting on their own. High social integration into a group as postulated by Durkheim can be the case, but is not a necessary precondition

[12] Stack (2004: 19), for example, correctly points out that Durkheim exaggerates the general acceptance of suicide in "primitive societies," albeit without questioning the dichotomy between "civilized" and "primitive" in general.

(Taylor 1982: 191). Although Durkheim's "altruistic suicide" is still a useful term (Jorgensen-Earp 1987: 83) as it indicates self-chosen dying for a collective cause, it is nevertheless important to stress that politically motivated suicide is a new and specific form of this type distinct from the historic cases he describes. As a result, Durkheim's explanatory frame is too narrow and dismisses the instrumental and communicative character of the phenomenon.

The same is true for suicidological and psychiatric approaches that focus almost entirely on the intra-psychic motivation of the individual. They tend to take models derived from "ordinary" suicide and apply them to self-sacrifice without considering the major differences between the two. Politically motivated suicide is therefore regarded as the result of a mental illness, such as depression or a personality disorder. The written testimonies of the deceased are regarded as nothing more than the manifestation of a troubled mind, thereby largely neglecting social causes and political effects.

Trying to go beyond these approaches, this chapter has looked at what these messages want to communicate and what social meanings are attributed to the suicidal act. Using death as an argument, sacrifice notes are directed at different audiences that can encompass kindred communities and potential sympathizers, as well as political opponents. When messages reach their audiences and the intended tasks are fulfilled, politically motivated suicide can be of enormous efficiency. It can draw attention to a political problem, initiate peaceful demonstrations or violent riots, and lead to drastic policy shifts. No matter how many people die for a cause, success is not always guaranteed. The desired results are often only partially realized, or the death fails to have any political impact whatsoever. Even if many people fall short of achieving their desired results, the wish to duplicate successful attempts—that is, those that have achieved their goal—is the reason for the overall high number of acts of political self-sacrifice and will be responsible for its persistence in the future.

Politically motivated suicide is in no way a homogenous field. Self-sacrifice can be pacifist or extremely violent, it can be secular or religious. In addition, it can be linked with almost any political movement. Yet sacrifice notes do share some common elements and metaphors, as they must address similar communicative problems. Another commonality of the various forms of political self-sacrifice is that orchestration by the media is nearly always a precondition to make death into a successful political weapon.[13] Suicide bombing can be committed for

---

[13] While this chapter deals explicitly with sacrifice notes and martyr videos, other sources of the communicative dimension of a political suicide can include slogans shouted before death, media interviews with surviving attempters and signs carried by suicide protesters. Communication can also be non-verbal and people can express themselves by carrying flags, via symbols, gestures,

military purposes alone—for example, harming the enemy army. Additional effects, such as destabilizing a political system by spreading fear and terror, can be brought about only when news regarding this event reaches a large audience.[14] On the contrary, fasting-to-death and suicide protest are entirely dependent on media orchestration. Otherwise they remain obscure and meaningless acts of self-murder that do not attract any public attention. If social science wants to make sense of suicide missions (Gambetta 2005), there is no other option than to listen to what the related messages actually say.

References

Anderson, Benedict (1989). *Imagined Communities: Reflections on the Origin and Spread of Nationalism*. London: Verso.

BBC (2008). "'Suicide videos': What they said," April 4. Accessed September 1, 2011. At <http://news.bbc.co.uk/2/hi/uk_news/7330367.stm>.

Bell, Vikki (2005). "The Scenography of Suicide: Terror, Politics and the Humiliated Witness," *Economy and Society*, 34(2): 241–60.

Biggs, Michael (2005). "Dying without killing: Self-immolations, 1963–2002," in *Making Sense of Suicide Missions*, ed. Diego Gambetta. Oxford: Oxford University Press, pp. 173–208.

— (2012). "How Suicide Protest Entered the Global Repertoire of Contention," *Sociology Working Papers*. Accessed November 5, 2012. At <http://www.sociology.ox.ac.uk/documents/working-papers/2012/repertoire.pdf>.

Breivik, Anders (2011). *2083. A European Declaration of Independence*. Accessed April 2, 2014. At <http://publicintelligence.net/anders-behring-breiviks-complete-manifesto-2083-a-european-declaration-of-independence/>.

Cook, David, and Olivia Allison (2007). *Understanding and Addressing Suicide Attacks*. Westport, CT: Praeger Security International.

De Leo, Diego, Shelley Burgis, José Bertolote, Ad Kerkhof, and Unni Bille-Brahe (2006). "Definitions of Suicidal Behaviour," *Crisis*, 27(1): 4–15.

DHKC Informationbureau Amsterdam (1996). Farewell Words from Hunger-striking Members of the DHKP-C. Accessed November 8, 2011. At <http://www.driftline.org/cgi-bin/archive/archive_msg.cgi?file=spoon-

how they behave in front of a camera (Murray Yang 2011), or their dying body in fasting-to-death scenarios (Wee 1991).

[14] Paradoxically, it is often the media of the "enemy country" that fulfill this function as demonstrated by Bell (2005), on the example of Chechen suicide bombers.

archives/marxism.archive/marxism_1996/96-09-marxism/96-09-02.203&msgnum=48&start=4173>.

Diez, Carl August (1838). *Der Selbstmord, seine Ursachen und Arten vom Standpunkte der Psychologie und Erfahrung*. Tübingen: Laupp.

Durkheim, Emile (1952 [1897]). *Suicide*. London: Routledge and Kegan Paul.

Elif Medya (2010). *Das islamische Urteil über die Zulässigkeit von Märtyrer Operationen*. Accessed June 21, 2010. At <http://www.ahlu-sunnah.com/threads/29527-Das-islamische-Urteil-%C3%BCber-die-Zul%C3%A4ssigkeit-von-M%C3%A4rtyrer-Operationen>.

Ezzedeen Al-Qassam Brigades Information Office (2006). "Hamas Question & Answer". Accessed September 1, 2011. At <http://www.qassam.ps/interview-1458-Hamas_Question__Answer.html>.

Gambetta, Diego (2005). "Can We Make Sense of Suicide Missions?" in *Making Sense of Suicide Missions*, ed. Diego Gambetta. Oxford: Oxford University Press, pp. 259–99.

Graitl, Lorenz (2012). *Sterben als Spektakel. Zur kommunikativen Dimension des politisch motivierten Suizids*. Wiesbaden: Springer VS.

Grojean, Olivier (2008). "La cause kurde, de la Turquie vers l'Europe. Contribution à une sociologie de la transnationalisation des mobilisations," PhD dissertation, EHESS Paris.

Hafez, Mohammed (2006). *Manufacturing Human Bombs: The Making of Palestinian Suicide Bombers*. Washington, DC: United States Institute of Peace Press.

— (2007). "Martyrdom Mythology in Iraq: How Jihadists Frame Suicide Terrorism in Videos and Biographies," *Terrorism and Political Violence*, 19: 95–115.

Halbwachs, Maurice (1978 [1930]). *The Causes of Suicide*. London: Routledge and Kegan Paul.

The Herald (2008). "Bomber Nicky Reilly's suicide note," November 21. Accessed September 13, 2011. At <http://www.thisisplymouth.co.uk/Bomber-Nicky-Reilly-s-suicide-note/story-11795579-detail/story.html>.

The Hindu (2011). "Youth 'ends life' for Telangana," August 19. Accessed August 19, 2011. At <http://www.thehindu.com/todays-paper/tp-national/article2371195.ece>.

Ho, T., P. Yip, C. Chiu, and P. Halliday (1998)."Suicide Notes: What to do they tell us?" *Acta Psychiatrica Scandinavica*, 98: 467–73.

Horowitz, Michael (2010). "Nonstate Actors and the Diffusion of Innovations: Suicide Terrorism," *International Organization*, 64: 33–64.

Hürriyet (1982). "Ermeni yurttas, Ermeni terörünü protesto için kendini yaktı," August 12.

Jacobs, Jerry (1967). "A Phenomenological Study of Suicide Notes," *Social Problems*, 5: 60–72.

Jan, Yün-hua (1965). "Buddhist Self-Immolation in Medieval China," *History of Religions*, 4(2): 243–68.

Joiner, Charles (1964). "South Vietnam's Buddhist Crisis: Organization for Charity, Dissidence, and Unity," *Asian Survey*, 4: 915–28.

Jorgensen-Earp, Cheryl (1987). "'Toys of Desperation' Suicide as Protest Rhetoric," *Southern Speech Communication Journal*, 53(1): 80–96.

Khoury, Elias, and Rabih Mroué (2006). "Three Posters. Reflections on a Video/Performance," *The Drama Review*, 50(3): 182–91.

Kim, Hyojoung (2008). "Micromobilization and Suicide Protest in South Korea, 1970–2004," Social Research, 75(2): 543–78.

Kim, Sun-Chul (2012). "Self-immolation in South Korea," Protest and Politics Workshop, City University of New York, October 25. Accessed November 5, 2012. At <http://politicsandprotest.ws.gc.cuny.edu/files/2012/07/PPW-7-Kim.pdf>.

Lahiri, Simanti (2013). *Suicide Protest in South Asia. Consumed by Commitment.* London: Routledge.

Leenaars, Antoon, B.C. Ben Park, Peter Collins, Susanne Wenckstern, and Lindsey Leenaars (2010). "Martyrs' Last Letters: Are They the Same as Suicide Notes?" *Journal of Forensic Sciences*, 55(3): 660–68.

Luckmann, Thomas (1989). "Prolegomena to a Social Theory of Communicative Genres," *Slovene Studies*, 11(1–2): 159–66.

Mauss, Marcel, and Henri Hubert (1981 [1899]). *Sacrifice: Its Nature and Functions*. Chicago, IL: University of Chicago Press.

Mayo, David (1992). "What is Being Predicted? The Definition of Suicide," in *Assessment and Prediction of Suicide*, eds. Ronald Maris, Alan Berman, John Maltsberger, and Robert Yufit. New York: The Guilford Press, pp. 88–129.

McClelland, L., S. Reicher, and N. Booth (2000). "A Last Defence. The Negotiation of Blame Within Suicide Notes," *Journal of Community & Applied Social Psychology*, 10: 225–40.

Merari, Ariel (2010). *Driven to Death: Psychological and Social Aspects of Suicide Terrorism*. Oxford: Oxford University Press.

Moghadam, Assaf (2008). *The Globalization of Martyrdom: Al Qaeda, Salafi Jihad, and the Diffusion of Suicide Attacks*. Baltimore, MD: Johns Hopkins University Press.

Movahedi, Siamak (1999). "The Utopian Pursuit of Death," *American Imago* 56(1): 1–26.
Murray Yang, Michelle (2011). "Still Burning: Self-Immolation as Photographic Protest," *Quarterly Journal of Speech*, 97(1): 1–25.
Osiander, Benjamin (1813). *Über den Selbstmord, seine Ursachen, Arten, medicinisch-gerichtliche Untersuchung und die Mittel gegen denselben.* Hannover: Hahn.
Özgürlük (2007). *Eyüp Beyaz.* Accessed 24 August, 2011. At <http://www.ozgurluk.org/sehitlerimiz/sehitler-html/Eyup%20Beyaz-ozgecmis.htm>.
Pape, Robert (2005). *Dying to Win: The Strategic Logic of Suicide Terrorism.* New York: Random House.
Park, B.C. Ben (2004). "Sociopolitical Contexts of Self-Immolations in Vietnam and South Korea," *Archives of Suicide Research* 8(1): 81–97.
Park, Byeong-chul (1994). "Political Suicide among Korean Youth," *Bulletin of Concerned Asian Scholars* 26(1–2): 66–81.
Pedahzur, Ami (2005). *Suicide Terrorism.* Cambridge: Polity.
Prague TV (2007). "Zdenek Adamec's Suicide Note". Accessed August 24, 2011. At <http://prague.tv/pill/article.php?name=adamec>.
Shibata, Shingo (ed.) (1977). *Alice Herz als Denkerin und Friedenskämpferin. Dialog und gemeinsames Handeln von Christen und Sozialisten.* Amsterdam: Grüner.
Shneidman, Edwin (1985). *Definition of Suicide.* New York: John Wiley and Sons.
Singh, Rashmi (2011). *Hamas and Suicide Terrorism: Multi-causal and Multi-level Approaches.* London and New York: Routledge.
Smith, Lacey Baldwin (2008). "Can martyrdom survive secularization?" *Social Research*, 75(2): 435–60.
Spivak, Gayatri (2004). "Terror: A speech after 9-11," *boundary 2*, 31(2): 81–111.
Stack, Steven (2004). "Emile Durkheim and Altruistic Suicide," *Archives of Suicide Research*, 8(1): 9–22.
TamilNet (2009a). "Last statement of Muthukumar," January 31. Accessed November 8, 2011. At <http://tamilnet.com/art.html?catid=79&artid=28208>.
— (2009b). "Eezham Tamil immolates himself to death in front of UN office in Geneva," February 13. Accessed March 6, 2009. At <http://tamilnet.com/art.html?catid=13&artid=28403>.

— (2009c). "Black Air Tiger urges Vanni youth to join for final battle," February 21. Accessed November 8, 2011. At <http://www.tamilnet.com/art.html?artid=28488&catid=13>.

Taylor, Steve (1982). *Durkheim and the Study of Suicide*. London: Macmillan.

Turner, Victor (1966). Review of *Sacrifice: Its Nature and Function*, by Marcel Mauss and Henri Hubert. *Man* 1(1): 116–17.

Wee, Lionel (1991). "The Hunger Strike as a Communicative Act," *Journal of Linguistic Anthropology*, 17(1): 61–76.

Yang, Bijou and David Lester (2011). "The Presentation of the Self: A Hypothesis about Suicide Notes," *Suicidology Online*, 2: 75–9.

YouTube (2008). "Black Tigers". Accessed January 29, 2009. At <http://youtube.com/watch?v=cCzlmzQ0Few>.

Part IV
Faux Suicide Cults

Chapter 11

Death by Whose Hand? Falun Gong and Suicide[1]

Helen Farley

Introduction

The teachings of Falun Gong explicitly forbid suicide; yet in 2001, five protesters set themselves ablaze in Tiananmen Square resulting in two deaths. The suicides' stated aim was to bring the world's focus onto the repression of the movement by the Chinese government. Falun Gong spokespeople were quick to defend founder Li Hongzhi, saying that the movement strictly forbids suicide in accordance with the traditional Chinese belief that suicide is an affront to the ancestors. They claimed that the Chinese government had staged the suicides in order to stir up public opinion against the movement. Indeed, the tide of public opinion did turn against Falun Gong and its founder (Bell and Boas 2003: 285).[2]

Yet despite Falun Gong's stated opposition to suicide, the movement does encourage its adherents to refuse medicine or medical treatment, and some regard this refusal of treatment to be suicidal. Chinese state media seized upon Li's writing in which he expressed that illnesses are caused by *karma*, and claimed that in excess of one thousand deaths were the direct result of adherents following Li's teachings. Authorities also claimed several hundred practitioners had cut their stomachs open seeking the Dharma Wheel that turns in response to the practice of the five meditative exercises characteristic of the movement. Indeed, many of their fellow followers had been arrested in Tianjin, following condemnation of their movement by physicist He Zouxiu of the Chinese Academy of the Sciences. He had claimed that Falun Gong had been responsible for several deaths (Bejsky 2004: 190).This chapter examines the complex relationship between Falun Gong and the

---

1 An earlier version of this chapter was published as Helen Farley, "Self-Harm and Falun Gong," *Journal of Religion and Violence*, 1(3) (2013): 259–75.

2 Some commentators deny that these self-immolations even took place. See Munro (2002: 267).

Chinese government, exploring the reality behind the claims and counterclaims regarding the former's stated opposition to suicide. This is contrasted with Falun Gong writings that encourage adherents to refuse medical treatments in order to rid themselves of *karma*.

On Sunday, April 25, 1999, Falun Gong first came to the attention of western media when some 15,000 adherents calmly surrounded the seat of the Chinese government at the Zhongnanhai compound adjacent to the Forbidden City in Beijing (Penny 2003: 643; Lee 2011: 209). The movement was outlawed in 1999, which signaled the beginning of a bipartisan propaganda war between Falun Gong adherents and the Chinese government, each claiming the other was responsible for deceptions, atrocities, and conspiratorial plots (Biggs 2005: 205). Falun Gong or Falun Dafa is a religious movement that arose from the *qigong* boom of the 1980s (Ownby 2003: 233). "*Qigong* fever" was the name given to the phenomenon that gained over one hundred million practitioners, some 20 percent of the urban population in China, practicing *qigong*'s characteristic breathing and meditation techniques (Palmer 2007: 6; Palmer 2008: 79). Falun Gong emerged in 1992 as part of this pre-existing *qigong* movement. Falun Gong means literally "Great Way of the Wheel" or the "Dharma Wheel Discipline" (Fisher 2003: 296).

This chapter begins with a brief overview of the history of attitudes to suicide in China. There are conflicting accounts of how the act is viewed; sometimes it is condoned as the act of a martyr or as a protest, and at other times it is clearly an affront to the ancestors and thus is roundly condemned. An examination of the emergence of Falun Gong from the larger *qigong* movement in the early 1990s follows. Most people in the West think of Falun Gong adherents as peaceful meditators, cruelly suppressed by the Chinese government. The veracity of this claim is scrutinized, along with the central tenets of Falun Gong belief and practice. Falun Gong adherents have a strong belief in fate, destiny and *karma* that is congruent with their attitude to death, but particularly to suicide. Though Falun Gong founder Li Hongzhi speaks against suicide, his teachings may inadvertently condone suicide in two particular circumstances: in self-immolation as a form of protest and in the refusal of adherents to accept medical treatment when ill, sometimes resulting in death.

Suicide in China

The suicide rate in China is one of the highest in the world and suicide has often played a prominent role in Chinese culture (Fei 2011: 213). Indeed, suicide has featured in accounts of defeated military leaders and monarchs during the shifting of dynasties, wars, the uncovering of corruption, and unfavorable family circumstances (Lo 1999: 624). Depending on the viewpoint of the narrator, suicide was variously depicted as an act of fervent loyalty, as an extreme form of moral protest, or as a strategy for escaping abusive or unjust social or familial situations (Lee and Kleinman 2005: 296, Fei 2011: 214). By way of example, in pre-Communist China, Mao Zedong wrote about women who took their own lives in order to escape forced marriages. These suicides he considered to be symptomatic of larger societal problems, such as the double standards around chastity and promiscuity in men and women, the inability to pursue love, and other facets of patriarchy that disempowered women. He viewed suicide as a symptom of a society that had caused people to lose hope (Lee and Kleinman 2005: 295). It is true that in contrast to most other countries, the suicide rate for women in China is significantly higher than for males (Zhang and Xu 2007: 185).

Suicide rates soared during the Cultural Revolution. During the mass arrests and detentions between 1966 and 1969 by the Red Guards, official reports claim that around 35,000 people died from all causes, though the actual figure is probably closer to 400,000 (Lester 2005: 100). Teachers jumped from windows and those detained in labor camps and prisons found ingenious ways of ending their lives (ibid.: 100–101). These suicides were acts of protest against a brutal regime, often precipitated by violence and torture. Even so, suicide is generally eschewed in the Chinese tradition as polluting. It is viewed as an unnatural death and, consequently, to be shunned. In some cases, the unfortunate victim is not to be mourned. The consequences of suicide also include economic hardship for the family through the loss of that person's productivity and reproductive power (Lee and Kleinman 2005: 296). Suicide notes are often characterized by a deep sense of remorse and a sense of unfulfilled filial responsibility towards parents and the family (ibid.: 297). In other contexts, Chinese cultural attitudes to suicide are to some extent ambiguous: it can be supported as pro-social or frowned upon as anti-social. In the context of Confucian thought, it is morally wrong to preserve one's life at the expense of benevolence and justice ("*ren*" and "*yi*"). Life is good, but is not the supreme good; death is evil, but it is not the supreme evil (Lo 1999: 626).

Suicide can also be viewed as a practical solution to a problem and in this context it is supported. For those who believe in reincarnation, the temptation to begin life anew is sometimes too great. Many women, especially in rural areas, wish to reincarnate as a man (Zhang and Xu 2007: 189). This tension between opposing viewpoints while allowing for creative ambiguity also encompasses the challenges of normlessness and hypocrisy. For this reason, the community and family members might view the suicide differently (Lee and Kleinman 2005:

295). Suicide can be viewed as a means of defying social power and as a strategy to respond to the inter-subjective struggles of commonplace social experience. Social forces may prevail in defiance of individual purposes and aspirations, and in turn, suicide may convey a resistance to the imposition of that authority (ibid.: 300–301). For example, Lucien Bianco wrote that one of the most common ways to exact revenge upon a callous creditor was to commit suicide in front of his door. In doing so, it caused the landlord to lose face (Bianco 1978: 280).

The reportage of suicide in an authoritarian state is rarely straightforward. In some instances, administrations have suppressed the real number of deaths ascribed to suicide in order to limit criticism of the state. Until the late 1980s, there was very little reliable data on suicide in China (Lee and Kleinman 2005: 295; Xin Ma et al. 2009: 159). In some cases, World Health Organization estimates of Chinese suicide rates are up to 40 percent higher than Chinese government estimates (Phillips et al. 2002: 835). Conversely, these same regimes may attribute suicides to a particular group or groups in order to discredit them or to garner public support against them. This is what Falun Gong practitioners have accused the Chinese government of doing in regards to several cases of self-immolation reported in the media both in China and the West. Certainly, Falun Gong attracted much criticism following the alleged self-immolation of practitioners (Bell and Boas 2003: 285).

The Birth and Substance of Falun Gong

Falun Gong emerged onto the Chinese religious landscape in 1992, founded by Li Hongzhi (Palmer 2007: 6; Penny 2012a: 35). It emerged from the *qigong* movement that had transfixed China since the 1980s. *Qigong* can be described as a system for improving and maintaining health based on ideas found in traditional Chinese medicine (TCM) and other aspects of Chinese culture. The practice of *qigong* involves practitioners observing a wide range of physical, mental, and breathing exercises. "*Qi*" can be translated as vital energy, and "*gong*" as skill, so *qigong* is literally the skill of developing vital energy so as to obtain good health (Xu 1999: 967; Rahn 2002: 41).

By 1991, there was considerable criticism and cynicism about *qigong*. The Chinese government began to vigorously monitor *qigong* masters, associated literature and *qigong* organizations with the goal of uncovering "false" or "unscientific" *qigong* (Ownby 2008: 166; Chen 2003: 509). It was amid this widespread disenchantment with *qigong* that Falun Gong emerged and was able to gain traction, attracting millions of adherents across China (Ownby 2000).

Li Hongzhi deliberately distanced Falun Gong from *qigong* by arguing that the aim of Falun Gong was not about the accumulation of extraordinary powers such as clairvoyance or supernatural healing, as had been the focus of much *qigong* practice. He also emphasized that it was not specifically about health, though good health was sure to follow rigorous practice. In contrast to *qigong*, the goal of Falun Gong was to purify one's heart and attain spiritual salvation (Lu 2005: 175; Palmer 2007: 219). The earliest writings about *qigong* described body postures and illustrated appropriate techniques, but did not contain any moral content. By way of contrast, the writings of Li Hongzhi contain moral content to accompany the somatic technologies (Ownby 2000). Supporters of both Falun Gong and *qigong* were equally strident in their protests that the two sets of practices were independent. Though it emerged from the ideas and practices of *qigong*, Falun Gong has characteristic exercises and ideologies that differentiate it from *qigong* (Irons 2003: 254; Palmer 2007: 27–8).

Given Falun Gong's interesting status within the People's Republic of China, it is useful to examine the background of its charismatic founder. Seen as an enlightened master by Falun Gong adherents, he is portrayed by authorities as evil incarnate, an unscrupulous liar and charlatan. Li Hongzhi completed his primary school education in Changchun in 1969, graduating from junior high school at eighteen and applying to join the Communist Youth League. Former schoolmates and teachers recall him as an ordinary child who was unexceptional academically in school (Thornton 2005: 260). The Chinese government is adamant that Li Hongzhi learned how to perform *qigong* exercises in 1988. Falun Gong sources dispute this, instead saying that he was drilled from age eight in those disciplines by various Taoist and Buddhist masters (Lu 2005: 178; Penny 2003: 648–9). Whatever the situation, it is certain that Li did travel to Beijing in 1992 to participate in research with a group at the China Qigong Scientific Research Society (Tong 2009: 8). Not long afterwards, Li founded the Falun Gong Research Society with his associates Li Chang, Wang Zhiwen, and Yu Changxi. Accreditation followed and the new organization was recognized as a branch of the larger organization, which in turn publicized Falun Gong training sessions (Tong 2002: 640). After 1994 when Li left China, these sessions were no longer conducted. According to Falun Gong sources, the reason for their discontinuation was to enable Li to devote all of his time to the study of Buddhism. But it is likely his departure had more to do with the mounting opposition Falun Gong was attracting within Communist Party and government circles (Ownby 2008: 167). By this time, Falun Gong had tens of millions of adherents enticed by its negligible admission criteria, lack of membership fees, simple exercises, and assurances of health and salvation (Chang 2004: 4; Irons 2003: 250; Penny 2012b: 7). Li Hongzhi finally left China for the United States in 1996, just ahead of government persecution. He established himself in New York, where he resides and actively directs Falun Gong's operations (Burgdoff 2003: 335).

Falun Gong adherents believe that Li possesses supernatural powers such as the capacity for levitation and that he is able to manifest miracles. In order to promote this image, he associates himself with characters in popular martial arts media and fantasy literature (Xiao 2001: 125, 6). Further, Li claims to use telekinesis to insert the *falun*, or the "wheel of the law," into the abdomens of those who follow him (Hongzhi 1999a: 130). Li claims that negative energy is expelled as this wheel turns, and positive energy is generated, ensuring sound health and an absence of disease (Fisher 2003: 295; Palmer 2003: 353). In order to keep the wheel turning, adherents must regularly perform the five characteristic meditative exercises of Falun Gong, thereby removing any accumulation of bad karma (Thornton 2005: 260–61). To further support this process of cultivation, Li directs "law bodies," or *fashen*, which are complete, independent, and realistic individuals which are flexible and invisible. He directs the *fashen* to protect followers suffering from illness, healing them in the process. Those practitioners serious about adhering to Falun Gong must uphold the purity of their devotion, ceasing any other sort of spiritual practice. Serious adherents must also avoid even reading about or thinking about other forms of spirituality in order to avoid deformation of the rotating *dharma* wheel (Lu 2005; 177–8, 180).

Falun Gong, also known as Falun Dafa, is an uneasy fusion of several pre-existing traditions—namely Taoism, Buddhism, and Chinese folk religion—which have been remixed into something never before seen in China (Thornton 2005: 260; Lu 2005: 174). The breathing and meditative aspects of Falun Gong closely resemble the breathing exercises used to increase potency and longevity in Taoism (Chang 2004: 39). Even so, there are numerous references to UFOs and science, giving the movement a more contemporary appearance (Ackerman 2005: 500). This is reinforced by Falun Gong's extensive use of modern communication technologies including email and the Internet (Leung 2002: 782). In the West, Falun Gong is known primarily as a harmless set of meditational exercises that are readily accessible to novice practitioners. In reality, it is first and foremost a rigorous system of morality (Penny 2003: 644; Chan 2004: 676; Ackerman 2005: 501; Burgdoff 2003: 336). Physical rejuvenation and good health are only the result of strict moral practice (Ownby 2000; Madsen 2000: 243). Followers strive to foster the time-honored spiritual values of truthfulness, compassion, and tolerance through the practice of particular exercises and meditation (Hongzhi 1999b: 59–61; Madsen 2000: 243). The practitioner directly experiences the supreme nature of the cosmos energized from within by the energy of the turning *falun* when he or she becomes suitably developed (Leung 2002: 764). The purging of negative *karma* accrued from this life and previous incarnations, together with the accrual of virtue as accepted in Falun Gong, allows the cultivation of spiritual advancement (Ownby 2008: 93). In spite of the extensive moral teachings in Falun Gong, followers and leaders alike claim that Falun Gong is not a religion, but a movement that encourages spiritual and moral cultivation (Keith and Lin 2003: 629–30; Madsen 2000: 243).

In Falun Gong, everything is either good or evil, and individuals are either true practitioners or ordinary people. Those who remain faithful to Li's teachings are true practitioners with a fated relationship to Falun Gong and access to the highest spiritual truth. If they are able to remain faithful to Li's teachings and resist seductions along the way, this elite group will attain enlightenment. Any deviance from this path and they will resume their pathetic lives as ordinary people, destined for annihilation at some time in the not-too-distant future (Lowe 2003: 268). To most observers, these apocalyptic and millenarian characteristics make Falun Gong resemble a religion (Chang 2004: 59, 60; Burgdoff 2003: 334).

Suicide and Falun Gong

Li Hongzhi has repeatedly criticized suicide as a sin, as part of a larger prohibition against taking life. According to the tenets of Falun Gong, God has a plan laid out for every individual. Not every detail of a life is planned out but the major milestones such as birth and death are planned to take place at certain immutable times. Obviously, Falun Gong practitioners are able to influence their own lives, but it is very difficult to extend a lifespan beyond an allotted time. By killing oneself before time, an individual is effectively sidestepping the divine plan. The act of suicide, while temporarily removing a person from suffering, is an act that accrues even more negative *karma* for an individual, which increases the amount of *karma* to be eliminated in a future incarnation. An individual would be better advised to endure the suffering, thereby helping to eliminate negative *karma* and not attracting more *karma* through suicide (Hongzhi 1999a: 27). Before a person dies, preparations are occurring for that individual's next incarnation. A mother is pregnant, awaiting the birth of her child and the fetus is awaiting the consciousness of the individual. If someone dies by their own hand before their designated time, then that individual must wait between lives in a nether world until they have spent the allotted time of their own predestined lifespan. Once that time has passed, the individual will move into the next incarnation but with an additional accumulation of *karma* (Penny 2012b: 116).

Though theoretically adherents of Falun Gong are opposed to suicide, there are two instances that confuse the situation. The first involves the self-immolations that took place in 2001 as a protest against the persecution of Falun Gong by the Chinese government. The crackdown that occurred after these events also sparked a number of mass suicides in detention centers. The second is in Falun Gong adherents' refusal to seek medical help when they are ill. This has resulted in a number of deaths from a variety of medical disorders that remained untreated. Though suicide is not condoned in Falun Gong, there are certain philosophies and circumstances that predispose followers towards suicide in particular contexts.

Self-immolation

Suicide by burning is an intensely dramatic method of terminating one's life (Romm et al. 2008: 988). Self-immolation, while involving an individual intentionally killing him or herself as with other forms of suicide, is usually done for or on behalf of a larger cause. An act of self-immolation is not about injuring anyone else or inflicting material damage. Rather, it is an extreme form of protest. Thus, it is usually done either in a public place or with an accompanying letter directed to the public or to specific political leaders (Biggs 2005: 173–4). These individuals are attempting to appeal to others and to incite potential sympathizers (ibid.: 201). This kind of protest in not unknown in China; there is a long history of suicide as protest in China, for example, women committing suicide to protest unfair or cruel familial situations (Lee and Kleinman 2005: 296; Fei 2011: 214).

On January 23, 2001, the eve of Chinese New Year, seven Falun Gong followers traveled over 550 kilometers from Kaifeng to Tiananmen Square, to set themselves alight in front of cameras and journalists from the Cable News Network (CNN) (Biggs 2005: 176; Thornton 2005: 266; Ching 2001). One of the protesters, a man sitting on the ground, was enveloped by fire; another four consisting of two mother and daughter pairs, lurched about with their arms raised as flames consumed their bodies. Police hurried to extinguish the flames and assembled a barrier to block the view of onlookers, but police were not fast enough; a 36-year-old woman died from her burns. Initially, the Chinese government attempted to quash news of the event, even though western journalists had been present and had recorded it; the tape was immediately confiscated by authorities (Chang 2004: 16–17). But soon the government realized they could use this as an opportunity to muster opposition to Falun Gong. A week after the incident had occurred, state television broadcast some footage showing the 12-year old daughter of one of the practitioners, rolling around in agony. The government framed the deaths as "cultic suicide," and discredited them as a form of protest (Biggs 2005: 205).

The leadership of Falun Gong were quick to deny any connection to the incident. From the United States, it released its own video, charging the Chinese government with fabricating the incident (ibid.: 206). Adherents abroad claimed that the self-immolators were not true practitioners (Thornton 2005: 266), because both Li and the movement had consistently opposed any form of killing, including suicide, as a means of reaching salvation (Chang 2004: 17–18). This attempt to disassociate itself from the act was probably counter-productive. In all probability, the leadership of Falun Gong did not encourage or sanction these actions; but it also seems unlikely that it was part of a Chinese government conspiracy to discredit the organization. Interestingly, some of the adults had participated in previous protests. Even in light of the government manipulation of the event's coverage to the detriment of Falun Gong, two more people set themselves alight in the months following (Biggs 2005: 205). On February 16, another adherent immolated himself on a residential street in Beijing. By the time the police arrived just a few minutes later, Tan Yihui, just 25 years old, a shoe-shiner from Hunan province, had died (Chang 2004: 17–18). The self-immolations continued when on July 1, Luo Guili set himself alight in a city square in Nanning in southern China. Barely 19 years old, he died the following day of severe burns and heart and lung failure (ibid.: 21).

Prior to the propaganda campaign resulting from the self-immolations, people marveled at the Chinese government's repression of such an insignificant and benign organization. Subsequent to it, people thought that the government's actions were justified. Authorities had shown the 12-year-old girl's face on television for more than a month, and public opinion shifted to oppose Falun Gong. It seems unlikely that the state could have attained such success if children had not been involved in the immolation. Such a move allowed the government to step up their repression of the organization, which included the systematic torture of its followers. The Chinese government claimed that around 1,700 Falun Gong followers had committed suicide; evidence, they reasoned, of Falun Gong's cultish evil (Bejesky 2004: 155; Biggs 2005: 206). The Chinese media carried many anti-Falun Gong diatribes. Children were compelled to attend anti-Falun Gong lessons, and 12 million school students contributed to a signature campaign, signing a declaration asserting their disbelief in cults and opposition to them. Thousands of workers attended mass meetings and signed petitions condemning the movement (Chang 2004: 18). Within just six months of the shocking incident, Falun Gong was effectively disempowered within China (Richardson and Edelman 2011: 380). During the course of 2002, the maimed survivors were paraded around and were part of a press conference. "Falun Gong is indeed an evil cult and it led me to this," uttered Chen Guo, the daughter of the woman who died (Thornton 2005: 266). Footage showing the young girl, her face badly burned and bandaged, calling out for her mother, was shown repeatedly on television (Chang 2004: 18).

In response to the crackdowns, on June 20, 2001, some sixteen Falun Gong followers held in a Harbin labor camp attempted suicide by hanging themselves with ropes created from bed sheets. Of these, ten women died. These followers were among thirty who had previously gone on a hunger strike, for which they had their sentences extended by six months. In addition, authorities conceded that eleven Falun Gong members in a re-education center had attempted mass suicide, with three dying from the effort. For its part, the Falun Gong leadership claimed that fifteen followers in that same camp died as a result of torture (ibid.: 28).

In light of the Chinese government's persecution of Falun Gong, Li Hongzhi fashioned an apocalyptic ideology to motivate his disciples to instigate and participate in civil disobedience. It was estimated that by February 2002, 365 practitioners had died while in custody, and more than 50,000 were either in prison, labor camps, or mental hospitals (Palmer 2003: 355). Would-be activists were not formally invited to become a member of an activist team. There were no formal instructions on how to dissent. Civil disobedience actions were planned at local meetings. The heroic roles of the protester and the martyr were exhibited via testimonials and stories at "Experience-Sharing Conferences" (Palmer 2003: 353–4). Li increasingly talked extensively about "*Fa*-rectification," the process by which the cosmos would be rid of evil. This process would ensure the annihilation of evil doers—in this context, those responsible for suppressing Falun Gong. The process had already begun on other levels and would soon come to humanity. This was the struggle before that final battle (Penny 2012b: 156–60). Hundreds of practitioners chose to place themselves in situations where they died painfully (Palmer 2003: 362).

After the political heat intensified in response to the immolations, Falun Gong adherents displayed posters on power poles in Shenyang City and dropped fliers in letter boxes in Beijing back streets, disputing the government's reports of the self-immolations and condemning them for turning a blind eye to poverty and unemployment. Residents were inundated with video footage and automated phone calls that played recordings criticizing the government. Angry followers also hacked into television broadcasts (Chang 2004: 21; Thornton 2005: 266; Rahn 2002). The apocalyptic teachings of Li Hongzhi could well have precipitated the self-immolations through a veiled call to civil disobedience and the promise of salvation for martyrs. Li teaches that the "Ending Period of Catastrophe" is almost here, that contemporary society is degenerate and will be purged. The only ones who will be saved are those who are genuine Falun Gong practitioners. Li called Jiang Zemin, then president of the People's Republic of China, "the highest representative of the evil force in the human world," who is being manipulated by higher beings to persecute Falun Gong. According to Li, only when evil is eliminated can practitioners return home through consummation to the Falun Dafa paradise (Rahn 2002).

Refusing Medical Treatment

Though not as dramatic as the self-immolations, many Falun Gong members have effectively committed suicide through a refusal to seek medical treatment when they were ill. There is considerable social pressure on Falun Gong followers to abandon conventional medicine, though not all inevitably do so. Li does not explicitly tell adherents not to consult doctors, saying each person must make their own decision (Hongzhi 1999a: 41–2). He asserts that disease is caused by negative *karma* (Palmer 2003: 363). In Falun Gong, *karma* is recognized as a discrete substance, and is black in color. The first goal of the process of cultivation is to transform this *karma* into another substance, called *de*, which literally means "virtue." In contrast to *karma*, *de* is white in color. Li himself then transforms *de* into a form of energy called *gong* that gradually infuses all the body's physical structures, converting it into what is known as a "pure white body" in Falun Gong texts (Penny 2012b: 42). This accounts for most of the *karma* in the body.

The process of the removal of the remainder of the *karma* is called "*xiaoye*" and is achieved through the practice of Falun Gong (Wessinger 2003: 221). According to the tenets of Falun Gong, physical disorders are actually precipitated by the ejection of negative *karma* from the body. To employ conventional medical treatment to treat the condition serves only to mask the pain associated with this elimination. In this way, *karma* can re-enter the body where it will lie dormant until it re-appears, possibly causing a more severe illness. Illness represents an opportunity to purge *karma* from the body. Hence the pain and suffering of sickness becomes a spiritual issue rather than a medical one (Burgdoff 2003: 341; Porter 2003: 157). A true practitioner does not suffer real illness, only *xiaoye*. Afflictions should not be approached with fear and dread but following the principles of forbearance, calm, and joy at the potential of being provided with an opportunity to progress spiritually (Fisher 2003: 300). Li considers that illness, along with birth, old age, and death, all have *karmic* reasons and demand *karmic* retribution. If a person is ill, then the *karmic* debt needs to be paid before wellness can be regained (Hongzhi 2003: 296).

In Li's opinion, dubious moral values have caused a variety of diseases that neither hospitals nor medicine can cure. The corruption of society has led to this situation (ibid.: 298). He further claims that medicines can poison a person and that they cannot remove the *karma* that is causing the illness (ibid.: 298–9). Instead, hospitals and medicine simply mask the spiritual illness, while healing the physical illness. The retained *karma* will cause the illness to reappear in the latter part of life (Porter 2003: 157). According to Li, when an individual dies, the *karma* is pressed into the reincarnated person and is not obvious to start with. The sickness will appear to be caused by some trigger in the physical world but this is really not the case. If the person dies again without having purged that *karma* through enduring the illness, then the illness will manifest in the individual in a subsequent lifetime (Hongzhi 2002: 38–40). He likens the human body to a tree in which the growth rings contain the sickness *karma*. He further asserts that no person is able to deal with all of the sickness *karma* at the same time and so it must be dealt with incrementally (ibid.: 40). Interestingly, Li does not confine his criticism to Western medicine. He also claims that conventional *qigong* also delays dealing with *karma*. Further, he warns that if a person has accumulated much negative *karma* over several lifetimes and continues to accrue more by doing bad things, then sooner or later heaven will not permit the debts to remain unpaid and the person faces the complete destruction of the body and soul, that is, complete annihilation (ibid.: 41).

In this context, Li also refers to his *fashen* who, as mentioned earlier, he can direct to take on the role of removing negative *karma* from practitioners. If the practitioners are ordinary people, he will not direct the *fashen* to help them; to do so would be a waste. A practitioner condemns him or herself to ordinariness by taking medicine instead of taking the opportunity to clear *karma*. Illness is a test and *fashen* are only to help those who pass that test (Lu 2005: 177–8; Hongzhi 1999a: 41–2). When adherents die of their illness even when they have refused medical care, Li covers himself by asserting that the person must have been an ordinary person and it would have been their time to die. It is not worth extending the life of an ordinary person. Li himself must acknowledge his disciples; conducting the meditation exercises and otherwise following the teachings of Falun Gong does not guarantee that Li will acknowledge that person as a disciple. The fundamental nature of that person has not been transformed because the practice was not approached with sufficient diligence (Hongzhi 1998: 33–5). Li has also expressly prohibited Falun Gong practitioners from healing others, which they would be capable of if they were advanced enough in their own cultivation. Healing others transfers the *karma* from the ill person onto the healer and, therefore, retards his or her own cultivation. It also robs the sick individual of the opportunity to begin cultivation themselves, the only sure way to health (Penny 2012b: 42).The Chinese government claims that more than 1,400 adherents have died because they rejected medical care due to their Falun Gong beliefs (Cheung 2004: 24).

Conclusion

The allure of Falun Gong lies in its claims to wed traditional Chinese culture to modern science and beyond, to the science of Master Li Hongzhi that would supplant the scientific knowledge crudely accrued thus far (Ownby 2008: 93). Falun Gong emerged from the larger movement of *qigong* through the 1990s, but is different in important ways. Both have a millenarian structure and the idea of a universal bliss in salvation. *Qigong*'s vision is of a blissful future for humanity, but Li Hongzhi tells of an apocalyptic end of the universe with salvation taking place in another dimension (Palmer 2007: 239). Body technologies are common to both and yet with *qigong* the path of accomplishment is based on paranormal powers, while in Falun Gong the way to salvation is via moral and spiritual discipline (Hongzhi 1999b: 7; Palmer 2007: 239).

Though Li Hongzhi and Falun Gong condemn suicide as an attempt to disrupt God's plan and because of the excessive negative *karma* accrued, certain philosophies and teachings predispose adherents to effectively commit suicide in certain contexts (Hongzhi 1999a: 27). The self-immolations of a number of Falun Gong practitioners in 2001, undoubtedly an act of protest against the Chinese government's crackdowns on the organization also became an appealing option for adherents because of Li's apocalyptic messages. He advocated "*fa*-rectification," increasingly focused on retribution against those who suppressed Falun Gong and the struggle that preceded it (Penny 2012a: 156–60). Though not explicitly encouraged, adherents heard stirring tales of martyrs, protesters, and the paradise that awaited them after death (ibid.: 353–4). Though the leadership of Falun Gong tried to distance themselves from the self-immolations of 2001, the mass suicides and immolations continued.

Falun Gong's teachings about illness have also encouraged large numbers of adherents to effectively suicide through their refusal of medical treatment. Though illness is seen as an opportunity to work through and expel *karma*, seriously ill adherents have died without medical treatment (Palmer 2003: 363). Li has covered himself by saying that those who died were not practicing the tenets of Falun Gong with the correct attitude and that their practice had not effected a real change in their psyches (Hongzhi 1998: 33–5). Though the aim of this practice is not to die but is to gain health, the reality is that a number of people are dying as a result, from diseases including cancer, heart disease, and diabetes. The open condemnation of suicide by Falun Gong's leadership is disingenuous given the number of followers who have died as a direct result of their adherence to Falun Gong's teachings.

References

Ackerman, Susan E. (2005). "Falun Dafa and the New Age Movement in Malaysia: Signs of Health, Symbols of Salvation," *Social Compass*, 52(2): 495–511.

Bejesky, Robert (2004). "Falun Gong and Re-Education through Labor: Traditional Rehabilitation for the Misdirected to Protect Societal Stability within China's Evolving Criminal Justice System," *Columbia Journal of Asian Law*, 17 (Spring): 148–90.

Bell, Mark R., and Taylor C. Boas (2003). "Falun Gong and the Internet: Evangelism, Community, and Struggle for Survival," *Nova Religio* 6(2): 277–93.

Bianco, Lucien (1978). "Peasant Movements," in *Republican China 1912–1949*, eds. J.K. Fairbank and A. Feuerwerker. Cambridge: Cambridge University Press, pp. 270–328.

Biggs, Michael (2005). "Dying without Killing: Self-Immolations, 1963–2002," in *Making Sense of Suicide Missions*, ed. Diego Gambetta. Oxford: Oxford University Press, pp. 173–208.

Burgdoff, Craig A. (2003). "How Falun Gong Practice Undermines Li Hongzhi's Totalistic Rhetoric," *Nova Religio* 6(6): 332–47.

Chan, Cheris Shun-Ching (2004). "The *Falun Gong* in China: A Sociological Perspective," *The China Quarterly* 179: 665–83.

Chang, Maria Hsia (2004). *Falun Gong: The End of Days*. New Haven, CT: Yale University Press.

Chen, Nancy N. (2003). "Healing Sects and Anti-Cult Campaigns," *The China Quarterly*, 174: 505–20.

Cheung, Anne S.Y. (2004). "In Search of a Theory of Cult and Freedom of Religion in China: The Case of Falun Gong," *Pacific Rim Law & Policy Journal* 13: 1–30.

Ching, Julie (2001). "The Falun Gong: Religious and Political Implications," *American Asian Review*, 19 (1 January): 1–18.

Fei, Wu (2011). "Suicide, a Modern Problem in China" in *Deep China: The Moral Life of the Person: What Anthropology and Psychiatry tell us about China Today*, eds. Arthur Kleinman, Yunxiang Yan, Jing Jun, Sing Lee and Everett Zhang. Berkeley: University of California Press, pp. 213–36.

Fisher, Gareth (2003). "Resistance and Salvation in Falun Gong: The Promise and Peril of Forbearance," *Nova Religio* 6: 294–311.

Hongzhi, Li (1998). "Falun Buddha Fa: Lecture at the First Conference in North America." New York.

— (1999a). "Falun Dafa: Lecture in Sydney." New York.

— (1999b). *Falun Gong*, rev. English edn. New York: The Universe Publishing Company.

— (2002). "Essentials for Further Advancement II." New York.

— (2003). *Zhuan Falun: Turning the Law Wheel*, English trans., 3rd edn. New York: The Universe Publishing Company.

Irons, Edward (2003). "Falun Gong and the Sectarian Religion Paradigm," *Nova Religio* 6: 244–62.

Keith, Ronald C., and Zhiqiu Lin (2003). "The 'Falun Gong Problem': Politics and the Struggle for the Rule of Law in China," *The China Quarterly*, 175: 623–42.

Lee, Sing (2011). "Depression, Coming of Age in China," in *Deep China: The Moral Life of the Person: What Anthropology and Psychiatry tell us about China Today*, eds. Arthur Kleinman, Yunxiang Yan, Jing Jun, Sing Lee and Everett Zhang. Berkeley: University of California Press, pp. 177–212.

— and Arthur Kleinman (2005). "Suicide as Resistance in Chinese History," in *Chinese Society: Change, Conflict and Resistance*, eds. Elizabeth J. Perry and Mark Selden. London: Routledge, pp. 294–317.

Lester, David (2005). "Suicide and the Chinese Cultural Revolution," *Archives of Suicide Research* 9(1): 99–104.

Leung, Beatrice (2002). "China and Falun Gong: Party and Societal Relations in the Modern Era," *Journal of Contemporary China* 11(33): 761–84.

Lo, Ping-Cheung (1999). "Confucian Views on Suicide and Their Implications for Euthanasia," in *Confucian Bioethics*, ed. Ruiping Fan. Boston, MA: Kluwer Academic Publishers, pp. 624–41.

Lowe, Scott (2003). "Chinese and International Contexts for the Rise of Falun Gong," *Nova Religio* 6(2): 263–76.

Lu, Yunfeng (2005). "Entrepreneurial Logics and the Evolution of Falun Gong," *Journal for the Scientific Study of Religion*, 44(2): 173–85.

Ma, Xin, Yu-Tao Xiang, Zhuo-Ji Cai, Shu-Ran Li, Ying-Qiang Xiang, Hong-Li Guo, Ye-Zhi Hou, Zhen-Bo Li, Zhan-Jiang Li, Yu-Fen Tao, Wei-Min Dang, Xiao-Mei Wu, Jing Deng, Sandra S.M. Chan, Gabor S. Ungvari, and Helen F.K. Chiu (2009). "Lifetime Prevalence of Suicidal Ideation, Suicide Plans and Attempts in Rural and Urban Regions of Beijing, China," *Australian & New Zealand Journal of Psychiatry* 43(2): 158–66.

Madsen, Richard (2000). "Understanding Falun Gong," *Current History* 99(638): 243–7.

Munro, Robin (2002). "On the Psychiatric Abuse of Falun Gong and Other Dissenters in China: A Reply to Stone, Hickling, Kleinman, and Lee," *The Journal of the American Academy of Psychiatry and the Law* 30: 266–74.

Ownby, David (2000). "Transnational China Project Commentary: 'Falungong as a Cultural Revitalization Movement: An Historian Looks at Contemporary China.'" Houston, TX: Rice University Asian Studies, History and the Center for the Study of Cultures.

— (2003). "A History for Falun Gong: Popular Religion and the Chinese State since the Ming Dynasty," *Nova Religio* 6(2): 223–43.

— (2008). *Falun Gong and the Future of China*. Oxford: Oxford University Press.

Palmer, David A. (2007). *Qigong Fever: Body, Science and Utopia in China*, ed. Christophe Jaffrelot (The Ceri Series in Comparative Politics and International Studies). London: Hurst & Company.

— (2008). "Embodying Utopia: Charisma in the Post-Mao Qigong Craze," *Nova Religio* 12(2): 69–89.

Palmer, Susan J. (2003). "From Healing to Protest: Conversion Patterns among the Practitioners of Falun Gong," *Nova Religio* 6(2): 348–64.

Penny, Benjamin (2003). "The Life and Times of Li Hongzhi: 'Falun Gong' and Religious Biography," *The China Quarterly*, 175: 643–61.

— (2012a). "Master Li Encounters Jesus: Christianity and the Configurations of Falun Gong," in *Flows of Faith: Religious Reach and Community in Asia and the Pacific*, eds. Lenore Manderson, Wendy Smith, and Matt Tomlinson. Dordecht: Springer, pp. 35–50.

— (2012b). *The Religion of Falun Gong*. Chicago, IL: University of Chicago Press.

Phillips, Michael R., Xianyun Li, and Yanping Zhang (2002). "Suicide Rates in China, 1995–99," *The Lancet* 359: 835–40.

Porter, Noah (2003). "Falun Gong in the United States: An Ethnographic Study," MA thesis, Department of Anthropology, University of South Florida.

Rahn, Patsy (2002). "The Chemistry of a Conflict: The Chinese Government and the Falun Gong," *Terrorism and Political Violence* 14(4): 41–65.

Richardson, James T., and Bryan Edelman (2011). "State Fostered Violence against the Falun Gong in China," in *Violence and New Religious Movements*, ed. James R. Lewis. New York: Oxford University Press, pp. 379–96.

Romm, Sharon, Heidi Combs, and Matthew B. Klein (2008). "Self-Immolation: Cause and Culture," *Journal of Burn Care & Research* 29(6): 988–93.

Thornton, Patricia M. (2005). "The New Cybersects: Resistance and Repression in the Reform Era," in *Chinese Society: Change, Conflict and Resistance*, eds. Elizabeth J. Perry and Mark Selden. London: Routledge, pp. 247–70.

Tong, James W. (2002). "An Organizational Analysis of the Falun Gong: Structure, Communications, Financing," *The China Quarterly*, 171: 636–60.

— (2009). *Revenge of the Forbidden City: The Suppression of the Falun Gong in China, 1999–2005*. Oxford: Oxford University Press.

Wessinger, Catherine (2003). "Falun Gong Symposium Introduction and Glossary," *Nova Religio* 6(2): 215–22.

Xiao, Hongyan (2001). "Falun Gong and the Ideological Crisis of the Chinese Communist Party: Marxist Atheism Vs. Vulgar Theism," *East Asia: An International Quarterly* 19(1/2): 123–43.

Xu, Jian (1999). "Body, Discourse, and the Cultural Politics of Contemporary Chinese Qigong," *The Journal of Asian Studies* 58(4): 961–91.

Zhang, Jie, and Huilan Xu (2007). "The Effects of Religion, Superstition, and Perceived Gender Inequality on the Degree of Suicide Intent: A Study of Serious Attemptors in China," *Omega (Westport)*, 55(3): 185–97.

Chapter 12
The Mount Carmel Holocaust: Suicide or Execution?[1]

James R. Lewis

Introduction

Hearts were pounding in tense expectancy when three National Guard helicopters swooped over the ridgeline and converged on Mount Carmel. There was an exchange of gunfire, during which at least some of the community's casualties were incurred. Shortly afterwards, two trucks pulling canvas-covered livestock trailers rushed up the driveway and stopped in front of the building, positioning themselves between the reporters who had gathered in the front lawn and Mount Carmel.

Hoping to avoid violence, David Koresh, unarmed, opened the front door, and began shouting, "Go away! There are women and children here! Let's talk!" According to some accounts, this gesture of appeasement was answered by a bullet, fired by Agent Steve Willis, who had been assigned to "take out'" Koresh. Willis, seated on the passenger side of an ATF vehicle,[2] fired at the Davidian prophet with a suppressed (silenced) machine gun in such a way that the gathered press would not see his act of aggression (Vinzant 1994: 49). At the same time, ATF agents in dark blue uniforms jumped out of the cattle trailers, tossing concussion grenades and screaming "Come out!" A lead agent shouted "It's showtime!" as he jumped from the trailer (Wessinger 2000: 61). Willis initially missed Koresh, who slammed the door and dived for cover as a fusillade of bullets crashed through the door. Koresh was hit twice, in the wrist and in the abdomen. The Davidians who had armed themselves when they became aware

---

1 My general approach in this chapter builds upon John R. Hall's analysis. See, for example, Hall (2002) and Hall et al. (2000).

2 ATF is an abbreviation for the Bureau of Alcohol, Tobacco, Firearms, and Explosives, a federal law enforcement organization within the US Department of Justice.

of the impending raid began shooting back, taking particular aim at Willis, who was the first agent to die.

The firefight then began in earnest. Hundreds of bullets filled the air, crashing through the buildings and vehicles, and throwing up geysers of dirt as they furiously buried themselves in the soft Texas earth. It happened quickly, like the crashing of a tidal wave over a sleepy costal village. Peter Gent, who had been scraping rust off the community water tower—the ATF subsequently dubbed it a "watchtower"—died as he turned his head to see what the commotion was all about. Jaydean Wendell, an ex-policewoman and mother of four, died when a bullet struck her in the top of the head. Winston Blake, who was sitting on the edge of his bed eating a late breakfast of French toast, was gunned down by unseen assailants firing wildly into the thin wooden walls of Carmel. The children, screaming in fear, hid themselves under the beds and any available cover as the undirected fusillade of bullets whizzed through the air.

The Davidians quickly called 911 for help. The details of this conversation reveal a community startled by the violence of the assault. At one point Koresh, speaking to the Waco police, shouted in anguish, "You killed some of my children!" "There is a bunch of us dead and a bunch of you guys dead now—that's your fault!" At other points in the conversation, Koresh made assertions like, "We told you we wanted to talk!" "Now we are willing and we've been willing all this time to sit down with anybody!" These assertions align well with the attitude of cooperation the Davidians had displayed in the past, and sharply call into question the necessity for a dramatic, military-style assault.

Two ATF casualties occurred when a team of agents went towards upper rooms believed to contain an armory and Koresh's bedroom. Video footage from this dramatic episode—showing an agent on the roof dodging bullets fired through an adjacent wall—appeared on the television news the same day. This clip was shown over and over again in subsequent weeks on television newscasts. Three agents were wounded and two killed in this tragically botched phase of the operation. Had the raid truly been a surprise, they could have effectively prevented the Davidians from arming themselves. Without a back-up plan, however, the agents charged blindly forward with this phase of the attack. Agents Todd McKeehan and Conway LeBleu were shot and killed. Other agents on the roof were wounded and escaped (Reavis 1998: 151–5).

The ATF did not see fit to end the assault until they were out of ammunition. Only at that point did they call for a ceasefire, which the community readily granted. The Davidians further allowed the ATF to remove wounded agents, even assisting them with this task. These acts of reasonableness and kindness, coming from a community that had been violently and undeservedly assaulted, were quickly forgotten. Both the agency and the media, motivated by different but convergent agendas, proceeded immediately to demonize the Davidians as evil fanatics.

Though the ATF repeatedly asserted they had been practicing the assault for months, at least some of the agents involved were not briefed until the preceding day, and were never told they would be facing high-power, assault-type weapons. Incredibly, the ATF did not even bring a doctor to treat wounded agents, a standard practice of more professional agencies like the FBI. These inept, 'Keystone Cop' antics of the ATF are difficult to understand unless we suppose that agency officials simply assumed the Davidians would give up at the first sign of a superior force, a fatal assumption that would have been immediately rejected by anyone knowing anything about survivalist religious groups. The stupidity of the attack was exceeded only by the stupidity of the explanation ATF spokespersons offered for the attack's failure: "We had an excellent plan and we practiced it for months. Everything would have been fine, except we were outgunned" (Richardson 1994: 181).

If the ATF was serving a search warrant to a heavily armed "cult" believed to have automatic weapons and perhaps even hand grenades, why were they surprised by the Davidians' powerful gunfire? Especially after they lost the element of surprise, why did ATF agents charge in with guns blazing? If Mount Carmel was such a dangerous place, why didn't they just lay siege to it from the very beginning rather than sacrificing the lives of their agents? The reason given to the public was that, in the words of one ATF official, "Either they were going to come out and attack the citizens of Waco or do a Jonestown, which was why an operation was staged that placed our agents between a rock and a hard place. Our information was that was how bad it was" (cited in Lewis 2000: 100).

The perception that Mount Carmel was another Jonestown waiting to happen is interesting from a number of different points of view. John R. Hall (2002; 1995; Hall et al. 2000) has argued that the ATF sincerely believed they were dealing with a suicide cult, which helps explain a number of aspects of the attack that are otherwise difficult to interpret. This initial attribution of being suicidal was later reinforced by the FBI who, following the deadly second attack, claimed the Branch Davidians had committed mass suicide, an explanation conveniently absolving them of any blame for the resulting deaths (Palmer 1994; Lewis 1994b; Bradford 1994).

The present chapter will focus on the "suicide cult" perception and how it helped shape the Davidian tragedy of 1993. Also, current theorists have stressed the important role hostile external forces play in the precipitation of much new religion-related violence. This line of thinking—which seems to have originated from careful reflection on the Jonestown murder-suicides—received considerable impetus from the Branch Davidians, who were for the most part victims rather than perpetrators of violence.[3] It will thus be useful to explore in some detail the "exogenous" factors (Robbins 2002: 58) that set the Mount Carmel tragedy in motion.

Another Jonestown

The first assault by agents of the Bureau of Alcohol, Tobacco, and Firearms was the end result of the differing but convergent agendas of the ATF and hostile former Davidians. Both of these groups drew heavily on the evocative power of the cult stereotype to legitimate (Lewis 2003: 198–213) their respective agendas. As analyzed by John R. Hall, "After Jonestown, 'mass suicide' became a term of general cultural currency, a touchstone for describing the stark danger posed by cults" (2002: 151–2). Davidian apostates raised the specter of Mount Carmel becoming a potential Jonestown more than a year before the raid (Breault and King 1993: 11–12). When the ATF became involved, they uncritically adopted the perspective of these disaffected ex-members.

Had it not been for these outside forces, it is highly unlikely the community would ever have been engulfed in violence. The Branch Davidians were infrequently a problem to their immediate neighbors, or to the residents of Waco. The only incident of note was the 1987 shoot-out with George Roden, the son of Lois Roden, from whom Koresh had inherited leadership of the Branch Davidians.[4] In the wake of this incident, the local sheriff, Jack Harwell, had telephoned Koresh and informed him that charges were pending from the shoot-out and that he would have to be placed under arrest and give up his weapons. Koresh promised the sheriff full cooperation. Two law officers were then dispatched to Mount Carmel where they arrested him and seven associates, and confiscated their weapons. (ATF officials could have learned some lessons

3 Even Robert Jay Lifton, whom no one can accuse of being a "cult apologist," has characterized the Davidians as "an armed but not violent" religious sect (Lifton 1999: 329).

4 Some years prior, George Roden had tried to trump Koresh in the spiritual arena by challenging him to a "resurrection contest." He dug up the casket of Anna Hughes, who had died twenty years earlier at Mount Carmel, and proposed that the two of them compete to raise her from the dead. Koresh lodged a complaint with the sheriff's office, but was told nothing could be done without evidence. So on the evening of November 3, 1987, Koresh and some others went to Mount Carmel to take photographs of the woman's remains that could be used as evidence to prosecute Roden. This led to a gun battle in which Roden received a minor wound. Koresh and his group were tried for attempted murder, but charges were eventually dismissed (Bromley and Silver 1995b: 153).

in etiquette, not to mention proper law enforcement procedure, from the McLennan County Sheriff's department.) The Davidians were eventually acquitted on charges of attempted murder.

As part of the community's gun-show business, the Davidians had purchased empty grenade casings. These were cut in half, mounted on frames, and sold as novelty items. The Bureau of Alcohol, Tobacco and Firearms initially turned its attention to the community in May 1992 after a UPS driver making deliveries to Mount Carmel saw some of the grenade casings and reported it to authorities (Kopel and Blackman 1997: 49). Possessing empty grenades is not illegal, but the UPS driver was either unaware of this or assumed he had seen live grenades. The ATF assigned Davy Aguilera to investigate, and he subsequently met with Waco Assistant US Attorney Bill Johnston and Gene Barber of the sheriff's office. Both Johnston and Barber had met with Geoffrey Hossack, a private investigator working for Davidian apostates, two years earlier. They were thus familiar with such accusations, and passed them along to Aguilera. It was at this juncture that the ATF began to become entwined in the "webs of discourse that had been spun by Koresh's opponents" (Hall 2002: 159).

The ATF, however, was not a disinterested player in the Waco drama. Before the Mount Carmel assault, the ATF had been investigated for discriminating against minorities in its hiring and promotion practices. The agency had also been accused of turning a blind eye to sexual harassment within its ranks. As discussed at length in the first chapter of Kopel and Blackman's *No More Wacos* (1997), the prospect of overcoming this tarnished image seems to have been a major impetus behind conducting a high-profile raid of the Branch Davidian community. It is also apparent in retrospect that ATF began searching for such a high-profile operation soon after it became clear that Bill Clinton would become the next president of the United States. Clinton had been broadcasting a strong anti-gun message, and certain ATF officials perceived an opportunity to expand the scope, power, and above all, the funding of their agency within the new president's anti-gun agenda. The Waco attack, if this suggestion is correct, was designed to attract positive attention to the ATF in a highly publicized raid. The raid seems to have been planned with an eye to the Senate Appropriations Subcommittee on Treasury, Postal Service, and General Government slated to meet in early March (Kopel and Blackman 1997: 47–8).

By October 1992, Aguilera was told to start drawing up an affidavit for search and arrest warrants. However, on November 2, ATF headquarters reported back to Aguilera that the evidence he had provided was insufficient justification for a search warrant. The agency then decided to establish direct contact with Davidian apostates and unhappy relatives of current members.

In order not to compromise the secrecy of their investigation, they "limited themselves to interviewing committed opponents of Koresh" (Hall 2002: 160). This self-limitation seems to have guaranteed that the ATF would come to perceive the Branch Davidians as a potential Jonestown. Recounting interviews with Breault and other hostile apostates, a US Treasury Department report noted that "Several former cult members ... noted the distinct possibility that Koresh might respond to a siege by leading his followers in a mass suicide" (US Department of the Treasury 1993: 46). This perspective was adopted and repeated to Treasury officials—officials who wanted to call off the raid—by Stephen Higgens, then-director of the ATF. Higgens explained that a forceful entry was necessary "because BATF feared that Koresh and his followers might destroy evidence or commit mass suicide if given the opportunity" (ibid.: 53, B126). The most aggressive approach was chosen, and, despite statements to the contrary, the ATF never intended to try peaceably to serve a search warrant (Tabor and Gallagher 1995: 2).

The extent to which ATF discourse about mass suicide at Mount Carmel reflected genuine concern versus the extent to which such discourse was simply rhetoric meant to legitimate a "dynamic entry" is difficult to determine. On the one hand, staging a dramatic raid immediately prior to the Senate Subcommittee hearing in combination with the agency's shameless courting of media attention indicate self-serving factors were the primary factors at work in the Waco tragedy. On the other hand, Hall's argument that the specter of mass suicide can explain a number of oddities about the assault, including why the ATF never contemplated siege as a fallback option, is also convincing (2002: 165). Probably the fear that Mount Carmel might become another Jonestown was a genuine but secondary influence.

Other, less direct, factors at work in the Waco stand-off were the media and the anti-cult movement. The notion that most "cults" are mass suicides waiting to happen is a standard component of anti-cult discourse, one that undoubtedly influenced the expectations of the ATF and later the FBI. The negative stereotype of alternative religions was also significantly responsible for shaping the attitudes of FBI negotiators, who seem never to have taken Koresh's religious views seriously: "The power of the term 'cult' ... render[ed] all other attempts at understanding unnecessary" (Ammerman 1995: 295, n.2). This view of the Branch Davidians dominated the interpretation of events in media coverage of the stand-off.

More generally, the journalistic penchant for sensationalism has been a decisive factor in promoting the cult stereotype to the larger society.[5] The mass media are not, of course, motivated primarily by the quest for truth, although some reporters have more integrity than others. Instead, the mainstream media is driven by market forces and by the necessity of competing with other newspapers, other television news programs, and so forth. This is not to say that reporters necessarily lie or fabricate their stories. Rather, in the case of New Religious Movements (NRMs), news people tend to accentuate those facets of these groups that seem to be strange, exploitative, dangerous, totalitarian, sensational, and the like, because such portrayals titillate consumers of news. This kind of reporting contributes to the perpetuation of the cult stereotype. In the words of British sociologist James Beckford:

> Journalists need no other reason for writing about any particular NRM except that it is counted as a cult. This categorization is sufficient to justify a story, especially if the story illustrates many of the other components which conventionally make up the "cult" category. This puts pressure on journalists to find more and more evidence which conforms with the categorical image of cults and therefore confirms the idea that a NRM is newsworthy to the extent that it does match the category. It is no part of conventional journalistic practice to look for stories about NRMs which do *not* conform to the category of cult. (Beckford 1994: 146)

Another important factor is the marked tendency of the mass media to report on a phenomenon only when it results in conflicts and problems. To again cite from Beckford:

> NRMs are only newsworthy when a problem occurs. Scandals, atrocities, spectacular failures, "tug-of-love" stories, defections, exposés, outrageous conduct—these are the main criteria of NRMs' newsworthiness ... And, of course, the unspectacular, non-sensational NRMs are permanently invisible in journalists' accounts. (Ibid.: 144–5).

The different media vary somewhat in their tendency to produce imbalanced reports. Television tabloids such as *20/20* and *Dateline* that have to compete with prime-time programming tend to be the most imbalanced. Rather than attempting to produce programs that examine the complex ramifications of

5 There are a number of illuminating analyses of how the media played into the Mount Carmel tragedy. See, for example, the treatments in Richardson (1995), Shupe and Hadden (1995), and Chapter 6 of Tabor and Gallagher (1995).

issues, news shows usually present melodramas in which people in white hats are shown locked in conflict with other people in black hats. On the opposite extreme are the major newspapers, such as the *Los Angeles Times* and the *Washington Post*, that tend to do the best job of presenting balanced articles on controversial subjects. Such "balance," however, usually only means finding the space for opposing views. The journalist appears to be objective when their story is two-sided rather than one-sided. The news magazines such as *Time* and *Newsweek* tend to fall somewhere in between, although on the "cult" issue they have generally been as bad if not worse than the worst of the television tabloids.

The Mount Carmel stand-off also instructively demonstrates the point that the anti-cult movement is simultaneously powerful and impotent. There were only a couple of *direct* connections between law enforcement authorities and the anti-cult movement. The testimony of deprogrammed former Davidians was used to support the contention that Koresh had to be served a search warrant (reports of deprogrammees about their former religious group are notoriously suspect). Also, Rick Ross, a deprogrammer, was consulted by the ATF prior to the attack. Before the blood had even dried in the Mount Carmel killing fields, Ross was busy promoting himself to the media on the basis of his advisory role to the ATF. Ross's only credentials, however, were that he was a deprogrammer who had deprogrammed several Branch Davidians. In common with almost all deprogrammers, he had no professional training in counseling. And as someone who made his living kidnapping cult members for money, Ross clearly had a vested interest in portraying non-traditional religions in the worst possible light. It is easy to see how ATF's distorted impressions of the Branch Davidians might have been influenced by information received from this individual.

However, beyond the consultation with Ross, which was probably minimal, the anti-cult movement exercised relatively little real direct power in Waco. Where it was most influential was in helping construct and reinforce negative stereotypes about non-traditional religions in the mass media. The three-decade-long interaction between the anti-cult movement and the media has been partially responsible for the widespread view that all non-traditional religions are dangerous organizations—this despite the fact that comparatively few such groups constitute a genuine threat, either to themselves or to society. The general atmosphere of distrust toward minority religions contributed significantly to public support for the ATF assault on Mount Carmel, and probably even explains why the ATF picked a group like the Davidians for their dramatic public raid.

What all this means for the Waco situation was that the Branch Davidians lost their chance for a fair hearing as soon as the label "cult" was applied and accepted by the general public. After that, it was only a matter of time before the media completely demonized Koresh and his followers. And after this demonization had been successfully carried out, the entire community—men, women, and children—could be consigned to the flames with little more than a peep of protest from the American public, a public that overwhelmingly approved (more than 80 percent) of the FBI's tragic final assault on Mount Carmel.

"A Bunch of Religious Fanatics Decided to Kill Themselves"[6]

On April 19, 1993, the day of the final tragedy, the FBI's workday began somewhat prior to the gas attack. As reported by a nurse interviewed on two different radio programs—one in Laporte and the other in Waco—the FBI dropped by the local hospital at 5AM Monday morning to find out how the facility was equipped to handle burn victims (Kelly 1995: 366). This incident indicates the FBI fully *expected* Mount Carmel to catch fire, and stands in sharp contrast to the agency's *apparent* lack of preparedness for the final fiery holocaust. The nurse's radio interview is, however, only the most glaring item of information in a rather lengthy laundry list of suspicious events and situations—bits of information that, while insignificant in isolation, together indicate that the Mount Carmel fire was intentionally set by the FBI rather than on the order of a suicidal cult leader.

Consider, for example, that, tactically, the best times for tear gas attacks are days on which the wind is still, allowing the gas to hang in the air around its target rather than being blown away. Instead of waiting for such conditions, the Feds chose to move on a day when the wind was blowing at a brisk 30 miles per hour. On top of that, they called the Davidians at 5:50AM and informed them *ahead of time* that the FBI was about to mount a gas attack (Linedecker 1993: 230–31). People inside the community responded by opening up the windows and doors, so as to allow the wind simply to blow the gas through the building and out the other end. This would have created a wind-tunnel effect, an effect *amplified* by the large, gaping holes the tanks created as they ripped into the building and inserted gas. Clearly, these were *poor* conditions for a tear gas attack, but *ideal* for setting fire to a wooden-frame structure.

The potential for Mount Carmel to go up in flames should have been readily apparent. Electricity had been cut off on March 12, compelling the community to use gasoline-powered generators, propane, and kerosene lamps. The building

---

[6] This statement was part of President Bill Clinton's remarks made in the wake of the FBI assault.

itself was a crudely built firetrap, constructed from plywood, both used and new lumber, and tacked together with tar paper. Bales of hay had been pushed against windows to help stop bullets.

On April 26, a team of arson investigators led by Paul Gray, assistant chief investigator for the Houston Fire Department who insisted his group of experts was independent of any federal law enforcement agency, issued their report. Gray and his team concluded the blaze must have been initiated by people inside the building in two or more different locations at about the same time. (Defending the scenario of several simultaneous starting-points was an important point in eliminating the possibility that one of the tanks tipped over a lamp that set the building on fire, which was the surviving Davidians' version of the story.) However, other authoritative sources assert that flames broke out at different points *within 50 to 120 seconds* of each other, which is not exactly "simultaneous" when we take into consideration a 30 mile per hour wind in a firetrap that burnt to the ground in less than 45 minutes.

Suspicions began to be raised on April 28, when *CBS News* correspondent Sarah Hughes broadcast the information that the "independent" arson team had close ties with the FBI. It was also discovered that the wife of arson team leader Paul Gray was an employee of the ATF. Gray responded indignantly to these revelations with the assertion that to "even suggest that any information we may be getting from the FBI is somehow tainted is absolutely ridiculous." However, on *Nightline* that same evening, lawyer Jack Zimmermann posed the question, "Why in the world did they bring in, as chief of this investigating team looking into the fire, a fellow who had been on an ATF joint task force for eight to ten years, out of the Houston office of the ATF, the office that planned and executed the raid?"[7]

In a situation already reeking with the stench of dissimulation and cover-up, choosing an individual with close personal ties to the very agencies he was hired to exonerate could only have the opposite effect of increasing rather than decreasing widely held suspicions. As if to *further* confirm critics' suspicions, the burned-out remains of Mount Carmel—along with any remaining evidence—were bulldozed on May 12. This action, which assured that no *truly* independent arson investigator would ever be able to sift through the charred remains and construct an alternative scenario, was justified on the pretext of safety and health concerns—filling holes, burying trash, and so on (Kopel and Blackman 1997: 227).[8]

---

7 Also refer to Zimmerman's more extended remarks, as well as remarks by Dick DeGuerin, who was Koresh's lawyer during the siege, cited in Kopel and Blackman (1997: 226–7).

8 As anyone who has studied the Branch Davidian fiasco in any detail knows, there were so many unusual aspects of the case that it is impossible to avoid the impression of a systematic

The government's interpretation assumes that, like Jonestown, the Davidians had actually planned a mass suicide. Given this assumption, it is plausible they set fire to Mount Carmel rather than surrender to government forces. Otherwise, the contention that Koresh's followers torched their own community is implausible. Prior to the initial ATF attack, the only sources for the view that Mount Carmel was another Jonestown were hostile ex-members, and self-appointed "cult experts" like Rick Ross (ibid.: 142–3), neither of whom were reliable sources of information. There is far more evidence to support the alternative contention, namely that the Davidians were not suicidal, and that Koresh and his followers were planning on living into the future.

From as authoritative of a source as William Sessions, then-director of the FBI, we learn that the agency had concluded before the April 19 assault that Koresh was *not* suicidal:

> ... every single analysis made of his writing, of what he had said, of what he had said to his lawyers, of what the behavioral science people said, what the psychologists thought, the psycholinguist thought, what the psychiatrists believed, was that this man was not suicidal, that he would not take his life. (US House of Representatives 1993: 124)

On April 29, Dr Murray Miron, a psycholinguistics professor consulted by the FBI, informed newsman Tom Brokaw that, with respect to the letters authored by Koresh that he had been asked to analyze: "All of his communications were future oriented. He claimed to be working on a manuscript. He was talking about the publication rights to that manuscript through his lawyer. He was intent upon furthering his cause."[9] Koresh even went so far as to retain literary attorney Ken Burrows to handle his story. He also requested another attorney to prepare a will that would protect Davidian property rights, as well as establish a trust for his children to safeguard any future income from books or movies.

Beyond Koresh himself, there are many indications that the other Davidians were not suicidal. For example, despite claims by the FBI that the community had not tried to save its children during the final fire, a May 14 report issued by the Associated Press revealed that "most of the children were found huddled in the concrete bunker, enveloped in the protective embraces of their mothers" (cited in Lee 1995), in what had clearly been an attempt to protect the children

---

cover-up. To take another particularly gruesome example, "there were thirty Davidian corpses stored in the Tarrant County medical examiner's refrigeration unit that somehow was turned off. All the corpses deteriorated, making additional examination impossible" (Wessinger 2000: 67).

9 Also refer to Miron's remarks cited in Tabor and Gallagher (1995: 169).

from the flames. These and many other particulars that could be cited indicate the Davidians were not suicidal.

Yet other kinds of questions are raised by the FBI's choice of tear gas. The gas used in the attack—a white, crystalline powder called CS (O-chlorobenzylidene malonitrile)—causes nausea, disorientation, dizziness, shortness of breath, tightness in the chest, burning of the skin, intense tearing, coughing, and vomiting. If dispersed in a flammable medium—as it was at Waco—it is also quite flammable. It is so inhumane that in January 1993, shortly before the ATF attack on Mount Carmel, the United States and 130 other nations signed the Chemical Weapons Convention agreement banning CS gas. This treaty did not, however, cover internal uses, such as quelling domestic disturbances.

On April 23, 1993, Benjamin C. Garrett, director of the Chemical and Biological Arms Control Institute in Alexandria, Virginia, was quoted in the *Washington Times* as saying that CS gas would have had the greatest impact on the children at Mount Carmel. "The reaction would have intensified for the children," Garrett said, because "the smaller you are, the sooner you would feel response" (cited in Lee 1993). According to the FBI, the anticipated scenario was that mothers, in an effort to protect their children, would leave the building with their offspring after the gas had thoroughly saturated it. White House spokesman George Stephanopoulos, speaking at a news conference, was unwilling (or unable) to account for why such a deadly form of tear gas—one that temporarily blinds and disables people—was selected over other possibilities.

Given the deadly choice of tear gas, the question of how the fires started on the plains of east Texas that fateful day becomes all the more intriguing. All of the survivors, despite FBI claims to the contrary, denied that Davidians had started the fire. Instead, they asserted the tanks had knocked over lanterns, which probably set the blaze. The Davidians were, however, being more generous to the FBI than the evidence indicates. As we have already noted, it seems the FBI took steps to guarantee flames would spread quickly, and could not be stopped once started. A dry, windy day was chosen for the assault, a day that, as pointed out earlier, would have been terrible for a tear gas attack, but perfect for incinerating a building.

Despite the obvious risk of a fire, fire trucks were nowhere near the scene when the assault began. When smoke began to appear, the FBI waited at least ten minutes before calling 911 to request firefighters from Waco. Clearly, stopping the fire was not a high priority on the agency's list. When fire trucks finally arrived, they were held at the checkpoint *under FBI order* for another 16 minutes—more than enough time to guarantee Mount Carmel would be reduced to a pile of embers before a drop of water touched the flames.

What does all of this indicate? Given the FBI's visit to the local hospital early that morning to enquire about burn facilities, given the conditions that were less than ideal for a tear gas attack, given the inadequate preparations for the possibility of a fire, et cetera, et cetera, it is impossible to avoid the conclusion that the agency *planned* to torch Mount Carmel from the very beginning. In the years following the tragedy, a wide variety of observers pointedly raised doubts about the government's claim that the Davidians had committed mass suicide (for example, Bradford 1994; Kopel and Blackman 1997; Lewis 1994b; Palmer 1994; Reavis 1998; Tabor and Gallagher 1995; Wright 1995). However, after over six years of denial, it finally came out that the FBI had misled everyone—government and public alike—about the use of "incendiary devices" on the final day of the assault (Wright 2002: 102; see also Handcock 1999). The FBI had even withheld parts of relevant documents from public scrutiny that had authorized the use of pyrotechnic military rounds (Kellman 1999). Whether intentionally or unintentionally, these rounds were almost certainly the proximate cause of the fire. Clearly, the FBI believed so, or the agency would not have gone to such lengths to hide the evidence.

Although the perpetrators of the Waco tragedy will likely never be brought to justice, these revelations definitively demolish the Branch Davidians' undeserved reputation as a suicide cult. And if there is a lesson here, it is that we should hesitate before unreflectively accusing other non-traditional religious groups of being potential Jonestowns.

Postscript: Kenneth Newport and the Mass Suicide Debate Revisited

If we set aside popular books, all of the serious books written about the Waco confrontation have been critical of the official conclusion that the Branch Davidians committed mass suicide. The community of researchers who have studied this tragedy were thus surprised when a British theologian, Kenneth G.C. Newport, published his *The Branch Davidians of Waco: The History and Beliefs of an Apocalyptic Sect* (2006) in which he argued strongly in support of the official conclusion. Stuart A. Wright, who had edited the most important scholarly volume published up to that point, penned a book review and then later a journal article demolishing Newport's argument regarding the mass suicide scenario.[10] Minus the argument for mass suicide, *The Branch Davidians*

---

[10] Wright's "Revisiting the Branch Davidian Suicide Debate" originally appeared as an article in November 2009, in the journal *Nova Religio*, 13(2): 4–24 .

of Waco is, as Wright also noted in his review, actually a fine account of the theology and history of the Branch Davidians.

In part for reasons of space, I will oversimplify Newport's argument by saying that that the cogency of his analysis depends upon accepting his contention that the imputed group suicide was the logical outcome of Davidian theology plus accepting the official account pretty much at face value. Newport also completely ignores or misrepresents contrary evidence, such as some of the items of information mentioned earlier in this chapter. This was possible, it appears, because he had reached a *theological* conclusion beforehand, and then selectively focused on gathering supporting data at the expense of disconfirming information. From my reading, the key to understanding Newport's approach to the mass suicide issue is contained in the last paragraph of his text (not counting appendices) where he asserted:

> In a post-modern intellectual climate it has become rather unfashionable in academic circles to say that people's religious beliefs or their interpretation of the Bible are wrong. But at Waco this was surely the case ... one could argue that most religious people are wrong in what they think. That might well be so. Unfortunately, however, in the case of Waco being right or wrong turned out to be a matter of life or death. (Newport 2006: 343)

It is difficult to read this passage and not infer that Newport had been convinced from the very beginning of his project that it was flawed theology which had led to the deaths of the Branch Davidians. With that conviction as a starting-point, he subsequently went about collecting evidence which would prove that this was indeed the case.

I will conclude by noting that one need not be a "fashionable post-modernist" in order to object to Newport's conclusion. Rather, to argue that an idea or that an ideology is false based on the negative results of adhering to such ideas is to commit the fallacy of *argumentum ad consequentiam*. Over the centuries, Christians as well as many other people with strong convictions have had to endure the "life or death" consequences of holding certain beliefs. If we applied Newport's style of reasoning to such historical cases, we would have to conclude that they were just as "wrong" as the Branch Davidians, a conclusion I doubt most of us, including Newport, would be ready to accept.

References

Ammerman, Nancy T. (1995). "Waco, Federal Law Enforcement, and Scholars of Religion," in *Armageddon in Waco: Critical Perspectives on the Branch Davidian Conflict*, ed. Stuart A. Wright. Chicago, IL: University of Chicago Press, pp. 282–96.

Beckford, James A. (1994). "The Media and New Religious Movements," in *From the Ashes: Making Sense of Waco*, ed. James R. Lewis. Lanham, MD: Rowman and Littlefield, pp. 143–8.

Bradford, R.W. (1994). "Who Started the Fires?: Mass Murder, American Style," in *From the Ashes: Making Sense of Waco*, ed. James R. Lewis. Lanham, MD: Rowman and Littlefield, pp. 111–14.

Breault, Mark and Martin King (1995). *Inside the Cult: A Member's Chilling, Exclusive Account of Madness and Depravity in David Koresh's Compound*. New York: Signet.

Bromley, David G., and Edward D. Silver (1995a). "The Davidian Tradition: From Patronal Clan to Prophetic Movement," in *Armageddon in Waco: Critical Perspectives on the Branch Davidian Conflict*, ed. Stuart A. Wright. Chicago, IL: University of Chicago Press, pp. 43–72.

— (1995b). "The Branch Davidians: A Social Profile and Organizational History," in *America's Alternative Religions*, ed. Timothy Miller. Albany, NY: State University of New York Press, pp. 149–58.

Hall, John R. (1995). "Public Narratives and the Apocalyptic Sect: From Jonestown to Mt. Carmel," in *Armageddon in Waco: Critical Perspectives on the Branch Davidian Conflict*, ed. Stuart A. Wright. Chicago, IL: University of Chicago Press, pp. 205–35.

— (2002). "Mass Suicide and the Branch Davidians," in *Cults, Religion and Violence*, eds. David G. Bromley and J. Gordon Melton. New York: Cambridge University Press, pp. 149–69.

—, with Philip D. Schuyler and Sylvaine Trinh (2000). *Apocalypse Observed: Religious Movements and Violence in North America, Europe, and Japan*. London and New York: Routledge.

Handcock, Lee (1999). "Waco: FBI to acknowledge use of pyrotechnic devices—New account on Branch Davidian fire expected," *Dallas Morning News*, August 25.

Kellman, Laurie (1999). "FBI Aware Early of Waco Tear Gas," *Associated Press*, September 11. Accessed November 15, 2013. At <http://www.cesnur.org/testi/waco10.htm> This article can also be found at <http://www.rickross.com/reference/waco/waco54/.html>.

Kelly, Dean M. (1995). "The Implosion of Mt. Carmel: Is It All Over Yet?" in *Armageddon in Waco: Critical Perspectives on the Branch Davidian Conflict*, ed. Stuart A. Wright. Chicago, IL: University of Chicago Press, pp. 359–78.
Kopel, David B., and Paul H. Blackman (1997). *No More Wacos: What's Wrong with Federal Law Enforcement and How to Fix It.* Amherst, NY: Prometheus Books.
Lee, Robert W. (1993). "Truth and Cover-up," *The New American.* Accessed November 15, 2013. At <http://www.thenewamerican.com/focus/waco/vo09no12_waco.htm>.
— (1995). "Waco Whitewash," *The New American* <http://reformed-theology.org/html/issue09/waco-whitewash.htm> accessed November 15, 2013.
Lewis, James R. (1994a). "Showdown at the Waco Coral: ATF Cowboys Shoot Themselves in the Foot," in *From the Ashes: Making Sense of Waco*, ed. James R. Lewis. Lanham, MD: Rowman and Littlefield, pp. 87–94.
— (1994b). "Fanning the Flames of Suspicion: The Case Against Mass Suicide at Waco," in *From the Ashes: Making Sense of Waco*, ed. James R. Lewis. Lanham, MD: Rowman and Littlefield, pp. 115–20.
— (2000). *Doomsday Prophecies: A Complete Guide to the End of the World.* Amherst, NY: Prometheus Books.
— (2003). *Legitimating New Religions.* New Brunswick, NJ: Rutgers University Press.
Lifton, Robert Jay. (1999). *Destroying the World to Save It: Aum Shinrikyo, Apocalyptic Violence, and the New Global Terrorism.* New York: Henry Holt and Co.
Linedecker, Clifford L. (1993). *Massacre at Waco, Texas: The Shocking True Story of Cult Leader David Koresh and the Branch Davidians.* New York: St Martin's Paperbacks.
Newport, Kenneth G.C. (2006). *The Branch Davidians of Waco: The History and Beliefs of an Apocalyptic Sect.* New York: Oxford University Press.
Palmer, Susan J. (1994). "Excavating Waco," in *From the Ashes: Making Sense of Waco*, ed. James R. Lewis. Lanham, MD: Rowman and Littlefield, pp. 99–110.
Pate, James L. (1993a). "Gun Gestapo's Day of Infamy," *Soldier of Fortune* magazine (June).
— (1993b). "Waco Standoff Ends in Disaster," *Soldier of Fortune* magazine (July).
Reavis, Dick J. (1998 [1995]). *The Ashes of Waco: An Investigation.* Syracuse, NY: Syracuse University Press.

Richardson, James T. (1994). "Lessons from Waco: Will We Ever Learn?" in *From the Ashes: Making Sense of Waco*, ed. James R. Lewis. Lanham, MD: Rowman and Littlefield, pp. 181–4.

— (1995). "Manufacturing Consent about Koresh: A Structural Analysis of the Role of Media in the Waco Tragedy," in *Armageddon in Waco: Critical Perspectives on the Branch Davidian Conflict*, ed. Stuart A. Wright. Chicago, IL: University of Chicago Press, pp. 153–76.

Robbins, Thomas (2002). "Sources of Volatility in Religious Movements," in *Cults, Religion and Violence*, eds. David G. Bromley and J. Gordon Melton. New York: Cambridge University Press, pp. 57–79.

Shupe, Anson, and Jeffrey K. Hadden (1995). "Cops, News Copy, and Public Opinion," in *Armageddon in Waco: Critical Perspectives on the Branch Davidian Conflict*, ed. Stuart A. Wright. Chicago, IL: University of Chicago Press, pp. 177–202.

Tabor, James D. (1994). "The Waco Tragedy: An Autobiographical Account of One Attempt to Avert Disaster," in *From the Ashes: Making Sense of Waco*, ed. James R. Lewis. Lanham, MD: Rowman and Littlefield, pp. 13–21.

— (1995). "Religious Discourse and Failed Negotiations: The Dynamics of Biblical Apocalypticism at Waco," in *Armageddon in Waco: Critical Perspectives on the Branch Davidian Conflict*, ed. Stuart A. Wright. Chicago, IL: University of Chicago Press, pp. 263–81.

— and Eugene D. Gallagher (1995). *Why Waco? Cults and the Battle for Religious Freedom in America*. Berkeley, CA: University of California Press.

US Department of the Treasury (1993). *Report of the Department of the Treasury on the Bureau of Alcohol, Tobacco, and Firearms Investigation of Vernon Wayne Howell, Also Known as David Koresh*. Washington, DC: US Government Printing Office.

US House of Representatives (1993). *Events Surrounding the Branch Davidian Cult Standoff in Waco, Texas*. Hearing before the Committee on the Judiciary, US House of Representatives, 103rd Congress, 1st Session, April 28.

Vinzant, Carol (1994). "ATF-Troop," *Spy*, March.

Wessinger, Catherine (2000). *How the Millennium Comes Violently: From Jonestown to Heaven's Gate*. Chappaqua, NY: Seven Bridges Press.

Willman, David, and Glenn F. Bunting (1995). "Agent Disputes Boss on Waco Raid Warning," *Los Angeles Times*, July 25. Accessed November 15, 2013. <http://www.waco93.com/latimes7_25_95.htm>.

Wright, Stuart A. (1995). *Armageddon in Waco: Critical Perspectives on the Branch Davidian Conflict*. Chicago, IL: University of Chicago Press.

— (2002). "Public Agency Involvement in Government-Religious Movement Confrontations," in *Cults, Religion and Violence*, eds. David G. Bromley and J. Gordon Melton. New York: Cambridge University Press, pp. 102–22.
— (2011). "Revisiting the Branch Davidian Mass Suicide Debate," in *Violence and New Religious Movements*, ed. James R. Lewis. New York: Oxford University Press, pp. 113–32.

Part V
Screen Suicide Cults

Chapter 13

Rescripting the Past: Suicide Cults on Television[1]

Lynn S. Neal

Introduction

On November 18, 1978, the world learned of the tragic murders and suicides at Jonestown. Filled with shock and horror, Americans asked a series of questions: "What happened at Jonestown?" "Why did it happen?" "How could this have happened?" As people struggled to make sense of this "revolutionary suicide," most blamed charismatic leader Jim Jones, claiming that he brainwashed his followers. This explanation shifted responsibility for the murder-suicides from members of Peoples Temple to Jim Jones, and offered many horrified observers a satisfactory explanation invoking existing stereotypes of cults and dangerous charismatic leaders (Chidester 1988: 28–46). Early press reactions to Jonestown reinforced how this movement "dissolved the thin line that separates the regions of religion and madness" (ibid.: 28). Every year in November, television networks, like the History Channel and CNN, revisit the question of religion and madness by airing specials, including "Jonestown: Paradise Lost" (2007) and "CNN Presents: Escape from Jonestown" (2008). With a focus firmly on the past, these specials seem to serve as cautionary tales to remind amnesia-prone viewers to "never forget."

If we shift our attention to fictional television, however, we can see that Americans do not have amnesia when it comes to groups labeled "cults." Since the late 1950s, the cult stereotype has been a staple of fictional television programming (Neal 2011: 95–9). Many of these programs emphasize the pain loved ones experience when a friend, lover, son, or daughter joins a cult, and the resulting commitment to rescue them from this tragic turn of events. Others focus on the alleged threat of ritual murder by crazy cultists or the seemingly

---

1 An earlier version of this chapter was published as Lynn Neal, "Suicide and Cultural Memory in Fictional Television," *Journal of Religion and Violence*, 1(3) (2013): 322–42.

unlimited potential for violence that these groups possess. These episodes explore the "thin line" between persuasion and coercion, religion and madness. Since the early 1990s, as the Branch Davidians at Waco and the Heaven's Gate members in Rancho Santa Fe further cemented the questions and fears associated with Jonestown, television programs have not shied away from the topic of cult suicide.

Television is the central storyteller in American culture (Gerbner n.d.), and television tells stories about cults and religious suicide, especially Jonestown, Waco, and Heaven's Gate. These events are not forgotten, but rather are told and retold, learned and remembered, in significant part through prime-time television shows. These narratives may not meet the standards of academic history, but as Steve Anderson writes, "American television has sustained an extremely active and nuanced engagement with the construction of history and has played a crucial role in the shaping of memory" (Anderson 2001: 20). As a result, this chapter does not focus on historical errors in television depictions of Waco or Jonestown, but, rather, examines how these traumatic historical and national moments are remembered in and through television. "Memory," Marita Sturken writes, "is crucial to the understanding of a culture precisely because it indicates collective desires, needs, and self-definitions" (Sturken 1997: 2). Thus, how television depicts the relationship between cults, suicide, and murder—the *cult*ural memories constructed about Jonestown, Waco, and Heaven's Gate—makes visible this history of desire. It reveals how Americans make sense of that "thin line" between religion and madness, life and death, government authority and divine revelation.

Television wields tremendous power to "promote and prefer certain meanings of the world, to circulate some meanings rather than others, and to serve some interests better than others" (Fiske 1987: 20). Television helps create shared meanings that reinforce the existing norms of a society, including those related to religion (Carey 1988: 18; Silverstone 1988: 37). Specifically, the portrayal of cults in televisual fictions promotes a certain understanding of religion, which privileges Christianity and "enhance[s] the values and structures of American society—independence, family, capitalism, [and] government" (Neal 2011: 93–4).

While these patterns continue to characterize fictional programs featuring cult-related suicide storylines, specific episodes also provide us with insight into the dynamic relationship that exists between historical event, cultural memory, and television narrative.[2] These relationships prompt us to ask what stories are

[2] Throughout this chapter, I use Marita Sturken's definition of cultural memory. In *Tangled Memories* (1997, 2-3), she writes that cultural memory is "a field of contested meanings in which Americans interact with cultural elements to produce concepts of the nation, particularly in events of trauma, where both the structures and the fractures of a culture are exposed. Examining

told, what meanings and memories are promoted, and whose interests are being served? To answer these questions, I examined six fictional television dramas that aired in the United States between 1999 and 2010, and referenced cults and suicide.[3] Cult-themed shows have aired since the late 1950s; however, episodes featuring cults and suicide do not appear prior to the early 1990s. It is only after the Branch Davidian disaster at Waco in 1993 and the Heaven's Gate suicide in 1997 that cults and suicide emerge as themes on fictional television. Television dramas began to examine this relationship, incorporate elements from historical events, and contribute to America's *cult*ural memory.

Approaching Cult Suicide: Television, Effects, and History

While most have examined the relationship between television and suicide from a media "effects" approach, which studies whether or not coverage of suicides relates to reported instances of suicide (Pirkis and Blood 2001; Stack 2000, Pirkis et al. 2007), the programs examined in this chapter lead to a different set of questions. How are historical elements of cult-related events (including suicide) incorporated into fictional television shows? What do these portrayals tell us about how American viewers are encouraged to remember these events? How do they frame our thinking about religion, violence, and the US government? These television dramas tell stories about cults and suicide that

---

cultural memory thus provides insight into how American culture functions, how oppositional politics engages with nationalism, and how cultural arenas such as art, popular culture, activism, and consumer culture intersect."

3 I used internet databases, TV.com and the International Movie Database (IMDb), to locate television shows featuring suicide-cult storylines. I then viewed the episodes and further narrowed the pool based on each episode's plot, the salience of the suicide cult theme, and genre. I limited my findings to television drama, although some episodes of *South Park* and *Family Guy* contain suicide cult references. In what follows, all descriptions and quotes come from the shows as cited here. *Touched by an Angel*, "Into the Fire," Season 5, Episode 20, first broadcast 4 April 1999 by CBS. Directed by Tim Van Patten and written by Brian Bird. *Law and Order: Special Victims Unit*, "Charisma," Season 6, Episode 7, first broadcast 16 November 2004 by NBC. Directed by Arthur W. Forney and written by Michele Fazekas and Tara Butters. *Cold Case*, "Blank Generation," Season 2, Episode 11, first broadcast 9 January 2005 by CBS. Directed by David Barrett and written by Meredith Stiehm and Chris Mundy. *CSI*, "Shooting Stars," Season 6, Episode 4, first broadcast 13 October 2005 by CBS. Directed and written by Danny Cannon. *Criminal Minds*, "Minimal Loss," Season 4, Episode 3, first broadcast 8 October 2008 by CBS. Directed by Felix Enriquez Alcalá and written by Andrew Wilder. *Flashpoint*, "The Farm," Season 2, Episode 19, first broadcast 18 June 2010 by CBS. Directed by Erik Canuel and written by Ian Weir, Melissa R. Byer and Treena Hancock.

incorporate elements from Jonestown, Waco, and Heaven's Gate. Drinking poisoned kool-aid, participating in "white night" drills, as well as dwellings that resemble the Branch Davidian compound, and references to UFO theology—all appear in one or more of these episodes. For example, in "Shooting Stars," an episode of *CSI*, the plot closely resembles Heaven's Gate, a notion reinforced when CSI Gil Grissom explains with increasing derision: "The mythology here appears to be similar to the Heaven's Gate cult in California several years ago. They committed mass suicide to shed their earthly bodies and hitch a ride on a spaceship hidden in the tail of the Hale Bopp comet." Further, while much of the *Criminal Minds* episode "Minimal Loss" echoes the events at Waco, they also include a "white night" drill and references to Jonestown. An agent informs his co-workers and the audience, "Jim Jones pulled the same stunt. They did a test run just like this years before they did the real thing." The plots of these episodes resemble traumatic cult-related historical events, a technique that enhances the realism and credibility of the unfolding drama, even as it prompts viewers to draw comparisons; to reinterpret the past in light of this present.

As a result, in this chapter I follow Marita Sturken's model in *Tangled Memories* (1997), and examine these episodes as "retelling[s] of the past in order to create narratives of closure and to promote processes of healing" (Sturken 1997: 24). This approach highlights how historical events have been re-imagined and re-told for the present (ibid.: 2). Thus, what these episodes excise and what they emphasize, what is forgotten and what is remembered, become clues in understanding what narratives are constructed about cults, suicide, and American culture. Through analyzing the episodes in this way, three dominant themes emerge—religion and madness, suicide and salvation, government authority and divine revelation—that show how Americans have grappled with and interpreted "suicide cults." First, cult leaders, led astray by their own power and delusions, deserve to die. Secondly, cult followers are the victims of charismatic cult leaders and must find a "good death." Third, the American government can be trusted to handle these situations in a responsible manner. Its authority, unlike claims to religious revelation, can be trusted. Through these themes, we can see how fictional stories "afford a means through which uncomfortable histories of traumatic events can be smoothed over, retold, and ascribed new meanings" (ibid.: 85).

Deserving of Death: Cult Leaders and Religious Madness

In the aftermath of Jonestown, Waco, and Heaven's Gate, the media's attention and the public's fury focused on the leaders of these movements. Allegations of corruption, coercion, brainwashing, and abuse abounded. People sought to make sense of these tragedies by assigning blame to the "crazy, charismatic cult leader," who abused his power and led innocent victims to their deaths. Given the way television shapes and reflects culture (Forbes and Mahan 2005: 4–7), it is not surprising that news and entertainment media utilized these ideas in the creation and maintenance of the "cult leader" stereotype.

In many ways, the episodes in this study reinforce existing stereotypes of cult leaders as greedy con-men and sexual deviants. In *CSI*'s "Shooting Stars" episode, viewers learn that cult leader Joseph Diamond has a history of repeatedly running the same con. He recruits college-age students to his cult-of-the-moment, has them solicit money from their parents, and then when it is time for the group to commit suicide as a sign of their devotion, Diamond drugs them with hallucinogens and absconds with the money. His followers awaken to realize they have been duped. Cult leader Abraham, in the "Charisma" episode of *Law and Order: SVU*, is also shown to be financially corrupt. Not only does he have a history of check forgery and counterfeiting, but he murdered one of his male followers to gain access to the man's daughter and heiress, Melanie. Both episodes depict Joseph Diamond and Abraham as sexual deviants. Abraham impregnated 12-year-old Melanie in a plot to get her money, and she is not his only victim. Later, the FBI psychiatrist tells the detectives: "A lot of cult leaders were known to have sexual relations with the children in their groups. David Koresh had a ten-year-old bride." While not as depraved as Abraham, Joseph Diamond is no saint. CSI Catherine Willows remarks, "Well, these earthly bodies got a good workout first. Big room, big bed, light show. This cult was about getting laid." To which, CSI Gil Grissom responds: "Well, Jim Jones and Charles Manson used sex to manipulate their followers." The inclusion of references to historical cult leaders reinforces the sense of accuracy in these fictional cult depictions, and encourages viewers to interpret the historical past in light of the televisual present.

Furthermore, even if the cult leader has not committed any sexual and financial misdeeds, deception and abuse of power remain prominent elements. Not only do Joseph Diamond and Abraham deceive their followers and wield unchecked power, but so too does Brother David, the cult leader in "Into the Fire," an episode of *Touched by an Angel*. As new convert Melina obeys Brother David's request to burn the mail, angel Monica challenges her unquestioning obedience. "These letters are addressed to people here, but Brother David never allowed them to be delivered." Melina responds: "Distractions from our past life confuse us, you know." Monica retorts, "He wants to control you like he controls everybody here. That's how cults work." However, Melina remains unconvinced.

Given the prominence and frequency of cult-themed television episodes, these stereotypical characterizations attract viewers (Neal 2011). This repetition also suggests that cults continue to be seen as deviant and or dangerous—that their stories have not been sufficiently "smoothed over" and "retold" (Sturken 1997: 85). More specifically, cult leaders remain problematic figures as their ability to wield seemingly unquestioned power and control over people's lives exists in stark contrast to the autonomy and individualism prized in American culture. How do these cult leaders gain power? Do they believe what they are saying? Does sincerity matter? Fictional television shows offer viewers a window into the cult leader's mind and motives.

As television shows attempt to render the "thin line" between religion and madness more visible, the depiction of the cult leaders' sincerity and ultimate fate is telling. One might imagine sincerity in a cult leader would highlight the religious aspects of these fictional cults; however, sincerity often becomes evidence of the cult leader's madness. This is most clear in "Charisma." During her interrogation of Abraham, Detective Olivia Benson has a stunning realization:

> You know, I thought that you were just another con-artist seeking out people who were starved for anything that would give them meaning in their life. They're easy marks. You talk about God and the apocalypse and they give you all their money. But you are much more pathetic than that. You actually believe your own hype. You've conned yourself.

This is confirmed through Abraham's maniacal appearance and his claim, at the end of the episode, that "I am greater than man ... I am greater than God." Whereas Joseph Diamond was a conman and criminal, he was not crazy, but Abraham, a man who believes in his own message, is much more dangerous. He crosses the line between religion and madness. This crossing also occurs in "Minimal Loss" and "Into the Fire." In both episodes, the cult leaders continue to quote biblical passages until the end, which demonstrates their continued delusion.

In all of these cases, the cult leader's belief in his own message precedes his death. After claiming that he is "greater than God," Abraham's young wife and victim Melanie shoots him because she recognizes his lie. "He said he was greater than God, but nobody is." In a similar way, after quoting from the gospel of Matthew, Ben Cyrus explains to Agent Reid that "No one had to follow. God could have stopped me." As he utters these words he is shot by a government agent, and Agent Reid provides the audience with the preferred interpretive lens: "He just did." Despite Monica's explanation that God has not forsaken Brother David and her attempt to save him, he remains in the burning building resolute in his belief that "I'm destined to sit at the right hand of God. I know he's coming for me."

Abraham and Ben Cyrus are shot, Brother David commits suicide, and Joseph Diamond is murdered. No matter their manner of death, these fictional television episodes affirm the stereotypical attributes of cult leaders, show that their religiosity is a form of madness, and portray death as a viable solution to the problem these men present. As Agent Derek Morgan explains in "Minimal Loss," "Cults are structured like pyramids. Got the leader at the top, die-hard believers, underneath, biggest group the base—the followers—women and children. These [the women and children] are the people we can save." Cult leaders because of their crimes, depravity, and their crazy religious beliefs deserve to die.

This message also emerges in episodes that do not specifically equate religiosity with mania. For example, even though Joseph Diamond does not believe his own con, he becomes a victim of it. He is murdered by devout follower, Abigail, for his lack of belief. She explains, "He always said we'd be tested," and a flashback shows her discovery of Diamond's duplicity as well as her response (hitting him over the head with a tire iron). Similarly, an episode of *Flashpoint* entitled "The Farm," features a "secular" cult that revolves around drug rehabilitation—the group resides on a secluded farm, has cut off ties with family members outside the group, and adheres to the rules of cult leader Charles. An exchange between members of the Strategic Response Unit makes this clear: "You should hear how they talk about this guy Charles, they're totally devoted to him," to which another agent responds, "This is sounding like a cult mentality." In many ways, "the farm" resembles a secular version of Jonestown complete with questions about the cult leader's sanity. Charles's behavior appears erratic, increasingly paranoid, and the threat of mass suicide looms. In addition, viewers see that Charles is taking some kind of drug. Reminiscent of debates about Jim Jones's state of mind in 1978, Charles's delusional and dangerous acts emerge from the realization that he is going to die from terminal cancer and his belief that mass suicide will keep his followers safe. While the Strategic Response Unit prevents the mass suicide, Charles, like Brother David, kills himself. Thus, even though Diamond does not believe in the religious teachings he promotes and Charles has transformed the "secular" enterprise of rehab into one that resembles a "religion," both still die.

If we think about these episodes and their portrayal of cult leaders as a form of *cult*ural memory, as a mechanism by which we make sense of the past for the present, then we must ask what memories are being constructed? How are the histories of traumatic events like Jonestown, Waco, and Heaven's Gate being "smoothed over"? These episodes emphasize at least three ways of thinking about and remembering cults, both fictional and historical. First, by drawing comparisons between fictional and real-life cult leaders, these programs not only enhance the realism of their fictional plots, but also affirm that Jim Jones and David Koresh, like Brother David, Ben Cyrus, and Abraham, were deceptive, deviant, and dangerous in numerous ways. As a result, they do not deserve concern, nor do their beliefs merit understanding. Secondly, these episodes make it clear that cults are not "real" religions. Rather, cults are creations of power-hungry men who distort the ideas and ideals of religion(s) for their own selfish reasons. Cults are shown to be flawed and dangerous human creations. The episodes make an implicit contrast with "real" religion, which presumably is divinely instituted, devoid of corruption, and safe. This message not only reinforces the illegitimacy of "cults" more broadly, but also promotes specific interpretations of Jonestown, Waco, and Heaven's Gate as the delusional creations of power-hungry men. These were not religious communities seeking enlightenment or salvation, but rather people led astray, brainwashed, and victimized, by charismatic leaders who perverted religion for their own ends. Third, just as the cult leaders in these episodes deserved to die, so too did Jim Jones, David Koresh, and Marshall Herff Applewhite. Whether their manner of death was murder, suicide, or the bullet of a government agent, these men needed to die. As cult leaders, these men are identified as responsible for the tragedies that occurred. The threat of their deviance can only be counteracted with deadly force. Ultimately, these cult leaders are consumed by the violence and havoc they caused. The episodes construct a *cult*ural memory in which only Jim Jones, David Koresh, and Marshall Applewhite are to blame for the tragic events that occurred. Neither the government nor the public is responsible. Culpability resides solely with the leader. As a result, these programs discourage empathy toward charismatic cult leaders, while promoting an understanding that men like David Koresh and Jim Jones deserved to die for their religious deviancy and abuses of power.

Finding a "Good" Death: Cult Followers and Victimization

The cult leader's responsibility for the events that unfold is further emphasized by the portrayal of cult followers as victims, rather than willing participants. This emerges clearly in how episodes portray their manner of death. None of the dramas examined in this study include an example of an adult cult follower committing religious suicide (an individual at least 21 years of age knowingly and willingly making the decision to take one's life for religious reasons). Three general patterns emerge that firmly situate cult members as victims. First, suicidal acts by cult members are explained by their victimization at the hands of the leader. Secondly, apparent suicides are revealed to be murders, and third, attempted mass suicides are thwarted.

In only two of the dramas, *Criminal Minds* and *Charisma*, is a suicidal action taken by a cult member. In both cases, the actions are committed by young women under the age of 21 who have been the victims of the cult leaders' sexual perversions. In the *Criminal Minds* episode "Minimal Loss," 15-year-old Jessie, the "wife" of Ben Cyrus, remains loyal to him, and at the end of this Waco-like scenario, Jessie sees Cyrus's dead body, picks up the detonator that has fallen from his hand, and blows up the building. She is seemingly the only victim left in the residence—a symbol of youth and innocence permanently scarred by the delusions and depravity of Ben Cyrus. In "Charisma," the investigation reveals that after the initial conflict with police, a 20-year-old female follower of Abraham shot the children and then killed herself. However, her actions are never depicted. She emerges in the story only as a corpse and a victim, a status that is heightened when Detective Munch remarks, "Abraham had total control over all of these kids. He orchestrated all of this." Like Jessie, this unnamed young woman represents innocence lost, normal childhood disrupted, and right religious thinking unraveled.

While *Cold Case* and *CSI* also depict cult followers as victims, they show this in a different way. In these episodes, initial interpretations of events are challenged to show that cult suicides did not really occur. For example, in *Cold Case*'s "Blank Generation," the team re-opens the case of Matthew, a young man who belonged to a cult and apparently committed suicide in December 1978. The episode firmly situates this case in the aftermath of Jonestown as an early scene indicates:

> Beth [Matthew's sister]: "This was '78, Jonestown had just happened."
> Detective Valens: "The kool-aid?"
> Beth: "We were scared that they were going to do the same thing."

As the investigation unfolds, the detectives discover that the cult had no mass suicide plan, and Matthew's status as a victim becomes clearer. He has not committed suicide for any reason. He is a sincere, yet troubled young man seeking answers—a spiritual journey cut short by his tragic death, his murder. The detectives discover that after a conversation with his family, Matthew rejected the group's violent plans and went back to the cult residence to "save" his girlfriend. There he fell victim to her perfidy: cyanide in his drink. Matthew tells his lover Allison, "I came back … to save you," only to be met with the reply: "I'm saving you." Thus, Matthew finds a "good" death. He is the victim of murder, but at least he has not committed suicide, which in the episode is described as a "defective thinking," "narcissism," and a "screw you to the world."

Similarly, in "Shooting Stars," what appears to be a mass suicide for religious reasons is revealed to be something else. The CSIs discover that, like Matthew, the cult members were victims of an overzealous fellow member, Abigail. While they were willing to commit suicide, the audience learns that these followers were only supposed to be the victims of a hallucinogenic drug. It is Abigail, a sincere believer in Diamond's teachings, who commits the crime. She replaces the hallucinogen with a lethal drug cocktail, and then watches her fellow cult members die. After her own unsuccessful suicide attempt, Abigail continues to believe in Diamond's teachings and her murderous actions: "I know they're all up there—happy, healthy, perfect." This plot frames Abigail as both a victim of Joseph Diamond, and the perpetrator of horrific violence caused by her deluded belief in a conman. At the same time, this depiction reframes the deaths of the eleven cult members. They may have been willing to take their own lives, but, in fact, they were the unknowing victims of Abigail. If Diamond had executed his con, then these young people would have had the chance to learn from their mistakes, to continue their life journeys. With this opportunity precluded, their deaths are framed as a tragedy, but ultimately the show undermines the idea that they committed religious suicide.

In *Touched by an Angel* and *Flashpoint*, one sees a different framing of events. In these two episodes, none of the cult followers die. All are rescued, by angels and government agents, respectively. In these scenarios, viewers also see these cult followers question and protest the cult leader's actions. Toward the end of *Flashpoint*'s "The Farm," cult leader Charles has led everyone into a barn, barred the exits, and his minions begin releasing poisonous gas. However, most of the followers are restive, fearful, and questioning ("What's happening?" "Why are you locking us in?"). As the gas spreads, people do not meekly acquiesce to their deaths, they struggle, demand to be let out, and pound on the barn door seeking an exit. The Strategic Response Unit arrives in time and the followers are saved. In *Touched by an Angel*, though Brother David's followers have clearly rehearsed for mass suicide with "drills" and pitchers of kool-aid, they change their minds when angel Monica reveals herself and shares her message:

> I am an angel from God, the true God, the Alpha, the Omega, Jehovah, creator of heaven and earth. Listen to me. This act, this taking of your own lives is not an acceptable sacrifice to God. Would it not be better to break the bonds of oppression? To feed the hungry, to clothe the naked, to let the homeless into your homes? Then will the glory of God break forth for you. Then will you cry out to Him and He will answer, here I am. Believe it. He is waiting for you here—in life—not in death as blind followers and the murderers of little children.

Monica assures Brother David's followers that life, not death, is God's plan for them, and they slowly, one by one, throw away their cups of kool-aid. Even when Brother David sets the building on fire, Monica uses her angelic powers to unlock the chained doors and lead the victims to safety.

Through these three patterns, we see cult followers defined as victims of cult leaders and fellow followers. These deluded zealots bear the ultimate responsibility for violent actions and tragic events. Thus, in these depictions, cult or religious suicide remains implausible. No sane adult would do such a thing. As a result, cult followers find a "good" death. The stigma of "suicide" is removed by the tragic, but more "acceptable" fact of murder, or the attempted "suicides" are thwarted by intervening forces so that the cult members can reclaim normal lives and die a "good" death in old age. As re-envisionings of Jonestown, Waco, and Heaven's Gate, these narratives create a preferred story that "smooths over" the possibility that some adults do, in fact, kill themselves for religious reasons. These fictional television shows create a past in which participants are absolved of responsibility by virtue of their victimization. They provide viewers with a history of desire, one in which the people of Jonestown fought back, threw down cups of kool-aid, and walked out. A past where most of the Branch Davidians survived, and those in Heaven's Gate were victims of a murderous conspiracy, rather than willing participants in their own deaths.

Trusting in Authority: The Federal Government and Religious Freedom

The portrayal of the US government, usually represented by some form of law enforcement, heightens the culpability of cult leaders and the victimization of cult followers. Caution, procedural adherence, and efficiency characterize their entrance into these cult events, and religious deviance never constitutes part of the rationale for their involvement.

In contrast to the irrationality and chaos caused by cult leaders, government agents and law enforcement do their jobs efficiently. They follow procedure, approach situations using logic and reason, and keep their emotions in check. For example, in *Flashpoint*, the Strategic Response Unit (SRU) takes every precaution to prevent loss of life and escalation of events. Throughout, the agents remain calm and in control. They exhibit empathy and understanding even as they wield guns and power. For example, when SRU Agent Lane is taken hostage, he attempts to reason with cult leader Charles's son Isaac. Lane pleads with Isaac:

> I understand that you love your father and you have been raised to follow him without question, but there comes a time in all our lives, son, when we have to think for ourselves. Now what your father's doing is wrong. Your mother knows that. Now, if you can help me, I can stop him. I can fix it.

Agent Lane doesn't denigrate "the Farm" or deride Charles, but rather rationally tries to talk with Isaac and convince him to claim his autonomy. Throughout, Lane remains calm knowing that his team is ultimately in control. By the end of the episode the SRU has indeed "fixed it." Charles is the only casualty.

The government's procedural carefulness and efficiency also emerges in *CSI, SVU*, and *Cold Case*. Every week, *Cold Case* highlighted the ability of the detectives to solve previously unsolved crimes. The case of Matthew's apparent suicide is no exception. Despite the passage of twenty years, these detectives find answers, and they continue to do their job even when threatened. For example, after a cult member breaks into Detective Rush's home, she remains unflappable and determined to find the perpetrator. Similarly, in *CSI*, despite the horror of confronting eleven deaths, the CSIs remain dedicated to the task of figuring out what happened and who was responsible for it. Furthermore, when an excess of emotion threatens one of these agents of the law, the episodes emphasize the agents' ability to overcome this threat or the system's ability to effectively deal with the problem. CSI Nick Stokes exhibits nervousness before entering the bunker containing the victims' bodies. For knowing viewers, his fear of going underground makes sense as he was buried alive in the previous episode; however, Stokes takes a deep breath, shakes off the fear, and does his job. Likewise, the detectives in *SVU* are not unaffected by seeing the dead bodies of Abraham's children, and are required to undergo therapy. Not only does this plot device make the detectives more three-dimensional and sympathetic, but it also emphasizes the checks and balances that exist within law enforcement agencies. In *SVU*, Detective Tutuola voluntarily removes himself from the case, while Detective Stabler's mental state is questioned and he is removed from the case. Similarly, in *Cold Case*, Detective Valens is required to hand over his gun and go on leave until he can better handle his emotions and job as an officer of the law. Thus, viewers see representatives of the government successfully handle their emotions, and if they fail to do so, viewers learn that mechanisms exist to prevent these individuals from participating in active cases.

In addition, the episodes clarify that religion is not the cause of these violent confrontations between government agents and cults. In *Criminal Minds* and *SVU*, concerns for and crimes against children prompt law enforcement to become involved. In *Flashpoint* and *CSI*, the authorities' response to one crime leads them to investigate the cults in question. In some episodes, the cults' violations of the law, justified by claims to religious authority, demand governmental action. For example, in *Cold Case* and *Touched by an Angel*, both cult leaders assert that their authority comes from God and takes precedence over the laws of the land. In *Cold Case*'s "Blank Generation," when asked about tax fraud and statutory rape, cult leader Warfield explains that "those are your laws," and "I don't accept your authority. I consider myself wrongly detained." Similarly, when confronted by the Department of Children Services in "Into the Fire," Brother David refuses to cooperate using a religious justification: "I answer only to God." Both episodes show these claims to divine revelation to be manipulative and self-serving. Warfield continually lies to the police and angel Monica challenges the authenticity of Brother David's link to God. She asks, "Brother David, what does God's voice sound like? Is it male or female? Or does it sound just like your voice?" Monica's incisive critique of Brother David's claims to authority and his defiance of the government highlight the madness and chaos created by cult leaders. Thus, the episodes firmly situate any government involvement as a necessary and expected response to violations of the law. They show viewers that law enforcement deserves one's trust and respect, while claims to divine revelation, often the basis of charismatic religious authority, should be met with suspicion.

All of these elements combine in the *Criminal Minds* episode "Minimal Loss." When BAU agents Prentiss and Reid go undercover as "child victim interview experts" in Ben Cyrus's cult, they explicitly deny any anti-cult or anti-religious motives. As Agent Prentiss explains, "We are not here because of your religious beliefs." However, when a mistake does occur and a siege ensues with Prentiss and Reid trapped inside, Prentiss and Reid's co-workers must put aside their concerns, control their emotions, and work the case. Agent Hotchner insists that Agent Rossi act as lead negotiator because of his expertise. When Rossi protests that he is too emotionally involved, Hotchner quickly responds: "This outcome depends as much on our ability to predict the moves of Prentiss and Reid, as Cyrus. That's why you're the best man for the job."

This scene assures viewers that government agents can control their emotions, and that their personal connection to the case could even be advantageous. Rossi's ability to handle this position is further enhanced by his character's negotiation experiences at Waco, Ruby Ridge, and the Freemen's stand-off. However, unlike these historical events, the episode places the blame for this debacle on state government, specifically a governor seeking reelection who ordered the raid leading to the hostage situation. The BAU, which represents the federal government, must rectify this state-level political corruption, rescue their trapped friends, and resolve this stand-off. As negotiations ensue, Agent Rossi remains calm and sympathetic, and, like Agent Prentiss, he assures Ben Cyrus that "I have no issue with your beliefs," and later tells a worried Cyrus that "This isn't Waco."

However, even as the Rossi insists that "this isn't Waco," Waco permeates the episode. The dusty isolated "compound" resembles the Branch Davidian headquarters at Mt. Carmel. Cult leader Ben Cyrus echoes the words of Branch Davidian leader David Koresh: "We're believers, Dave. We believe that God says what he means and means what he says." Cyrus also explains: "They stay for now while I pray for God's guidance. Please don't try to force us out." And later, "Tell them I'm not crazy. Tell 'em I'm just a man living by God's law." Further, the episode features a little girl on the phone with negotiators asking in a plaintive voice: "You killed my Mommy and Daddy. Are you goin' to kill me too?" Similarly, the Waco negotiation tapes include the voice of a little girl asking negotiator Jim Cavanaugh, "Are you comin' to kill me?" And Agent Rossi, like real-life Jim Cavanaugh, assures her "no one is going to kill you, honey." Even the climax of the episode, in which Jessie pushes the detonator and fire engulfs the building, resembles the flames that consumed Mt. Carmel. The scene is shown to viewers through the camera lens of a news crew covering the Ben Cyrus cult similar to the way Americans saw the events at Waco end on 19 April 1993.

The resemblances between the fictional and the historical affirm the episode's status as a retelling of the past, as do the alterations to this history. For example, Rossi's insistence that power not be cut off to Cyrus and his followers is the opposite of what happened at Waco. Similarly, Rossi and Hotchner's orders to de-escalate the situation differ drastically from the tactics utilized in the Branch Davidian siege. Throughout the episode, the BAU continues to act cautiously and patiently. They do not rush to judgment, nor do they act recklessly.

The episode constructs a history of Waco in which the federal government acted with care and lives were not needlessly lost. It is a *cult*ural memory in which government intervention in cult affairs remains guided by logic, procedure, and due process. Rather than ask what the government could have done to prevent Jonestown or Waco, these television shows offer a narrative of the past that affirms one's faith in the nation-state. These episodes assure viewers that the government acts justly, that the good of law enforcement will triumph over the evil of crazy cult leaders, and that one should trust in the government's authority. Further, these episodes "smooth over" any suspicion that the government unduly targets minority religious groups by framing involvement in terms of violations of the law. The checks and balances on law enforcement agents within these episodes emphasize the trustworthiness of the system, as well as its efficiency in solving highly emotional and dangerous situations. Thus, these television shows construct a vision of history in which viewers are taught to question claims to religious authority and divine revelation (especially those that justify defiance of the law), while simultaneously exhibiting unquestioning obedience toward governmental authority. Through this lens, these plots demonstrate to viewers that despite the tragic events at Jonestown, Waco, and Heaven's Gate, the government acted as it should. It did what needed to be done, and by framing the past in this way, these episodes highlight the government's commitment to the First Amendment and its ability to balance religious freedom with protecting citizens from harm.

Thus, these episodes reinforce a central motif in American culture—the triumph of religious freedom and liberty. These shows demonstrate that religious freedom is not about blind obedience to a crazy, deceptive cult leader, who causes death and destruction, but rather it is represented by the courageous men and women of law enforcement who put their lives on the line for their country. These are the people who risk their lives to ensure that religious freedom remains triumphant. In this history of desire, viewers are encouraged to re-interpret potentially problematic past governmental actions as the tragic consequences of events caused by crazy, charismatic leaders. In the end, it is not government authority and power that should be in doubt, but rather claims to religious revelation and defiance of laws that create violent confrontations and endanger religious freedom.

Conclusion

The episodes encourage viewers to let go of the historical past and embrace this history of desire through their blending of elements. By combining fictional plots with elements mined from Jonestown, Waco, and Heaven's Gate, the shows highlight their verisimilitude and encourage viewers to interpret the fictional and the historical in light of one another. Further, these dramas not only blend the historical with the fictional, but they also combine features of different cult events. "Minimal Loss" moves back and forth between elements from Jonestown ("white night" drills, loyalty tests, and comparisons of Cyrus with Jones) and Waco (weapons, a Mt. Carmel-like setting, and comparisons of Cyrus with Koresh). The blending that occurs in this episode and others fosters a homogenization of these religious movements and their histories. Jonestown, Waco, and Heaven's Gate become equivalent events in this pick-and-choose past, rather than distinctive historical moments.

This erasure of historical context and nuance promotes a *cult*ural memory in which the act of cult suicide is relegated to the realm of a few crazy, charismatic cult leaders. These fictional television shows deny the possibility that cult followers would willingly take their own lives for religious reasons. Rather, these innocents are the victims of foul play or fortuitously rescued by trustworthy government agents (or the occasional angel). These television shows assure viewers about the role of both religion and government in American society. Through these fictional scenarios, the audience learns and re-learns that unlike cults, "real" religions do not require individuals to commit acts of violence against themselves or others, that claims to revelation and hearing God's voice are more likely signs of delusion than proximity to divinity, and that religious rationales for violating the law should be met with suspicion. Further, these episodes reinforce the idea that cults are not real religions unfairly persecuted by law enforcement, but rather harmful scams which necessitate governmental intervention. And government authorities can be trusted given their rationality and efficiency, as well as the checks and balances that govern the system. Thus, any fears that "real" religion requires extraordinary measures of devotion, disrupts the norms of family life, leads to violence, or questioning of the law are alleviated. Concerns that the government unfairly targets minority religions or that government agents abuse their power are written out of the *cult*ural memory. These television dramas create a history of desire—a past in which both religion and government adhere to the ideals of rationality and moderation while upholding the value of religious freedom.

References

Anderson, Steve (2001). "History TV and Popular Memory," in *Television Histories: Shaping Collective Memory in the Media Age*, eds. Gary R. Edgerton and Peter C. Rollins. Lexington, KY: University Press of Kentucky, pp. 19–36.

Carey, James W. (1988). *Communication as Culture: Essays on Media and Society*. New York and London: Routledge.

Chidester, David (1988). *Salvation and Suicide*. Bloomington, IN: Indiana University Press.

Fiske, John (1987). *Television Culture*. London: Methuen.

Forbes, Bruce and Jeffrey Mahan (2005). *Religion and Popular Culture in America*, rev. edn. Berkeley, CA: University of California Press.

Gerbner, George (n.d.). "Society's Storyteller: How Television Creates the Myths by which We Live". Accessed November 12, 2012. At <http://www.medialit.org/reading-room/societys-storyteller-how-tv-creates-myths-which-we-live>.

Neal, Lynn S. (2011). "'They're Freaks!': The Cult Stereotype in Fictional Television Shows, 1958-2008," *Nova Religio*, 14(3): 81–107.

Pirkis, Jane and R. Warwick Blood (2001). "Suicide and the Media: Portrayal in Fictional Media," *Crisis* 22(4): 155–62.

—, Philip Burgess, R. Warwick Blood, and Catherine Francis (2007). "The Newsworthiness of Suicide," *Suicide and Life-Threatening Behavior*, 37(3): 278–83.

Silverstone, Roger (1988). "Television Myth and Culture," in *Media, Myths, and Narratives: Television and the Press*, ed. James W. Carey. Newbury Park, CA: SAGE Publications, pp. 20–47.

Stack, Steve (2000). "Media Impacts on Suicide: A Quantitative Review of 293 Findings," *Social Science Quarterly*, 81(4): 958–71.

Sturken, Marita (1997). *Tangled Memories: The Vietnam War, the AIDS Epidemic, and the Politics of Remembering*. Berkeley, CA: University of California Press.

Chapter 14

Why Muslims Kill Themselves on Film: From Hollywood's Racism to Girard's Victimage Mechanism[1]

Christopher Hartney

Introduction

The philosopher of film Stanley Cavell makes the (somewhat obvious) point that films must come from somewhere. And that somewhere for Cavell is other films (Cavell 1979: 7). That is to say the style and grammar of a particular film is based on its predecessors, whether resting on stylistic precedents or breaking away from those precedents. Additionally, the experience of watching films over time also conditions how an audience reads new films. As basic as Cavell's pronouncement seems, it has powerful political consequences when one studies a topic such as Islam, terror, and suicide on film. When I was asked to write on this nexus, I realized that one clear (but too well-trodden) path would be to examine Hollywood re-creations of Middle Eastern political and religious complexities via films such as *The Siege* (1998), *Syriana* (2005), *The Kingdom* (2007), and *Traitor* (2008). Then, after providing a reading of these films, illustrate how Muslims are presented in these tales and investigate the mechanisms of their motivation. To do *just* this, however, would be to encode a political statement about the singularity of the connection between Islam, terror, and suicide.

Yet I am at pains here to stress that there is a very long history of terror and suicide in films that mainly concern the lives of westerners. We see this, for example, in the multiple versions of *Romeo and Juliet* (Zeffirelli's 1968 production, Luhrmann's of 1996, and Carlei's of 2013), where the two lovers sacrifice themselves and, in a sense posited by René Girard, bring a new level of peace to the Verona of the playscript. Or we see this in films that use suicide to

---

[1] An earlier version of this chapter was published as Christopher Hartney, "Why Muslims Kill Themselves on Film," *Journal of Religion and Violence*, 1(3) (2013): 276–302.

develop a mystery or aporia such as Sofia Coppola's *The Virgin Suicides* (1999) or Sion Sono's *Suicide Club* (2001) where the plot refuses to explain the ultimate reasons for the suicide. Similarly the sacrifice of these characters can also be read in a Girardian sense if we, as audience members, commit ourselves to these characters only to experience the terror of their demise. Their sacrifice becomes our vicarious spill of emotions. What distinguishes these films from how Muslim suicide is usually depicted is that when a non-Muslim turns to thoughts of suicide, the camera provides them with the time and space to examine their inner life before the fateful decision is made. As audience members, we are given the time to empathize with the character. Conversely, in gun-filled Hollywood re-imaginings of terror, we tend to be presented with Muslims who are inherently suicidal. Here I will demonstrate this point through a selection of Hollywood and non-Hollywood inspired films.

First, however, there is a point to stress. As with many who will read this chapter, my life has been touched by suicide. It is a painful topic for those who have encountered it, but here I hope the reader will permit me to speak of suicide as it operates in the game-space of the cinema. This significantly changes the discourse. Throughout this chapter, we should reflect on the fact that narrative cinema's first duty is to provide an engaging spectacle and an intense emotional experience. In cinema, we enter a liminal gamespace where cognitive-subjunctive possibilities can be played within a zone that is, by the film's end, politically and socially restorative and thus ultimately non-challenging to the status quo (Turner 1982: 43). For this reason, suicide provides tensions on screen that must be, in the last count, emotionally satisfying for the audience. Regarding the operation of this sort of engaging emotional rollercoaster, I will argue that René Girard's 'victimage mechanism' is a generally satisfying model. I will additionally suggest that this Girardian approach needs methodological amplification to suit more precisely the realm of death on film, and suicide in particular.

A Brief History of Terror

"Extreme fear" is the simplest way of describing terror at an individual level—that is, a fear that may not derive from events simply *within* our quotidian lives but rather a fear that is generated from events and perceived threats that affect the very basics *upon which* our quotidian lives progress (Solomon 1993: 253–4). Thus, terror links immediately to political systems and the worldviews these systems maintain. Terror is generated as our accepted reality is threatened, or as our worldviews quickly mutate, particularly through threats of radical change.

There is little discussion, however, on the specific differences at a personal level between terror and horror, and I hope to make this more explicit. The continuum between these emotions becomes important when Freud's writings on horror are considered later in this chapter.

Ortega y Gasset has referred to this worldview threat as the fear of being without a world, for the social topography can change during periods of crisis so radically that individuals in a society can end up with no conceptual map by which to understand that world (Ortega y Gasset 1956: 92–3). Terror therefore remains a major, and sometimes *the* defining, emotion behind radical political change. The primordial and archetypal example of this in the context of modernity is that stage of the French Revolution known as *la terreur.* "The Terror" as a historical-political precedent is defined by the period from June 1793 to July 1794 when the Committee for Public Safety considered that the Revolution could only be protected by a state-sponsored reign of terror centered upon mass executions. The number of those executed by guillotine around this period numbered over 16,000, with additional summary executions across the country (Dunn 1990: 350). This is reflected in the growth of language on terror that expanded our concept of its use emotively and politically. In its supplements, the *Dictionnaire de l'Académie française* charts the development of the concept and its derivations. "Terrorists" (*terroristes*) was in use by 1794, and "to terrorize" (*terroriser*) was in common usage by 1796 (Académie Française 1796).

These words did not necessarily have a pejorative dimension at the point of their origins in the way they do today. The revolutionary leader Robespierre linked state-sponsored terror with a special kind of virtue that would cleanse the new republic of traitorous elements. His attitude then translates into numerous purgatory stages of revolutions and coups that have occurred ever since, especially where a new regime stamps its control on a community through a period of "white" or "pure" terror:

> [Robespierre] became in the 1790s—and has been ever since—a popular personification of terrorist evil. In one of his most important speeches on the policy of terror, he proclaims its adoption with republican pride. He knew full well the resonance of the word used to elevate violence to transcendent significance. In the sense here employed, terror is a manifestation of *vertu*, a republican quality sacralized in the nation. (Maniquis 2000: 372)

We encounter here a special link between terror and a sense of beauty, as manifest in the virtue of social transformation that Robespierre made in his speech of February 5, 1794. As a severe, inflexible, and sudden form of justice, terror also contains a sense of transcendence that is as sublime as it is political. It is this connection that keeps terror in the zone of political activity and, one might argue, a sort of metaphysical political activity at that (Gauchet 1998: 9–12).

An archeology of political terror, based on the original French terror, may be developed throughout the twentieth century as a major part of the process of political transformation. Episodes in the history of terror can include the manifestation of the Nazi totalitarian state from out of the Weimar Republic (Gellately 1991: 23–38). and the purgation of Cambodia after the declaration of a "Year Zero" by the Khmer Rouge (Um 1998: 131–54). In both these incidents, the dominant power structure sought to radically re-imagine the nation. A similar lineage can be developed to examine the use of terror by colonial powers that employed fear-laden tactics to hold colonized peoples in thrall during the twentieth century (Baker 2009). A final significant lineage outlines movements to counter state terror, built predominantly from the legacy of the anti-Spanish guerrilla tactics developed during the Rif War (1920–26) by Abdul Karim (Courcelle-Labrousse and Marmié 2009). His terrorist strategies had a strong influence on other operatives in the Muslim world, as well as figures such as Ho Chi Minh and Che Guevara (Abdelkrim 1927: 59–123). Although these archeologies of terror remain in the background of the following films as real-life sources for various narrative structures, this chapter seeks only to examine terror and suicide in its fictional cinematic field.[2] This brings this particular emotion back to a personal register and of how terror is used to problematize the relationships of fictional characters dealing with the problematic of suicide.[3]

Girard posits that one of the great failures of psychologists and ethnologists is their refusal to comprehend the paradoxical relationship of socialization and mimesis (copying others as we develop as social beings and therefore claiming a competitive stance against them in that need to copy). This mimesis, which is essential to socialization, also encourages a powerful tension that we find against societal prohibitions that prevent us from repeating others specifically. This

---

[2] I cannot make the same boundary blur that Brym and Hamlin make by confusing the field of cinema with the field of real human action. After a sociological reading of suicide motivations in relation to terrorism, they provide a reading of *Paradise Now* (2005). The article suggests the film highlights the theory they expound. I maintain that narrative film operates under its own rules of engagement and should not be appreciated for its possible documentary dimensions and its ability to highlight real human behavior (Brym and Hamlin 2009: 83–96).

[3] I carry out this task in the knowledge that between 1981 and 2008, 1,840 suicide attacks claimed the lives of more than 21,000 people. See Wright (2008), "Since 2001, a dramatic increase in suicide bombings," as quoted in Brym and Hamlin (2009: 83).

includes the failure by such scholars to make a "connection between conflict and acquisitive mimesis." Girard continues:

> Inevitably we imagine that the prohibitions covering imitative phenomena must be quite distinct from those against violence or intense rivalries. But this is not the case. What is impressive in imitative phenomena is that those who participate in them never cease imitating one another, each one transforming himself into a simulacra of the other ... An examination of our own terms, such as competition, rivalry, emulation, etc., reveals that the traditional perspective remains inscribed in the language. Competitors are fundamentally those who run or walk together, rivals those who dwell on opposite sides of the same river etc. (Girard 1978: 11–12)

We have a perfect picture of Girardian mimetic crisis in the seemingly unstoppable conflict between, for example, the two warring houses of Verona. What breaks—or at least significantly interrupts—such conflicts, Girard argues, is sacrifice.

That is to say, an act of violence that unites rather than divides the warring factions. Girard defines the victim thus:

> The community finds itself unified once more at the expense of a victim who is not only incapable of self-defence, but is also unable to provoke any reaction of vengeance ... The sacrifice is simply another act of violence, but it is the final act of violence, its last word. (Girard 1978: 24)

Girard states that such a sacrifice becomes most important in societies where a legal mechanism for justice, such as a complex court system meting out finally balanced and socially acceptable punishments, has not developed or is for political reasons non-operational (Girard 1978: 30). This fact is vitally important when describing the world of cinema, which easily gives itself over to vigilantism and a focus on the moral choices of individuals, rather than examining the machinery of extended court processes. Free from such justice mechanisms, this absence of vengeance occurs because the victim has, while still alive, become liminal to his/her/its society. In the world of Shakespeare's Verona, where justice systems seem barely able to touch the city's most prestigious families, the sacrifice of the lovers certainly reunites the community. In the final lines of the play, Capulet calls Montague his brother as they plan to build a memorial for the lovers.

What I wish to do, however, is demonstrate how a Girardian sacrificial journey takes place in the gamespace of cinema. Here it may seem as though characters kill themselves. The truth is, the scriptwriter, director, and the extended production process of a film all support the act of suicide as a representational process, ultimately, of entertainment. The self-killer on film is a sacrifice generated by the film coming into being and which presents us both the terror and the resolution that Girard speaks of as happening also in real-world scenarios.

Between Muslim and Arab

In this chapter, I am focusing the use of clearly identified "Muslim" characters. But I must first acknowledge the work of Jack Shaheen, who focuses not on "Muslim" but "Arab" characters who are, in the eyes of Hollywood, *ipso facto* Muslims. In Shaheen's research (and via his Arab/racial paradigm), we find our first and most basic answer as to why Muslims/Arabs kill themselves on screen throughout the history of cinema; it is because they have undergone a century-long process of pseudo-speciation in the cinematic field (Grossman 1995: 156–70). Shaheen demonstrates how Arabs have been "framed" by Hollywood as radically other to the West. If the West is *ipso facto* reasonable, it follows that Arabs have no sense of reason. Thus their status as complete humans is constantly challenged by their cinematic portrayal. He argues that Hollywood's attitude to Muslims/Arabs has remained unchanged throughout its history:

> When colleagues ask whether today's reel Arabs are more stereotypical than yesteryear's, I can't say that the celluloid Arab has changed. That is the problem. He is what he has always been—the cultural "other." Seen through Hollywood's distorted lenses, Arabs look different and threatening. Projected along racial and religious lines, the stereotypes are deeply ingrained in American cinema. From 1896 until today, filmmakers have collectively indicted all Arabs as Public Enemy #1—brutal, heartless, uncivilized religious fanatics and money-mad cultural "others" bent on terrorizing civilized Westerners, especially Christians and Jews. (Shaheen 2003: 171)

It follows that if the Muslim/Arab represents something completely other to the West, then the terror that flows from their suicidal urges is chaotic and without a deep sense of reason or justification.

In opposition to, in particular, the ideal of the western middle classes, Muslims, it is imagined, simply cannot control their emotions in public. As such, they are able to burst into ferocious bloodthirsty action on any sort of emotive whim. This accords with Edward Said's paradigm of Orientalism. A system of "truths in Nietzsche's sense of the word [where it is] correct that every European, in what he could say about the Orient, [is] consequently a racist, and imperialist, and almost totally ethnocentric" (Said 1991: 204).

Said is talking about a grand tradition where westerners appropriate the Orient by means of descriptions that are intertwined with political and societal assumptions and esthetically this is very much the case in the following examples.

An entertaining proof of this is a short film inspired by Shaheen's research, which consists of edited scenes of Arabs from a range of Hollywood films and is called *Planet of the Arabs*.[4] The unsophisticated ease with which Muslims/Arabs are roused to raging emotions is such a definite dimension of their character as to be *beneath* understanding for a westerner. This fits nicely into Shaheen's paradigm. In western films, suicide victims tend to be the main characters, or suicide tends to deeply affect the main characters of a plot. In films by Hollywood that address Muslim suicide, often very little narrative focus is given to the Muslim characters, as if suicide is not a personal or social tragedy in itself, but an intrinsic part of being Muslim. It is a characteristic that needs no deep explanation or consideration on the part of a western audience. Thus our chances of examining a character's mental state, as Zunshine suggests in her exposition of theory of mind (Zunshine 2006), can be blatantly truncated by the focus of the camera away from the Muslim character. This lack of focus is determined by the way previous films have been made (again Cavell) and, of course, the cultural biases of the plotmaker and the director.

This attitude is very much the case in *The Kingdom* (2007) where the director's focus provides us with significant screen time to consider, and seek to understand, the motivations of the Americans in the film. The camera dwells with them as they plan, it stays with them on their flight to Saudi Arabia, it "hangs out" with them as they wait in their quarters after they have landed. We are given, however, very few opportunities to guess at what the Saudi Arabians may be thinking, for the camera gives them very little time at all.

The Kingdom (2007)

"The Kingdom" of the title refers to Saudi Arabia, and the film opens in a semi-documentary style by addressing the strange relation that exists between this feudal state and the United States. It gives an overview of the development of the country after the fall of the Ottoman Empire and the discovery of oil. It hints at the internal fighting for oil resources and links the 9/11 bombings to Saudi

---

4 Accessed 30 September 2012. At <http://www.youtube.com/watch?v=Mi1ZNEjEarw>. *Planet of the Arabs* is done very much in the style of film artist Tracey Moffatt who edits together scenes from Hollywood productions to reveal startling biases in the constancy of cinematic tropes. See Smith (2007).

nationals. Such an opening suggests that it will be a semi-factual documentary-style examination of the geopolitics of the United States and the Kingdom. Nothing, of course, could be further from the truth.

The film then switches to a group of Saudi terrorists sitting on the top floor of a tall building. From here they have an expansive view over a foreigners' compound. An older man (who we later discover is the terrorist mastermind Abu Hamza) tells a young boy (his grandson) to watch the carnage that is about to erupt. In the compound, the westerners are playing softball. Operatives disguised in police uniforms storm the compound and start shooting the westerners. A suicide bomber, again in police uniform, calls confused westerners to him as if offering protection before blowing himself up. Finally, the carnage brings emergency services to the compound, including a random FBI investigator. Another bomb, hidden inside an ambulance is then exploded, ripping the front off a residential apartment block and killing many more. The message is clear: playing softball in Saudi Arabia can be lethal.

The film has some history behind it. In May 2003 in Riyadh, a series of western compounds were attacked. Thirty-five people, many of them westerners, were killed and a further 160 were injured. *The Kingdom* makes no attempt to recreate these attacks per se, but the Riyadh attacks lurk as a real event backgrounding the film's plot and adding to the possibility that *The Kingdom* is partially a documentary. What we get up front in this film is a significant dose of suicidal horror. Once the bombing is over, there is a chance to direct our thoughts to why these suicide bombers may have done what they did. But no. Instead, the film rips our attention back to Washington and onto the distress that FBI agents are going through because of the loss of one of their own. The film is not particularly interested in the Arabs, or even in exploring the emotions or reactions of those westerners who were killed or injured in the blasts.

What is compelling about the direction of the narrative is that immediately after this overture of carnage, director Peter Berg turns the film into an FBI police procedural, one that just happens to take place on foreign soil. In fact, the screenwriter, Matthew Carnahan, summed up the film by posing the question: "What would a murder investigation look like on Mars?" (Cielty 2007). This is a statement that, in its own special way, links Saudi Arabians to Martians. A film that is billed as being about "The Kingdom" suddenly switches to become an exploration-cum-celebration of the corporate mystique of the Federal Bureau of Investigation.

As a police procedural, *The Kingdom* thus operates in a form made famous by the television detective shows like *Columbo* (1968–2003) and *Cracker* (1993–2006): the initial crime is committed and the perpetrators are shown to the audience. The tension lies in whether or not the superior intelligence of the insightful detective/police psychologist will work out whom the perpetrators are before, as the tired cliché has it, "they kill again." This comparison falls down in one powerful respect. The television dramas of *Columbo* and *Cracker* were powered by the slow, and dramatic, unveiling of the motivations and psychologies of those who had committed the murders. Here the focus is quite different and yet the culture of what a Hollywood film has become means that this difference can go mostly unexplained.

Much of the running time following the opening scenes of the film are spent dealing with the problem that the FBI is a homeland policing organization and has nothing to do with on-the-ground actions outside the US. In fact, why would the Saudis invite operatives of a foreign police force into their country? Why would the US government allow an organization not trained in geopolitics, or the local culture or language, into that foreign land? This issue is solved when lead investigator Special Agent Ronald Fleury (Jamie Foxx) jumps the Saudi ambassador to the United States in Washington and blackmails him into letting his team access the blast site. We then move into another cliché of the police procedural as Fleury and his team carry out their investigation despite the prevailing power structures; in this case, both the Saudi and the US governments remain reluctant to have the FBI team at the site.

Fleury's team know no Arabic, but this is almost beside the point. The FBI has the universal language of scientistic forensic reason and justice. The film seeks to demonstrate that this process of investigation and justice remains superior to anything culturally connected that the Saudis might achieve. The cast list announces that Fleury's team consists of Special Agents Grant Sykes (bomb technician), Janet Mayes (forensic examiner), and Adam Leavitt (intelligence analyst). These agents have brought their evidence bags, their autopsy kits, and their police crime-scene tape. Because of their science, they do not need to connect with the local culture, and thus do not need to problematize reasons for why suicide bombers may have attacked the compound.

Arriving at the destroyed compound, all four watch in anguish as the Saudi forces march back and forth across the crime site. If anything in recent popular narrative structures defines sacred space, it is the space of the crime scene. Roped off and minutely investigated, the crime scene is the start, the locus, and font of the detective's journey towards a (sacred but truly rational) explanation of "whodunit." The Saudis' desecration of this scientistically sacred site is another sign of their barbarity, as is the scene where Special Agent Janet Mayes is only permitted to carry out autopsies on the western bodies, not the Muslim ones. Only after long negotiation is the team finally allowed to gather evidence and piece together a scenario. They do this by slowly winning over the local police agent, Colonel Faris Al-Ghazi (Ashraf Barhom), who is assigned to be their babysitter. He is the only Saudi who gets to see and appreciate the rational efficiency that the American agents bring with them. Only he is elevated to the same status as family man Agent Fleury, when we watch a short scene of Al-Ghazi at home with his son.

In order to return the film to a spectacular action ending, the four agents are ordered out, but have their road convoy attacked as they proceed to the airport. In chasing the attackers, the FBI agents and Al-Ghazi are forced to fight an OK Corral-type shoot-out in an unknown town. This conflict brings them face to face with Abu-Hamza, the terrorist mastermind we saw at the start of the film coordinating the initial attack. While attempting to arrest this man, Colonel Al-Ghazi is fatally wounded. That is, using Girard, although Al-Ghazi does not kill himself, he is nevertheless a liminal figure sacrificed by the plot for our emotional satisfaction. He may remain an Arab (albeit one that the film has sought to humanize/westernize), yet he has also seen the "scientific" ways of the foreigners. He has grown to be *like* a westerner, thus the audience can be shocked at his death, which "retards" him and those around him back into an unscientific "Arabness." His death is thus terrifying because it ends the possibility that he may bring something of the FBI ethos to "Mars" as it were.

At the end of the film, the four agents return to America, their heroic immortality reconfirmed.[5] The sacrifice of Muslims, however, occurs in two distinct registers. They self-sacrifice at the start of the film, yet we are given no space to consider why. Their deaths are not presented as aporias, but rather, as a consequence of something that Muslims just do. The other register of sacrifice, as in the case of Al-Ghazi, allows us to see the victim sacrificed by the plot. He is killed for being pseudo-American, yet remaining, in the end, intractably Arab.

It is by a rather unbelievable plot twist (an FBI agent successfully blackmailing a Saudi ambassador) that *The Kingdom* seems to address issues in Saudi Arabia, but soon becomes an American film about Americans. It is not surprising then that the film was shot in Arizona, thus obviating the need to negotiate with Middle Eastern or North African communities about the weirdly American content of the film. *The Kingdom* assumes, without giving space for contemplation of their motivations, that Saudi Arabian Muslims kill themselves

[5] Whereas heroes and heroines in non-Hollywood national cinemas will give their lives in an act that they hope will improve their society, Americans, as they are represented on film, increasingly want to risk their lives to achieve a boon for their communities and to come away with their lives, as though they are immortal. This feeds into much research about the denial of death in the West. See in particular Becker (1997).

because they are Saudi Arabian Muslims. It re-affirms a worldview in which western rationality in detective work overrides the sort of connected community policing that locals may carry out. *The Kingdom* is in the end a film that uses suicide and terror, as it uses Islam, to demonstrate that reality as constructed by FBI agents, is far superior to how the locals on Mars may conceive of their own worldview and their own terrain.

Syriana (2005)

In 2006, Monica Eng from the *Chicago Tribune* wrote, "The tagline for the critically acclaimed film *Syriana* was: 'Everything Is Connected.' But for those who saw it flash by in theaters, it was more like 'Everything is confusing'" (Eng 2006). The film weaves together four plotlines (the script proposed a fifth plot which was deleted, perhaps for the sake of clarity). Although a single viewing gives a particular image of United States-Middle Eastern relations, the impression remains hazy. The film is inspired by episodes from former Central Intelligence Agency (CIA) case manager Bob Baer's memoir *See No Evil*. Roger Ebert sees the confusion as a part of the powerful political message of the film:

> *Syriana* is a movie that suggests Congress can hold endless hearings about oil company profits and never discover the answer to anything, because the real story is so labyrinthine that no one—not oil company executives, not Arab princes, not C.I.A. spies, not traders in Geneva, understands the whole picture. (Ebert 2012a)

Ebert declares the film to be his second favorite of 2005 (Ebert 2005b), and additional critical responses agreed that the film was noteworthy. There are aspects of the film that are only understandable because they function in the field of cinematic cliché. The CIA operative Bob Barnes (George Clooney) becomes a morally ambiguous figure who, by the end of the film, seeks to save the life of Gulf State Prince Nasir (Alexander Siddig). He does so despite the US government ordering Barnes to kill the prince.

In a reflection of Barnes, Prince Nasir is revealed as a "good Arab" who declares his wishes to bring democracy and liberalism to the totalitarian state his father the emir operates with the US's blessing. As these two figures become liminal to their home cultures by seeming to be too deeply engaged with the culture of the other, it is not surprising to find them both sacrificed in one of two bomb attacks at the end of the film. In this case, a drone attack by the American military hits a motorcade in which the prince is traveling and which Bob Barnes is approaching in order to deliver his warning to the prince. Barnes dies in the film, despite the fact that Bob Baer is still alive and well today: the present rules of plot-making dictate that the character based on him must die as he becomes liminal to the worlds in which he operates. Barnes and Nasir are sacrificed to cancel out the hope that change may come to this region. In this way, the film provides us with an emotional punch and leaves the political order ultimately unchallenged.

The second bomb attack in the film is carried out by a Pakistani guest worker, again somewhere in a Gulf State. The storyline of this character called Wasim (Mazhar Munir) begins when the oil refinery he works for lays him off because of a change in ownership. Here we come face-to-face with the concept that "everything is connected" as global company politics result in local staff cuts and immediate political consequences. Told he needs to learn Arabic to get a new job and stay in the country, Wasim begins attending an Islamic school where he meets a fundamentalist cleric. I found this storyline to be the weakest of the four. Although the film pays some attention to the relationship between Wasim and the cleric, there is simply too much going in the rest of the film to allow us into this character's mindset with any depth. We do not know enough about him to intuit his motivations (theory of mind). We are not sure why he becomes a devoted disciple of the cleric, nor why he does not return to his native Pakistan and carry out his terrorist plotting there. We do not know why he agrees to martyr his life by sailing a fishing trawler armed with a missile into a natural gas tanker. By leaving this aspect of the story undercooked, writer-director Stephen Gaghan unfortunately falls back once more on the Hollywood trope that a Muslim is more likely to kill himself than not. For all the critical acclaim heaped upon it, *Syriana* has a little too much in common with *The Kingdom*, although its hectic flow of multiple plots may, at first, obscure the connection.

Taste of Cherry (1997)

When we move away from Hollywood and consider how directors in the Muslim word represent the suicide of Muslims on film, we find, in at least two significant examples, the phenomenon being treated with a care and consideration that westerners apply to the subject when it is westerners who are killing themselves. *Taste of Cherry* (1997) is a masterwork in minimalism by the Iranian director Abbas Kiarostami. Its slow pace almost makes it a visual meditation on the last days of a man called Mr Badii (Homayon Ershadi). He drives around a city asking various men if they will come and cover his body with earth after he has committed suicide. The tension created between Mr Badii and the three men he asks is potent.

The first man, a young soldier, flees from the car. The second, a seminarian, reminds Badii of religious proscriptions against suicide and refuses to help. The last man, a taxidermist with an ailing daughter, accepts the money Badii offers, agrees to cover his body with earth, but nevertheless tries to convince him not to kill himself. The story he tells of his own suicide attempt is deeply touching and, in the end, life affirming. Mr Badii, however, will not be swayed.

The care that Badii displays for the posthumous state of his body is fascinating. That he requires his body to be covered with earth links his death to a general monotheistic apocalyptic scenario. It may be that Badii simply does not want to be found, but with the presence of the seminarian, we are reminded of the Last Day, the Resurrection of the Dead, and the Final Judgment. It may be the case that Badii believes in these things, but believes that when he is called before Allah on the last day, he will be able to justify his suicide. The film is an aporia, but Kiarostami never lets the camera stray far from Ershadi's fascinating face, as viewers look for hints, and build on their own theory of mind as to why he might want to die.

The final scenes of the film are compelling and terror-filled because of both the simplicity and the monumental nature of his act. Badii takes pills in his bathroom, closes his apartment and takes a long taxi ride to the gravesite at the back of the city. On the edge of his own grave, he smokes a final cigarette. He then lies in his grave. In one sense, because we know so little about him, he becomes an everyman figure. Which is to say that, to some extent, it is ourselves who are in the grave. Here is the source of the terror we feel from this movie. A thunderstorm approaches. In one flash of lightening, we see him alive; in the next flash, his eyes are closed and he seems to be gone. Having been sacrificed by Kiarostami to make a compelling film, once the character of Mr Badii is dead, the film ceases to exist. A low-quality camera shows Kiarostami and crew packing up the film in the area of the grave. The actor Ershadi is standing about. A troop of soldiers marches by. Are the soldiers a hint to Badii's reasons for killing himself? Or are they simply there?

The power of *Taste of Cherry* comes from the ample time the film gives us to try to understand how the world might seem to Mr Badii. As he seems justified in leaving this earth, is it love that compels him? Is he doing his best to escape from Iran in a political sense? As we ask these questions from our own subjective position, the film also provides us time to contemplate ourselves, and those things that hold us to life, or which would justify our departure in such a way. At a deeper level, the film also works as a corrective to Hollywood's serious anti-Islamic biases; Badii kills himself not because he is a Muslim, but because of his humanity and the complexities that come with being human. Although we might not know what they are, after seeing *Taste of Cherry*, we have no doubt that Badii has his own complex, rational, and sophisticated reasons for wanting to die, Muslim or not.

Paradise Now (2005)

The first film to be accepted for competition at the Academy Awards as a *Palestinian* film, *Paradise Now* received nomination in 2006 for Best Foreign Film. It won a Golden Globe award in the same category. Directed by Hany Abu-Assad, the film is shot in Nablus on the West Bank and in Nazareth. It tells the story of two childhood friends who agree to be suicide bombers in Israel: Said (Kais Nashef) and Khaled (Ali Suliman). The plot is built from a number of transcripts of interrogations carried out by the Israeli Army upon suspected suicide terrorists, and with people who had known successful suicides. Thus in locality and in research, the script seeks to draw out human qualities and thinking from a deep understanding of the reality of life in this troubled area.

The film gives us a great deal of time to consider the depths of Said's and Khaled's convictions as we see them prepare for their attack. They are washed and cleaned by their fellow operatives, given a final meal and asked to record a declaration of purpose into an aging video camera. The scene with the video camera is most stark. At one stage, the camera does not work and Said must repeat his declaration. As he does so, the others nibble at their lunch. While on tape, Khaled reminds his mother about some shopping. That is, even in this moment of heightened political drama, the real world is ever-present, even comically so. These sorts of details go a long way to humanizing Said and Khaled. They are not robots, their suicide is not a given, they doubt until the end. The terror from this film comes not from the illogical emotions that power the two potential killers, but that their reason would lead them in this direction. As Dan Glaister in *The Guardian* put it:

> *Paradise Now*'s depiction of the bombers has generated powerful positive and negative reactions, although neither as harsh as Abu-Assad expected. For some, it does not treat the two characters with the respect suicide bombers should be afforded; for others it humanises them, even glorifies them. "They are human, like it or not," says Abu-Assad. "It's a human reaction. It's not that these people are different genetically." (Glaister 2006)

Moreover, this care links the motivations of the characters to some of the saner academic investigations of suicide bombing.

As Robert Pape in his powerful examination of suicide-terrorist motivations writes:

> Most suicide terrorism is undertaken as a strategic effort directed towards particular political goals; it is not simply the product of irrational individuals or an expression of fanatical hatreds. The main purpose of suicide terrorism is to use the threat of punishment to compel a target government to change policy, and most especially to cause democratic states to withdraw forces from land the terrorists perceive as their national homeland. (Pape 2005: 27)

In stating this, Pape is seeking to redress the sort of myths and misconceptions that the West, and Hollywood in particular, have been perpetrating against the reality of terrorism and suicide. Instead of a wildly emotive *other* moved to unreasonable acts of violence, Pape reveals the rational and mundane strategies behind suicide terrorism. So it is not surprising that practical political concerns form a significant part of Said's and Khaled's motivations as well. What separates these two friends' overall worldviews comes back to the history of their fathers. Khaled's is still alive and, we assume, a respected member of his Palestinian community. Contrariwise, Said's father was killed by operatives within the community for working as an Israeli informant. The camera lingers on Said enough that we can see he is tortured by the shame of this execution and is powered by the additional motivation to prove himself in the eyes of the community. The issue of fatherly prestige is elevated by the presence of Suha, to whom Said is attracted. She doubts violence can be any sort of answer, but ironically, she speaks with the authority of one whose father was extremely prestigious in the fight against the Israeli occupation. Unlike Khaled, Said has something very particular to prove and this motivation seems both practical and personal to us. Moreover, he is a figure that will remain forever on the outskirts of his community because of the actions of his father. He fits the victimage model of Girard.

Said and Khaled make a first attempt to enter Israel. It is thwarted. Said makes it to a bus stop just inside the boarder, but cannot find the will to get on the bus. He returns and ends up on his father's grave, angst ridden and about to kill himself by triggering the bomb he has been wearing all day. He is discovered by Khaled and, after a long discussion, they decide to return to Israel. The drama reaches its climax as the two have a second chance to detonate the bombs they wear. This *Hamlet*-like delay in the action of the film also allows us to further consider the tenuousness of their resolve. The final scene gives us a shot of Said sitting on a bus in Israel. Having made his objective, the camera slowly focuses on his eyes as Israelis sit around him talking. The screen then whites out. We assume, but do not know, that he has pulled the trigger on his explosive belt. We do not get to see the dramatic events that follow his suicide/sacrifice. Said is in one sense not sacrificed at all, we are left in some doubt as to what he does indeed do.

The aim of the director, Abu-Assad, was to focus on the humanity of the characters and the mundane atmosphere behind the terror they seek to create. In this he succeeded, although he felt he lost sight of his artistic intent in the heady moments during his acceptance speech for the Golden Globe Award, as he explained in an interview to the *Guardian*,

> While he doesn't regret his words at the celebration, they have given him pause for thought. "I believe I made my film artistically less important when I said the Palestinians need their liberty. But that was my feeling at that moment. I turned the film into a kind of political statement, which it is not. The film is an artistic point of view of that political issue. The politicians want to see it as black and white, good and evil, and art wants to see it as a human thing." (Glaister 2006)

It is this "human thing" that makes *Paradise Now* a particularly valid investigation into the motivations of suicide bombers, and puts in sharper contrast the strange assumptions Hollywood continues to make about Arabs, Muslims, suicide, and terror. As Brym and Hamlin observe:

> The decisions that Khaled and Said make are fascinating because they are shot through with ambivalence, as decisions often are when real flesh-and-blood men and women make them. Khaled and Said think their action will bring political benefits—but they are not sure. They clothe their decision in terms of religious rectitude—but they are not very religious themselves, fear death, and are uncertain they will enter paradise when they complete their task. They seek revenge—but the inhumanity of their plan troubles them and causes one of them to experience a change of heart. Above all, Khaled and Said understand that they can choose how to act. They know they can change their mind. Their plans are in effect only until further notice, as it were. (Brym and Hamlin 2009: 95–6)

What Said is about to do at the end of the film is not presented as esthetically beautiful, nor is it framed as virtuous, but simply as the point at which the film refuses to follow his character any further. If there is terror in the final scene of *Paradise Now*, it is the message that individuals under extreme pressure will react, after much thought, in an extreme way.

It is here that Freud's theory on the uncanny becomes useful. In his article on the uncanny, Freud examines the feelings of horror and terror put forward first by Jentsch where they were linked to a de-familiarization of the homeland:

> The German word *unheimlich* is obviously the opposite of *heimlich*, *heimisch*, meaning "familiar," "native," "be-longing to the home"; and we are tempted to conclude that what is "uncanny" is frightening precisely because it is *not* known and familiar ... so that the uncanny would always be that in which one does not know where one is, as it were. The better orientated in his environment a person is, the less readily will he get the impression of something uncanny in regard to the objects and events in it. (Freud 1919)

This theory returns the schema of this chapter to both Ortega Y Gasset and Pape, who examine remedial actions that an individual and a society can take to ensure that in times of crisis the familiar space of our dwelling area conceptually operates as such. When it does not, when we feel un-homed and un-powered, we feel the uncanny through both horror and terror. It is this feeling of unease that Said attempts to reconcile through his own sacrifice.

Conclusion

The clearest conclusion we can draw on motivations to suicide by Muslims on screen is deeply effected by an Orientalist perspective through Hollywood. Muslims on screen are easily depreciated as a radical and overly-emotive "other," less than human, due to a very long tradition of treating them in this way in the tropes of plot making and film making in the West. When attention is directed to films outside of this racist and pseudo-speciating bias, I have argued here that to understand suicide motivations amongst Muslims, it is most sane and fair to examine how various cinemas deal with suicide. Girard's victimage model becomes a very sustainable framework for examining why plot makers and film constructors sacrifice characters on screen: for a sense of resolution and also emotional affect. It is in part because suicide works to heighten the horror and confusion that a film might seek to have us experience. As audience members, we accept the validity of the lives of fictional characters and when we see some of these characters die, their sacrifice becomes a point where we can exercise our emotional distress, and occasionally terror. I have argued that Lisa Zunshine's exposition of the theory of mind approach shows how we do deeply intuit the motivational possibilities of characters and that their deaths can lead to deep considerations that are horror and terror-laced. It is a terror that at its most basic level threatens how we understand the world. For when our worldview does not operate in the way that we hope, we can develop a sense of terror-filled unhomeliness as Freud describes it. This sense of unhomeliness is not only the site of motivations for figures across cinematic history to sacrifice themselves, from Juliet to Said, but it also stirs the deepest senses of unhomeliness in ourselves. Yet, as I have stated throughout this article, it is the cinema's ability to stir these deep emotions that lays at the heart of its power as a vehicle of overwhelming and challenging entertainment. In order to remain aware of the political dimensions of that entertainment we should constantly consider what it is about the terror of watching suicide on screen that, ironically, gives us the sort of pleasure that it does.

References

Abdelkrim (1927). *Mémoires d'Abd el Krim/recueillis par J. Roger-Mathieu.* Paris: Librairie des Champs Elysées.

Académie Française (1796). *Dictionnaire de l'Académie française,* Supplément. Paris: Académie Française.

Asad, Talal (2007). *On Suicide Bombing.* New York: Columbia University Press.

Baer, Robert (2003). *See No Evil.* New York: Three Rivers Press.

Baker, Nicholson (2009). *Human Smoke.* New York: Simon and Schuster.

Beach, Christopher (2009). *The Films of Hal Ashby.* Detroit, MI: Wayne State University Press.

Becker, Ernest (1997). *The Denial of Death.* New York: Simon and Schuster.

Brym, Robert J. and Cynthia Hamlin (2009). "Suicide Bombers: Beyond Cultural Dopes and Rational Fools," in *Raymond Boudon: A Life in Sociology,* eds. Mohamed Cherkaoui and Peter Hamilton. Oxford: Bardwell Press, pp. 83–96.

Cavell, Stanley (1979). *The World Viewed.* Cambridge, MA: Harvard University Press.

Cielty, Michael (2007). "'The Kingdom' Gambles that Entertainment can Trump Politics," *New York Times,* June 19. Accessed May 4, 2014. At <http://www.nytimes.com/2007/06/19/movies/19king.html?ref=movies&_r=0>.

Courcelle-Labrousse, Vincent and Nicolas Marmié (2009). *La guerre du rif: Maroc 1921–1926.* Paris: Points.

Dunn, S. (1990). "The French Revolution and the Language of Terror," *The Partisan Review,* 57: 345–53.

Durkheim, Emile (19580. *Suicide*, trans. J. Spaulding and G. Simpson. Glencoe, IL: The Free Press.

Ebert, Roger (2005a). "Syriana," review. Accessed September 21, 2012. At <http://rogerebert.suntimes.com/apps/pbcs.dll/article?AID=/20051208/REVIEWS/51130002/1023>.

—— (2005b). "Ebert's 10 Best Movies of 2005". Accessed September 27, 2012. At <http://rogerebert.suntimes.com/apps/pbcs.dll/article?AID=/20051218/COMMENTARY/512180302>.

Eng, Monica (2006). "Dazed? Confused? Tribune Answers Syriana's Tough Questions," *Chicago Tribune*, July 20.

Eugenides, Jeffrey (2011). *The Virgin Suicides*. London: Bloomsbury.

Freud, Sigmund (1919). *The Uncanny*. Accessed October 2, 2012. At <web.mit.edu/allanmc/www/freud1.pdf>.

Gauchet, Marcel (1998). *La Religion dans La Démocratie*. Paris: Gallimard.

Gellately, Robert (1991). "Rethinking the Nazi Terror System: A Historiographical Analysis," *German Studies Review*, 14(1): 23–38.

Girard, René (1978). *Things Hidden Since the Foundation of the World*. Stanford, CA: Stanford University Press.

Glaister, Dan (2006). "It was a joke I was even nominated," *Guardian*, January 20. Accessed September 1, 2012. At <http://www.guardian.co.uk/film/2006/jan/20/israelandthepalestinians.comment>.

Grossman, Dave (1995). On Killing. New York: Back Bay Books.

Khatharya, Um (1998). "The Broken Chain: Genocide in the Reconstruction and Deconstruction of Cambodian Society," *Social Identities: Journal for the Study of Race, Nation and Culture*, 4(1): 131–54.

Maniquis, Robert M. (2000)."Filling Up and Emptying Out the Sublime: Terror in British Radical Culture," *The Huntington Library Quarterly*, 63(3): 369–407.

Ortega y Gasset, José (1956). *En Torno a Galileo*. Madrid: Revista de Occidente.

Pape, Robert A. (2005). *Dying to Win: The Strategic Logic of Suicide Terrorism*. New York: Random House.

Planet of the Arabs (2005). Accessed September 30, 2012. At <http://www.youtube.com/watch?v=Mi1ZNEjEarw>.

Said, Edward (1991). *Orientalism*. Harmondsworth: Penguin.

Shaheen, Jack G. (2003). "Reel Bad Arabs: How Hollywood Vilifies a People," *Annals of the American Academy of Political and Social Sciences*, 588: 171–93.

Shakespeare, William (1988). *Complete Works*. Oxford: Clarendon Press.

Smith, Sarah (2007). "*Lip* and *Love*: subversive repetition in the pastiche films of Tracey Moffatt," *Screen*, 49(2): 209–15.

Solomon, Robert C. (1993). *The Passions: Emotions and the Meaning of Life*. Indianapolis, IN: Hackett.

Sugrue, Thomas J. (2005). *The Origins of the Urban Crisis: Race and Inequality in Postwar Detroit*. Princeton, NJ: Princeton University Press.

Turner, Victor (1982). *From Ritual to Theatre*. New York: Performing Arts Journal Publications.

Zunshine, Lisa (2006). *Why We Read Fiction: Theory of Mind and the Novel*. Columbus: Ohio State University Press.

Index